CONTENTS

July

August

September

October

November

December

ACKNOWLEDGMENTS

We want to say thank you to:

- Kevin Johnson for his hard work and ability to "youthenize" these devotionals as he edited each page, making them more fun and easy to read.
- Betty Swanberg for her editing talents as she molded and shaped, trimmed and cut each devotion.
- Dave Bellis for guiding this project through the many details to get this work published and released.

Josh McDowell
Ed Stewart

HERE'S A DEEP QUESTION: Can you imagine anything ever happening in your life that would rattle your trust in God? Or would you ever swap your Christian faith for another belief—a belief you think makes more sense or works better in your life?

God wants to make your faith in him unshakable. He wants you to understand the undeniable reasons your beliefs are worth hanging on to. Sure, Christianity promises you eternity in heaven with God. But it also provides you with a relationship with the God who holds you tight right here and right now. No matter what you face, you're never alone. When you belong to God, you've got a solid rock now and forever.

In *Josh McDowell's One Year Book of Youth Devotions 2,* you'll come face-to-face with the truths all of us need to keep from "forever changing our minds about what we believe because someone has told us something different or because someone has cleverly lied to us and made the lie sound like the truth" (Ephesians 4:14). You'll be convinced that your faith is true. And you'll know why your faith matters for every moment of your life.

Each page of this book brings you a short Bible reading, a key verse, a brief prayer, and a few questions or suggestions to help you apply the truth of that day's reading. You'll take quizzes and read stories. You'll get true-life accounts and fiction—and some selections that are stranger than fiction. You might laugh or cry. You'll need to think, but nothing will bust your brain, because the goal of each daily adventure is to understand the "God who is passionate about his relationship with you" (Exodus 34:14).

As you use *Josh McDowell's One Year Book of Youth Devotions 2* on your own, you can also go through *Josh McDowell's One Year Book of Family Devotions 2* with your family. And you can look for many other "Beyond Belief" resources.

1 No Way? No Way!

Bible Reading: John 14:6-7

I am the way, the truth, and the life. No one can come to the Father except through me. John 14:6

YOU'VE MADE UP your mind. Instead of splitting your summer between lazing on the beach and scraping together odd chores to make money, you want an adventure. You want to go where none of your friends has gone before. You want to visit your cousin.

The attraction—and the problem: Your cousin lives on the other side of the planet in Borneo, where his scientist parents study insects. You don't know how to get there or where to find him. So you ask around.

You get all kinds of advice, but not all the responses you hear are helpful:

"Go to China and turn south for a few thousand miles. Lotsa luck."

"Take the Bornean Flying Cockroach Airline."

"Your cousin and his family must have misplaced their brains—and it sounds like it runs in the family."

But finally your search pays off. "Borneo? You want to get to Borneo? I was born and raised in Borneo!" a professor at a nearby college tells you proudly. "And I'm headed back there for the summer. I know your cousin, and I'll be happy to take you right to him."

Suppose you were actually hunting for a far-off cousin. Which bit of advice would help you most? It's no contest! You want to link up with someone who not only knows where you are going and how to get there but also knows your cousin and precisely how to find him.

You might never attempt an adventure to a hard-to-find location. But if you're a Christian, you are already on an all-important adventure. God the Father has invited you to come to him. James says, "Draw close to God, and God will draw close to you" (4:8). The Father invites you to enjoy a close relationship with him right now. Your life's destination, in fact, is *God*. He's the one you want to find.

But how do you get to him? Who can show you the way? Can you get to God without Jesus? No way. Not even close. Without Christ you can't get there from here, because to know the Father, you have to know the Son. To love the Father, you have to love Jesus Christ. To serve the Father, you have to serve Christ.

Jesus doesn't just *show* the way to the Father; he *is* the way! He's not a road map; he's the road. And he welcomes you to come through him to the loving Father.

REFLECT: How does it feel knowing that Jesus cares enough about you that he came to lead you to the Father?

PRAY: *God, thanks that I don't have to stumble through life to find you. Thank you for sending your Son, Jesus, to show me the way to yourself.*

2 Like Father, Like Son

Bible Reading: John 14:8-11
Anyone who has seen me has seen the Father! John 14:9

HOW WOULD YOU feel if someone said to you, "You're so much like your dad!"? It all depends on what your dad is like, right? If Dad has movie-star looks and Nobel prize–winning brains, you might pat yourself on the back because people think you're like him. But if he's like most dads—wiry hairs sprouting from his ears—you might hope you're *not* like him, at least not in *that* way.

So just how similar are you and your father? Check (✔) any statements below that describe how you are alike. (If you prefer, compare yourself to your mother, older sibling, or another relative.) Do you have . . .

- ☑ the same eye color?
- ☑ the same hair color?
- ☑ the same body type and facial features?
- ☑ the same basic personality traits?
- ☑ the same musical and artistic talents—or lack thereof?
- ☐ the same spiritual goals in life?
- ☐ the same wiry hairs growing out of your ears?
- ☑ the same taste in TV, movies, and music?
- ☑ the same food likes and dislikes?
- ☑ the same sense of humor?

If you resemble your father closely enough, even people who don't know him will get a good idea of what he is like by looking at you.

If you asked Jesus if he was a lot like his Father, he would answer, "Absolutely!" Jesus not only is your way to *get* to his Father, he also is your way to *know* what God the Father is like. Jesus is "the visible image of the invisible God" (Colossians 1:15). So the more you know about what Jesus said and did, the more you know about God. When you see Christ's compassion for people, for example, you know God is compassionate. Or when you read Christ's words of truth, you know God is truth. God the Father wants you to know him.

You might not show a striking, obvious resemblance to how your dad looks or acts or talks. But Jesus shows you exactly what God is like. Get to know the Son, and you get to know the Father.

REFLECT: What do you know about God because you have seen it in Jesus? What do you see in Jesus that attracts you to God?

PRAY: *God, you could have hidden yourself and made it tough to get to know you. I'm grateful that Jesus shows me what you are like.*

3 Ask for Something Outrageous

Bible Reading: John 14:12-14

You can ask for anything in my name, and I will do it, because the work of the Son brings glory to the Father. John 14:13

DERRICK GLANCES across the cafeteria to where a girl sits with her friends. *Dear God,* he prays silently, *let me go out with her and I'll witness to her so much she'll for sure want to become a Christian.*

Natalie lays her hand on the exam paper she has just completed. Closing her eyes, she prays without moving her lips. *God, I don't expect a perfect paper. But please make enough answers right to get me a B.*

What's the most outrageous thing you have ever asked God for? That a twenty-pound sack of money would spill at your feet? That the pimple growing like a third eye in the middle of your forehead would disappear by morning? That your parents would slip you a Ferrari for graduation—or sooner?

Jesus said we can ask him for anything. That's right, he said *anything!* John 14:13 says he had a good reason to extend this invitation. Jesus—our only way to the Father and our only way to know what the Father is like—also wants to teach us to show off God's greatness. Here's the formula:

Your prayer for anything in Christ's name
+ Christ's perfect answer to your prayer

= Glory to the Father.

When we pray *in Christ's name,* we are asking for our requests to be fulfilled *in Christ's will.* Since Jesus knows how to bring glory to God, he will answer our prayers in his best way so that God receives the glory he deserves.

So even though you might ask Jesus to miraculously change the answers on your exam, he knows you could grow more and bring greater glory to God by trusting him as you study. The result? Your prayer helps you recognize that God will help you when you study!

Jesus himself asked his Father for something outrageous, wondering aloud if he could avoid going to the cross. But he quickly added to his request, "Yet I want your will, not mine" (Matthew 26:39). Skipping the cross was not the Father's will, for he wanted salvation for us.

So go ahead—ask for anything. But ask in Christ's name. If you don't get the exact *anything* you pray for, it's because Christ knows a better way to give God glory.

 REFLECT: Is there anything that stands in the way of your wanting to bring glory to God?

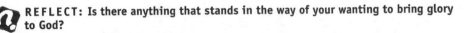 **PRAY: God, it's a privilege to ask for what I want—and to know you will answer my prayers in ways that change me for the better and give glory to you.**

4 What a Way to Go!

Bible Reading: John 14:1-4

I am going to prepare a place for you. . . . I will come and get you, so that you will always be with me where I am. John 14:2-3

WHERE'S YOUR HOME? Finger? Eyebrow? Coldfoot? (Those are real towns in Tennessee, Saskatchewan, and Alaska.) But a Christian's better-than-Worms hometown is only a temporary residence. (Worms is in Nebraska.) It's not temporary because you can't wait to get out of Boring (in Oregon), but because Christ is preparing a permanent home in heaven. Paul said, "We are citizens of heaven, where the Lord Jesus Christ lives. And we are eagerly waiting for him to return as our Savior" (Philippians 3:20).

Way back in the dark days, Christian youth groups used to gather around a large, floor-mounted acoustic instrument called a "piano" and sing a peppy little chorus about our other "home":

This world is not my home, I'm just a-passin' through;
My treasures are laid up somewhere beyond the blue.
The angels beckon me from heaven's distant shore;
And I can't feel at home in this world anymore.

Where is "heaven's distant shore"? And how do you get there?

Once again Jesus Christ steps in to show you the way. Jesus is the way to the Father. He's the way to know what the Father is like. And he's the way to bring glory to the Father as you pray in his name. But after all this, he won't leave you stuck in this place where at times you "can't feel at home." He won't abandon you with no hope of finding your way to heaven. When his time is right for you—either when he returns or the moment you die, whichever comes first—Jesus promises to take you to where he is. He's your way to go home.

Do you realize that Jesus couldn't show you how to get home if he hadn't come down to earth? See, you need more than a *map* to find your way to God. You even need more than somebody to *tell* you the way. You need somebody to *meet* you where you are. Jesus finds you and takes you to where you need to be. The Son of God left his home in heaven and came into your world to show you the way home. And he came looking for you because he loves you.

REFLECT: Since Jesus came all this way, doesn't it make sense to follow him to that heavenly home?

PRAY: *Jesus, I want to make your way my way. I want to follow you—through life, to heaven.*

5 Down in Lonesome Town

Bible Reading: John 15:9-16

The greatest love is shown when people lay down their lives for their friends. John 15:13

"I DON'T KNOW what my problem is," Tamara blurts through tears. "I have friends. It's not like I ever have to sit alone. But I still feel lonely in a crowd. I'm not sure anyone understands me—or wants to. Even my teachers. I think I could die and nobody would even notice I'd left."

Making it through middle school or high school minus feelings of loneliness is like darting through cold season without getting a runny nose. Sooner or later you're probably going to feel like a giant drip.

Like a runny nose, lonely feelings tell you something is amuck. Loneliness might seem like it's about popularity or looks. It's actually more about a God-given desire to be loved and accepted. That's a deep, healthy need everyone has. When that need goes unmet, you feel lonely.

Most folks try to get rid of loneliness in one of a couple ways.

Approach #1: *Act like a worm by crawling away from the crowds.* Here's how worms think: "I'm lonely because nobody loves me. Nobody loves me because I'm not lovable. The safest thing I can do is burrow underground. I'm never going to get close to others." The worm approach pushes you even further from people.

Approach #2: *Act like a puppy by doing anything to get people to like you.* Puppies think, "I'm lonely because nobody loves me. Nobody loves me because I'm not trying hard enough. I'm going to get the attention of others, even if I make a fool of myself or go against my standards." The puppy approach pushes you to do things you later regret.

Here's a better plan for dealing with loneliness: *Act like the child of God that you are.* Feeling loved and accepted starts with your relationship with Christ, who is the only one able to meet the deepest needs of your life. Talking to Jesus and reading his Word—the Bible—are steps to strengthening your friendship with him. He laid down his life for you, so it's obvious that *he* regards you as a friend worth dying for (see John 15:13). That's powerful comfort when you wonder if anyone cares.

God, of course, wants to help you behave better than a worm or a puppy dog—more on that later. But your first step to crawling out of loneliness is to get close to the God who wants to be your best friend.

REFLECT: Like any true friend, Jesus is ready to hear your concerns about loneliness and friendship. So when in your life have you felt loneliness?

 PRAY: Take a few minutes to tell God about times you feel lonely.

6 A Friend in Need

Bible Reading: Proverbs 17:17
A friend is always loyal, and a brother is born to help in time of need.
Proverbs 17:17

"A FRIEND knows you totally and likes you anyway."

"A friend is always there for you."

"A friend loans you money and doesn't bug you to get it back."

"A friend knows how you're feeling just by looking at you."

So how would *you* describe a "friend"? You might say, "Anyone I know." Or "Only those I can share my secrets and feelings with." Huge difference? That's because there are different levels of friendship.

Casual friendship is the first level. Casual friends are your next-locker neighbors, other classmates, neighbors you chat with but don't know well, and perhaps many of your teachers. (You wouldn't call all of them enemies, would you?) Anyone you talk with qualifies as a casual friend.

Close friends are the second level of friendship. Your close friends include people you eat lunch with, the ones you choose to sit by in class, and the ones you want time with on weekends.

Committed friends take you to a much deeper level of friendship. These are people you allow to see the real you. You trust them with your secrets, hurts, and joys. Most people have a group of casual friends, fewer close friends, and just a handful of committed friends.

If you have lots of casual friendships but come up short on committed friendships, you'll feel lonely. Only on that third and deepest level of friendship are your needs for love and acceptance truly met. It's committed friends who take away your loneliness.

Some days you want to go into worm mode and inch away from *everyone*. But if you get close to an inner circle of a few trusted friends, you find those friends comfort, counsel, and challenge you. When you hurt, your committed friends might not know what to say, but just being there for you helps. When you have to make a decision, friends let you bounce ideas around. Sometimes their advice doesn't really help, but just having them around gives you confidence that everything will work out.

And when there's something in your life that needs to be changed—a bad attitude, a harmful habit, or a risky behavior—committed friends lovingly push you toward doing what you know is right.

REFLECT: Good friends can impact your life in countless ways, so it's vital you choose your friends wisely. What friendships are you willing to work hard at today?

PRAY: Ask God today to guide you to a few trustworthy friends.

7 Bad Apples in the Barrel

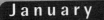

Bible Reading: 2 Timothy 3:2-5
Bad company corrupts good morals. 1 Corinthians 15:33, NASB

"MY PARENTS are always ripping into my friends," Hailey burned. "They say I shouldn't hang out with 'those kind of people.' I know my friends aren't perfect. But plenty of my parents' friends are a mess—and they still get together. It's like my dad and mom think I'm a four-year-old."

Ever had your parents clamp on you because of people you chum with?

Here's what is likely happening. Parents don't just look at what your friends are like right now. They try hard to peer into your future. And sometimes they see that someone you're close to is steering into a ditch and may cause you to crash and burn (see 1 Corinthians 15:33).

Being smart in how you choose your friends goes a long way toward keeping your parents happy. It also helps make you the person God wants you to be because close friends have incredible influence on you.

How can you tell a good friend from one who might run you off God's road? One sure way: Notice how friends alter your behavior. Let's assume you are a sweet, kind, obedient, thoughtful, responsible, even angelic person. Suppose you find a new friend, and after a few weeks or months of hanging out with that person you're blowing off school or mouthing off at home. What happened? You might feel your new friend is just helping you lighten up. But "friends" who negatively affect your behavior are not good for you no matter how much fun you have together.

You can befriend people who get into trouble, as long as you are a positive influence on them. Jesus was known as a friend to sinners (see Matthew 11:19). But he never let their attitudes or actions pull him in the wrong direction.

When someone starts steering you away from God, it's time to back off from that friendship. That's tough—but not as tough in the long run as continuing in a relationship that hurts you. You can explain: "You know, my commitment to Jesus Christ is really important to me, and I don't want to disappoint him anymore by doing the things I've been doing. If you want to do those things without me, that's up to you. But I can't join you anymore. I would like you to get closer to God with me. If you would like to get closer to God with me, that would be great. What do you think?"

REFLECT: When have you had a friend who influenced you in the wrong direction? Do you have friendships you need to reconsider right now?

PRAY: Talk to God about your questionable friendships today—and ask him what to do about them.

8 To Find a Friend You Have to Be a Friend

Bible Reading: Proverbs 18:24

There are "friends" who destroy each other, but a real friend sticks closer than a brother. Proverbs 18:24

LOOK AT THESE guaranteed ways to gather a crowd and get new friends:

1. Throw a party and give away your parents' credit cards as door prizes.
2. Let the kid who sits next to you snooze through school—while you cheerfully do all of his homework, write all of his papers, and take all of his tests.
3. Hack into the school PA system and announce that you've booked the world's hottest band for the next school dance.
4. Drag a crate of Twinkies to school and fling them to the crowds.

Any of those would get you friends, but not friends who will last. There's a better approach to finding friends:

- Start with *being yourself.* If you're not real in your relationships you have to pretend every day to be somebody you are not.
- *Get involved.* Relationships start the most easily in small groups.
- *Be open.* Be willing to have relationships with people different from you. Deciding ahead of time how your perfect friend should look or act will keep you from some valuable friendships.
- *Don't grump.* If you always look like your cat was just pancaked by a truck—unless it was—people will avoid you.
- *Talk to people.* Every person you speak to is a potential friend.
- *Ask questions.* Almost everybody likes to talk about himself or herself. Get it? People will think *you* are fun to talk to if you invite *them* to talk.
- *Look interested.* Suppose you meet the most boring person on the planet. Show interest. Listen. Look him in the eyes and ask questions. Maybe that person isn't as boring as you thought.
- *Don't be a bore.* If people doze off as you expound on the fundamental principles of applied thermodynamics and kinetics, consider changing the subject—no matter how interesting it is to you.
- *Don't give up.* You might suffer embarrassment and even rejection as you seek out new friends. But don't let anything keep you from trying. After all, Christ didn't give up on the human race—even when we spit on him, whipped him, and nailed him to the cross. He persisted. And he turned us into friends.

REFLECT: Who in your world might make a good new friend? What can you do to get to know him or her?

PRAY: *God, teach me how to reach out and make new friends. Help me make friends by being a friend.*

9 Happy Re-Birthday to You!

Bible Reading: Romans 8:1-4, 11

The power of the life-giving Spirit has freed you through Christ Jesus from the power of sin that leads to death. Romans 8:2

THEIR EYES MEET just minutes after the umbilical cord is cut. The young husband and wife can't believe that cradled in their arms and looking up at them is a tiny baby, their firstborn child. They have never seen anything so beautiful, wonderful, pure. They have never felt such total responsibility. And they can't remember ever being so happy.

Ponder for a few seconds the feelings and thoughts rushing through these new parents' minds. They expect nothing less than a bright future—sharing life together, watching their baby grow up. Sacrificial love, devotion, and commitment all burn in their hearts. As they tenderly enfold the helpless bundle of life, they dedicate themselves to raising their child.

And then their little boy grows up into a serial killer.

Not really. The point isn't that some lives turn out with unhappy *endings,* but that some lives start out with unhappy *beginnings.*

Maybe you have grown up in a happy home where you felt loved, cared for, accepted, and valued. On the other hand, maybe you lie awake at night wondering if your parents really love you and want you. Not every newborn baby is lovingly welcomed into the world. Some children were unwanted. Some have parents who neglect or abuse them. Others never meet their birth parents. Year after year they hear others sing, "Happy birthday to you. Happy birthday to you." But they wonder if there was anything happy about the day of their birth.

No matter how your birth was welcomed at home, there is no question about the happiness that surrounded the day of your re-birth, the day you trusted Christ as Savior and Lord. (Read Jesus' description of the re-birth process in John 3:1-21.) God eagerly awaited your re-birth. The Holy Spirit planted the seed of God's love in your heart. He nurtured it and waited for the day you would bow to Christ's lordship. Then, as you trusted Christ, the Holy Spirit was right there, setting you free from sin. He entered your life to "raise" you in the totally loving and accepting environment of God and his children. Thanks to the Holy Spirit's ministry in your re-birth and growth, you can count on nothing but happy re-birthdays ahead.

REFLECT: If you have felt less than welcomed by the people who should love you most, find a caring adult you can talk to about your feelings. But if you *are* welcomed, ask God how you can help anyone in your life who needs an extra dose of friendship because he or she isn't as fortunate.

PRAY: Say thanks to God for the Holy Spirit's activity in bringing you to Christ and bringing you up in Christ.

10 Free at Last, I'm Free at Last

Bible Reading: Romans 8:5-13

You are not controlled by your sinful nature. You are controlled by the Spirit. Romans 8:9

SHE WAS A SLAVE. She hadn't believed the rumors of people snatched from their huts and abducted to an unknown land until it happened to her. Chained for months in the dungeon-like hull of a ship, she feared she would die in bondage. After she endured years of hard labor and merciless beatings, the Union army marched into her town. Now an officer stands before her. "You are no longer controlled by your master. You are free."

He was a gang member. Not by choice. As gangs warred in his neighborhood, he needed protection. Trying to stay neutral brought threats to him and his family. Soon after he joined, he was forced to make his first drug run. Later came gang fights, vandalism, robberies. Late one night, while holding a loaded gun to the head of a boy from a rival gang, his heart screams, *I don't want to be controlled like this anymore!*

He was addicted. The first drink slid down easy. So did the second. A year later, getting drunk was a way of life for this high school senior. Without it he couldn't have any fun, couldn't fit in, couldn't escape ugly stuff at home. But when one of his drinking buddies landed in a coffin after a wild party, this student decided enough was enough. As he stands before a group at the finish of a rehab program, he declares, "I'm an alcoholic, but I no longer drink. I'm free!"

She was a victim. Three years had passed since her stepfather first hit her. Each year got worse. She had feared what he would do if she reported his abuse, so she kept quiet. But with a close friend's encouragement, she called the police. *He won't ever touch me again,* she thinks as the officers escort her stepfather to the car. *I'm free.*

Some people get the freedom they want. Others only hope for it. But the great news in Romans 8 is that the *strongest* chains known to humanity have been broken. All of us, the Bible says, were born as slaves to sin, shackled by a habit of evil we can't escape on our own (see Romans 8:5-6).

But Jesus changed all that. When you trusted him, the chains fell off. Because of the power of the Holy Spirit living inside you, you don't have to sin anymore. Yep, you *will* sin from time to time because of your own weakness when you're poked by temptations from the world, the flesh, and the devil. But you don't *have* to sin. You can *choose* to be controlled by the Holy Spirit instead of by sin. You are *free*.

REFLECT: What freedoms do you enjoy because Christ and the Holy Spirit are active in your life?

PRAY: *Jesus, you died to set me free from sin. I want your freedom in every area of my life.*

11 I'm Your Daddy Now

Bible Reading: Romans 8:14-17
All who are led by the Spirit of God are children of God. Romans 8:14

AMANDA HAD NEVER met her birth father. The moment her mom told her boyfriend she was pregnant, he walked out for good.

Life with Mom was more than okay, and Amanda assumed it wasn't part of God's plan for her to have a father. Then Scott came along. He started dating Amanda's mom when Amanda was twelve. Now she was fourteen, and the couple had been married for two months. Amanda loved Scott like the dad she never had. She had always thought it was too big of a wish to ask God for a father, but God had given her one. And Scott was incredible. He was kind, fun, and tight with God.

Still, a dark fear lurked in a back corner of Amanda's brain. She worried that one day Scott would leave her too. Why wouldn't he? Her real dad had left, and she was his child by birth. Nothing forced Scott to take any fatherly responsibility for Amanda. He could leave whenever he wanted, and she couldn't do anything to stop him. Then one day Scott and Amanda's mom took her out for dinner. They said it was important to them that Scott legally adopt Amanda. The thought both terrified and excited her. If he went through with it, he would be her legal father. She would finally have a real dad. But what if he backed out?

Day after day Amanda awaited news that her adoption was final and official. One day she came home from school and spotted Scott's car in the driveway, earlier than usual. When Amanda walked in the door, Scott and Mom were waiting. Scott stood. "The adoption papers came through today, Amanda," he said. Tears filled his eyes. "I'm your daddy now."

Amanda dove toward him with a gigantic hug. "Thank you for choosing me," she said through her own tears. "Thank you, thank you . . . Daddy."

Scott took a one-of-a-kind step to demonstrate his love for Amanda and his desire to be her father, making their relationship official through adoption. Similarly, God finalizes and formalizes his relationship with us by adopting us as his children. Do you have an inner sense that you're part of God's family? That's the quiet, reassuring voice of the Holy Spirit telling you that God has adopted you (see Romans 8:16). You don't ever have to worry when it comes to your relationship with your heavenly Father. He will never leave you. The adoption papers have come through. He's your daddy.

REFLECT: How do you feel knowing that God has permanently adopted you into his family?

PRAY: *Thank you for choosing me to be your child, God. Thank you for adopting me. Thank you that you will never leave me.*

12 Just a Few More Hours

Bible Reading: Romans 8:18-25
Even we Christians, although we have the Holy Spirit within us as a foretaste of future glory, also groan to be released from pain and suffering. Romans 8:23

"JUST A FEW more hours, Sara."

For months the Mexico mission team from the youth group had been working to prepare for this day. In just a few more hours—at least that's what the youth pastor kept telling Sara—the bus would arrive in Tecate in Baja California, across the border from California. There the team would spend two weeks repairing a church building and sharing the love of Christ with as many people as possible. Sara couldn't wait. "How much longer?" she asked her youth pastor again.

Sara couldn't believe she was so close to her destination. Not only was she glad for the privilege of serving Christ, but she got to work with thirty of her closest friends. That's why she applied to be part of the mission team over six months ago— and agreed to grueling fund-raising activities like car washes and rent-a-youth workdays, time-consuming homework assignments (from church of all places), and weekly training meetings and prayer sessions. That's why she spent at least half an hour each night trying to learn Spanish on a computer software program. And that's why she endured a twenty-hour ride on a school bus. She knew something valuable was waiting for her. She knew it was worth the work and the wait.

As soon as the bus crossed the border, all her hard study, all the time spent learning how to share Christ in Spanish, all the prayer, all the fund-raising work, and all the Bible study would pay off. God was going to use her, and her life would make a difference . . . in just a few more hours.

For each of us, the end of our whole life's journey—the spectacular day Christ returns and takes us to heaven to be with him for eternity—will arrive, poetically speaking, in just a "few more hours." But until it does, there's a pile of work here on earth.

Your bus ride on this planet and all you do to get ready for glory may seem long and difficult at times: there are people to love; unbelievers with whom you need to share the Good News; and Satan, whom you can't allow to keep you from succeeding. No one ever said the Spirit-led life would be trouble-free. Remaining faithful in the face of the temptation to flow with the crowd can be tough.

But the journey will end. Can you tough it out? One great comfort is the Holy Spirit's presence to sustain you and comfort you.

REFLECT: God helps you endure by sending his own Spirit to be your constant companion. Do you serve a great God or what?

PRAY: Talk to God today about things that are tough to wait for—and thank him for his loving care.

13 God, Please Help My Friend

Bible Reading: Romans 8:26-30
The Spirit pleads for us believers in harmony with God's own will.
Romans 8:27

"DEAR GOD, please help my friend Tyler."

Chris had prayed this prayer for months. His Christian friend, Tyler, was having an incredibly difficult time saying no to temptation. Tyler had a history of drug use and alcohol abuse. He had often shared his struggles with Chris, and Chris always promised that he would pray. So pray he did. No one knew Tyler's problems and needs better than Chris, and Chris took his responsibility to pray very seriously.

"Dear God, please help my friend Laura."

Ashley wouldn't give up. No matter how thin Laura got, Ashley simply wouldn't stop praying for her friend. Ever since her youth pastor had first asked her about Laura's eating habits, Ashley had sensed God's call to pray for Laura. "Only God can rescue my friend," she told her small group leader, "so we've got to pray." And she did pray. No one knew Laura's problems and needs better than Ashley, and Ashley took her responsibility to pray very seriously.

Isn't it great to have Christian friends who pray for you? And isn't it a special privilege to pray for your friends? Things happen when you and your friends pray for one another. God responds and acts!

There's only one thing more powerful than friends praying for one another, and that's the Holy Spirit praying for us. Do you realize that the Holy Spirit prays for you to God the Father? That's right. The Spirit of God who lives inside you is constantly talking to God the Father about your needs, your hurts, and your struggles. And his prayers are even more effective, because no one knows you like the indwelling Spirit of God—not your parents, not your friends, not even your youth leaders know you and your needs like the Holy Spirit does. Knowing your needs as he does, he can pray for you better than anyone.

Do you ever feel so hurt or confused or angry that you don't know how to pray? You sigh, cry, or groan, but you just can't get any words out? Well, relax. The Holy Spirit is taking your sighs and groans and translating them for you, because he knows exactly what they mean. And he takes your hurt and concern straight to the Father's throne. Pleading with a passion words can't express, the Holy Spirit prays, "God, please help my friend." And remember this: He takes prayer for you very seriously.

REFLECT: What does it mean to you when a friend prays for you? How about when the Holy Spirit chimes in with prayers that never cease?

PRAY: *Father, thank you that even when I can't find the right words to pray that your Holy Spirit knows exactly what to say.*

14 The Biggest No-Brainer of Them All

Bible Reading: Romans 8:31-39

Nothing in all creation will ever be able to separate us from the love of God that is revealed in Christ Jesus our Lord. Romans 8:39

LET'S TAKE a little quiz. For each statement below, check (✔) either true or false.

☐ True ☐ False Fire is hot.
☐ True ☐ False Water is wet.
☐ True ☐ False A rock is hard.
☐ True ☐ False The sky is up.
☐ True ☐ False Pickles are disgusting.

All right, how did you do? Now, you may have a different opinion about pickles than other people—though that doesn't mean they're not disgusting—but all in all that was a pretty easy quiz, right? What made it so easy? The statements represent basic facts and knowledge. Every statement—okay, except maybe the last one—are no-brainers. Everyone knows they are true simply because they are.

Here are a few more statements. Check (✔) true or false for each.

☐ True ☐ False God loves you.
☐ True ☐ False God will always love you.
☐ True ☐ False Nothing can separate you from God's love.

Do you think those statements are still no-brainers? You should. They are even more true than the first set. As you live the Spirit-filled life with its difficulties, the reality of God's constant love is your anchor.

Now let's try one more quiz. Check (✔) true or false for each statement.

☐ True ☐ False God's love runs out when you sin.
☐ True ☐ False God stops loving you if you eat too many pickles.
☐ True ☐ False The devil can cut you off from God's love.
☐ True ☐ False God doesn't love you if you think bad thoughts.
☐ True ☐ False You lose God's love if you sleep in church.

No-brainers to be sure, because they are all totally false. You might need to seek God's forgiveness for some of these acts, but you will never lose out on his love for you.

REFLECT: How do you react to the fact that God's love for you never quits?

PRAY: Spend some time today worshiping the God whose love for you is total and unending.

15 Mobilizing a Rescue Operation

Bible Reading: Matthew 9:35-38

The harvest is so great, but the workers are so few. Matthew 9:37

DEVIL HORNS don't stick out of the heads of non-Christians. Halos don't circle the heads of Christians. When you look at a football team, believers and unbelievers all wear the same uniform. Sitting around you in algebra, chem lab, band, and German class, believers and unbelievers just look like kids trying to get a decent grade and fit in with the crowd.

But there's a difference—a critical, eternal difference. Unbelievers don't wear prison jumpsuits, but they are imprisoned in darkness, separated from God and eternal life. They live under the rule of Satan. They are chained to their sinful nature and follow its desires and thoughts (see Ephesians 2:1-3). But those of us who have trusted Christ live in the kingdom of light (see 1 John 1:5-7). God in his love has rescued us from the darkness. He brought us into the eternal kingdom of his Son, Jesus Christ (see Colossians 1:13).

Many have heard about this difference so often that its reality bounces off. You might doze uncaringly because that difference isn't as sharp to you as the similarities you share with non-Christians. But God hasn't forgotten the difference. He's very aware that millions of people still live in the dark without Christ. He's incredibly concerned for each one—*so* concerned, in fact, that he took the ultimate step for every student, mom, and dad. He became a human being and gave his life.

The lostness of the people around you is serious business to God. He doesn't want any to perish (see 2 Peter 3:9). He died to rescue the lost, and his rescue operation didn't stop at the cross. God gives you the privilege of being involved in it. God could save the world single-handedly if he chose to. But he's appointed the rescued, who have trusted Christ, to work with him as rescuers.

Jesus compared God's rescue mission to a grain harvest. He challenges you to pray for more harvesters (see Matthew 9:37-38). We are God's ambassadors, official messengers with the ministry of taking his good news of salvation to others (see 2 Corinthians 5:18-20).

Will all those chained in darkness be rescued? No. Tragically, many have refused to be rescued in the past, and many others will refuse in the future. But there are countless others waiting for someone to tell them that Christ has set them free.

REFLECT: How do you view the students around you? Are you concerned that many of them are lost and in need of rescue?

PRAY: Ask God today to touch your heart with his compassion for your non-Christian friends.

16 Get the Word Out

Bible Reading: Matthew 28:18-20
Go and make disciples of all the nations. Matthew 28:19

GOD HAS a huge rescue mission going on. And your part is called *evangelism*—communicating the good news of Jesus to lost people. You might freeze with fear at the thought of becoming an "evangelist," but spreading God's good news isn't about getting a TV program or a slicked-back hairdo. Actually, the Bible reveals that real evangelism is made up of three activities:

1. Tell the facts (1 Corinthians 15:1-4). Sure, how you act around non-Christians shows the importance of Christ in your life. If you're living by the Bible's guidelines—you don't cheat, you aren't into drugs or alcohol or premarital sex, and you respect adults—that's superb. But don't mistake all that for evangelism. The good news centers on what God has done to free us from sin and introduce us to his love. At some point, you have to *tell* people how Jesus' death and resurrection has provided forgiveness for their sin and won them eternal life—and how they must trust Christ to claim what God has done them. You haven't started to evangelize until you spill the facts.

2. Call for a decision (2 Corinthians 5:11, 20). Imagine you just discovered a pill that cures cancer. If your best friend was dying of cancer, you wouldn't be content just to *tell* your friend about the cure. You would do everything in your power to persuade her to *take* the pill. The fact that a cure exists isn't enough. Your friend has to swallow the pill, or your wonder drug does no good.

Just like that, you need to persuade your non-Christian friends to respond to God's provision for their rescue. Knowing the facts isn't enough. If they don't trust Christ personally, then the good news isn't good news for them. Sharing the facts and persuading non-Christians to respond doesn't mean you threaten or pester people or bicker with them until they can't stand to be around you. Instead, reason calmly with them and convince them about the facts, lovingly challenging them to change their minds about God and trust Christ.

3. Make disciples (Matthew 28:19-20). Jesus left no doubt that the ultimate result of evangelism is that people become his steadfast followers. Once your friends trust Christ, they need teaching and encouragement to grow up in the faith. Introducing your non-Christian friends to Christ includes telling them the facts and calling them to trust their lives to Christ. But God likely also wants to use you over the next weeks and months in helping your new Christian friends mature.

 REFLECT: As you think about God's rescue mission today, what non-Christian friends or family members does God want to reach through you?

PRAY: Pray for those people by name, asking God to show you how to share Christ with them.

17 Call Yourself a Rescue Ranger

Bible Reading: 1 Corinthians 9:19-23
I try to find common ground with everyone so that I might bring them to Christ. 1 Corinthians 9:22

"ISN'T IT a bit much," Kalie argued, "that Jesus tells us to reach the world? I mean, there are five hundred kids just in my grade at school. How can I even make a dent in that—much less do something good for the rest of the world? Where am I supposed to start?"

Great question.

Think about your best friends. Are any of them non-Christians?

Think about the people you spend the bulk of your time with each day at school. Are any of them non-Christians?

Think about your neighbors. Are any of them non-Christians?

If you nodded yes to any of those questions, you're in the perfect spot to join God in his rescue mission. But there are some crucial things to remember as you respond to God's invitation to share Christ with others:

1. Be sensitive to God's Spirit leading you. Think about it: God has already put people all around you who don't know him. Are you asking God to help you see these people through his eyes? Are you catching the Holy Spirit's compassion for non-Christians? Ask God to give you his heart of love and alert you to chances to share with people around you.

2. Be a friend to non-Christians. Do you just hang out with people who have already trusted Christ? There are good reasons for spending the majority of your time with other Christians. The Bible, in fact, commands that (see Hebrews 10:25). But if you have a circle of non-Christian friends also, you are in a far better position to lead others to Christ.

Look for common interests as you build relationships with non-Christians. Don't agree with any who drink or take drugs, but applaud and affirm their good qualities. That's how Jesus managed to be friendly with sinners (see Matthew 11:19) without once compromising his standards.

3. Take the initiative, but be patient. Don't wait for non-Christians to ask you about spiritual questions—ask *them.* As you tell your non-Christian friends about God's love and forgiveness, God works through your words and example to bring them to Christ. Whether or not they agree with you or trust Christ personally, show them that you're a friend.

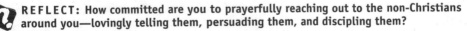

REFLECT: How committed are you to prayerfully reaching out to the non-Christians around you—lovingly telling them, persuading them, and discipling them?

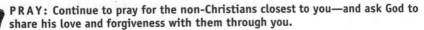

PRAY: Continue to pray for the non-Christians closest to you—and ask God to share his love and forgiveness with them through you.

18 The Liberator

Bible Reading: Matthew 4:18-22

Come, be my disciples, and I will show you how to fish for people!
Matthew 4:19

YOU PROBABLY DON'T picture yourself as a spiritual commando decked out to battle the forces of evil. You might use words like "saved" or "born again" to describe yourself as a Christian. But here's what you are to the kids around you who don't know Christ: a liberator. When you evangelize and disciple others, you liberate them from the power of sin and Satan.

God's Word is clear: He intends for you to be involved in his rescue operation. There are several reasons why you should consider yourself a freedom fighter in your school and community.

1. Jesus calls you to be a liberator. Jesus told his first disciples to tell others about him from home—for them, that was Jerusalem—to the ends of the earth (see Acts 1:8). He also said to them, "Come, be my disciples, and I will show you how to fish for people!" (Matthew 4:19). If you're like most Christians, you like the idea of following Jesus. You see how great it is to have a trustworthy leader who protects you and drenches you with wisdom. But Christ also calls you to be a witness (communicating the good news) and people-fisher (pulling others out of darkness). God intends for us to share our relationship with him with others.

2. The non-Christians around you need to be set free. It's a life-and-death fact: No matter how hip and happy people might look, if they haven't trusted Christ they're headed in only one direction: eternal separation from God. Jesus has compassion for the people around you who are chained in darkness. They are "harassed and helpless," he said, "like sheep without a shepherd" (Matthew 9:36, NIV).

3. You are indispensable in God's rescue plan. Someone needs to speak the good news to people you know well—and not-so-well. The apostle Paul asked how people can hear about Jesus "unless someone tells them" (Romans 10:14). God wants you to be that someone!

4. You want to rescue others because God rescued you. Paul said that he was compelled by Christ's love to join him in his rescue mission (see 2 Corinthians 5:14). Ponder this: What would your life be like today without Christ? If you are grateful that God lovingly invited you to be his child, then join him in inviting others to trust him. The more deeply you fathom God's love for you, the more you will want to help others find him.

REFLECT: Are you ready to call yourself a liberator? Why or why not?

PRAY: Talk to God about your hopes and fears about telling others about him.

19 Breaking Down the Barriers

Bible Reading: 2 Timothy 1:3-8
> *God has not given us a spirit of fear and timidity, but of power, love, and self-discipline. 2 Timothy 1:7*

"I JUST KNOW IT," Tyler erupted. "If I say anything about Jesus to my friends, I'm going to be an instant reject. Last year a friend of mine from church started witnessing to the guys on the soccer team. By the time they got done making fun of him I practically had to peel his lips off the floor."

No one likes to get mocked. But for each of God's commands to communicate the good news about Christ, Christians cook up excuses to not get involved in God's rescue mission. Here are four big ones:

1. *"I'm not capable."* Feel that way? Check out Ephesians 2:10, which calls you "God's masterpiece." God has given you special abilities, talents, and gifts. He's made you a new person in Christ and equipped you for what he wants you to do. He also has good works lined up for you. Boldly step out and do what God has made you capable of doing.

2. *"I'm not living a very good Christian life."* If you've become tangled in sin, realize that God wants to set you free. He has everything you need to enjoy a rich, Spirit-filled life. Confess your sin and let the Spirit lead you daily. You don't have to be perfect to be a liberator, but you do have to start letting God remake your life.

3. *"I don't know what to say to non-Christians."* You might think you don't have what it takes to communicate your faith and encourage others to trust Christ. It's true: Knowing what to say comes through training and practice. But it's not overwhelmingly hard to get the knowledge and skills you need, and there are great resources to help you. Ask your youth leader to point you to them.

4. *"I'm afraid of how non-Christians will respond."* That's what most often keeps Christians from sharing Christ. Satan and the world around you try to make you believe that what people think is more important than the message of freedom you have to share with them. As long as you focus on yourself instead of others, you'll be ineffective as a liberator.

Fear isn't from God. If you quake at how non-Christians will react, tell God about your fear. Trust God to give you his confidence. Then take a step of faith and talk with others. As you do, you'll discover God's courage in your life—just when you need it. In fact, you usually won't experience God's power until you put yourself in a position where you need it! You'll probably even get to keep your lips.

 REFLECT: Are you hiding behind these excuses instead of boldly moving out to fulfill your rescue assignment?

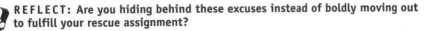 **PRAY:** Talk to God about barriers that hold you back from being a liberator. He'll give you the breakthrough you need.

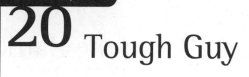
20 Tough Guy

Bible Reading: John 2:13-16
Don't turn my Father's house into a marketplace! John 2:16

BARELY AWAKE, you struggle to your feet in church. You turn to page 473 in your hymnal, open your mouth, and croak these lines: "Gentle Jesus, meek and mild, look upon that little child."

Wait a second! Exactly what kind of picture of Jesus do you get from those lyrics? Was your Lord really meek and mild? Was he so sweet he wouldn't swat a fly? Was he the kid who always got picked last—wimp of his Nazarene neighborhood?

Well, you're mistaken if you think Jesus Christ was weak. True, Jesus spoke gently of the birds of the air and the lilies of the field. True, he spun yarns of women baking bread and fishermen hauling in a catch. True, he bounced little children on his lap and made them laugh. True, he also stood quietly before kings, suffering bitter insults without uttering a word.

But Jesus was still a guy's guy. He was a carpenter with callused hands. He was an outdoorsman capable of spending long periods in the wilderness. He was a leader who courageously spoke against the corrupt authorities of his day, calling them "blind guides," "blind fools," and "snakes" (see Matthew 23).

The common perception of Jesus as soft and sentimental is a myth. He was gentle. He was meek. But that gentleness and meekness wasn't the absence of strength. It was *strength under control!*

According to the Gospels, Jesus stormed into the temple in Jerusalem—maybe more than once—to single-handedly drive out a mob of crooked merchants and money changers. *Not one* dared to protest or fight back against the red-hot blaze of his righteous anger. Jesus even dared to stay there—not only to teach on the temple steps but, as Mark says, to prevent the money changers from returning. Jesus didn't deal mildly with evil. He didn't react gently to hypocrisy. He didn't smile serenely at wickedness.

Jesus loves you dearly, but he can also act powerfully. And as his follower, at times you'll feel his tough love. He hates and opposes your sin, for example, because it separates you from the blessings and growth he wants for you. When he storms into your life to challenge your wrong thoughts, words, and behavior, he does it because he's *for* you, not *against* you, and he wants the best in your life.

REFLECT: Do you think Jesus is strong? Why or why not?

PRAY: *Jesus, thanks for your gentleness. Thanks, too, for your strength.*

21 The Nitty-Gritty Savior

Bible Reading: Mark 6:1-6

A prophet is honored everywhere except in his own hometown and among his relatives and his own family. Mark 6:4

"LISTEN," DANIEL SAID as he shook a wrench in my face, "you can't tell me that some guy who lived two thousand years ago and walked around in a white robe telling stories is going to make a difference to me today." He swept his arm around him to indicate the garage and the cars on blocks.

"I don't have time," he continued. "I mean, this Jesus stuff is okay for some people—like women and kids who like the stories and might even get something out of them. But for me? I don't think so. Jesus has nothing to do with a guy who has a timing chain to set on one car and a cracked block to replace on another."

Daniel echoes the way lots of people feel about Jesus. They see him like a plastic statue on a car dashboard—smiling, robed, a halo suspended above his head. "Jesus is fine," they say, "for people with their heads in the clouds. But he really doesn't have much to do with people who work in factories or take two jobs to pay for their kid's braces." They think Jesus has as much to do with your real life as that dashboard statue.

That's a myth. Jesus was a carpenter. You can picture him in a shop that opens onto a dusty Israel street, with a sign over the door that reads, "Jesus ben Joseph, Carpenter." Imagine him bending over a cedar plank clamped to a bench. He wears a leather apron, and perspiration drips off his face. He reaches for a knife, then a mallet. The shop is filled with the fragrance of cedar and cypress shavings that cover the floor.

Jesus of Nazareth toiled as a carpenter for eighteen years or more, growing muscles in his arms and calluses on his hands. He knew the demands of business—estimates to make, orders to take, prices to quote. He knew the pressures of family. Jesus had younger brothers and sisters who, upon the death of their father, Joseph, became Jesus' responsibility. He undoubtedly knew what it was like to keep clothes on kids and try to wrangle a fair price out of the merchants at the marketplace.

Jesus of Nazareth was no plastic saint. His world was gritty, smelly, and dirty. And when his life ended, he suffered a filthy, sweaty, bloody death. Because he lived a nitty-gritty life, he understands the nitty-gritty of your life. He knows about your struggles with life and work and problems because he had to deal with them too. He's a real-world kind of Savior.

REFLECT: What in your world do you worry that Jesus wouldn't understand? How can you be sure he can relate to you firsthand?

PRAY: Talk to God about the tough stuff of your life in the real world.

22 What Color Is Your Jesus?

Bible Reading: Galatians 3:26-28

There is no longer Jew or Gentile, slave or free, male or female. For you are all Christians—you are one in Christ Jesus. Galatians 3:28

MOST AMERICANS and Europeans picture Jesus looking something like a youngish Harrison Ford—brown hair, brown eyes, handsome. Oh yeah—and he's also white. Caucasian. Tan, most likely, but definitely white.

That's a racist myth—a falsehood spread by people and movements for centuries. The Ku Klux Klan, for example, preaches the supremacy of white Protestants over blacks and Jews, among others. They think that Jesus was white like them, so he must be on their side. In the early days of Hitler's Nazi movement, Jesus' death was used to incite the masses against Jews. The Nazis expounded white Aryan supremacy, also assuming that Jesus was white, so he must support their cause.

This racist myth persists today. People still characterize Jesus as an Anglo-Saxon Savior, painting him with pink and peach tones and ascribing to him the complexion, class, and customs of their Anglo-Saxon imaginations. But Jesus was neither white nor middle class. In all probability, Jesus was far darker in complexion than the average white American or European. As a Jew, his swarthy Middle Eastern heritage was probably accentuated when he stood beside Pilate, a fair-skinned Roman.

Even though Jesus possessed specific racial characteristics, he is bigger than barriers of race and color. He was a Jew, yet he spoke freely and respectfully to a Samaritan woman (see John 4:4-30). As a Jew, custom prohibited him from entering the home of a Gentile—a non-Jew. Yet when a Roman army officer asked for help for his servant who lay sick at home, Jesus went to the home and healed him (see Luke 7:2-10). When he was hounded by a Canaanite woman—Canaanites were historic enemies of the Jewish people—Jesus commended her faith and healed her daughter (see Matthew 15:21-28). He was a victim of racial prejudice too. On one trip through Samaria, he was rejected because the Samaritans knew he was Jewish (see Luke 9:53).

Jesus lived in a society that determined people's rights, privileges, and status by their race (Jew or Gentile), class (slave or free), and sex (male or female). As Paul points out in Galatians 3:26-28, Jesus turned those prejudices upside down. As Jesus' follower, you have the chance to be like him—not in matching his skin color or racial characteristics, but in accepting and loving people regardless of sex, class, or race.

REFLECT: What kind of a picture do you have of Jesus' physical appearance? Is he just like you?

PRAY: Ask Jesus to help you overcome prejudices of race, class, and sex.

23 How Will You Know If You Don't Ask?

Bible Reading: Colossians 4:2-6

Let your conversation be gracious and effective so that you will have the right answer for everyone. Colossians 4:6

MICHAEL HAD finally talked Emma into going out with him—provided they made it a double date, she said. Michael brought his best buddy, Eric, and Emma dragged along her cousin Heather. While Michael, Emma, and Heather tried to talk about things like sports and school, Eric sat like a lump on his chair, uttering nothing. He acted as if he was bored and wished he wasn't there. And Michael could see that the deadly silence was going to ruin his chance for a second date with Emma.

After the guys dropped off the girls, Michael slugged Eric hard in the arm—and Eric had no idea why. "Your conversation didn't exactly sparkle," Michael explained. "You looked like a corpse and made *me* look stupid. If bringing you was all the better I could do, Emma will never want to go out with me again."

Guess what? Meaningful friendships take meaningful conversation. How close can you get to someone whose entire vocabulary consists of grunts?

Here's how you start a good conversation and keep going: Ask questions. So look over the questions below and pick out four or five you really like. Memorize them. Practice using them tomorrow. And to help these stick in your brain, the first letters of the words from the various categories form the word FRIENDSHIP.

Faith: How did you become a Christian? When?
Reasonable plan: What goals do you have? What do you want to do in life?
Involvements: What extracurricular activities are you involved in?
Experiences: How do you spend your summers?
Needs: How can I help you? What can I do for you?
Dreams: What kind of impact would you like to have on the world?
School: Which is your favorite class? Least favorite? Why?
Home: What do you like best about your parents?
Interests: What do you most like to do in your free time?
Prayer requests: How can I pray for you?

See it? If you can ask good questions, you don't even need to do much talking. You just need to know how to listen.

 REFLECT: What do you talk about when you meet strangers? How good are you at showing an interest in others by asking questions?

PRAY: Ask God to help you pay attention to others—not just to make friends, but to make a difference in their lives.

24 Becoming Best Buddies

Bible Reading: 1 Samuel 18:1-4

After David had finished talking with Saul, he met Jonathan, the king's son. There was an immediate bond of love between them, and they became the best of friends. 1 Samuel 18:1

IT'S A QUESTION that may have puzzled you ever since you got socially burned back in first or second grade. You know, when you didn't get invited to the party everyone else in school got invited to. You might still be wondering, "Is there really such a thing as 'best friends'?"

The best way to find out is to look at two totally committed Bible-time friends, David and Jonathan. The story of their friendship is found in 1 Samuel 18–20. In these chapters you will discover that a best friend is someone who . . .

- loves you no matter what (20:17)
- speaks positively about you when others don't (19:4)
- listens to your problems (20:1-2)
- does things for you, regardless of the inconvenience (20:4)
- protects you from the bad guys (20:19)
- hurts when you hurt (20:34)
- understands your deepest feelings (20:41)
- is committed to you (20:42)

It would be great if you could have hundreds of best friends. But in real life, you can only be that kind of friend to just a few people—it takes time and skill to develop and keep those friends. But making friends isn't a mystery. Apply these skills and they will help you form friendships that will last a lifetime:

Feel good about yourself. Develop a good self-image. If you don't like yourself, it's tough to like others.

Accept people for who they are. Each of us is unique. Sometimes we're obnoxious and offensive. You have to look past people's faults.

Be positive and encouraging. You'll be a breath of fresh air to people if you can back off the constant criticism most people hear. Learn to build people up.

Practice confidentiality. You've probably heard yourself saying, "So-and-so told me not to tell anyone, but I know she won't mind if I tell you." Stop talking!

Be patient. It takes time to build close and committed friendships.

Be a good listener. Be interested. Reflect on what's being said. And don't think you always have to jump in with your own stories.

REFLECT: How are you doing at being a great friend?

PRAY: Check out the friendship qualities listed above. Which do you lack? Ask God to help you develop them.

25 The Friendship Killers

Bible Reading: Ephesians 4:31-32
Be kind to each other, tenderhearted, forgiving one another, just as God through Christ has forgiven you. Ephesians 4:32

FRIENDSHIPS ARE as easy to squash as bugs crawling on the sidewalk. If you want to make and keep friends, avoid these friendship killers:

Jealousy. Instead of envying your friend's achievements and good fortune, why not celebrate them?

Gossip. It's the teeter-totter principle: You try to lift yourself up by tearing others down. But sooner or later *you* end up splattered on the ground.

Disloyalty. You say you're her friend—but you've been known to turn on her. Real friendship stays true at all times.

Competition. You and your friends aren't running as competitors. Friends cheer each other on.

Negativism. Constant moaning leaves you minus your friends.

Comparison. If you compare yourself to your friends—trying to look better than them—you're asking for friendship hassles.

Selfishness. Make time to serve your friend's interests, not just your own.

Insecurity. This is a mammoth friendship stomper. It often sounds like this:

- What if he doesn't like me?
- What if I say the wrong thing?
- What if she laughs at me?
- What if I do something dumb?

If you have ever had those negative thoughts tromp through your mind, you know that they keep you from going any deeper into a friendship. Why? They paralyze you. You can break loose from this paralysis by meeting your fears head on. Every time you catch yourself dwelling on a *negative fear question,* change it to a *positive faith statement:*

- I know he will like me.
- I am confident I will say the right thing.
- She will accept me.
- I will do something intelligent.

When you move out in faith instead of fear, you will be a quality friend.

REFLECT: Think about how you get along with the people around you. What bad habits get in the way of good friendships?

PRAY: Tell God you want to do friendship his way.

26 Fairly Good Friends Fight Fairly

Bible Reading: Luke 6:37-38
Stop criticizing others, or it will all come back on you. If you forgive others, you will be forgiven. Luke 6:37

ANGELICA AND RENEE had been best friends since they sat next to each other in kindergarten Sunday school. But what started as a gleeful partnership on a science report nearly stomped out their friendship. Angelica liked to chat as much as anyone, but when the workload got serious, she wanted to split up the project and get her part done alone. Renee figured Angelica was irked—and she was—when Renee took charge and told Angelica what to do. And neither of the girls did well meeting deadlines—which led to nasty slams like "You're lazy!" and retorts of "Well, you're stupid!"

If you haven't experienced any conflict with your best friend, either (a) your best friend exists only in your imagination; (b) your best friend is a pen pal and you don't speak the same language; (c) one or both of you is an alien; or (d) you and your friend aren't as close as you think. Whenever you know another human being really well, conflict is inevitable.

When you have a conflict with a friend, you have a choice: resolve the conflict or dissolve the relationship. Here are some guidelines for keeping your fights fair:

Work at openness. You won't get anywhere thinking you're always right.

Choose your timing. Arguments break out at awkward times. Wait to settle them until both of you have the time and attention you need to talk things out.

Pick the right words. Think before you speak. Scan your words ahead of time and ask if they will help or hinder working out the problem.

Watch your tone of voice. You can say the right words in the wrong way. If you reek of sarcasm or criticism, your friend will smell you out.

Study your friend's point of view. See the conflict through your friend's eyes. Think of how he or she feels instead of how you feel.

Pinpoint the problem. The real issue that started the fight might be more than meets the eye. Your friend, for example, might blow up at something you say—but she was already upset yesterday when you spent time with another friend.

Figure out a solution. Once you identify the problem, decide on a practical, realistic solution. Talk about how to keep the conflict from happening again. Don't give up until you have worked things out.

Pray for your friend. It's tough to stay mad at someone you pray for regularly. Tell God you want him to make your heart tender—and ask him to help you love your friend.

REFLECT: What conflict do you have flaming up right now that you need to extinguish?

PRAY: Ask God for a tender heart and a love that won't let go.

27 A World of Friendship Opportunities

Bible Reading: Matthew 11:16-19

He [Jesus] is a friend of tax collectors and sinners. Matthew 11:19, NCV

FOURTEEN-YEAR-OLD Megan became a Christian three weeks ago. Now she's faced with tough choices in living out her new life. Some of her new friends at church, for example, are telling her to drop her non-Christian friends. "They'll influence you the wrong way. You need Christian friends now," they insist. Do you agree?

Admit it: Relationships are a major influence. So it's no minor point when people argue that you need close Christian friends. You need them because you can count on them for strength and encouragement while you grow as a Christian.

But your non-Christian friendships are important also—for different reasons. First, you are the best person to win your non-Christian friends to Christ. And there's a second reason to stay friends: If you ditch them, they could blame Christ for losing you as a friend. Then if someone tells them about becoming a Christian, their response could be, "Yeah, sure, and trash all my friends? No way!"

An exception to that rule: If your non-believing friends are a negative influence on you, you have to distance yourself enough to play it safe. When you back off, give them the option of coming closer to Christ. Let the rejection come from them, not the other way around.

One warning: If you spend time with non-Christians to win them to Christ, you might catch it on both ends. Non-Christians may mock you because you won't get involved in some of their activities, and Christian friends might reject you because they assume you're diving into sin. If that happens, take heart. You're in great company.

Because he spent time with a tough crowd, some people saw Christ as "a glutton and a drunkard, and a friend of the worst sort of sinners!" (Matthew 11:19). And because he spent time with sinners, the self-righteous Pharisees criticized him.

The best way to shut down that gossip, of course, is to win at least one of your non-Christian friends to Christ. The new believer will set the record straight. But in the meantime, don't stop reaching out to your non-Christian friends—and don't get mad at your Christian friends. Just press on and do what Jesus did. Show God's love to all of them.

 REFLECT: How well does it work for you to have both Christian and non-Christian friends?

PRAY: Ask God to help you deal with the tensions of living like Jesus did—loving both believers and non-believers.

28 Friends in a World of Hurt

Bible Reading: 2 Corinthians 1:3-7
If they are sad, share their sorrow. Romans 12:15

YOU SEE PAIN all around you. If you scan any crowd of your peers, you're almost guaranteed to see students struggling in some area—broken or strained relationships, the death of a relative or friend, a romantic breakup, or a family separation or divorce. You can be sure they face the losses and disappointments of everyday life—misplacing a textbook, earning a bad grade, losing a sporting event, or getting cut from a team.

What can you do to ease the pain and hurt?

You're on the right track if your mind flies to any of these ideas—be available, speak encouraging words, pray for your friend, do acts of kindness, point your friend to helpful Scripture passages. All of those responses are great. Yet God has one more way to use you to ease the grief or trouble of a hurting friend. Maybe you can understand it best through this illustration.

Imagine you're really down. Your girlfriend or boyfriend dumped you today, and you got slammed hard. You feel unwanted and unlovable—things couldn't be worse. You get together with your best friend and pour out your frustrations, anger, and feelings of betrayal. Eventually, you find words to explain exactly how badly it hurts. Which of the following responses by your friend would make you feel better?

(a) Your friend zonks and goes to sleep while you're talking.

(b) Your friend gets steaming mad at your boyfriend or girlfriend and starts plotting total revenge on him or her.

(c) Your friend listens carefully—maybe even choking back tears—then says something like, "I'm sorry this happened to you. I feel bad that you are hurting. I know this relationship meant a lot to you. I'm going to be here for you."

If you went for the third option, you have a good idea of how God wants to involve you in bringing comfort to a hurting friend. Romans 12:15 encourages you to share the sorrow of those who feel sad.

When you identify with the pain and hurt of a friend—speaking compassionate words and showering your friend with care—God miraculously reduces your friend's pain. It's as if your compassionate caring allows you to pick up some of your friend's pain. You make his or her burden lighter. And that's a Christlike thing to do.

REFLECT: Who around you is hurting? What can you do about it?

PRAY: Pray for and watch for opportunities to decrease the sorrows of others by sharing their pain.

29 A People-Centered Focus

Bible Reading: Mark 2:13-17

I have come to call sinners, not those who think they are already good enough. Mark 2:17

ONE SUNDAY morning a couple in their late teens wander into a church and sit down. They're dressed in chains and black leather. Later the pastor finds out they are new Christians, fresh out of a life of drugs and immorality.

Get this: After the service, several church members are discussing the visitors. While most hope that the couple felt welcome, one person is silent. He wears a sour scowl. Finally he can contain his opinion no longer. "God is not going to bless our church," he blurts angrily, "if we allow a woman to attend wearing pants instead of a dress!"

Huh? This brother was so focused on observing his interpretation of an Old Testament rule prohibiting Israeli women from wearing men's clothing (see Deuteronomy 22:5) that he missed the opportunity to wrap a loving welcome around two people desperately needing a home in the body of Christ. The man was rule-centered at a point where he should have been people-centered.

To be a Christian means to put people before rules. No one was ever more people-centered than Jesus. He taught, healed, blessed, lived, and died for people. He came to help people see that the Old Testament rules they had made cold, brittle, and brutal were actually guidelines for loving God and people. The conflict that ignited in Mark 2 between the people-centered Savior and the rule-centered Jewish leaders is what led those leaders to nail Jesus to the cross (see Mark 3:6).

You don't have to be stuck on Old Testament dress codes to have the same exclusive attitude as the sour man. If you have only Christian friends, attend only Christian events, and buy only from Christian-owned stores, you're totally missing the chance to be people-centered "salt" in the world—to communicate God's love firsthand, as Jesus did, to those who need it most.

Jesus said of his followers then and now, "You are the salt of the earth" (Matthew 5:13). Salt can't accomplish its purpose while sitting in the salt shaker. It needs to be sprinkled on food to bring out the flavor. Just like that, Christians must sprinkle themselves among the world's unbelievers in order to affect them.

Look again at Jesus. "We don't party with sinful scum," his critics seemed to say, "because we don't want their sin rubbing off on us." Jesus, though, saw things from a people-centered perspective. Why did he spend time with tax gatherers and sinners? So his love could rub off on them.

REFLECT: Are you afraid to hang out with non-Christians? Why or why not?

 PRAY: *God, remake my attitude. Help me love the people you died for—whatever they look like.*

30 Busted for Taking a Day Off

Bible Reading: Mark 2:23-28
The Sabbath was made to benefit people, and not people to benefit the Sabbath. Mark 2:27

PETER, ANDREW, JOHN, and the other disciples were still chewing on some of the raw grain they had picked when they saw the red lights and heard the sirens. It was the Sabbath police. The Pharisees were on them like a SWAT team on a terrorist bust. "You picked grain on the Sabbath, and that's a religious felony," they might have said, flashing their badges of religious knowledge. "You're in big trouble now. You have the right to remain silent. Should you forfeit that right, anything you say can and will be used against you . . ."

Well, maybe it didn't happen quite that way. But in Mark 2, Jesus and his disciples *were* accused of breaking highly esteemed rules regarding the Sabbath. Over the centuries, the Jews had established an elaborate network of regulations concerning what a Jew could and couldn't do on the seventh day of the week. The legalistic leaders had their noses so glued in their religious rule books that they had missed the purpose of the Sabbath commands. God simply wanted his people to take a day off each week for worship and rest (see Exodus 20:8-10). But the rule-centered Jews had made the Sabbath a day of no-no's rather than a day of rest.

People were more important to Jesus than man-made rules for religious behavior. "The Sabbath is a day to enjoy, not a rule to keep," he seemed to say in Mark 2:27. For his hungry disciples, the Sabbath meant picking handfuls of grain to eat, even though it was unlawful to "harvest" grain on the seventh day.

Lots of Christians today are trapped in rule-centered living rather than people-centered living. They decline an invitation to a class party just because there will be unbelievers there—and one of their Christian rules is "Thou shalt not party with pagans." With that rule-centered approach to life, unbelievers figure out that they don't matter to us or to God until they shape up to our religious code. How many people do you know who gag on Christianity because all they see in the church are crusty do's and don'ts?

Take a quick inventory of yourself. Are you rule-centered or people-centered? Do your unbelieving friends see you as an open, accepting person or as a holier-than-them judge perched high in a tower of religious rules?

Some of the most vile people in Palestine came to Jesus and were transformed because he was open, loving, and accepting toward them. That's the result of people-centered living. Can you argue with that kind of success?

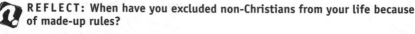

REFLECT: When have you excluded non-Christians from your life because of made-up rules?

PRAY: Ask God to help you discern which rules you follow are truly biblical—and which are made-up rules that keep you from showing people God's love.

31 Putting Your Life in His Hands

Bible Reading: Mark 4:35-41

Why are you so afraid? Do you still not have faith in me? Mark 4:40

THE AFTERNOON SUN dipped behind the rolling hills as a small boat carrying Jesus and his disciples set out across the Sea of Galilee. After a day of teaching, the Master was exhausted. So he found a quiet spot in the stern and was soon asleep.

The gentle breeze that had launched their boat quickly mounted to a stiff wind that filled the sails and rippled the surface of the water with whitecaps. Within minutes fierce downdrafts howled through the riggings, and huge waves crashed against the side of the boat. The disciples frantically tied down the sail while the boat tipped and water sloshed in by the gallons. But Jesus slept on undisturbed.

The disciples panicked. They shook Jesus awake and screamed at him over the roaring wind and crashing waves, "We're about to go under! Don't you care?"

The Master rose and shouted back at the wind, "Be quiet," and to the sea, "Be still." Almost immediately the killer gale dwindled to a whisper and the vicious waves subsided to a great calm.

"Why were you so stressed?" Jesus asked as the trembling disciples stared out over the suddenly tranquil lake. "Haven't you learned to trust your lives to God in such a simple thing as a storm?" The disciples hadn't trusted God. They were too worried about losing their lives.

You possess a drive to preserve your life—everyone does. You're born with the will to survive. But the *will* to survive is not always enough to keep people alive, for most people die against their own will. Your survival instinct tells you to drive on the correct side of the road, but you can't control whether the driver coming toward you will stay in his lane. Face it: You aren't all-powerful, so sometimes tragic events will overpower you. At some point in your life, you have to learn to say honestly—and reverently—"Lord, my life is in your hands."

And that's one truth Jesus wanted his disciples to learn from the storm. Nothing that will ever happen to you is a surprise to God. He knows what your life holds, including its duration (see Psalm 139:16). And since you can't stretch your lives beyond what he plans (see Matthew 6:27), you need not fear death. The Lord of life won't let your life end until his plan for you on earth is complete.

Are you scared to die? Jesus wasn't angry with his disciples for panicking in the storm, and God isn't angry with you for pushing out of your mind the thought of your own death. But he wants you to grow in trust. As you learn to trust him, you can face any storm, no matter how terrifying.

REFLECT: How does it comfort you to know that your life is in God's hands?

PRAY: *Lord, when storms brew in my life, I trust you to take care of me. My life is in your hands.*

1 Sometimes I Feel So Lonely

Bible Reading: Genesis 2:15-25

It is not good for the man to be alone. I will make a companion who will help him. Genesis 2:18

I'M SO LONELY I can hardly stand it. I want someone to care about me. I can't remember anyone smiling at me or wanting to be with me. I feel so empty inside.

I hate going home. My parents constantly fight with each other. The tension is awful. If I do anything wrong, they jump on me. When I go to my friend's house, it's just the opposite. Everybody is friendly. They laugh and joke at the supper table. Why can't my family be like that? Why do I have to feel lonely whenever I go home?

I'd really like to have a better relationship with Jesus. Everybody at church talks about "knowing" him and how close they feel to him, but I don't feel close to him at all. I try to read my Bible and pray, but it doesn't help. Is something wrong with me? I wish I could have Jesus for a friend because I don't have anyone else to talk to.

Ever had any of those thoughts simmer in the back of your brain? Or ever have someone come to you and spill those feelings?

You might claim you never feel lonely. But most students ache for a friend who lets them say *anything*—about their ideas, dreams, or problems. They want someone who makes them feel good about themselves, glad to be who they are.

God made you to enjoy relationships with others. When he created Adam, God made a perfect person. Yet he said, "It is not good for the man to be alone" (Genesis 2:18). Then he created Eve from Adam's rib to provide ultra-close, intimate companionship with him. See it? Friendship and companionship are normal, healthy needs everyone has. That's how God built you.

But even before Adam had Eve, he had God. The first way the Lord wants to meet your need for close friendships is by helping you get close to him. From the beginning, God pursued a relationship with humankind. After Adam and Eve were created, God enjoyed coming to the Garden of Eden to talk with them. That hasn't changed today. The ultimate solution to loneliness is knowing Jesus Christ. Only a real, meaty, daily friendship with Jesus Christ—the ultimate Friend—will satisfy your inner craving to be loved.

You need people. But you need Jesus most of all.

REFLECT: Are you enjoying an intimate friendship with Jesus Christ, your dearest friend? How would you like to get closer to him?

PRAY: Talk to Jesus today about the kind of relationship you want with him.

2 You Don't Go through Tough Times Alone

Bible Reading: Isaiah 43:1–7

When you go through deep waters and great trouble, I will be with you.
Isaiah 43:2

PONDER THIS: If Jesus materialized out of thin air and sat in the seat next to you while your fifth-period teacher droned on, what do you suppose he would say? You know that he's incredibly interested in a close, personal friendship with you. So maybe he would say something like this:

"I'm your Friend. Even though you can't see me, I'm with you all the time. About two thousand years ago Matthew wrote down in chapter 11, verses 28-29, something I said that's still true today: 'Come to me, all of you who are weary and carry heavy burdens, and I will give you rest. Take my yoke upon you. Let me teach you, because I am humble and gentle, and you will find rest for your souls.' Isn't that what you're really looking for—someone who will face life with you as your Friend? I refer to it as being yoked together. We're like a couple of water buffaloes plowing in the same direction.

"You might not guess that I know what loneliness, discouragement, and sadness are all about. Isaiah reminds you in chapter 53, verses 2-3, that the way I looked didn't wow people. I was also 'despised and rejected—a man of sorrows, acquainted with bitterest grief.' Doesn't that tell you that I know what it's like to be looked at as a loser?

"When I called twelve disciples and began to minister in public, my own brothers didn't believe in me. Mark tells about that in chapter 3, verse 21. So I know what it's like to be rejected by your own family. I was mocked and ridiculed when I did what I knew was right. In fact, I lived for long stretches of my adult life on earth among people who didn't like me at all. The religious leaders hated me. They lurked around me, looking for information they could use to slander me—or worse yet, to have me killed.

"I spent forty days and nights in the wilds with no one else around, so I know what it's like to be alone. A lot of that time was great, because I enjoyed my Father's presence. But I faced fierce temptations from the devil himself. I know how it feels to have negative thoughts hurled at you by the evil one.

"You know what? I wasn't afraid of being alone because I knew my Father was always present. I wasn't ever really alone. I want you to know that you're not alone either. I promise you I am with you whether you feel my presence or not. If I say it's true, you can count on it. I don't lie. I *am* with you."

REFLECT: What does Christ know about the tough times you face? How does it help you that he has promised that you won't go through your tough times alone?

PRAY: *When I feel alone, Jesus, help me remember that you're right here with me.*

3 When Friends Go Away

Bible Reading: Matthew 26:36–46

My soul is crushed with grief to the point of death. Stay here and watch with me. Matthew 26:38

LUIS WAS CRUSHED when the girl he liked moved with her family to another state. Loneliness haunted Laurel after her best friend, Samantha, died from leukemia. Ryan felt utterly rejected when two of his non-Christian friends decided he was too "holy" to be their friend anymore. Kara felt ditched when she wasn't invited to a sleep-over with other girls in the youth group.

Loneliness happens when others pull away from us. Do you know that feeling? Jesus does. Here's what he might say about it:

"You've maybe experienced loneliness—or even grief—because someone you love has moved away or died. I know what that's like too. My close friend Lazarus died, and I shared the sorrow, pain, and loss that his sisters, Mary and Martha, felt. I cried. Losing Lazarus cut through my soul like a knife. I understand how it hurts when you break up with a friend, when someone turns on you, when someone moves away.

"One of the ugliest experiences of my life happened just before I died on the cross. I had spent three intense years eating, traveling, and ministering with my twelve closest friends. During that time something began to eat away at Judas, finally leading him to betray me. Have you ever stopped to think how I felt when someone so close sold me out?

"But that wasn't the end of it. The other eleven disciples went with me to the Garden of Gethsemane. I was hurting because I knew I'd soon be facing a situation worse than I could imagine—dying for the sins of all humankind. So I asked Peter, James, and John to pray with me. *They fell asleep!* In that awful time of grief, anxiety, and loneliness, they let me down.

"When I bore the sins of humankind on the cross, it was an indescribable agony. You can't begin to understand the sheer hell I endured. In the midst of this awful moment, when I was desperate for my Father's love and companionship, *he was gone!* He couldn't look at me because I was bearing the sins of the world—including *your* sins. I asked God, my Father in heaven, why he had forsaken me.

"I know what it's like to be left by the closest person I know. My heart is touched when you cry because you're lonely. I feel your loneliness. That's why I will always be with you. I don't want you ever to be totally alone."

REFLECT: Are you lonely for someone special right now, someone you are separated from? How would you like God to help you?

PRAY: Tell Jesus that you trust him to stick with you when you feel separated from people you love.

4 He Knows Just How You Feel

Bible Reading: Hebrews 5:7-9

Even though Jesus was God's Son, he learned obedience from the things he suffered. Hebrews 5:8

SOME CHRISTIANS can't believe God feels their pain and loneliness. Maybe they figure that the God of the universe can't be touched by human emotions. But here's how Jesus might answer that thought:

"Something bothers me. People think I'm isolated—way up here in the sky somewhere, far removed from the cares of the world. They think I don't have any emotions. Well, I'm not made of cardboard. I feel joy. I feel sadness.

"If you read the Bible, you know how often my heart spilled over with compassion for every lonely, hurting, empty person. John tells you in chapter 4 how I felt the emptiness of the woman of Samaria who came to the well by herself. My love and tenderness satisfied her spiritual thirst because she learned her life could overflow with my love.

"And then there was Zacchaeus—hated by nearly everyone for being a tax collector. Like today, people back then didn't like tax collectors. But Zacchaeus had another problem. He was a little guy, the brunt of jokes. When I spotted him squatting on a tree limb as I passed along a road, I knew he was lonely. That's why I invited myself to lunch at his house. I wanted him to know that I cared about him.

"Here's what I'm trying to say. I know what's going on inside of you even when no one else does. You can't hide your feelings from me. I was there when you did poorly on that last exam. You probably didn't know it, but I felt your hurt. And when your dad yelled at you and accused you of not studying, I saw it—just like I was there for the woman at the well and for Zacchaeus.

"I've already told you I know what it's like to be lonely. I've told you just a little of my experience on the cross. But do you realize that I've already been part of *your* experiences of loneliness? Know it or not, I was there all along.

"I was there when you broke up with that person you liked. I was there when you screamed into your pillow. I felt you sweating when your parents were arguing and threatening each other. I've always been there! And I always will be.

"Just as my Father and I live in a unbroken state of companionship, I want to live *exactly the same way with you*. Our friendship will get deeper as time goes on. But right now you can begin to make new discoveries about who I am. I just want you to know how I feel about you. I'm Jesus. I'm your Friend, now and always."

REFLECT: How would your relationship with God be different if you thought about the fact that he is present with you every moment of your life?

PRAY: Tell God you believe that he will be with you—right now and always.

5 Fads and Facts about Faith

Bible Reading: Romans 10:8-17
Faith comes from listening to this message of good news—the Good News about Christ. Romans 10:17

WELCOME TO THE imaginary—yet entertaining—Carnival of Faith.

A guy in a shiny suit holds up a jar as he waves you over. "Ladies and gentlemen, gather around! Is your faith weak? Do you give up on God? Well, your days in the dumps are over. Introducing Faith-amins, the vitamin guaranteed to fire up your faith."

A woman in another booth is skinned in neon Lycra. "Hey, get over here!" she orders. "That's right, you with the puny faith muscles. You have flab where you should have faith because you don't work out. Twenty minutes a day on my patented Faith-asizer will build your trust tone and belief stamina."

The next guy offers you a plate of what looks like twigs and bark. "Eat right. It's as simple as that, folks. Eat from our Faith-Builder Diet, then watch your unwanted distrust and disbelief disappear."

Here's reality: You can't get faith in a bottle. You can't even hide faith in a tuna-fish hot dish. Sure, you know faith is a vital and necessary quality in the Christian life. Hebrews 11:6 gets right in your face: "It is impossible to please God without faith." Jesus praised people with great faith (see Matthew 8:10) and scolded people with small faith (see Luke 12:28). He promised that even mustard-seed-sized faith can move mountains (see Matthew 17:20). No wonder his disciples said to him, "We need more faith; tell us how to get it" (Luke 17:5).

That's the important question: How *do* you get more faith? Your spiritual life would be predictable and trouble-free if there was a special pill or plan that would increase your faith. But that's not where faith comes from. Neil Anderson offers this great insight: "If you want your faith in God to increase, you must increase your understanding of Him as the object of your faith. If you have little knowledge of God and His Word, you will have little faith. If you have great knowledge of God and His Word, you will have great faith . . . The only way to increase your faith is to increase your knowledge of God, your faith-object."* That's why Paul wrote: "Faith comes from hearing the message, and the message is heard through the word of Christ" (Romans 10:17, NIV).

Takes some of the mystery out of faith, doesn't it? The more you know about God, the more you grow to trust him. And the more you are involved in the Bible—reading, studying, memorizing, meditating—the more your knowledge of God grows. The Word of God is your key.

REFLECT: What do think about a God who requires you to have faith—and then gives you his Word so you can know him and believe him? Cool, huh?

PRAY: Tell God what you think about him.

---

*Neil T. Anderson, *Victory Over the Darkness* (Eugene, Ore: Harvest House Publishers, 1990), 112.

6 I Feel the Need for Seed

Bible Reading: Matthew 13:3-9,18-23

The good soil represents the hearts of those who truly accept God's message and produce a huge harvest. Matthew 13:23

"WELCOME TO the employment office, Mister . . . ?"

"My real name is Germinate, ma'am, but you can call me Nate."

"And you're a seed, is that right, Mister . . . er, I mean . . . Nate?"

"Yes, ma'am, I'm a seed. And I'm ready to fulfill my great potential."

"And what is your potential, Nate?"

"Tons of fruit, ma'am. Plant me in the right spot and watch the fruit fly."

"Fruit fly? What do fruit flies have to do with seeds?"

"Just a little humor, ma'am."

"All right, Nate, let me see what I have for you here. Ah, there seems to be a lot of openings down on the footpath. Very easy work, and you can start today."

"Sorry, ma'am, but to be fruitful, I have to get deep into the soil. Too many distractions on the surface. Besides, my friend Bud was eaten by a bird down there."

"Mmm, I see. Okay, the foreman in shallow soil is calling for more seeds."

"I can't do my best work in shallow soil, ma'am. Too many rocks. I need to send down deep roots and grow tall to be fruitful. What else do you have?"

"Well, there's always the weed patch, Nate. Things seem to grow well there."

"Are you kidding? Those bad boys choke out the competition before it can get started. Dropping into the weed patch would be asking to be strangled."

"You're being awfully picky, Nate. Do you want work or not?"

"Ma'am, with my potential for fruitfulness, I deserve the best environment possible. Don't you have some good, rich soil all plowed and ready for planting?"

In Christ's story about the farmer, the seed and the soil are co-stars. They can't be fruitful without each other. That's the way it is with *spiritual* fruit—not apples and oranges and squash and asparagus—but the positive character qualities like love, joy, peace, patience, and kindness. (See Galatians 5:22-23.)

You grow those Christlike qualities by welcoming the "seed" of his Word in your life—reading the Bible faithfully, listening to it attentively, and thinking about it frequently. As you do, the Word planted does its amazing work in you. It miraculously produces the fruit of Christlike character you long for—"even a hundred times as much as had been planted" (Matthew 13:23).

REFLECT: God sends his Word to cause spiritual growth and fruitfulness in you. What are you doing to receive that seed?

PRAY: *God, I choose today to spend time reading and thinking about your Word. Thank you that you will grow fruit in me.*

7 Something to Chew On

Bible Reading: Psalm 1:1-6
His delight is in the law of the Lord, and on his law he meditates day and night. Psalm 1:2, NIV

YOU BUTTER your toast. You peel a string of gooey pizza cheese off your chin. You gulp milk straight out of the carton. But answer this: Do you ever think about the brave, generous cow who provided the raw material for all this good stuff? Do you properly appreciate the time-consuming process old Bessie went through?

Here are some interesting facts about how dairy products make it from moo to you: When Bessie eats grass or hay, she chews her food just enough to swallow it—just like you do when you're in a hurry. That blob of soggy grass travels into the first two of her four stomachs. The larger stomach holds almost fifty gallons of food. When Bessie is full, she rests, but the four-stage milk factory inside her keeps working. Undigested food from the stomachs, called cud, burps back up into the cow's mouth for her to chew again.

When Bessie swallows the cud, it passes into stomachs three and four, where some of it is digested to nourish the cow. The rest is transformed into the makings for butter, cheese, eggnog, ice cream, and all that good stuff.

Bessie's digestion is so important to her that she spends a third of her entire life chewing cud. This process is called *ruminating.*

God designed you to be a "ruminant." He made you to "ruminate" on his Word. When you spend time in Scripture, you fill your mind with God's truth, turning it over in your thoughts and "chewing" on it. That's the kind of "rumination" or "meditation" on the law of the Lord that David urged (see Psalm 1:2). When you thoughtfully mull Scripture in this way, God will make your life fruitful (see Psalm 1:3).

Meditating on Scripture can be simple. Let's use Psalm 23:1 for now: "The Lord is my shepherd." Find a quiet place where you won't be interrupted, maybe in your room at bedtime. Read or recite the verse several times, emphasizing a different word each time. As you do, take time to think about the word you have emphasized and its meaning to you. It might sound something like this:

" 'The **Lord** is my shepherd.' *The God who sent Christ to die for me is my shepherd.* 'The Lord is my shepherd.' *He's my shepherd right now.* 'The Lord is my shepherd.' *He is interested in me personally.* 'The Lord is my **shepherd**.' *A shepherd feeds and protects his sheep, and that's what God does for me.*"

Don't hurry through it. Like Bessie, allow plenty of time to "chew on" each word. As you do, talk to God about what you are thinking. Let God's Word grow in your heart, and you will grow and be fruitful.

REFLECT: Try meditating and praying through a verse of Scripture right now.

PRAY: Tell God what you thought of that experience—and ask him to teach you how to meditate on his Word.

8 The One and Only

Bible Reading: James 1:19-25
Remember, [God's Word] is a message to obey, not just to listen to.
If you don't obey, you are only fooling yourself. James 1:22

YOU'VE PROBABLY HEARD it more than once. In a tone of voice that makes you feel like you have only half a brain, someone blurts, "You read the Bible? What for?" Or maybe you've run into a teacher or another adult who boasts of having the King James Version of the Bible on a shelf at home—covered with dust probably, but right there alongside the complete works of Shakespeare. He or she claims the Bible is one of the great works of literature.

That's a myth. The Bible isn't *one of many* great books. It is *the one and only* great book. There is no other book like it. In *All About the Bible,* Sidney Collett cites Professor M. Montiero-Williams, who spent forty-two years studying Eastern books. He said, "Pile them, if you will, on the left side of your study table; but place your own Holy Bible on the right side—all by itself, all alone—and with a wide gap between them. For . . . there is a gulf between it and the so-called sacred books of the East which severs the one from the other utterly, hopelessly, forever . . . a veritable gulf which cannot be bridged."

The Bible isn't like any ordinary book. It's a book you practice and obey. The positive difference the Bible makes in your life—like building your faith and making your life fruitful, meaningful, and productive—never happens just by *owning* a Bible or *reading* the Bible or *believing* the Bible or *carrying* a Bible. You benefit from this unique book when you *experience* it by allowing it to impact your thoughts, words, and actions.

You might have read or done research from a grand set of books called the *Great Books of the Western World.* One day a salesman for that series came to my house. He spent five minutes talking to me about the Great Books series. Then I spent the next ninety minutes talking to him about the greatest book, the Bible. I asked, "If you introduced a controversial subject, would ten authors from the Great Book series agree?"

The guy paused, then answered, "No."

Then I reminded him that the Bible was written over a period of 1,600 years on three continents by more than forty authors from every walk of life. Yet this astoundingly diverse book speaks with astonishing continuity. It tells one story from beginning to end: God's working to save humankind. Two days later, that guy committed his life to Christ because he recognized the uniqueness of the Bible and its life-altering message.

 REFLECT: Just think: God has carefully preserved the Bible so, today, you can take it in and live it out. What do you think of a God that good?

PRAY: Praise God today for providing his Word for you.

9 What's on Your Wish List?

Bible Reading: Luke 12:13-21

Beware! Don't be greedy for what you don't have. Real life is not measured by how much we own. Luke 12:15

SIXTEEN-YEAR-OLD Zachary had it all. When his bedroom-based dot-com started making him money, he dropped out of high school to run a business that gave him a big-buck paycheck. He soon could buy almost anything he wanted. He sloshed through the mud in his own SUV. He whizzed over the snow in his own snowmobile. He sped across the lake in his own speedboat.

At first, Zachary's friends envied him. Then business dried up and Zachary lost it all—the boat, the snowmobile, the SUV. Worse, he didn't know what to live for anymore. He had been so wrapped up in accumulating stuff that getting more and more of it had become his goal in life. Zachary thought that buying the right things—and having enough things—would bring him utter happiness.

So what's on your wish list? Exactly how much does it take to make *you* happy? What kind of car or entertainment system or other collection of toys would stuff you so full that you wouldn't want anything more? Can you imagine obtaining everything on your wish list—so you could finally say, "I've made it. I'm happy"? Or would you start a new bigger-and-better list?

Paul, in his letter to the Philippians, sounds like a man who had it made. He had what it takes to be happy. He exults, "Always be full of joy in the Lord. I say it again—rejoice!" (Philippians 4:4). Not only that, but his brief letter mentions joy or rejoicing seventeen times! Paul had it all.

But wait a minute! Paul was in prison when he wrote all those words about joy and happiness (see Philippians 1:12-14). By any measure we would use, he had nothing. But he was happy. That's why later he could write in his letter, "I have learned to get along happily whether I have much or little. I know how to live on almost nothing or with everything. I have learned the secret of living in every situation, whether it is with a full stomach or empty, with plenty or little. For I can do everything with the help of Christ who gives me the strength I need" (Philippians 4:11-13).

Real joy has nothing to do with the things you accumulate. The reason you can be joyful—whether you're wealthy or poor—is because you can have the peace and contentment that come only from Jesus Christ. And here's why: Christ is your most prized possession. You can't lose him. He can't be stolen from you. He can't be broken. He won't go out of style. And knowing him can give you joy that no mere thing can bring.

REFLECT: How happy are you with what you have? How are you letting Christ be your most prized possession?

PRAY: *Jesus, teach me to be content with what I have. And help me realize the joy of knowing you.*

10 Nice Guys Finish Last— But Not Always

Bible Reading: Luke 14:7-11

The proud will be humbled, but the humble will be honored. Luke 14:11

LEO "THE LIP" Durocher played shortstop for the Brooklyn Dodgers, New York Yankees, Cincinnati Reds, and St. Louis Cardinals in the 1930s and 1940s, then went on to become a successful major league manager. But Durocher is most famous for his flaming temper—and as the source of a saying he used to defend his behavior: "Nice guys finish last." As a manager, Durocher growled and scratched his way to three National League pennants. He expected his players to kick and claw, bite and bump, hit and hurt if they wanted to win.

Compare Leo Durocher with another major league ballplayer: Orel Hershiser was the pitching ace of the 1988 World Champion Los Angeles Dodgers. He won twenty-three games that year and pitched a record-setting fifty-nine consecutive scoreless innings. He earned the Most Valuable Player award in the League Championship Series and in the 1988 World Series. And to top off his great season, he won the Cy Young Award as the National League's best pitcher.

Orel Hershiser is a nice guy. And a Christian. After setting the scoreless-innings record, he knelt on the mound to thank God. In the locker room after the final World Series game, he told reporters that he had sung hymns to himself during the game to stay calm and keep focused. On national television that night he said, "This isn't a religious show, but I want to thank God." His baseball accomplishments remain in the record books as proof of his talent and hard work.

If nice guys are losers, how did Orel Hershiser get to the top of the heap? Leo Durocher says, "Nice guys finish last." But grab a look at what God says: "God blesses those who are gentle and lowly, for the whole earth will belong to them" (Matthew 5:5). Leo Durocher says, "Kick and claw your way to the top," but God's Word says, "When you bow down before the Lord and admit your dependence on him, he will lift you up and give you honor" (James 4:10). Leo Durocher says, "You have to step on other people to make it to the top," but the Bible says, "God sets himself against the proud, but he shows favor to the humble" (James 4:6). Leo Durocher says, "Strut your stuff. If you've got it, flaunt it." Jesus says, "The proud will be humbled, but the humble will be honored" (Luke 14:11).

Sometimes nice guys do finish last. So do some not-so-nice guys—like Durocher. He took first place three times in his career as a major league manager. Twenty-one times he didn't. Some seasons his teams even finished dead last.

Don't forget that sometimes nice guys work hard—and finish first.

REFLECT: What kind of satisfaction do you feel when you win in the best possible way—through hard work, perseverance, determination, and humility?

PRAY: *God, I like to win. I want to win, though, by doing things your way.*

11 You Have Friends in Weird Places

Bible Reading: John 15:9-16

Now you are my friends. . . . You didn't choose me. I chose you.
John 15:15-16

THEY WALK the halls of high schools all over America. Dorks. Gearheads. Skinheads. Jocks. The names change from time to time and place to place, but the idea stays the same. There's a right group and a wrong group, an in-crowd and an out-crowd. And everyone says that your job in life is to hang with the right people.

First, there are the dorks, dweebs, geeks, or nerds. Tacky, mismatched clothes. Hiked-up pants. Pocket protectors, too. And they actually *like* math and science.

Then there are the skinheads and hardnoses—the racist types fascinated by firearms. They wear army fatigues and can't wait for the next war.

Another group is the grease monkeys or gearheads. When they say "baby" they're more likely to be talking about cars than cute girls, as in, "This baby can do zero to sixty in eight seconds."

And there are always the jocks. They have the grace of a gazelle on the court or playing field, but off their home turf some have the intelligence of a doorknob.

Your whole world tells you that there are people you can afford to be seen with—and there are people you can't be caught dead with! The reasoning is this: If you're actually seen being friendly with a dork, for example, some of that dorkiness might rub off on you. Or at least some people will associate you with them. And you can't have that, can you?

Jesus had the same problem. He was a Jewish teacher, so he was only supposed to associate with other teachers and really religious people. A group called the Pharisees had especially rigorous rules about the right crowd to hang out with. But Jesus broke their code. He ate with tax collectors, touched lepers, and talked to a Samaritan woman—all from the wrong crowd. As a result, Jesus was called "a friend of the worst sort of sinners" (Luke 7:34).

But Jesus let the scorn of the Pharisees slide off of him. In the end, it turned out that many of his most loyal friends came from the wrong crowd. Matthew, a despised tax collector, was among his twelve disciples. And Mary Magdalene, from whom Jesus had cast out seven demons, was one of the few who didn't desert him through the crucifixion.

Who knows? Maybe a friend is waiting to be discovered among the dweebs, skinheads, and grease monkeys at your school.

REFLECT: What will it cost you to cross lines and make friends outside your current group? What are the possible rewards—for you and for others?

PRAY: Ask God today to help you befriend those who need it, no matter what group they belong to.

12 Know the Score about "Scoring"

Bible Reading: Genesis 39:1-9

How could I ever do such a wicked thing? It would be a great sin against God. Genesis 39:9

MANY LOCKER-ROOM conversations—on the guys' side, anyway—aren't the kind you want your mom to hear.

A towel snaps at you. "Hey, how'd the date with Andrea go?"

The guy next to you elbows you. "Well, was she hot or what?"

Then come screeches, gestures, and caveman noises.

Most guys know the pressure of that locker-room situation. If you don't give the impression that you "scored," there may be rumors that you're not a man. Or on the gals' side, the rumors might be that you're just an immature little girl.

But that's just not true.

Having sex has nothing to do with being grown up. It doesn't take maturity or strength of character. Taking a stand alone in the face of the crowd takes character, strength, and guts. A twelve-year-old kid can have sex, but it takes a mature person to say no. It takes boldness to be right up front and say, "Look, I don't want to be sexually involved right now."

Virginity is something you can be proud of, not ashamed of.

The Bible relates some down-and-dirty accounts of sexual temptation and sin. In one of them, a guy named Joseph worked for a high Egyptian official named Potiphar. The Genesis account puts it bluntly: "Now Joseph was a very handsome and well-built young man. And about this time, Potiphar's wife began to desire him and invited him to sleep with her" (Genesis 39:6-7).

Joseph could easily have let himself be seduced. He could have grabbed his chance to prove he was a "man." He would have had a story to tell as he strutted around the locker room at Potiphar's palace, bragging about his conquest! But the Bible says he refused—more than once, in fact. Joseph's refusal of Potiphar's wife's come-on landed him in prison. But Joseph had character, strength, and guts. Joseph—now there was a man.

It takes maturity like that to stand up to locker-room pressure. It takes someone with steel-bending strength to follow his or her conscience. It takes a mature person to say no and refuse to conform to the crowd.

 REFLECT: How much have you bought the idea that having sex makes you a real man or woman? Why is that idea messed up?

PRAY: Talk to God today about your conviction to say no in the face of ridicule from others.

13 Love Makes the World Go 'Round

Bible Reading: Philippians 2:1-4

Don't think only about your own affairs, but be interested in others, too, and what they are doing. Philippians 2:4

LOVE—THE WORD slides into conversations almost unnoticed.

- "You love her. Admit it."
- "I saw a great movie. You'll love it."
- "Yeah, I'd love a burger slathered with onions."
- "I love the acceleration and handling of this car!"
- "My kitten is so cute. I just love him."

The word *love* has a multitude of different meanings. So when we talk about love these days, it's important to know exactly what kind of love people mean. For example, if a guy can't spot the difference between loving his dog, loving his favorite baseball glove, and loving his girlfriend, he's in deep trouble—with his girlfriend, not the dog. And a girl had better know that her love for her prom dress and for her parents are two totally different things.

The apostle Paul dedicated a whole chapter to the topic of love. What he wrote in 1 Corinthians 13 describes what love *does* and *doesn't* do. And from this description and other examples in the Bible, we can come up with a concise statement defining what love *is:* Love wills and works for the good of the one loved. Love is making the health, happiness, and growth of another person as important to you as your own.

Is your well-being important to you? Of course! We all work hard at staying happy, safe, secure, and prosperous. Anyone with even a few ounces of ambition wants to grow as a Christian, do well in school, and have fun with friends.

It's part of everyone's makeup as a human being not only to survive but to flourish in every possible way. But true love demands that we want others to succeed as badly as we want to do it ourselves. That was Paul's instruction in Philippians 2:4: "Don't think only about your own affairs, but be interested in others, too, and what they are doing." He also wrote, "Love does no wrong to anyone" (Romans 13:10). Instead of doing harm, we are to do what is good and right to others. Love simply says, "Treat others right, the way you want to be treated." It all goes back to the Golden Rule given to us by Jesus (see Matthew 7:12).

That's what real love is like—even if it isn't the kind of love you usually hear about in the halls at school.

REFLECT: There is a lot of "I want what I want when I want it" in what people call love today. How do you see that false kind of love in the world around you?

PRAY: Ask God to flood you with his kind of love—because that's the only kind that will bring fulfillment to you and to those you love.

14 What Kind of Love Are You Talking About?

Bible Reading: 1 Corinthians 13:1-13

There are three things that will endure—faith, hope, and love—and the greatest of these is love. 1 Corinthians 13:13

TURN ON THE radio or TV at any time. You can't get way from love. It's sung about on music stations, dramatized—often *melo*dramatized—in soap operas, humorized in sitcoms, and mocked in trash-talk shows. Here's what you hear:

- "Love can't be wrong if it feels so right."
- "If you can't be with the one you love, love the one you're with."
- "I love what you do for me."
- "If you really love me, show me."

If love means making the health, happiness, and growth of another person as important as your own, here are some examples of what that might look like:

- If it's reasonable for your sister to baby-sit your little cousin while you go to a party, love requires that you do the same for her sometime.
- If you expect your teachers to treat you with respect, love requires that you treat them with respect and not bad-mouth them to other students.
- If you think your youth leader should be more attentive to your spiritual needs, love requires that you do your part to meet his or her needs—starting by praying for him or her consistently.

The loving thing to do in most situations isn't hard to figure out. Just put yourself in the shoes of the people involved and ask, "What's the best I could wish for if I were in that spot?" When you figure out the answer, love requires you to do the best that you have the opportunity and ability to do.

When you make the health, happiness, and growth of others a priority, you're following the example of the God of love. God wills only the best for every person. You see it in how he has treated the world.

First, he created you in his image and likeness (see Genesis 1:27). What better model of kindness could you ask for than to be formed in God's image?

Second, God wills your best by using his loving power to keep this planet going. Paul wrote, "Everything has been created through him and for him. He . . . holds all creation together" (Colossians 1:16-17).

Third, God proved that he wills the best for you—even at your sinful worst—by redeeming you at great cost. When Jesus Christ died on the cross, he did so for all people (see 2 Corinthians 5:15), even those who never respond to his love.

REFLECT: Since you are to make the health, happiness, and growth of others a priority in your own life, how does being loved by God help you do that?

PRAY: *Father, give me a love for others that is like the love you have for me.*

45

15 When Love Is a One-Way Street

Bible Reading: John 1:10-13

If we are unfaithful, he remains faithful, for he cannot deny himself.
2 Timothy 2:13

HOW DO YOU treat people who trash you?

Let me guess. Maybe not quite as kindly as God treats us when we reject him?

See, God loves us whether we receive that love or not. You probably know that "God so loved the world that he gave his one and only Son, that whoever believes . . ." (John 3:16, NIV). The key word there is *whoever*. When God gave his Son, he knew that some would believe and others would not. John wrote, "Even in his own land and among his own people, he was not accepted" (John 1:11). God knew that a sizable chunk of humankind would stomp on his gift of salvation and hoof it away from him. Yet he keeps on loving us.

If you ever doubt that God's love persists even when we snub him, consider how Jesus displayed love. He knew Judas would betray him, but he loved Judas and called him to be a disciple anyway. When the crowd cried, "Crucify him!" Jesus responded, "Father, forgive these people, because they don't know what they are doing" (Luke 23:34). Christ died for all, even those who turn their backs on him. Think about it: Even your freedom to choose for or against God is a gift from him. He *wants* you to love him, but he won't *make* you.

If giving with no demand for payback is how God loves, that's what true love looks like. That's the love God commands you to show in all your relationships.

When you decide to love like God loves, you might face the same rejection Jesus did. You might do to others what you hope they would do to you, only to have your kindness ignored or even tossed back in your face. Suppose you volunteer to feed, exercise, and even pick up after a friend's dog when your friend heads out of town. That seems like the loving thing to do. But when you ask your friend to do the same for you, she claims she doesn't have the time to look after your big, slobbering, mess-making doggy.

That's the kind of treatment that tempts you to quit looking for opportunities to love your friend. But genuine love doesn't give with a payback in mind. Love gives because it cares about the health, happiness, and growth of others—*period*. Whether or not its actions or words are appreciated, love keeps on giving. If you refuse to love because someone ignores your love or even mocks it, you're not loving with the love that comes from God.

REFLECT: When have you loved someone and felt your kindness was rejected? How did you handle it? In that kind of situation, how can you love like God loves? Are you asking God to help you love as he loves?

PRAY: *Lord, help me to love and keep on loving—like you do—no matter what.*

16 Loving When It Hurts

Bible Reading: 1 John 2:1-6
Those who say they live in God should live their lives as Christ did.
1 John 2:6

HUGE QUESTION: How do you know if you truly love someone?

Despite what you hear all around you, love is more than a good *feeling*. When you truly love, it becomes an *action*. You give yourself to others as God does.

If you accept God's challenge to love others like Christ loves you, then you will help them deepen their dedication to God and protect them from the stain of sin and hurt. If you're wondering if you really love someone—whether it's someone of the opposite sex, a family member, a classmate, a neighbor, or a stranger—ask yourself these questions:

- Am I making that person's health, happiness, and growth as important to me as my own?
- Am I trying to help that person mature in every possible way—mentally, physically, spiritually, and socially?
- Am I protecting that person from anything that threatens his or her well-being—or slows his or her growth?
- Am I prodding that person toward holiness and godliness?
- Am I adding to his or her beauty as a person—not leading him or her into ugly stuff?
- Is he or she more pure and gung-ho about God because of me, instead of stained with sin because of things we have gotten into?

If you can answer these questions with a confident "yes," you're truly loving that person. But get this: All your right, loving actions might not be accompanied by a flood of warm, fuzzy feelings of love or affection.

You don't always feel like obeying your parents, doing your homework, or brushing your teeth. But most of the time you manage to do those things because you have made a decision to do what's right.

Love is the same way. It isn't something you always *feel;* it's something you *do.* God says to do loving deeds whether you feel like it or not. Jesus didn't feel like giving his life to save the human race. The night before he was crucified, Jesus agonized in the garden, looking for a way to avoid the cross (see Matthew 26:38-39). But he chose to follow God's plan and sacrificed himself for our sin.

And there's a bonus. When you begin to love people you don't feel like loving, you often learn to like—or even love—them.

REFLECT: Who in your life needs love—even if you don't feel like loving them?

PRAY: Ask Jesus to love that person *through* you with the love he demonstrated *for* you.

17 The <u>Right</u> Right and Wrong

Bible Reading: Proverbs 16:25
There is a path before each person that seems right, but it ends in death. Proverbs 16:25

"YOU CAN'T TELL ME what's right and what's wrong!" Stephanie snapped. "I'm almost eighteen. You can't push your morals off on me. Just because it's wrong for *you* doesn't mean it's wrong for *me!*" Stephanie stormed out of that confrontation with her parents to find her own version of "right" and "wrong."

Stephanie has bought the lie that says, "Right and wrong, good and bad—it's all relative. You need to find what is right for *you*. You need to define your *own* morality." Stephanie isn't alone, of course. Most students entering college today believe that truth is "relative," not "absolute." They think it varies in different places and times. What that means is lots of people—including students your age—think they can decide for themselves what's right and true for them.

But morality isn't relative. Right and wrong aren't negotiable. C. S. Lewis wrote in *Mere Christianity:* "Whenever you find a man who says he does not believe in a real Right or Wrong, you will find the same man going back on this a moment later. He may break his promise to you, but if you try breaking one to him he will be complaining 'It's not fair' before you can say Jack Robinson."

It seems, then, we are forced to believe in a real Right and Wrong. People may be sometimes mistaken about them, just as people sometimes get their sums wrong; but they are not a matter of mere taste and opinion any more than a multiplication table is.

Paul pointed out that even those who have never heard of the Ten Commandments "demonstrate that God's law is written within them, for their own consciences either accuse them or tell them they are doing what is right" (Romans 2:15).

Even so, lots of people insist that what is wrong for you isn't necessarily wrong for them. They're like Pontius Pilate, who muttered the famous question to Jesus, "What is truth?" (John 18:38). The ugly irony of Pilate's question is that Pilate pretended to give Jesus a fair trial, and all the while Truth was standing right in front of him! Jesus—who had unveiled himself as "the way, the truth, and the life" (John 14:6)—was the answer Pilate sought. But Pilate failed to recognize Truth in human form. The best way to know what's right and wrong is to grow in your relationship with Christ and your knowledge of his Word.

REFLECT: Rightness and truth originate in the person of God and his principles for living. How are you learning more?

PRAY: *Father, help me draw close to you so I can know and feel the difference between right and wrong—and tell the difference between truth and lies.*

18 Does God Grade on the Curve?

Bible Reading: John 3:1-8

I assure you, unless you are born again, you can never see the Kingdom of God. John 3:3

"HEY, I MIGHT NOT be the greatest person in the world, but I'm not as bad as *him!* I'm Judas, and I could tell you stories about this guy Peter. He was always cocky and arrogant. I kept my mouth shut most of the time. He had a police record; I was very cooperative with the authorities. He once attacked a man right in front of a priest! I might not be a saint, but I'm not as bad as Simon Peter!"

You know the rest of the story. Judas betrayed Jesus—and hung himself. Peter denied Jesus—but repented of his sin. Peter received Jesus' forgiveness, and he became one of the greatest leaders the church has ever known.

The words we put in Judas's mouth aren't much different from the statements some people make to justify their less-than-good actions: "Yeah, I drink beer," they say, "but I don't get sloshed like so-and-so." Or, "I have my problems, but I don't stab people in the back like she does." Or, "I admit I'm not perfect, but if *he's* a Christian, then I shouldn't have any trouble getting into heaven."

But that's not how it works.

Some people think God must grade on a curve. That's a myth. Everybody loves teachers who grade on the curve—they take all the test scores, find the average, and give grades according to how many students scored above or below that average. There may be a brainiac, of course, who throws the curve off for everybody else—but if everyone else does badly, you can slack off and still probably pull a B.

The Bible makes it clear that God isn't going to do that. He won't compare Lauren to Brandon and decide, "Well, Lauren, you weren't quite as bad as Brandon, so come on into heaven. Sorry, Brandon, you didn't do as well as others. You lose."

Jesus explained to a man named Nicodemus what it took to get into heaven. Nicodemus was a Pharisee, a guy who did all the right things, said all the right things, even believed all the right things. Jesus didn't say to him, "Hey, Nick, if anybody is going to get into heaven, you will!" Jesus simply said, "I assure you, unless you are born again, you can never see the Kingdom of God" (John 3:3).

It doesn't matter if you're a better person than someone else, drink less than that person, or go to church more than anyone. What matters, according to Jesus, is being born again.

REFLECT: How can you explain to a non-Christian friend that God doesn't grade on a curve—that the standard to get into heaven is the same for all of us?

PRAY: *Lord, I don't claim to be better than other people. Thanks that Jesus died to bring me close to you.*

19 It's God's Way or the Highway

Bible Reading: Matthew 7:13-14

The gateway to life is small, and the road is narrow, and only a few ever find it. Matthew 7:14

SIXTEEN-YEAR-OLD TANISHA stunned her Sunday school class with this pronouncement: "The way I figure, Christians, Buddhists, and Muslims are all headed for heaven. We're just taking different roads."

Tanisha might not know it, but lots of people agree with her. Some won't come right out and say it, but they buy the idea that the devoted followers of every religion will somehow end up in heaven. That belief—universalism—is rooted in another belief: "It doesn't matter what you believe, just as long as you believe *something.*" There are "Universalist Churches" that make this doctrine a centerpiece of their teaching. But even many people in solid Christian churches have this idea rattling around in the back of their heads.

No matter how many people buy into universalism, it's still a myth. Jesus said that the road to heaven isn't a wide road that everyone will travel. Rather, it's a narrow road to a small door that few people will find.

Think about it: God became a man to suffer and die on the cross so people can find forgiveness and enjoy eternity in heaven. All through the centuries people have accepted or rejected his love. There are countless thousands whose faith in Jesus' sacrifice for their sins caused them to be thrown into prison, tortured, even killed. So imagine this picture at the end of time, when everyone stands before God: He surveys the throng of people who have accepted Jesus' dying love on one side, and the multitude of those who rejected him on the other. Then imagine God says with a shrug, "Oh, well. Everybody come on in."

That's not going to happen. And not because God enjoys seeing anybody face eternity in hell. After all, the Bible says God "does not want anyone to perish, so he is giving more time for everyone to repent" (2 Peter 3:9). Universalists say they can't see how a loving God could send anyone to hell. But God doesn't *send* people to hell. He provides eternal life for everyone who believes in him. People can spend eternity wherever they choose, but the Bible makes it clear that those who stubbornly and completely refuse God's love are choosing hell.

God has given Christians a command to "go and make disciples of all the nations" (Matthew 28:19). And that's because someday the opportunity for repentance will be past. Your friends need to hear *now* the great and indisputable news that Christ is that narrow way.

REFLECT: Who around you can you start praying for and sharing your faith with? How about making a list?

PRAY: Pray for opportunities to share Christ with the people you put on your list.

20 Getting to Know You

Bible Reading: Matthew 27:41-44
I am the Son of God. Matthew 27:43

MICHAEL AND STEFAN compared favorite teachers while standing in the registration line at their university.

"Would you believe I have to take Standish for Western Civ?" Michael moaned. "The guy is a beast. At least I got Nelson for English Comp."

"I got Warren again," Stefan said.

"Oh yeah? For what class?"

"All of them."

"All of them? Really? Does he give a lot of tests?"

"No."

"You have to memorize his material?" Michael asked.

"No," Stefan answered.

"Well, then, what *do* you have to do for this guy?"

"Just get to know him and develop a relationship with him."

It's hard to imagine a teacher like that, isn't it? But there is one. Christianity isn't just a religion; it's a relationship. Christianity isn't just a system of beliefs or doctrines; it's a person. In fact, that's what made the trial of Jesus unique. In most trials, the accused is tried for something he or she *did*. Jesus, however, was on trial for *who he was*. In the Bible Mark tells how several false witnesses came forward at Jesus' trial, but their testimony was conflicting and inconclusive. But then the high priest asked Jesus, "Are you the Messiah, the Son of the blessed God?" Jesus answered, "I am" (Mark 14:61-62).

The issue at the trial of Christ was his identity. That is a key difference in Christianity. Your faith isn't a bunch of beliefs you put in your brain and forget. It's all about Jesus—and how you relate to him every day.

Some of the biggest arguments in the Bible were between Jesus and the Pharisees, who thought that strict observance of their rules was utterly important. Jesus said in effect, "No, that won't do. Following God's rules has to come from a relationship with me. Obeying my teachings won't make you a Christian. Only having a personal relationship with me can do that."

Are you growing in your relationship *with* Christ or only in your knowledge *about* Christ? It's crucial that you understand what Jesus taught, but that doesn't make you a Christian. You become a Christian and grow in your faith through trusting Christ.

REFLECT: What are you doing to get to know Christ himself?

PRAY: *Jesus, don't let me turn my faith into a bunch of rules and ideas. I want to know you personally and follow you totally.*

21 Don't Check Your Brains at the Door

Bible Reading: Romans 1:16-17

I am not ashamed of this Good News about Christ. It is the power of God at work, saving everyone who believes. Romans 1:16

WALDO STROLLED DOWN the city sidewalk, lost in thought. He was going to church. He had decided he had run from God long enough. *I can't stand it anymore,* he thought. *The guilt, the conviction, the feeling that my life is missing something.* After walking for blocks, he reached a church and walked inside. He stood for a moment to let his eyes adjust to the dark. "Will you be coming in?" The voice startled Waldo. He turned and saw a man standing beside him.

"Uh, yes," Waldo answered. "I want to come in."

"Your brains, please, sir," the man said.

"My brains?"

"Yes, your brains. You have decided to become a Christian, haven't you?" the man continued. Waldo nodded. "Well, then, you have to drop off your brains here at the door. You won't be needing them anymore."

No, there isn't really a guy named Waldo who was forced to fork over his brain. But that story shows what many people think becoming a Christian is like. They think that believing in Jesus requires you to chuck your intellect and ignore your ability to think and reason. That's a myth. Being a Christian doesn't cut off your intellect; it completes it.

In his autobiography, C. S. Lewis, author of the Chronicles of Narnia, tells how he resisted the Christian faith as a young man because he considered Christianity a nonintellectual system. He quit fighting, though, and found that his conversion ignited his imaginative and creative powers.

Others have discovered the same truth. Lew Wallace set out to refute Christianity with his huge intellect. But the power of the truth made a believer out of the author of the classic novel *Ben Hur.* And British trial lawyer Frank Morison meant to write a book disproving Jesus' rising from the dead. He researched widely, gathered historical evidence, and worked hard at his task. Finally, all his brain power showed him that Jesus had risen from the dead! He became a Christian.

Trusting in Jesus doesn't require that you ditch your brains. Actually, it demands you use all of your intellect until you can say with confidence, "I am not ashamed of this Good News about Christ. It is the power of God at work, saving everyone who believes" (Romans 1:16).

REFLECT: Do you think that you have to check your brains at the door when you become a Christian? Why or why not?

PRAY: Ask God to use your mind to help you understand him and his good news.

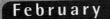

22 Check Your I.D.

Bible Reading: Psalm 8:1-9
You made us only a little lower than God, and you crowned us with glory and honor. Psalm 8:5

WHAT MAKES YOU who you are? The way you look? Your performance at school? Your hobbies, sports, and after-school busyness? Your spiritual gifts?

You're way more than any of that. Who you are is also more than your race, family pedigree, or skill at computer games. Those are important pieces of your identity. But they're just the outer layers.

People say, "Clothes make the person," but you no doubt know better than that. Clothes might *enhance* you or *disguise* you or *promote* you, but they don't *make* you. There's more to your identity than how you decorate your body or shockingly accessorize your ears, nose, or belly button.

And then there are all those diet and fitness infomercials promising to make you into a total man or woman: you'll shed pounds, tone up flab, and watch your life change. But does a transformed body affect your true identity? Of course not. You might like your new looks. But your true identity has slim-to-none to do with whether you're buff—or bulge in a few places.

So if these outer layers are just layers over your true identity, who are you underneath it all? That's something you want to figure out, because your core identity—especially how you see yourself—plays a huge role in how you carry yourself in daily life, how happy you are, how you treat other people, and how you respond to God. It's vital that you know who you are apart from what you look like and what you do.

Maybe you've never pondered the question "Who am I?" Maybe you've worked so hard on your outer layers that you've missed the big truth that you're a person of great value and worth, made in the image of the Creator and crowned with glory and honor (see Psalm 8:5). One girl said this about her friend: "She's one of the prettiest girls in the world, but she thinks she's incredibly ugly. She feels grotesque. That's why she can't trust anyone who says they love her. It's as if she's saying to God, 'God, if you love me, you must be a real jerk.' " This girl's thinking is flawed because she fails to realize that a loving God holds the key to her identity. Only he knows her real worth.

Truth is, when you're a Christian your innermost identity is this: You're a child of the King. And when you get close to the King, you begin to see yourself as the princess or prince you are.

REFLECT: God wants you not only to understand who you are but also to enjoy being that person. What gets in the way of seeing yourself first as God's child?

PRAY: Ask God to teach you a biblical view of yourself.

23 There's More to You than Meets the Eye

Bible Reading: 1 Samuel 16:7

People judge by outward appearance, but the Lord looks at a person's thoughts and intentions. 1 Samuel 16:7

NIKKI, straight out of college, works in a high-powered career. Her job requires her to be around other attractive women all the time. She's great-looking by most people's standards, but she doesn't see herself that way. Since she was a teenager, she's been told by her mother that she isn't shaped right. Nikki doesn't spend much time thinking about her value and worth as God's creation. Instead, she tells herself she's ugly. She's convinced no man will ever like her because her figure is imperfect. Working around women she considers gorgeous only makes Nikki feel worse about herself, and her lack of confidence in her appearance is starting to affect the quality of her work.

Allen's problem is similar. When Allen looks in the mirror, all he sees are scars—the result of a childhood accident that left his face permanently disfigured. In school he suffers rejection from his peers, especially the girls. His warped sense of identity tells him he is worse than ugly. He is a freak. And to cope, Allen has withdrawn from people. He spends up to twenty hours a week watching movies, escaping into the darkness of the movie theater—where no one can see the freak he considers himself to be.

Looking good is hugely important in our culture today. We spend a staggering amount on clothes, cosmetics, jewelry, and physical fitness, and hundreds of millions of dollars are spent every year to *change* physical appearance through cosmetic surgery, liposuction, tattoos, and body piercing. The closer we get to appearing "picture perfect," the more we feel we're worth to ourselves and others.

But it's a myth that how you look determines who you are, because your identity as God's creation goes far deeper. That doesn't mean physical appearance doesn't matter. There's nothing wrong with wearing clothes you like and caring for your body so you look your best. The mistake is when you do those things to *be* someone. As God's unique creation—no matter how you look—you already *are* someone with infinite worth.

How do you feel about how you look? Do you have to look good to feel good? God couldn't love you any more if you were the most "beautiful" person on earth. He already loves who you are.

 REFLECT: How is your view of yourself deflated when you think you look less-than-best? How do you feel knowing that God is looking at something far deeper than your appearance?

PRAY: *Father, it does matter to me what other people think about how I look. But more important than that, I thank you for making me your unique creation.*

24 Big Person on Campus

Bible Reading: Matthew 23:1-12

The greatest among you must be a servant. But those who exalt themselves will be humbled, and those who humble themselves will be exalted. Matthew 23:11-12

BEN AND MARCY were a brother-sister pair that started attending youth group at a small church. The struggling group was glad to get them, because they seemed like strong Christians and showed up at everything right from the start. After a few months Ben volunteered for a vacant spot on the youth group leadership council; the council enthusiastically welcomed him. And by now Marcy was deep into a midweek girls' Bible study group.

But soon Ben and Marcy started taking charge. They insisted that things get done their way. They bragged about how they had led other groups and said their ideas would really help the group grow. At first the adult volunteers went along with them. But Ben wanted more and more control in the youth group, and Marcy pushed hard to further her ideas of what her girls' group should study. When the adults asked the pair to back off, Ben and Marcy got huffy. Two weeks later they left the church without a word.

See it? Some people don't feel good about themselves unless they have power, influence, or control over others. Who they are is wrapped up in the status they achieve. And when these people want to give themselves a shot of self-worth, they grab leadership in school, church, clubs, and friendships. For Ben and Marcy, their personal worth and identity are wrapped up in status and a sense of importance. They aren't content just to be available and to serve wherever they can. They have to exert influence to feel like they matter.

So what's the problem with that—besides the fact that most people gag when you try to control them? Well, if your identity as God's child and your worth to him is based on the importance you achieve, you're likely out of luck. A church youth group can have only so many student leaders. A government can have only so many officials. And most of us will never get the opportunity to rule the world.

The Bible is clear: Your identity doesn't depend on the status you attain. Jesus picked ordinary people to be his disciples—and passed over the religious leaders overblown with status and self-importance.

Whether the world thinks you're a somebody or a nobody in your family, school, or church, you are special to God. Whether you achieve great things or small, you can't change your pricelessness to him.

REFLECT: What does the status or power you attain have to do with God's love for you?

PRAY: *Father, you control the universe. Help me to understand that I don't need to control my world to impress you.*

25 Break Free from Those Flimsy Chains

Bible Reading: Ephesians 1:3-8

Long ago, even before he made the world, God loved us and chose us in Christ to be holy and without fault in his eyes. Ephesians 1:4

YOU DON'T HAVE TO wonder why many kids grow up with a warped sense of their worth to God and to others—and a twisted sense of their true identity. Parents, teachers, the media, advertisers, and marketers can pummel into you the idea that your identity depends on how good you look, how well you perform, and how well you succeed. You can know better than that and still have a hard time shaking thoughts that put you down or control how you act.

We're like the circus elephant whose leg is held to a stake with a bicycle chain. How can a flimsy chain control such a brawny animal? The elephant is locked up by a memory. As a baby, the elephant tried to break loose but wasn't strong enough. It was burned into the elephant's brain that the chain was stronger than he was, and he hasn't forgotten that lesson. Even though the elephant could break the chain with a small yank, he rarely tries. He's conditioned to captivity. But notice this: If he *does* break away, he is almost impossible to control again.

How you think about yourself works the same way. Most of us are trained to think that how we look, perform, and achieve is all-important—so even when we know better, we're chained by that dumb idea. But God wants to set you free from the flimsy chains that keep you from realizing your full potential as God's unique, valued creation. God's truth is stronger than those chains. You can break free to be—and be glad to be—who God made you.

An important part of understanding who you are involves getting into your head what God says about who you are.

First God tells you that you are his child. John 1:12 says, "To all who believed him and accepted him, he gave the right to become children of God." Try putting yourself in this verse: "I have believed God and accepted him. He has given me the right to be his child." Write these words on a card and place it where you can see it when you feel put down.

Then God says that you are chosen. Ephesians 1:4 tells us, "He chose us in him before the creation of the world to be holy and blameless in his sight" (NIV). Personalize that verse too: "I was chosen by God, before he even created the world, to be holy and blameless."

When you let these Scripture truths dig their way deep into your heart, you see yourself afresh. You're bigger than the chains that bind you.

REFLECT: Who shouts louder—the people around you who hand you a warped view of who you are, or God with his true view of you? Why?

PRAY: Say thanks to God for what he has shown you about yourself.

26 Your Inner Self-Portrait

Bible Reading: Jeremiah 31:3

I have loved you, my people, with an everlasting love. With unfailing love I have drawn you to myself. Jeremiah 31:3

GOT ANY PICTURES in your wallet or purse—you know, pictures of friends, parents, or siblings—or some girl or guy? You probably are proud to show off those pictures of people you love. But how do you feel about flashing that other picture you drag around—the photo of you on your student ID card or driver's license? Do you cringe even thinking about it?

You might not know that those photographers get paid to take the worst possible photos. Really. Well, maybe not. But grab hold of this good news: That picture doesn't represent what you really look like.

Did you know you carry another personal identification photo, one far more important than any portrait in your pocket? It's the picture you hold of yourself in your mind—your concept of who you are. Like your ID photo, your inner self-portrait might or might not accurately represent the real you. But like that ID photo, it's the only one you have.

Take Alex, for example. The big message he heard growing up was, "Alex, you can't do anything right." Was that an accurate description of Alex? No! True, there are some things Alex doesn't do well, just like with any of us. But to say he can't do *anything* right is completely wrong. Yet that message was flashed onto the film of Alex's heart, and today Alex carries that distorted self-portrait wherever he goes. It's the picture of a young guy who sees himself as a failure waiting to happen. And he is so embarrassed by it that he's shy and antisocial.

On the other hand, think about Theresa. Her perception of her identity is suitable for framing. She grew up in a home where she was cherished and nurtured by loving Christian parents. She learned early that she was God's unique, dearly loved creation. As a result, she is entering adulthood confident—but not cocky—about her worth to God and to others. She meets new people easily, and God has used her to bring a number of her new friends to Christ.

Your goal isn't to become Theresa. It's to get God's true view of you—a view that captures your real identity as God's child. No matter how you see yourself right now, here's a truth that can start to rearrange your self-portrait into a truer picture of who you are. Jeremiah 31:3 says you are loved by God—*eternally.* That's right. God is committed to love you forever. Try that verse on personally: "God loves me eternally, and in his love he draws me to be close to him."

REFLECT: How does God's view of you capture your real identity?

PRAY: *God, show me areas where my view of myself doesn't match how you see me. Help me get your true view of me.*

27 Death, Taxes, and Temptation

Bible Reading: James 4:7-10

Humble yourselves before God. Resist the Devil, and he will flee from you. James 4:7

THE ONLY CHRISTIANS who don't face temptation are the ones parked in heaven. The rest of us face temptation—sometimes subtle, sometimes slamming us in the face—every single day of our lives. The fact that you've become a Christian won't make Satan decide the game is over with you and stop picking at you. In fact, a person's problems with temptation never really begin until he or she starts to respond to God's Holy Spirit.

That's cheery news, isn't it? Actually, though, knowing Jesus gives you great power to handle temptation. You don't have to get slapped around. When you face temptation, here's how you fight back:

1. Be on your guard. Expect temptation. Benjamin Franklin was wrong when he said, "In this world nothing is certain but death and taxes." There's at least one more certainty: temptation.

2. Hit back at temptation quickly. The biggest danger in temptation is *entertaining* it—wallowing in it and telling yourself how much fun evil is—instead of dealing with it. It's like playing with a lion cub. It might be fun for a while, but it soon grows up, turns on you, and tears you to pieces. Notice that the account of Jesus' temptation in Matthew 4 seems to indicate that he responded to each temptation quickly—as in immediately!

3. Submit to God. You are wise to get to your knees and submit control of the situation to God. It's not enough to turn from the temptation—you must also turn to God. Tell him about your temptation and ask him for the help he is willing and able to offer: "Since he himself has gone through suffering and temptation, he is able to help us when we are being tempted" (Hebrews 2:18).

4. Resist the devil. Once you recognize a temptation and ask God's help in overcoming it, put your running shoes on and get out of there! Resist and rebuke the devil, and claim victory in the name of Jesus Christ.

5. Say thanks. And once God has helped you overcome, don't forget to praise him for keeping his promise, because "he will keep the temptation from becoming so strong that you can't stand up against it. When you are tempted, he will show you a way out so that you will not give in to it" (1 Corinthians 10:13).

 REFLECT: What are the biggest temptations you face? How do you deal with them? And does your current strategy work well?

PRAY: *Father, thank you for your presence and the strength you give me to resist temptation. Help me not to give the devil a way to defeat me. Turn my mind to prayer at the first sign of temptation.*

28 Someone to Watch Over Me

Bible Reading: James 5:16-18
Confess your sins to each other and pray for each other so that you may be healed. James 5:16

"ACCOUNTABILITY" is a six-syllable word for having someone who kindly but directly tells you when you're messing up—and what you need to do. Accountability means having teachers who give assignments, grade them, then pat you on the back or slam you into detention. Accountability means having coaches who make you run wind-sprints until you heave and who call for a stretcher when you break a body part. Like it or not, accountability keeps you on track.

There's also spiritual accountability. You need to be accountable to another Christian—a *mature* Christian—who can help you when you hurt and correct you when you're headed for a crash and don't know it. You might never have thought about that, but it's a major step to help you grow in your Christian life.

James 5:16 shows two pieces of a good accountability partnership. Number one: An accountability partner is someone you can talk to about your temptations and sins—and who won't treat you like you're stupid even when you fail. Number two: An accountability partner is someone who will pray with you about your weaknesses and stick with you as you grow up in God.

Got any Christian friends like that? Here's more of what you want to look for—a checklist of characteristics for someone who can keep you accountable in your spiritual life:

A mature Christian. You can learn from young Christians. But you can only grab wisdom from a mature Christian who has known both success and failure.

Someone you trust. Your confession and prayer partner must be someone you can trust with your darkest secrets, as well as someone who will trust you. You must also be able to feel certain that your partner will keep all the confidences you share.

Someone of the same sex. Some of your closest friends are probably of the opposite sex. But for accountability it's best that guys seek a guy partner and girls, a girl partner. Meeting with someone of the same sex gives you an advantage in being honest and understanding—and also prevents, well, distractions.

Someone nearby. Your best friend who moved two thousand miles away last year can still help you grow. But look for someone nearby who can get together with you often. It's ideal to have this be someone you see nearly every day.

REFLECT: That's a tall order—who in your life can fit that description of an accountability partner?

PRAY: Ask God to guide you to someone who will be a helpful confession and prayer partner.

29 A Habit You Can Live With

Bible Reading: 1 Timothy 4:11-13
Focus on reading the Scriptures to the church, encouraging the believers, and teaching them. 1 Timothy 4:13

UNDERSTANDING. Enjoyment. Satisfaction. Are those the words to describe how your heart pitter-patters when you put your nose in God's Word? Maybe you know you *should* read the Bible. Maybe you even *want* to read it. But actually *reading* and *enjoying* it seems as possible as tying a rope to your family roadster and dragging it to church.

Getting into a habit of Bible study is like getting physically fit. Honestly, stretching spiritual muscles isn't any easier than motivating a backside that's molded a comfortable spot in the couch. But like physical exercise, reading God's Word *regularly* produces great results—results that show. And after a while you won't like the sluggish feeling you get when you take a day or two off.

Ponder this: If you were to begin a habit of daily prayer and Bible study right now, what would you look like spiritually one year from today? What will you look like if you *don't* spend time developing as a Christian? Take a few moments to picture yourself as you *can* be, and ask God to fulfill that vision according to his will.

One huge reason people who want to read the Bible still find it so difficult is they've never learned these simple guidelines for personal study:

Spend 15-30 minutes a day in Bible study. If that sounds odious, start with 5 minutes. You'll usually find you read more.

As you sit down to read, ask the Holy Spirit to help you understand. Look for a Bible translation that's easy to read and that makes sense.

Start with the clear, basic parts. You don't have to plow through the Old Testament first. Start with the book of Mark, John, or Romans.

Keep a notebook and pencil close by. For each section you read, jot notes: What is the main point of this section? What does it teach me about God, Jesus Christ, and the Holy Spirit? What does it tell me about myself? What am I going to do about what I learned?

Finish by thanking God for what you learned. Pray something like, "Father, I thank you that the Bible gives me patience and encouragement. Please help me not just hear your Word, but do it. Amen."

REFLECT: What keeps you from getting into God's Word daily?

PRAY: Ask God for the confidence and power you need to put his Word into action in your life.

1 What Part of Perfect Don't You Understand?

Bible Reading: Romans 3:10-20

No one can ever be made right in God's sight by doing what his law commands. Romans 3:20

YOU STRUT into Spanish class wearing a triumphant smirk. Your first exam is due back from the teacher today, and you're sure you aced it big-time. But when your teacher, Mr. Chalupa, drops the paper on your desk, you slap your hand over your mouth to keep from crying out in horror. The word "Fail" is scrawled across your paper. Leafing through the test, you find only one tiny mistake. Your teacher has a reputation for being tough, but this is ridiculous.

You storm up to his desk. "Mr. Chalupa, I could understand an A- or maybe a B. But how can you fail me for one picky little mistake?"

The teacher points a bony, accusing finger at you. "The 'picky little mistake' wasn't the only error on your paper," he says. "You were required to write your answers on narrow rule paper; you used wide rule. Besides, I only give passing grades to members of the National Honor Society who have memorized the Encyclopedia Britannica. Didn't you read the class rules?"

You vaguely remember receiving on the first day of class a thirty-page, single-spaced document printed in Spanish. You used the pages to line the bottom of your parakeet's cage. "Uh, not yet, sir," you say. "I'll start today."

"Don't bother," Mr. Chalupa snarls. "You can't pass my class without passing all my exams, and you already failed the first one. Better luck next year."

Would you walk out of Mr. Chalupa's class feeling a little hopeless? Try *totally* hopeless! This teacher's standards are way out of reach. It's obvious that pleasing Mr. Chalupa by obeying his rules is impossible.

Hopefully you don't have teachers as tough and unreasonable as Mr. Chalupa. But that's what you're up against if you try to please God by obeying his rules. It can't be done. The point isn't that God's rules are *unreasonable,* but that keeping them perfectly is *unreachable.* No one can go through life without committing one little sin, and the Bible says, "The person who keeps all of the laws except one is as guilty as the person who has broken all of God's laws" (James 2:10).

Is God as heartless as Mr. Chalupa? No way! God didn't give his commandments to make you fail. His standards only prove that you need another way to come to him. A way to please him that doesn't depend on your performance. And a way where you can't fail!

 REFLECT: One of the first steps to trusting God is admitting you can't perfectly keep all of his rules. Do you really believe that?

PRAY: *God, thank you for providing a way to yourself through the sacrificial death of your own Son, Jesus.*

2 Here Comes the Judge

Bible Reading: Romans 3:21-23

We are made right in God's sight when we trust in Jesus Christ to take away our sins. Romans 3:22

"WILL THE defendant please rise," drones the court bailiff.

The young man at the table in the center of the courtroom slowly stands. The lawyer beside him has done everything she can. The young man is now at the mercy of the judge for sentencing. A roomful of spectators quiets to listen.

The elderly judge looks intently at the defendant. "Do you acknowledge that the actions you have confessed to are wrong?"

"Yes, Your Honor," the young man says softly, his head bowed in shame.

The judge glances at the documents on his desk, then returns his gaze to the defendant. "On the basis of the evidence in this case and your admission of guilt, this court sentences you to a fine of $10,000 or one year in jail."

"But Your Honor," the defendant says, "I don't have $10,000."

"Young man," the judge says firmly, "the law requires that you pay the fine or spend a year in jail." Then he raps the gavel once, signaling that court is dismissed.

As the crowd files out of the courtroom, the judge steps down from the bench and approaches the young man. "Come with me," he says.

The defendant follows the robed judge to the court cashier. As the young man watches, the judge reaches beneath his robe and pulls out his personal checkbook. He carefully writes a check to the court in the amount of $10,000, signs it, and hands it to the cashier. Then he turns to the defendant with a smile. "You're free to go, Son."

Tears fill the young man's eyes. "I don't deserve this, but thank you, Dad." Then the two embrace.

That's a picture of how God loves us! We can't fully obey God's law. Our sin has earned us a sentence we can't pay. God, the righteous Judge, can't forgive the sin until the fine is paid. But the righteous Judge, who is also our loving Father, steps down from the bench and pays the fine himself. All we have to do is accept his generous gift by trusting Jesus Christ to take away our sins. Then all is forgiven and we are made right with our totally just and totally loving God.

There's no other way. If God hadn't stepped in to make things right through Christ, we would have been forever trapped by the penalty and power of sin. But he did step in, and he saved us!

 REFLECT: What if God hadn't provided Jesus to make things right between you and him? How would you feel to be still under the penalty for sin?

PRAY: Spend some time today thanking your loving Judge.

3 The Egg and I

Bible Reading: Romans 3:24-26
We are made right with God when we believe that Jesus shed his blood, sacrificing his life for us. Romans 3:25

WANT TO ASTOUND your friends with your dynamic stage presence, manual dexterity, and biblical insight—all at the same time? Try this.

You'll need a few simple supplies: a raw egg, an empty tin can, a small piece of scrap wood, and a hammer. Practice your presentation ahead of time, then gather a group of friends around a table.

Place the scrap wood on the table and carefully set the egg on it. Lay the hammer on the table, but keep the can out of sight for now. Announce, "This egg represents you and me. The Bible says that all of us have sinned, and God's punishment for sin is death." Pick up the hammer. "This hammer represents God's punishment for our sin." Lift the hammer menacingly above the egg and say, "What is going to happen when I hit the egg with this hammer?"

Your friends will probably say something like, "Major splattage!" or "Scrambled egg" or "The yoke will be on us." But before they start covering themselves in plastic wrap, bring out the empty tin can and cover the egg with it. Take a good, hard whack at the top of the can with the hammer. The loud *thunk* will probably make your friends jump. If all goes well, you'll have one nastily dented can—but when you lift it up, you should find that fragile egg still intact.

Here's where you impress your friends with your spiritual insight: "See, Jesus took the hit for us, just like the can took the hit for the defenseless egg. The Bible says that by dying on the cross in our place, Christ stepped between us and God's judgment for our sin. We couldn't survive God's anger against our sin any more than an egg could live through a blow from the hammer. But we can escape God's wrath. It's a gift we receive simply by trusting Christ."

As you and your friends look at the dented can, think about what it cost to forgive your sin. During the last hours of his life, the sinless Son of God was cursed, mocked, spit upon, and mercilessly beaten. A crown of thorns dug into his head. He was nailed to a wooden cross with spikes driven through his wrists and feet. The cross was dropped into the ground with a jolt, and for three hours Christ hung from those spikes as his life faded away.

That's the price for your sin. That's what you're worth to God. You're worth the humiliating, excruciating death of his only Son. He loves you so much that he allowed his Son to die.

REFLECT: How do you feel about yourself when you think about the loving sacrifice Jesus made for you? Are you humbled?

PRAY: Tell God how you are feeling right now.

4 Credit Check

Bible Reading: Romans 3:27-31
Can we boast, then, that we have done anything to be accepted by God? No, because our acquittal is not based on our good deeds. It is based on our faith. Romans 3:27

HERE ARE SOME QUOTES from famous people that you will never read:

"My famous sculpture of David, the beautiful fresco I painted on the ceiling of the Sistine Chapel, and the stunning St. Peter's Basilica are all the products of my ingenuity. I received no external inspiration or ability." *Michelangelo Buonarroti, sixteenth-century Italian sculptor, artist, architect, and poet.*

"Musical talent? Are you kidding? Anybody can compose symphonies that will live on for centuries. If you want to spend your life driving a truck or filling teeth, that's your problem. I decided to become famous for composing music." *Wolfgang Amadeus Mozart, eighteenth-century Austrian composer.*

"Some people have called me the greatest basketball player of all time. Becoming a basketball superstar is nothing more than willing yourself to be tall and talented. Just start thinking *six-feet nine, six-feet nine, six-feet nine.* It worked for me." *Michael Jordan, NBA superstar.*

You won't find these quotes anywhere, because those famous folks never uttered them. Most great achievers admit that they're at best only partially responsible for their success. A surprising number of famous people give God the credit for their ability, intellect, or talent. Late in his life Michelangelo, for example, wrote, "I believe that I have been designated for this work by God. . . . I work out of love for God and I put all my hope in him."

For anything you accomplish, you have to give credit where credit is due—starting with acknowledging God. Get honest: If he hadn't created you and gifted you with all sorts of talents, you could accomplish *nada.* You might pump and sweat to develop your natural abilities, but you got those abilities from God—along with the ability to persevere, by the way. It all goes back to God.

And when it comes to the gift of forgiveness, you especially had nothing to do with it. You didn't create it, devise it, earn it, buy it, or win it. It wasn't your brainchild or work of art. It's something God did for you and offered freely to you. You can't improve on it and you can't take any credit for it; you can only receive it by trusting in Christ's sacrifice on the cross for you.

 REFLECT: How do you feel about a God who has done everything necessary to bring you into right standing with himself?

PRAY: How will you tell God today that he deserves all the credit?

5 Who's Right about Right and Wrong?

Bible Reading: Genesis 3:1-7

You will know the truth, and the truth will set you free. John 8:32

"HEY, EVE," said the serpent, his forked tongue flicking out of his mouth with every hiss. "Why haven't you tried that luscious-looking fruit dangling on that tree in the middle of the Garden?"

"God said not to," she answered. "Isn't that obvious?"

The serpent frowned. "You can't dine on any of these fruity trees, huh?"

Eve shook her head. "No, God said we can't eat from *that* tree—can't even touch it, he said, or we'll die."

"You won't die," the serpent hissed. "God doesn't want you to eat that fruit because he knows it will make you like him. You'll know right from wrong. And he has the gall to inflict his rules on you. That's not right, Eve. You've got brains enough to decide for yourself whether the fruit is good or evil. You've got the right to make up your own mind about what's good for you and what's bad."

The serpent's wiliness worked, of course. Eve and then Adam ate the fruit. Satan convinced them they didn't need God to pick right and wrong for them, because they were smart enough all on their own.

Know what? Human beings are all part of Adam and Eve's family, and Satan hasn't changed his tactics. He wants to prevent you from looking to God as the only true judge of right and wrong—and prompt you to look to yourself to decide what is right to do in your own eyes.

For centuries, that plan fizzled. People didn't always obey God, but most people still saw God as the objective, righteous Judge. But in recent centuries, people have slid into a significantly different way of thinking. Society today has largely rejected the notion of God's truth and morality. Instead, people have inserted their own ideas of right and wrong. They rely on their own standards.

That approach is like an oceangoing sailor who determines his location by pointing himself in a random direction and calling it north. It won't be long before he's lost if he calculates his position by what he picks willy-nilly as north instead of looking to the heavens and charting his course by the North Star.

North isn't a matter of opinion. It's not a personal preference. If you ignore the reality that north is north, you're bound to get lost. If you ignore the fact that God alone gives you direction, you're bound to go astray.

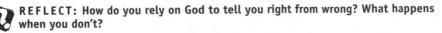

REFLECT: How do you rely on God to tell you right from wrong? What happens when you don't?

PRAY: *Lord, you alone know right from wrong. Each moment of today and always, help me look to you for direction.*

March

6 Self-Appointed Judges

Bible Reading: Psalm 9:3-10

The Lord reigns forever, executing judgment from his throne. He will judge the world with justice and rule the nations with fairness.
Psalm 9:7-8

IT FEELS SO WARM and cozy that you almost sweat when someone says that all people have the right to decide right and wrong for themselves. "Religion is a private thing," they argue. "You shouldn't be allowed to impose your idea of truth on someone else."

This brand of tolerance has become so big in our culture that it pretty much defines what it means to be a good person. To take any other view is to be close-minded, intolerant, and bigoted.

But that trendy way of thinking doesn't catch the true meaning of tolerance. The true definition of tolerance says you act considerately toward people whose practices differ from your own. You stay courteous and kind even when someone doesn't see things like you do. Tolerance keeps you from judging others. And why? Because God is the only Perfect One. He's the only one capable of judging flawlessly. Scripture makes it clear that we aren't to judge but to leave that to God. (See the passage listed above.)

Just because we aren't to pass judgment on another, though, doesn't change the fact that truth is absolute. Tolerance is simply supposed to guard us from getting ugly with each other. It wasn't meant to be twisted into a cultural "law," forcing people to applaud another person's view even if that view clearly violates God's absolute commands, which are true and right in every time and every place.

God calls you to be loving. Sometimes the best way you can love a friend is by not letting the wrong she's doing slide by. You can still accept a person while warning her that how she's acting is wrong.

The wrong kind of tolerance says you should ignore or even applaud when someone lives in a harmful way. God's kind of tolerance cares too much to let the hurt go on. He can show you the best and most caring time and way to confront a friend, because anything less than speaking up isn't real love.

God has given each of us freedom to accept or reject his truth. So people who reject God's absolute truth aren't rejecting you. They're rejecting God. It's God's job to worry about that. And it's your job to live according to God's truth and to share his truth in love and compassion.

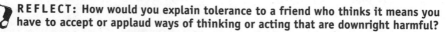

REFLECT: How would you explain tolerance to a friend who thinks it means you have to accept or applaud ways of thinking or acting that are downright harmful?

PRAY: Ask God to help you know when to confront a friend whose behavior may be harmful—and ask God for grace and compassion to confront without judgment.

7 How Do You Measure Truth?

Bible Reading: 2 Thessalonians 2:13-17
We are thankful that God chose you to be among the first to experience salvation, a salvation that came through the Spirit who makes you holy and by your belief in the truth. 2 Thessalonians 2:13

"HEY, PEDRO, here's that board you wanted," Devin says to his friend. "I was on the arm saw anyway, so I cut it for you."

Pedro looks at the board. "Thanks. But it looks longer than a meter."

Devin shakes his head. "It's a meter exactly. I measured twice, cut once."

"Let's see," Pedro says. He finds a meterstick and lays it on the board. "I was right. It's four centimeters too long."

"That's crazy," Devin retorts, pulling out his own meterstick. "Check it out. According to my stick, the board is exactly one meter long."

When the two friends compare metersticks, Devin's is four centimeters longer than Pedro's. How can they know which meter is really a meter? Well, they do have some options. They could take a vote, flip a coin, or appeal to an absolute, unchanging standard of measurement. It so happens that there exists a totally authoritative benchmark for measurements in Sèvres, France, at the International Bureau of Weights and Measures. That bureau establishes and guards the international standards for metric measurements. To learn what a meter really is, all you need to do is compare it to the original—the standard.

Webster defines *truth* as "fidelity to an original or to a standard." Just like you need a consistent stick when measuring meters, you also need a standard to tell right from wrong. To decide what's good and true, you need to ask how something stacks up against the original, *the standard.*

The only reason you can recognize that some things are right and some things are wrong is that there is a Creator: God. He is so righteous, so just, so true that he alone sets the standard for right and wrong, justice and injustice, truth and lies. The reason you know love is good and hatred is evil is that the God who made you is a God of love. Honesty is right and deceit is wrong because God is true. Sexual purity is moral and sleeping around is immoral because God is pure.

It's God and God alone who determines absolute truth—what is right *for all people, for all places, for all times.* That perfect truth is *objective* because God isn't just a figment of our feelings. It's *universal* because God is above all. And it's *constant* because God is eternal. Absolute truth is absolute because it originates from the original—God, *the* Standard.

REFLECT: Can you explain to a friend why God's standard of right and wrong—and truth and falsehood—is the one to use?

PRAY: *Lord, the world gives me all kinds of standards to judge actions and ideas. I submit to you as the perfect Judge of what is good and right.*

8 Getting to the Bottom of the Rules

Bible Reading: Romans 13:8-10

Love does no wrong to anyone, so love satisfies all of God's requirements. Romans 13:10

IF YOU HAD TO figure out for science class whether rolling friction slows an object faster than sliding friction, what would you do? Well, the fate of animals that scurry in front of your car on slick roads depends on your answer.

You could climb into an older car and drive thirty-five miles per hour across an icy, empty parking lot. (Do NOT try this near a cliff or without a license.) Jam on the brakes and skid to a stop. Then go back to the starting point, accelerate again to thirty-five miles per hour, and at the same spot pump the brakes hard while keeping the wheels rolling. You'll discover that rolling stops an object faster than sliding—which is why cars now have anti-lock brakes.

But suppose you wanted to figure out whether sex between two unmarried people who love each other is right or wrong. How would you decide that?

Well, you can follow the pattern God has used to teach people truth throughout history. God began his revelation of right and wrong with the Ten Commandments. So you can compare your attitudes and actions to God's spoken commands—his *precepts*. His spoken Word (the Bible) points to universal moral *principles*, which in turn spring from the *person* or character of God himself.

Precept. God has spoken some totally clear precepts—or commands—in the Bible. Like the fact that sexual involvement outside marriage is wrong (see 1 Corinthians 6:18; 1 Thessalonians 4:3). But those precepts aren't just a long list of dos and don'ts. They also point to bigger moral principles.

Principle. A principle is a standard you can apply to more than one situation. They help explain the "why" behind a precept. God's law that says sexual immorality is out of bounds isn't intended to squash your fun. That "don't" also tells you that *the biblical standard for sex is love.* True love—as defined by God—sets clear boundaries for sex, requiring that you care for the happiness, health, and spiritual growth of the other person.

Person. But having your head stuffed full of God's precepts and principles means nothing if you don't know the Person who provides them. God's ultimate purpose in every precept is to help people know him. Apply that once again to sex outside marriage: It's wrong not only because it violates God's precepts and principles but because it violates his character of love, purity, and faithfulness.

That's a little more complicated than skidding your car on ice. But it's how you know if something is right or wrong.

REFLECT: Look at what God teaches about sex through his precepts, his principles, and his person. Do you want to honor God by obeying him?

PRAY: Talk to God about your desire to follow his best for your life.

9 Whose Rules Will Rule?

Bible Reading: Deuteronomy 10:12-16

He requires you to . . . obey the Lord's commands and laws that I am giving you today for your own good. Deuteronomy 10:12-13

"YOU KNOW," Carmen insists, "I want to do what's right. But I hear so many things from so many people that I don't know what's right anymore. I'm like a little kid playing baseball. I've got coaches and teammates and my parents and the other team all yelling at me at once. I need to know what God wants."

Confused as Carmen is, she's taken a huge step toward obeying God: *She wants what God wants.* Truth is, the struggle isn't figuring out right and wrong. It's deciding God's version of right and wrong is better than your own or anything anyone else yells at you. Once you have decided to follow God's absolute best, here's a step-by-step plan to figure out what he wants:

1. *Consider the choice.* Through Jesus Christ and the words of Scripture, God has revealed his absolute standards for right and wrong. You have many big choices to make in life, but the biggest is deciding whose version of right and wrong you will live by.
2. *Compare it to God.* Your next step is to compare an attitude or action to who God is and what he has said about it.
3. *Commit to God's way.* God has promised that when you submit to him as Savior and Lord of your life, he will pump you full of his power to live according to his ways. Here's how to get filled:
   a. *Turn from your selfish ways and confess your sin* (see 1 John 1:9). Sincerely turn your back on sin and claim God's free forgiveness.
   b. *Turn control of your life over to the Lord.* If God can keep planets spinning, rivers running, and seasons coming and going, don't you think he can keep your life in order if you give him control?
   c. *Trust God to fill you and lead you by his Holy Spirit.* Being filled with the Holy Spirit means he directs your life and gives you his power to resist temptation, gain courage, make right choices, and deal with whatever happens to you.
   d. *Keep walking in the power of the Spirit.* As you live in the power of the Holy Spirit, you can live more consistently day after day.
4. *Count on God's protection and provision.* Living according to God's way brings countless spiritual blessings—like freedom from guilt, a clear conscience, the joy of sharing Christ, and, most importantly, the love and smile of God.

REFLECT: Are you seeking God's version of right and wrong for your life? How do you see that happening in your daily decisions?

PRAY: Ask for help to apply God's standards to your attitudes and actions.

10 Do Yourself a Favor and Love Yourself

Bible Reading: Matthew 22:34-40
Love your neighbor as yourself. Matthew 22:39

THEY'RE OUT THERE. They think you don't see them. But you do. And it makes you gag. Unless you happen to be one of them . . .

- A guy struts in front of a locker room mirror and flexes and poses like he's Mr. World Champion Bodybuilder.
- A girl pauses to admire herself in a shopping mall window. She fluffs her hair, then lays a lip print on her reflection.
- A guy won't shut up about how great and tough he is.
- A girl splashes her bedroom walls with blown-up photos of herself modeling all her outfits.

When the Bible commands you to love others like you love yourself, that's not exactly what God meant. Yes, there's a healthy kind of self-love, but bragging about your greatness or being infatuated with your looks is conceit, not love.

Matthew 22:39 implies that you won't love *others* in the right way unless you love *yourself* in the right way. Is that okay? Look at it this way: God loves you, so you can love yourself. God accepts you, so you can accept yourself. God cherishes you as his unique creation, so you can cherish yourself. Liking yourself like that isn't just okay, it's great. It's what God wants.

Seeing yourself as God sees you—no more or no less—is a *healthy* self-image. That's an uplifting thing. It's also a humbling thing—because you recognize that every gift you possess comes from the Lord Jesus Christ.

Another kind of self-image is *unhealthy*. An unhealthy self-image can be either negative or positive. People with a negative self-image get down on themselves. People with a positive self-image get high on themselves. What warps these two views is their reliance on the world's system of value and worth—that what matters most about you is your looks, abilities, intelligence, possessions, etc. When you think well of yourself based on the world's standards, you easily slide into pride.

You can be sure you're loving yourself in the right way when you love others more as a result. And when you make loving others your goal, everything then falls into place. Life—and liking yourself—makes sense. You put others, beginning with Christ, smack at the center of your attention. And when that happens, God is pleased.

REFLECT: Describe in your own words a healthy self-image.

PRAY: *Father, teach me to love myself in the right way so I'll love others as a result.*

11 Looking for a Pony

Bible Reading: Philippians 4:6–9
Fix your thoughts on what is true and honorable and right.
Philippians 4:8

THERE ONCE WERE a mom and dad having trouble with their twin boys. One was abnormally happy all the time—a total optimist. The other boy was continually depressed and finding something bad about everything—an absolute pessimist. When the parents ran out of ideas, they decided it was time to seek professional help. So they took their two sons to a psychiatrist.

The psychiatrist claimed to have the cure for this family dilemma. He took the optimist and put him in a room filled with horse manure and a pitchfork. Figuring this would cure the boy's over-joyful spirit, the doctor told him to dig. Then he left the boy alone. He took the pessimist into a room filled with new toys and candy. He was free to play with it all. "That should cure him of his dark outlook on life," exclaimed the psychiatrist. "We'll come back in a few hours and see."

When the doctor and parents returned to the room full of toys and candy, they were shocked to see the little boy sobbing. "I might hurt myself if I play with these toys," he cried, "and the candy might give me a tummy-ache." All the wonderful things around him hadn't snapped him out of his pessimistic attitude.

"Well, surely your other boy will be cured," claimed the psychiatrist, trying to sound confident. Peering into the second room, the adults were astounded to see the optimist pitching manure in a fury. The boy's mom tried to get him to slow down, but he was so busy that he only paused to say, "With all this manure, there must be a pony in here somewhere!"

You've got to admire positive thinking; and if you don't have it, you've got to get some. Negative thinking won't get you anywhere in life. Thinking positively draws out potential—in you and in the people around you. But positive thinking can't produce something that doesn't already exist. Positive thinking is only an advantage when you focus on what is true and positive according to God's Word.

And the problem with negative thinking (besides the fact that it makes you a crab) is how it keeps you from ever having a healthy self-image. It blocks out all the good things God says about you. But as you believe God's Word and what God says about your being his special child, you will discover gifts God has prepared for you far bigger than finding a pony.

 REFLECT: Do you find yourself thinking negatively and pessimistically about your life? Make a list of positive things to think about from Philippians 4:8.

PRAY: Ask God to give you a positive outlook on life based on his Word. Start praying about it today.

12 Guess What I Heard about You

Bible Reading: Proverbs 19:19-23

Get all the advice and instruction you can, and be wise the rest of your life. Proverbs 19:20

YOU TELL YOUR FRIEND you signed up for the football team. "Are you kidding?" he snorts. "The only position the coach will let you play is left end—*of the bench!*"

You come home and announce that you're trying out for the chorus in your school's spring drama production. Your older sister scowls. "Why are you doing that? You couldn't carry a tune if it came in a bucket."

You walk into a party proud of your new outfit. Two students eye you up and down. You hear one of them say, "She always wears cheap outfits."

Criticism stings. And if you don't deal with the hurt you feel, it makes your self-image stink. No one escapes getting stung by others. But with God's help you can take the unkind words of others as opportunities to become wise. Here's how.

First, *decide if the criticism is deserved.* If it is, you have something to work on. Sometimes criticism is what it takes to make us correct flaws, change motivations, and learn to be sensitive to others.

Second, sometimes your critic was honestly trying to help, so *say thanks for the input.* But it won't help anyone if you sass something like, "Thanks. I so very much value the opinion of a jerk like you."

Third, *remember who you are*—God's much-loved child. You are valued, accepted, and gifted. Don't let the criticism damage that view of yourself.

So what do you do when someone compliments you? It's easy to go to one of two extremes. One extreme? False humility. You deny any positive quality or accomplishment by saying something like, "No, no, no. I'm just a dung-burrowing worm." That makes people sick. Everyone knows that inside you're screaming, "Say it again! Tell me again how great I am!"

The other extreme is to agree with the person who compliments you to the point of bragging. You know people like that. You say one nice thing and they remind you of twenty other things they do well.

When you get a compliment, first *see if it is deserved.* If it isn't, pass the credit on to someone else. If it is, simply say, "Thank you."

For every compliment, *whisper a thanks to Jesus.* After all, he is the source of your gifts, abilities, looks, and personality. If you hold on to the compliments instead of giving credit to God, you forget that he is your source and you start believing that you're the source. That's pride.

REFLECT: Have you been criticized or complimented recently? How did you react?

PRAY: Ask God to help you receive criticism and compliments with grace.

13 Keep Blooming Where God Plants You

Bible Reading: Philippians 1:3-6

I am sure that God, who began the good work within you, will continue his work until it is finally finished on that day when Christ Jesus comes back again. Philippians 1:6

SUPPOSE YOU WANT TO communicate to someone that he or she is totally special to you. You don't say it with stinkweed. You don't dial a florist and have a dozen dandelions delivered. You buy a gorgeous long-stemmed rose. Bigger and better yet, you buy a bunch of roses. Why? Because roses are the crowning achievement of God's work in the flower department. Here's the surprise: A rose left to itself stays small and thorny. But with loving care from a gardener, the rose reaches its full potential.

Perfect as you are, you're still not all you're capable of becoming. There are some things you can do to let God train you to become all you are capable of becoming. These training tactics don't increase your value as God's child, but they prepare you to serve Christ in greater ways than you could ever dream. Try these:

- Don't label yourself negatively (like "I'm stupid," etc.). You tend to live down to negative labels you stick on yourself.
- When you fail, admit it to God. And then refuse to browbeat yourself.
- Be as kind to yourself as you want to be to other people.
- Don't compare yourself to others. You are unique. God enjoys your uniqueness, so have a similar attitude toward yourself.
- Focus on God's grace, love, and acceptance, not on criticism from others.
- Help other people see themselves as God sees them by accepting them, loving them, and encouraging them.
- Be positive. See how long you can go without saying something noxious about another person, situation, or yourself.
- List the things you *can* change and what you *will* change, along with *how* you will change and *when* you will change.
- List the things you would like to change but can't, and how these facts of who you are can benefit you.
- Look your best. Take care of yourself by getting rest, good food, and exercise.
- Use and develop your talents, like playing a musical instrument, working with wood, playing a sport, etc.
- Develop your God-given spiritual gifts and ministries.

REFLECT: Aren't you grateful that God is always with you to help you grow to your fullest potential?

PRAY: Pray through the above list. Ask God to empower your efforts.

14 One Gigantic Sign from God

Bible Reading: Acts 17:19-28
In him we live and move and exist. Acts 17:28

A FEW WEEKS AGO you were turning over dirt. But then your mom planted seeds and your little sister watered them and you all watched day by day for them to sprout. Warm spring sunlight coaxed green from the moist earth. And now raindrop beads rest on the leaves in your backyard. The garden promises tomato, zucchini, lettuce, and carrot taste sensations later in the summer.

The amazing point is this: From dirt, water, sun, and seeds comes God's provision. Daily. In abundance.

You have likely never seen lightning torch your mom's vegetable garden. It probably doesn't flood with every rainfall. And most summers the wind doesn't blow the asparagus into oblivion. God does allow natural disasters to strike sometimes, but he is a God who cares about the earth he created and the creatures who live on it.

Paul once told a group of unbelievers that God "has not left himself without testimony: He has shown kindness by giving you rain from heaven and crops in their seasons; he provides you with plenty of food and fills your hearts with joy" (Acts 14:17, NIV). God promised Noah, "As long as the earth remains, there will be springtime and harvest, cold and heat, winter and summer, day and night" (Genesis 8:22). God provides signs of his love from the lavish ripeness of a garden to the intricate design of the tiniest cell swimming happily in a mud-splat.

Each of us totally depends on the love of the God who made us. Paul said this to another group of non-Christians: "Human hands can't serve [God's] needs—for he has no needs. He himself gives life and breath to everything" (Acts 17:25). And Paul told the people who received his letter in Rome that we can see enough about God in nature to convince every human being that God exists—and that he made us and cares for our needs. Paul wrote that even unbelievers "can clearly see [God's] invisible qualities—his eternal power and divine nature. So they have no excuse whatsoever for not knowing God" (Romans 1:20). Nature is constantly telling us that God's love is true.

Maybe you never thought of a zucchini or a carrot or a falling star or a snowcapped mountain as proof of God's love. But that's what creation cries out. What God made is a huge sign of love.

REFLECT: When you look at the way God has provided a wonderful world for you, do you feel loved?

PRAY: Take some time to express your love to God for the beauty he has put all around you.

15 Can You Feel the Love?

Bible Reading: 2 Corinthians 5:11-15
Whatever we do, it is because Christ's love controls us.
2 Corinthians 5:14

OKAY, MAKE A quick list in your head of everyone you love. Who makes it onto your list? Parents and grandparents? Siblings—at least some of the time? A boyfriend or girlfriend? Close friends? A pastor or youth leader? Favorite teachers? Your drooly dog, Bosco? You might be able to generate a fairly long list of people for whom you have genuine love in your heart.

So who loves you? Maybe the same list of people—and Bosco too, who shows his affection when he jumps up to lick leftovers off your chin.

What you know about God's love doesn't just come from nature. God also demonstrates his love for you through the people he made. The apostle John put it this way: "Love comes from God. Anyone who loves is born of God and knows God" (1 John 4:7). Parents change messy diapers, referee fights, and provide you with food, clothes, and lots more. Husbands and wives commit to love each other till death do them part. Even some of the friendships you make right now might last a lifetime. And every time someone runs errands for a shut-in, provides meals for a sick friend, donates money or materials for disaster relief, helps a neighbor move furniture, or performs some other loving deed, God's love shines through human behavior. The love you see tells you something about God's love.

As a Christian, you're like an instrument of God's love to others. And people who experience true love, whether believers or not, sense God cares.

Droughts, floods, earthquakes—and twisters that toss cows into the air—sometimes make it tough to look at nature and see God's care. Just like that, the human love you see in your world is sometimes warped. Sick and sinful human hearts twist love into pride, hatred, and revenge. Fighting, envy, and bitterness split individuals, families, friends, races, and nations. And yet human love shows up all around you. The most violent cultures have some piece of decency and respect in human relationships. They have laws and moral codes—and even Attila's savage Huns loved their own spouses, children, and friends.

You have to hunt out the world's most hard-boiled evildoers to find a person who doesn't love *someone:* a parent, a kid, a brother or sister, a teacher, a husband or wife. And even the faintest glimmer of love in a human heart shows the fingerprint of the loving God who created you.

REFLECT: God has surrounded you with human love so you will know he loves you. How do you best see God's message of love to you?

PRAY: *When people love me, God, help me remember that you are the source of that love. Thanks for showing me your love in solid ways.*

16 God Wrote the Old Book on Love

Bible Reading: Exodus 34:5-7

I am the Lord, the merciful and gracious God. I am slow to anger and rich in unfailing love and faithfulness. Exodus 34:6

YOU REALLY WANT TO know about God's love? Look at the Bible. That's where you spot more specifics about God's love than anywhere else.

Hundreds of references in both Testaments fill you in on God's affection for you. Some entire chapters, such as 1 Corinthians 13—called "the love chapter"—are devoted to love. Love is the big theme in books such as Hosea, the gospel of John, and John's skinny first letter toward the back of the Bible. And according to Jesus, love is the overall theme of Scripture (see Matthew 22:37-40).

In the Old Testament, the Law (the first five books) and the Prophets (the last seventeen books) summarize God's instructions about how to have a deep, radically loving relationship with him and others. How those relationships panned out is related in the Old Testament books of history (Joshua, Judges, Kings, Chronicles, etc.) and celebrated in the books of poetry (Psalms, Proverbs, etc.).

When Jesus talked about "commandments" and "prophets," he was saying that God's love fills the Old Testament. Catch these rich words about how your loving God described himself in the Old Testament:

- "The Lord is slow to anger and rich in unfailing love, forgiving every kind of sin and rebellion" (Numbers 14:18).
- "You, O Lord, are a merciful and gracious God, slow to get angry, full of unfailing love and truth" (Psalm 86:15).
- "The Lord is kind and merciful, slow to get angry, full of unfailing love" (Psalm 145:8).
- "Return to the Lord your God, for he is gracious and merciful. He is not easily angered. He is filled with kindness and is eager not to punish you" (Joel 2:13).

And do you remember Jonah? He's the guy who was swallowed by a big fish for refusing to spread God's love. Jonah hated the Ninevites, but he had to admit *God* loved them: "I knew that you were a gracious and compassionate God, slow to get angry and filled with unfailing love" (Jonah 4:2).

See a pattern here? The good news of God's eternal love permeates the Old Testament from Genesis to Malachi. God isn't first and foremost about judgment. He's about love. And you are at the center of his loving heart.

REFLECT: Which of those messages in God's Word makes you most sure of his love for you?

PRAY: Tell God thanks for shouting his love for you through the Bible.

17 God Wrote the New Book on Love

Bible Reading: 1 John 3:11-17

We know what real love is because Christ gave up his life for us. And so we also ought to give up our lives for our Christian brothers and sisters. 1 John 3:16

IF THE MESSAGE of God's love is strong in the Old Testament, it's a bone-crushing bear hug in the New Testament. God's love is all over the New Testament. You spot it in the Bible's most famous verse: "For God so loved the world that he gave his only Son, so that everyone who believes in him will not perish but have eternal life" (John 3:16). John later said the same thing in slightly different words: "God showed how much he loved us by sending his only Son into the world so that we might have eternal life through him" (1 John 4:9).

Jesus said, "The greatest love is shown when people lay down their lives for their friends" (John 15:13). The apostle John echoed that thought, pointing out that Jesus himself showed us how: "We know what real love is because Christ gave up his life for us. And so we also ought to give up our lives for our Christian brothers and sisters" (1 John 3:16).

Paul was shocked that God would love us while we were still warring with him: "But God showed his great love for us by sending Christ to die for us while we were still sinners" (Romans 5:8). The way God sacrificed his Son to save the sinful human race is the maximum expression of love. No wonder John cheers, "See how very much our heavenly Father loves us, for he allows us to be called his children, and we really are!" (1 John 3:1). And Romans 8:35, 38-39 lists all the things that *can't* separate you from God's love.

The love of God reverberates through the New Testament. You see God the Father's love for his Son (see Matthew 3:17; Mark 9:7) and the Son's love for his Father (see John 14:31). Jesus tells us that his love for us is modeled after the Father's love for him (see John 15:9). We are commanded to respond to God's love for us by loving God (see Matthew 22:37) and by loving others (see John 13:34-35; Romans 13:8; 1 Peter 1:22; 1 John 4:7), including our enemies (see Matthew 5:44). And our ability to love comes straight from God and his loving nature: "This is real love. It is not that we loved God, but that he loved us and sent his Son as a sacrifice to take away our sins" (1 John 4:10).

You can't read the New Testament and miss God's message of love unless you're blind in one eye and can't see out of the other. God's love is everywhere.

REFLECT: What do you think of a God who heaps so much love on you?

PRAY: Pray today for your non-Christian friends who need to personally know God and his love.

18 The Book of Love

Bible Reading: 1 Peter 4:7-11
> *Continue to show deep love for each other, for love covers a multitude of sins. 1 Peter 4:8*

JACOB RAN HOME after school, feeling like he'd been kicked by his classmates. *If I'm just a dirtball as they say,* he thought to himself, *then no one wants to be around me. Fine. I don't want to be around them.* He went into his room, shut the door, and slipped on his headphones. With the music blasting loud enough to blow his eardrums, he tried hard to think about anything but people.

There's a problem with Jacob's approach to life: You can't resign from the human race. God custom-designed you to be involved with people of all kinds—even those who get on your nerves and make that feat look impossible. You're made to help people, work through difficulties with them, enjoy them, comfort them, and guide them to Christ.

But God didn't design you to do good to people and then leave you clueless how to do it. His Word is the manufacturer's handbook for how you're to live.

The key is love—and God wrote the book on love, literally. God's Book *invites* you to experience his love for you through his Son, Jesus. It *commands* you to put love into practice as you get along with the world around you. And it *instructs* you on how to show that love. Unless you put the Bible's lessons into practice, you miss out on the true reasons you exist.

Here are honest facts you need to understand in order to cooperate with God's priority of love in relationships:

- *Love is a "universal moral absolute."* To love is always right. Not to love is always wrong.
- *Love is more than hearts, flowers, and drippy songs.* Love is a choice. A conscious action. A real response.
- *Love isn't an option.* The Bible's supreme command to Christians is to love God and love people.
- *Love is often hard.* Sometimes figuring out the loving thing to do is tough. Sometimes doing the loving thing is even tougher.
- *Love never fails.* But sometimes we fail—at loving God and others. Despite our best intentions, we sometimes act unloving.

All around you every day there are people who need God's real, life-changing love. You're not an island. You're made to swim in the ocean of God's love.

REFLECT: When have you wanted to pull away from your world? How does God's law of love make that *not* a long-term option?

PRAY: Ask the God of love to keep teaching you what it means to love him and others.

19 The All-Time Right Thing to Do

Bible Reading: Luke 6:27-36
Do for others as you would like them to do for you. Luke 6:31

YOU MIGHT SEND your heart into a spasm figuring out what to wear to a party. You might not know the music you're supposed to have memorized for your next concert. You might have dropped your script book for the class play in a sewer. And you might discover your brain is dry when you try to squeeze out a few drops of geometry during your next math test.

But you can know the right way to live life—*every time.* There's only one overarching, always-right, basic moral absolute. Here it is: *Always love.*

God's command to love is an absolute because it has no exceptions. It applies to all people at all times in all places. Know how you know? Because even people who are hateful or indifferent object when others treat them hatefully or indifferently. In other words, you might feel okay about ignoring others or spinning rumors about them or calling them names. But if they do any of that stuff to you, you feel wronged. That's how you know love is an absolute—and that anything less than love is wrong.

The law of love even crosses lines of culture and faith. People everywhere want to be loved—to be treated with fairness, respect, courtesy, and honesty. People—except for a few who are mentally unhinged—aren't happy when they are assaulted, abused, slandered, lied to, cheated, robbed, made fun of, or ignored. Those things make everyone angry! People everywhere expect better than that.

Think about yourself. You no doubt hope for positive, loving treatment from people. And you no doubt get a little heated when you fail to receive the treatment you expect, right? When you help your little brother with his homework, for example, you expect him to appreciate your help—and you feel disappointed, hurt, or frustrated when he takes you for granted. You expect your teachers to grade fairly—and you go ballistic when they play favorites.

People demand nothing less than to be loved—and that demands nothing less from us than we *should* love. We know it's right. If you admit that you hope for and insist on loving treatment from others, then your expectation demands you love others with the same love you expect for yourself.

Jesus said it all when he spoke the Golden Rule: "Do for others what you would like them to do for you" (Matthew 7:12).

REFLECT: What does it mean that God's law of love is an "absolute"? How do you know that?

PRAY: *God, I want to love others as I need to be loved. Help me to love as you love.*

20 A Love That Is More than Human

Bible Reading: 1 John 4:16-19
As we live in God, our love grows more perfect. 1 John 4:17

NINA HAD BEEN Felicia's best friend for most of their lives. Nina was really nice. When Felicia became a Christian and announced to her best friend that she needed Jesus, Nina answered that she was just as good as Felicia.

Nina's challenge isn't a surprise. Even Christians wonder what the Golden Rule looks like in real life. Here are three big questions that pop up:

1. Can non-Christians really obey the Golden Rule when they don't know God? Yes. You don't have to be a Christian to live out biblical truth. In fact, sometimes unbelievers follow the Golden Rule more feverishly than some Christians! Unbelievers can live out the Golden Rule without knowing that God is its source simply because treating others like you want to be treated makes sense. Here's the catch: As kind and loving as an unbeliever can be, salvation comes through faith in Christ alone, not through following the Golden Rule. Loving others isn't enough. People need a friendship with God, the source of love.

2. What does the Holy Spirit have to do with treating others like I want to be treated? You can't deny that lots of people—unbelievers included—manage to follow the Golden Rule on brute willpower. But to live this "love ethic" day-in and day-out takes supernatural power from inside—the Holy Spirit's power.

You see the difference when loving gets hard. When nasty, negative people challenge your determination to treat others according to the Golden Rule, it's way easier to flip-flop the rule—to dish back to them what they dished out to you! Or when you get tired or stressed, your willingness to love wears thin. You can *know* what's right, but you still need the Holy Spirit's power to *do* what's right.

3. What's the difference between how the Bible defines love and how my conscience and common sense tell me to act? You might be able to trust your conscience and common sense most of the time, but they aren't perfect. Your conscience can take its cues from influences around you, urges from inside you, and even temptations from the devil. "Common sense" just means something is widely accepted—crowds of people and whole countries can be twisted by the same ungodly pressures that affect personal conscience. Without a changeless standard for behavior—those moral "absolutes" anchored to God himself and expressed in the Bible—eventually you miss the mark.

REFLECT: How would you have answered Nina?

PRAY: *God, there are great people all around me. Show me how to help them see that they still need to know you.*

21 The Great Pretender

Bible Reading: Romans 8:28–30
For God knew his people in advance, and he chose them to become like his Son. Romans 8:29

WHAT DO THE following words have in common? Masquerade. Impersonator. Impostor. Cover-up. Actress. Mimic. Disguise. Costume. Camouflage. Actor. Copycat. Mask. Impressionist. Pretender. Your final answer? Yes! They all have something to do with trying to *be* like or at least *look* like someone else.

Ever wish you were like someone else? Pretending to be someone else might be fun for a few hours at a costume party, but in everyday life it's more exciting to be the unique person God made you to be. Maybe you're as gorgeous as a homecoming queen, as brainy as a valedictorian, or as hunky as the captain of the football team. But if you don't fit into any of those pre-defined categories, you don't have to fake your "fabulousity."

You're great just the way God made you. You don't have to be anybody else. You don't have to compare yourself to anybody else.

Face it: You compare yourself to others because you want to know how you measure up. If you're doing well, you soar. If you aren't as gorgeous, brainy, rich, or hunky as the other person, you crash. The trouble with comparisons is the fact that you're using the wrong measure—other people. Every person is different, so you're guaranteed to find someone you think is better or worse than you are, filling you with either frustration or pride.

There is, however, someone even God wants you to copy. And that's his Son. God wants you to be like his Son in your character—that is, what you're like on the inside. God is looking for you to match an inward ideal, the way Jesus looks on the inside. Galatians 5:22-23 lists the qualities you possess when you imitate his perfection: "When the Holy Spirit controls our lives, he will produce this kind of fruit in us: love, joy, peace, patience, kindness, goodness, faithfulness, gentleness, and self-control."

God doesn't want you to remake yourself in the mold of anyone but his Son. To do that he wants you to allow his Spirit to control you. Instead of asking, "Am I as good as so-and-so?" quiz yourself on this: "Do I have the character of Christ, which is what God wants me to have?" When you can say yes to that question, you won't be pretending. You'll see proof in your life that you're just like him.

 REFLECT: Who do you want to be like? Why?

PRAY: *Father, I don't have to remake myself in the mold of anyone but your Son. To do that, I give your Spirit control of my life.*

22 There's a Price on Your Head

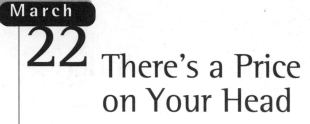

Bible Reading: 1 Corinthians 1:26-29

God chose things despised by the world, things counted as nothing at all, and used them to bring to nothing what the world considers important. 1 Corinthians 1:28

A SCIENTIST once stated that every dry pound of human being is worth about $112,247. Since about 68 percent of your body is water, you can calculate your dry weight by multiplying your full weight by 0.32. Then figure your total value by multiplying that dry weight by $112,247. If you weigh 125 pounds, for example, your 40 pounds of dry weight is worth a whopping $4.5 million!

You might wish that you could hunt down that scientist and make him cough up the money. Being worth $4.5 million doesn't matter, of course, if no one is willing to pay the price.

Fact is, most of us have times when we don't feel worth much at all. You feel useless to yourself, to others, and to God. When you judge your worth by the world's standards, you discover that you don't measure up. When you compare yourself to people around you, you seem foolish and weak.

Well, God has a smashing plan for you. Not to smash *you,* but the system of thinking that calls you stupid and scrawny.

According to 1 Corinthians 1:27, God has chosen the foolish things of this world to shame the wise, and he has chosen the weak things to shame the strong. This means that God can use your "foolishness" (your lack of brilliance, popularity, or experience) and your "weakness" (lack of strength, good looks, or abilities) to discredit the world's system. How? By demonstrating his power through you. God's power makes you adequate for every responsibility he's given you. Second Corinthians 3:5 says, "It is not that we think we can do anything of lasting value by ourselves. Our only power and success come from God."

A price far bigger than mere bucks has already been paid for you—the infinitely valuable blood of Jesus Christ. He died on the cross to bring you to God.

So how can you tell how much you're really worth? Just figure up how much the life of Christ was worth. First Peter 1:18-19 gives you a hint: "For you know that God paid a ransom to save you from the empty life you inherited from your ancestors. And the ransom he paid was not mere gold or silver. He paid for you with the precious lifeblood of Christ, the sinless, spotless Lamb of God."

You are exceedingly valuable. You are worth Jesus! Ponder that—and when you do, the fact of your worth will revolutionize your life.

REFLECT: So what are you worth? What does Christ's death have to do with your worth?

PRAY: Spend some moments with Christ right now asking him to flood your mind with the reality of your value to him.

23 Hey, You with the Fluorescent Orange Hair!

Bible Reading: Hebrews 13:5
God has said, "I will never fail you. I will never forsake you."
Hebrews 13:5

CHECK (✔) any of these embarrassing situations that have happened to you:

- ☐ Tried to bleach your hair and it turned fluorescent orange.
- ☐ Discovered your jeans had a revealing rip up the backside.
- ☐ Got a red zit on your forehead that looked like a third eye.
- ☐ Figured out that your socks didn't match.
- ☐ Was told your wardrobe was really lame.
- ☐ Smelled an awful odor nearby, then discovered it was you.

You wouldn't like walking down a crowded hallway in school in any of those conditions. You would hear whispers and worse. You definitely wouldn't feel confidence oozing out of your pores.

When you wonder whether you are going to feel accepted or not, you feel insecure. When you look at yourself and all you see is shortcomings, you start wondering why anyone would ever want to spend time with you.

But you don't have to feel that way. Why? You are accepted by the one who matters most—Jesus Christ. He takes you just as you are—fluorescent orange hair, red zit, ripped pants, mismatched socks and all. He's promised never to ditch you because he wants to be with you no matter how you feel about yourself.

If Jesus Christ—Creator of the universe—accepts you, what does it matter if nobody else accepts you? You don't stop needing people. But you do stop needing their acceptance to make you feel okay. If valuing yourself depended on being accepted, Jesus himself and most of the disciples wouldn't have done very well. They weren't exactly popular among their peers.

When you realize that Christ accepts you unconditionally, you don't have to focus on yourself. You can shift your attention to others. Most all of your friends feel insecure, whether they act that way or not. They need someone to help meet their needs by reaching out to them and pointing them to Jesus. Knowing that Christ accepts you cuts you loose from insecurity and lets you be a confident, accepting friend.

REFLECT: How does knowing that Christ accepts you make you more accepting of others?

PRAY: Tell Jesus now how grateful you are that he accepts you completely.

24 It's Not How Good You Are, It's How Good He Is

Bible Reading: 2 Corinthians 5:21

God made Christ, who never sinned, to be the offering for our sin, so that we could be made right with God through Christ. 2 Corinthians 5:21

YOU MAY HAVE heard of PDA (personal digital assistant—or public display of affection), PBJ (peanut butter and jelly), and PDQ (pretty darn quick). But have you ever heard of PBA (performance-based acceptance)? Probably not. But you can figure out what it is and recognize the feelings it causes. It's the lie that our worth is based on what we do, not who we are.

PBA often starts at home. Did you ever show your parents your grades, and instead of bragging about the five B's you got, they start nagging about the one C? Or they start in with comments like, "Why can't you be like your older sister? She never . . ." You go away thinking that your only hope of being accepted is to do better. You're being hit with performance-based acceptance. It's PBA.

The great thing about belonging to God is that you don't have to be a whiz at anything to get him to like you. Jesus has already performed perfectly for you. When you became a Christian, he took your failures and gave you his sinlessness (see 2 Corinthians 5:21). God sees the perfection Christ provided for you.

That makes it okay to fail, because you can be sure that God won't reject you. That means you can stretch to reach your full potential, because he accepts you unconditionally. That means you can truly find out what you're capable of, because he frees you to try—and to fall on your face.

And when you succeed, it doesn't matter if you don't get all the credit. You may *want* the credit because you have bought into the PBA lie. And in the back of your brain, you think you need people to like you and think you're special because you don't feel special. But as you realize your true value to God, you can yank yourself out of that mucked-up thinking. You can put your focus back on the God who loves and accepts you just as you are.

If you never succeeded at another task, Christ would still accept you. He doesn't sit up in heaven tabulating points on your performance each day. There is no quota of goodie-goodie points you have to reach for him to accept you.

You want to excel at what you do. But you already have God's love and approval. Like Colossians 3:23-24 says, "Work hard and cheerfully at whatever you do, as though you were working for the Lord rather than for people. Remember that the Lord will give you an inheritance as your reward."

 REFLECT: God accepts you totally because you are righteous in him. How does that make you feel?

PRAY: Tell God about times you doubt he accepts you—and thank him that he really does.

25 A Day in the Life of Whoever

Bible Reading: 1 Thessalonians 5:9-11

So encourage each other and build each other up, just as you are already doing. 1 Thessalonians 5:11

7:45 A.M. You miss your ride to school, so your mother has to take you. All the way to school she lectures you about punctuality.

8:12 A.M. You confess that you left your assignment at home, so your teacher writes your name on the chalkboard under the heading "No Clue."

11:47 A.M. You carry your lunch to the table where your friends are sitting, but there isn't a spot for you—and nobody moves to squish you in.

2:06 P.M. You receive a note from your best friend: "I never want to see you again." The note is taped to a small bottle of mouthwash.

4:33 P.M. Your dad forgets to come to your game—again. But it doesn't matter because the coach won't let you play—again.

After your lousy day, what would encourage you? Check (✔) the things that would lift your spirits and help you see the bright side of life.

☐ A friend says, "You think *you* have problems. Let me tell you about mine. (Blah, blah, blah.)"

☐ A friend explains, "Here's why that happened, Dummy, and here's what you need to do so it doesn't happen again. (Blah, blah, blah.)"

☐ You receive this e-mail from a friend: "Sorry to hear about your discouraging day. I'm praying for you."

☐ A friend shows up with a new Christian music CD. "I heard you had a tough day. I thought we could listen to this together."

Everybody you know has days much like the one described above. And everybody needs encouragement. To encourage means to lift people's spirits and cheer them up by helping them focus on the positive, good things in life. But only a couple of choices from the list of responses really fit that definition, right?

Are you a true source of encouragement when your friends are down? Or do you only try to point out why things are so bad?

REFLECT: When your friends are down, do you help, or do you add to their hurt?

PRAY: *God, show me how to encourage the people who need it most.*

26 A Moment-by-Moment Friend

Bible Reading: Ephesians 4:25-29

Let everything you say be good and helpful, so that your words will be an encouragement to those who hear them. Ephesians 4:29

THERE'S A TIME and a place for every expression of friendship. Sometimes cheery thoughts and words help lift a friend's spirits. But at other times they make your friend want to slug you. Another translation of today's key verse tells you to use your words to build people up and be helpful to them "according to the need of the moment, that it may give grace to those who hear" (Ephesians 4:29, NASB). It's important to tune into what your friend needs *at the moment.*

For each scenario below, circle the response that you feel best meets your friend's "need of the moment."

1. My friend who seems discouraged but has said nothing needs:
   a. Medication
   b. Time just to get over it
   c. Someone to care enough to listen
   d. To hear that no one likes a loser

2. My friend who has suffered a serious loss and is hurting needs:
   a. Someone to hurt with him or her
   b. To stuff the hurt and get on with life
   c. Pain medication
   d. A place to hide and hurt alone

3. My friend who is struggling in a class and is facing a big exam needs:
   a. To get smarter
   b. To learn how to cheat without getting caught
   c. Someone to help him or her study for the exam
   d. To sign up for easier classes

Instead of getting stuck in one way of reacting to a friend—always whipping out a joke or busting loose with some personal experience—take a few seconds to think through some better options. Being a loving, helpful friend means being alert to what your friends are going through and determining just what they need at that moment.

REFLECT: What is your usual reaction to a friend who is hurting? What are some other options?

PRAY: Ask God today to help you develop the discernment to be a supportive friend when and how your friends need you most.

27 Dinner in a Time Machine

Bible Reading: Mark 14:17-26
This is my blood, poured out for many, sealing the covenant between God and his people. Mark 14:24

MAYBE YOU SIT on the couch experiencing brain-crushing jealousy every time you watch the Starship Enterprise go to places you will never go. Little known fact: When Jesus gathered with his disciples in the upper room to celebrate the Passover, they entered a time warp—though not exactly of the sci-fi kind. And every time you participate in the Lord's Supper, you enter that time warp too.

Flash to the past: The Passover meal transported its participants some fifteen hundred years back into Israel's history. On the eve of God's saving Israel from slavery in Egypt, he told every family to sprinkle lamb's blood on the door posts of their homes and gather inside for a meal of lamb, unleavened bread, and bitter herbs (see Exodus 12). God dealt a death blow to the firstborn sons of godless Egypt, saving only those gathered inside homes marked by lamb's blood. As Jesus and his disciples ate the Passover meal together, their thoughts traveled back to Egypt, remembering how God delivered their ancestors from slavery.

Flash to the future: When Jesus took bread and wine from the Passover table, the disciples looked ahead to his crucifixion. The Passover meal that pointed back to a sacrificial lamb and deliverance from Egypt *also* pointed forward to "the Lamb of God who takes away the sin of the world" (John 1:29).

Today, all believers who celebrate the Lord's Supper also enter a time warp. The bread and cup take you back 2000 years to Christ's sacrifice on the cross for your sin. "Every time you eat this bread and drink this cup," Paul wrote, "you are announcing the Lord's death until he comes again" (1 Corinthians 11:26).

But the same bread and cup fling you forward to an event Jesus referred to when he said, "I will not drink wine again until the day I drink it new with you in my Father's Kingdom" (Matthew 26:29). The Lord's Supper lets you look ahead to the end of human history. It's when Christ will return to invite all believers to a celebration feast where we can thank him personally for his sacrifice that won our salvation.

It's mind-stretching to look back to the cross and ahead to Christ's return, because both events have a bearing on your present life. Looking back you say, "Lord, because you were so willing to give your life for me, help me daily give my life back to you in loving service." Looking forward you say, "Lord, the prospect of meeting you face-to-face encourages me to make my life count for you!"

REFLECT: How can you make every Communion celebration a feast to remember?

PRAY: *God, don't let me take Communion for granted. When I look back, I remember your death for me. When I look forward, I can't wait for your return.*

28 When the Pressure Is On

Bible Reading: Mark 14:32-42

Please take this cup of suffering away from me. Yet I want your will, not mine. Mark 14:36

EVER FELT PRESSED and pained in the process of doing something you know is right—but you still don't want to do it? Jesus knows exactly how you feel.

As your Lord walked into the Garden of Gethsemane to pray, he was totally committed to giving his life to save lost humankind. But he knew his task would be difficult beyond imagination.

The Greek word for "Gethsemane" means "oil press," a device for squeezing oil out of olives. Ponder that irony—that Jesus spent the last evening before his death in the oil press. Like the olives, he was about to be crushed through crucifixion. And just as the crushed olives yield oil used to light lamps, so Christ's sacrifice provides light for your soul.

Doing right isn't always easy, even for the Son of God. In choosing to go the Father's way, Jesus made the difficult choice of enduring—painfully—alone.

Even today, doing what is right isn't always easy or fun. Suppose you're parking your dad's new car. You crunch the taillight of another car. No one saw your booboo, so you can speed away and avoid the humiliation of admitting your fault and paying for the damages. Will you do what's right or take the easy way out? That's a "Gethsemane moment"—a tough choice to do what's right in the face of unpleasant consequences.

You're wise if you handle these tough situations in the same way Jesus did. His prayer in Mark 14:36 is the kind of response you want to show—a prayer you can use in your Gethsemane moments.

"Father . . . everything is possible for you." Acknowledge that God can do anything he wants to do—eliminate the painful consequences of doing right or supply the strength you need to survive.

"Please take this cup of suffering away from me." God won't be offended by your respectful request to change unpleasant circumstances.

"Yet I want your will, not mine." Being an obedient follower of Christ means being willing, just as Jesus was, to do whatever God says is right no matter what the consequences may be.

And when you walk out of your place of prayer and do the difficult right thing, realize you're in very special company.

REFLECT: When have you wanted to do what's right—but had huge second thoughts because of the cost?

PRAY: Take a tough situation you're in right now and pray about it, using Jesus' prayer.

29 Are You or Aren't You?

Bible Reading: Mark 14:66-72
"That man is definitely one of them!" Peter denied it again. Mark 14:69-70

WHEN THE JEWISH LEADERS put Jesus on trial for claiming to be God's Son, a few yards away in the courtyard another trial—an unofficial one—was going on.

Only a few hours earlier Peter had boldly told Jesus, "Even if everyone else deserts you, I never will" (Mark 14:29). But as Jesus faced the Sanhedrin, Peter huddled in the shadows near a fire outside, hoping to learn the fate of Jesus.

At Peter's "trial" three witnesses spoke up about his connection to Jesus: "You were one of those with Jesus"; "That man is definitely one of them"; "You must be one of them" (Mark 14:67, 69-70). Three times Peter denied he followed Jesus: "I don't know what you're talking about"; "Peter denied it again"; "I swear by God, I don't know this man you're talking about" (Mark 14:68-71). Then a rooster's crow reminded Peter that Jesus had predicted this denial the night before. Peter was shattered with grief "and he broke down and cried" (Mark 14:72).

Know it or not, your identity as a believer in Christ is called into question almost daily. A friend of yours messes up and needs a Christian friend to pray and give biblical advice—Do you say anything? A representative of a cult wants you to take their literature—Do you share Jesus? Or a group of Christians at your school wants you to join them in sponsoring a Christian band at a campus outreach—Do you let yourself be spotted as part of the group?

As a committed Christian, you will step forward and be Christ's representative in each situation no matter what it costs you. But if you just follow a religion—the same way you might belong to a political party—then you might, like Peter, avoid any Christian activity that inconveniences or threatens you.

Peter, of course, was rescued from the despair he felt after he betrayed Jesus. After Jesus rose from the dead, he sought out Peter to encourage him (see John 21:15-19). And after the Holy Spirit came down at Pentecost, Peter was a new guy with a new identity. He wasn't just a companion of Christ. He was *one* with Christ because Christ's Spirit lived in him. Peter's boldness on the Day of Pentecost (see Acts 2) is a clue to how his devotion had radically deepened.

Identifying with Christ can make that huge difference in you too—whether you're counseling a friend, confronting a cult member, or taking part in an outreach rally. If you're empowered by the Holy Spirit and someone puts your faith on trial, you won't stand a chance of being acquitted.

REFLECT: Answer this pointed question: If you were arrested for being a Christian, would there be enough evidence to convict you?

PRAY: *Lord, I face situations almost every day that tempt me to shrink from admitting I know you. Make me fearless and bold.*

30 100 Percent Faithful

Bible Reading: Mark 16:1-11

He has been raised from the dead . . . just as he told you before he died!
Mark 16:6-7

"I MEANT WHAT I said, and I said what I meant; an elephant is faithful one hundred percent." Recognize those immortal words?

If you're a Dr. Seuss fan, you'll know those words of Horton the elephant. In Horton's story, a mother bird complains to Horton that she is tired of waiting for her eggs to hatch. Goodhearted Horton agrees to take her place on the nest while the mother bird flies off for a vacation.

Days pass while Horton keeps watch atop the nest. Opportunity after opportunity tempts him to ditch his post, but each time he responds firmly with his committed words: "I meant what I said, and I said what I meant; an elephant is faithful one hundred percent."

Finally the mother bird returns to the nest, Horton's duty is done, and the baby birds are hatched. The moral of the story? Like Horton, you should be faithful to do what you say you will do. That's often tough to do.

Mark 16 opens with the stupendous news that Jesus meant what he said and said what he meant about coming back to life after his crucifixion. From the disciples' point of view, things looked darker than the inside of the tomb. Their loving teacher had been brutally executed. And now they feared that they would be killed for following him. Nothing in the Bible tells us the disciples either remembered or believed Jesus' prediction in Mark 9:31 that he would rise from the dead. They were grieving over their great loss.

When some of the women who had followed Jesus arrived at the tomb, they were astonished to find the huge stone rolled away—not to mention Jesus' body missing and an angel waiting to tell them that the Savior was alive, "just as he told you before he died" (Mark 16:7). True to form, when the disciples heard the news, "they didn't believe her" (verse 11). If you had watched your friend and leader die the no-doubt-about-it death of crucifixion, you might have had a hard time believing the truth of his resurrection too.

But Jesus meant what he said and said what he meant. He conquered death, burst out of the tomb, and lives today as Lord and King.

Jesus has never failed to keep a promise. Every promise in Scripture is made by the one who keeps his Word 100 percent.

REFLECT: How does Christ's keeping his promise to rise from the dead make all of his other promises more believable to you?

PRAY: Ask God to help you trust his Word. Talk about times it's tough to trust.

31 A Reservation for Your Destination

Bible Reading: Matthew 25:31-46

Come, you who are blessed by my Father, inherit the Kingdom prepared for you from the foundation of the world. Matthew 25:34

BELINDA CARLISLE topped the charts a few years ago with the hit song, "Heaven Is a Place on Earth." Nice song. Nasty theology.

You overhear a girl on a bus talking to the guy beside her. "You know what I think?" she says. "I think heaven is what you make it. I think it's a state of mind."

You may also have heard the flip side. "Listen," says the dude in the donut shop, "No hell can be worse than what I have already been through."

It's true that some human experiences can be such a riot that you can't imagine anything better or higher. It's also true that some experiences are so tormenting that you wonder how hell could be any hotter. But the Bible teaches that a *real* heaven and a *real* hell exist.

Jesus told his followers he was going to prepare a place for them (see John 14:2). The apostle John provides some details about heaven, describing it as a place in the presence of God where there will be no more death or tears or pain (see Revelation 21:4). It's a place where God's people will serve him, be in his presence, and reign with him forever (see Revelation 22:3-5).

God's Word is just as clear that the future holds punishment for evildoers in a place we dub hell (see Matthew 25:41). John also describes in Revelation the punishment waiting the ungodly (21:8). The Bible says a whole lot about the subject of hell, addressing the subject over and over in utterly severe terms, like a truck without brakes on a steep hill blasting its horn to warn of a danger that can't be stopped.

Unfortunately, not enough people heed the Bible's warnings of hell or its promise of heaven. But like the writer of Hebrews says, "We must listen very carefully to the truth we have heard, or we may drift away from it. The message God delivered through angels has always proved true, and the people were punished for every violation of the law and every act of disobedience. What makes us think that we can escape if we are indifferent to this great salvation that was announced by the Lord Jesus himself?" (Hebrews 2:1-3).

If you have trusted Christ, your future is heavenly—and will be in a totally real place where you will enjoy God's presence forever. For those who refuse Christ, the future will be just as sure—but in a totally real place where God will be absent forever.

REFLECT: Doesn't the Bible give enough reasons to pray and share Christ now so others may also find their home in heaven? What do you think?

PRAY: Pray for your friends who don't believe in heaven—or hell.

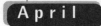

1 A Family Affair

Bible Reading: Romans 1:6-7
God loves you dearly, and he has called you to be his very own people.
Romans 1:7

THE MIDDLE-AGED HUSBAND and wife moved carefully between the rickety cribs and makeshift beds of the crowded Romanian orphanage. The room was dimly lit. The walls, floors, and furnishings were less than sparkling and sanitary. The stench of a dozen unchanged diapers clouded the air.

From each bed the couple passed, an infant or toddler gazed at them, eager for love and attention. Behind each small, angelic face was a gut-wrenching story of neglect, abandonment, and glaring need. Tears streamed down the couple's cheeks. They already had five sons at home in America—four biological and one adopted. They had come to Romania to adopt another child. If they could, they would take them all. But they could take only one. But which one?

Then they saw her—a girl only a few weeks old. She stood out from all the other children, as if God was pulling the couple to her. She was the one, they decided. After enduring days of bureaucratic red tape, the couple left Romania with their sixth child. Tiny Andrea was totally unaware of the miraculous change that had begun in her life.

Andrea today is eight years old. She lives in a loving, secure, Christian family with five older brothers and two younger sisters—her parents adopted two more orphaned girls! The care, affection, and protection of her new home have all but wiped away any memories of her tragic start in life.

You have something in common with Andrea—not that you were a literal orphan, though maybe you were. In a spiritual sense, you came into the world without "parents." The sin we inherited from Adam and Eve separated us from God. It was like being born in an orphanage.

Then God came along—not just to visit, not just to drop off gifts and leave, but to take us home to join his family. He loves you so much that he has invited you—orphaned by sin—"to be his very own people." And your change in status was even more remarkable than Andrea's. The apostle Peter put it this way: "Once you were not a people; now you are the people of God" (1 Peter 2:10). When you trusted Christ as your Savior, you went from having no family to being a member of God's family through faith in Christ!

Can you imagine how Andrea will feel when she grows to understand what her adoptive parents have done for her? Do you have some of those same feelings when you realize God has adopted you into his family?

REFLECT: Where would you be if God hadn't adopted you into his family?

PRAY: *I'm grateful, God, that I can be your child.*

2 A Knight to Remember

Bible Reading: Romans 1:13-17

This Good News tells us how God makes us right in his sight. This is accomplished from start to finish by faith. Romans 1:17

LET'S SAY YOU LIVE in England. You think it would be totally cool to become an official knight. You've heard about Sir Lancelot and Sir Winston Churchill and Sir Elton John and all those other sirs. You decide you want to be called Sir–(Whatever Your Name Is). You want everyone to bow to you.

So you jump on the Internet to find out how to apply. You learn that only after decades of service to the crown will the queen invite you to Buckingham Palace, tap you on the shoulder three times with a sword, hand you a nifty medal, and–*shazzam!*–make you a knight.

But you have a little problem: Serving the crown for decades means you won't get to hang out at the mall most afternoons. And you're way too busy doing homework and playing computer games for all that noble and meritorious stuff that aspiring knights do. So you try cutting corners on your way to knighthood.

You start passing around your own business cards which say in bold letters, "Sir (Whatever Your Name Is)–Don't Forget to Bow." You buy some cool knight clothes, get a bunch of official looking medals at the pawn shop, and make sure you watch the knightly news on TV. You tell all your friends, "Call me Sir from now on–or else." You so much start feeling like a knight that you conclude you must be as knightly as anybody who is called Sir.

The big question is, "Are you really a knight?" You know the big answer is "No!" You can dress like a knight, talk like a knight, act like a knight, and swing a sword like a knight. But there is only one way to become a real knight, and that's to be picked by the Queen of England.

Many people try to look and act like Christians, but it's God who invites us into his family. The Bible clearly explains that God makes you right in his sight and knights you–makes you a member of his family–when you confess your sin and trust him for salvation. Faith–believing and trusting in God–is the way you receive family standing with God. You don't become God's child by what you do and say–or *don't* do and say–or by how much you know, how much you give, etc.

One reason the Good News of the gospel is *good* news is because God has done everything necessary to make you right and keep you right. When by faith you accept his righteousness as your own, he welcomes you into his family. You don't have to do anything to earn admission.

REFLECT: How do you feel toward a God who loves you enough to make you right by faith—not by your effort—so he can be your Father?

PRAY: Tell God what you're thinking and feeling right now.

3 Getting to Know Him

Bible Reading: Romans 1:18-20

The truth about God is known to them instinctively. God has put this knowledge in their hearts. Romans 1:19

THE BIG DAY ARRIVES. Your parents take you down to the local home electronics megastore and empty their wallets for a brand-new computer: the XL Hyperflash 6000 Super-Plus. This box comes equipped with more bytes and bits and megs and gigs than you'll ever use. It can play CDs and DVDs in HD. It can communicate by phone, fax, and e-mail in sixty different languages and dialects, including Pig Latin.

Once you have your Hyperflash 6000 hooked up in your room, a few simple modifications let you turn all the lights in the house on and off, take the blender for a spin, flip TV channels, boost the electric blanket in your parents' room up to ten, and nuke burritos in the microwave. And thanks to remote access, you can control everything from a friend's house too.

Of course, the Hyperflash 6000 also comes loaded with tons of software—like the Encyclopedia Galactica, Games-a-Gazillion, and programs for accessing your school's grade records.

Computers are techno-wonders. They arrive at stores with fully functioning brains. They get operating systems and a big selection of software installed at the factory, so all you have to do is pop open the carton and hook up the hardware.

But the most killer advanced computer ever created—or yet to be created—will never beat your brain. The gray, spongy "hardware" crammed inside your cranium isn't much to look at, but the factory-installed software is fantastic. Every movement you make, every task you complete originates in the complex neurological system God built into you. Your brain, bundled with your soul and spirit, is how God equipped you for life even before you came out of the crate.

At the core of your internal operating system is a unique feature—a built-in capacity to know and relate to your heavenly Father. He put it there, not just in you, but in every human being. Why? Because God wants you to know him as your loving Father. This God who called you into his family wants you to thoroughly know him. But even your marvelous, complex brain couldn't comprehend God unless he gifted you with that capacity. So he did!

And when you turn to him in faith, it's like he activates that inner program and lets you know him better. Anybody with half a brain would go for that deal.

REFLECT: God built you with a built-in capacity to know him. How much of that capacity are you using?

PRAY: *Thank you, God, that I can know you. Help me to know you better.*

4 Is There an Elvis in Your Life?

Bible Reading: Romans 1:21-23

Instead of worshiping the glorious, ever-living God, they worshiped idols made to look like mere people, or birds and animals and snakes.
Romans 1:23

WEIRD: THE DEATH on August 16, 1977, of rock 'n' roll legend Elvis Presley "morphed" him into something of a god. Shrines built to Elvis encourage worship of the legendary singer often called "The King."

"The First Church of Jesus Christ, Elvis" is a Web site picturing the head of Elvis Presley superimposed on a painting of Christ. The caption proclaims, "For unto you is born this day in the city of Memphis a Presley, which is Elvis the King."

Members of the First Presbyterian Church of Elvis the Divine are encouraged to face Las Vegas daily and make a pilgrimage to Graceland (Presley's home in Memphis, Tennessee) at least once in their lives. One of the ministers says, "Truly, Elvis has a hunka-hunka burning love for whosoever believeth in him."

The First Congregational Church of Elvis was founded by a hairdresser from West Virginia who claims she has been filled with the peaceful spirit of Elvis.

Most of this Elvis "worship" is done in fun, of course. People say they believe in Elvis like you used to believe in Santa Claus, the Easter Bunny, and the Tooth Fairy—or still do.

Worship literally means to *declare the worth* of something. That's where the word *worthy* comes from. Something is *worthy* if it's *worth* a lot. You declare what a thing is worth to you by its priority in your thoughts and time and by its influence on your decision-making.

It isn't likely you would ever turn into a foaming-at-the-mouth worshiper of Elvis, or even that you would worship any "idols made to look like mere people, or birds and animals and snakes." Worship is for God alone. Nobody loves you like he does or has his power, so only he is worthy of your worship.

But there can be other things in your life that carry too much weight. How important is it to you, for example, to spend time with friends or play computer games or watch TV? Is that stuff a higher priority than spending time with God in prayer and in his Word?

Many things can rule your thoughts and time—schoolwork, music, sports activities, a boyfriend or girlfriend. But you can have only one all-important priority in your life, one thing worth your worship. So enjoy your activities. Keep close to people. But only God gets to be King.

 **REFLECT:** What in your life competes with God for your time, energy, and affection?

PRAY: Talk to God about things that might get in the way of your worshiping him.

5 He Became One of Us

Bible Reading: Romans 1:1-5
It is the Good News about his Son, Jesus, who came as a man.
Romans 1:3

"HUMAN TRANSFORMED into Ant."

That headline was the theme of a Christian film several years ago. No, it wasn't a horror movie about a missionary subjected to a curse. It was a parable about Christ's incarnation—his being born in the flesh as a human being.

As the film opens, a man and his adult son are tending a lush jungle garden at the top of a mountain. From the base of the mountain they hear faint cries of anguish and distress. The gardener and his son realize that the ants on the desert floor below are in deep pain from generations of conflict, hatred, and war. Father and son yearn to bring peace to the ant colony. But how? They decide that they need to visit the colony in a form the ants will understand. The gardener's son agrees to leave the beautiful garden, descend to the desert, and enter the ant colony as an ant.

When he arrives at the base of the mountain, the son is transformed into an ant—through the use of special effects, of course! This one-of-a-kind ant enters the colony and begins to teach the ants about the gardener's love for them. Many listen and are changed, but eventually the gardener's enemies kill his son. He rises from the dead as a winged ant and returns to his father in the garden. All the ants who believe in him sprout wings like his and continue to spread his message of the gardener's love and peace.

Bizarre as it sounds, that's a graphic illustration of what Jesus did when he came into this world. Romans 1:7 says that God loves us and calls us to belong to his family. Romans 1:17 informs us that nothing we can do qualifies us for God's family—we become his children by faith alone. Romans 1:19 says that our loving Father has equipped us with the capacity to know him and relate to him. And Romans 1:23 teaches that our loving father deserves top priority in our lives and is worthy of our worship.

So what do those Bible verses have to do with ants? Well, we couldn't have become members of God's family if his Son, Jesus, hadn't left heaven, put on human flesh, and entered the human race as a man. His sinless life, sacrificial death, and victorious resurrection smashed sin and opened the door to new life through faith. And because Christ came to our world and provided forgiveness for sin, those of us who trust him can enter God's world as his beloved children. The next time you see an ant crawling down the sidewalk, squat down and contemplate this life-changing truth.

REFLECT: What hits your heart hardest about the price Jesus paid for your sins?

PRAY: Spend some time thanking Jesus for the steps he took to get close to you.

6 Clues to the Big Surprise

Bible Reading: 1 Corinthians 15:1-4

Christ died for our sins, just as the Scriptures said. He was buried, and he was raised from the dead on the third day, as the Scriptures said.
1 Corinthians 15:3-4

AN EAGER YOUNG PREACHER was assigned to his first church. The old folks who had attended this little church all their lives had seen dozens of ministers come and go, but this young preacher was determined to make a good impression.

He decided to preach his inaugural sermon on the second coming of Christ, knowing that it was a popular subject with most church folk. As he stood to speak, he slammed his fist on the pulpit and shouted the words of Christ from Revelation 22:7, "Behold, I come quickly!" (KJV).

Well, the sleepy congregation barely twitched. But the young minister wouldn't be discouraged. He stepped back from the pulpit. He cleared his throat. And then he sprang to the pulpit and shouted even louder, "Behold, I come quickly!" Result? Not an eyebrow of interest from the congregation.

The preacher wasn't about to let the stone-faced congregation beat him. This time he backed up to the rear of the platform and huffed deeply. Then he raced to the pulpit screaming, "Behold, I come quickly!" He crashed into the pulpit, tipping it off the platform and onto the flower arrangement. The preacher tumbled over the fallen pulpit and landed in the lap of a little old lady.

He jumped up, red-faced with embarrassment. "Dear ma'am, I am so very sorry. Please forgive me."

"No need to apologize, Reverend," the old lady replied. "After all, you warned me three times that you were a-comin'."

A surprise isn't much of a surprise if somebody tells you about it ahead of time. But sometimes a surprise is too good to keep. Remember what it was like to be a tiny tyke at Christmastime? Your dad probably helped you pick out and wrap a simple gift for your mom. But you were too bubbly to keep from babbling: "Look, Mommy, I bought you a Power Rangers pot holder!"

God has a hard time keeping a secret too. Picture him in heaven planning to send Christ to earth to die for you and then rise from the dead. He oozed excitement about his plan and the new life you would receive through it. So centuries before Jesus was born, God burst. He just had to start talking about his surprise. The Old Testament contains hundreds of prophecies about Christ, such as his birthplace (see Micah 5:2), his suffering and death (see Isaiah 53), and his resurrection (see Job 19:25). God had good news for you that wouldn't keep!

 REFLECT: Don't you feel jazzed about a God who was so eager to share Christ with you that he couldn't keep silent?

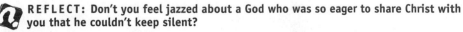 **PRAY:** Express some of your excitement in a prayer of thankfulness.

7 Eyewitness Account

Bible Reading: 1 Corinthians 15:5-9
He was seen by more than five hundred of his followers at one time.
1 Corinthians 15:6

EZRA P. WAFFLE WALKED into the local police station looking like he had seen a ghost. The eyeballs of the Nebraska farmer were half out of his head and his wispy white hair was standing on end. "One of them flyin' saucer contraptions just landed in my cornfield again, Officer," Waffle reported.

The officer had been through this with old Ezra a few times before. "So what did it look like this time, Mr. Waffle?"

" 'Bout the size of my combine, 'cept it was flat and kind of round and all shiny-like, with little Christmas lights a-blinkin' from the inside."

"And did somebody talk to you this time, Mr. Waffle?"

"Sure did," Ezra said, almost bragging. " 'Bout six of them critters, looked kind of like the Muppets on TV."

"What did these Muppets from outer space want, Mr. Waffle?"

"They wanted some of my corn to take home. Elmo and Oscar and the bunch picked a couple of my stalks clean and—*whoosh*—they was gone."

The officer leaned forward, looking serious. "Mr. Waffle, did anybody else see this flying saucer or the Muppet creatures? Your wife? Your kids?"

Ezra shook his head slowly. "By the time I got to the house to tell Bessie Lou, they was long gone into outer space."

"Well, thanks for telling us about it, Mr. Waffle," the officer nodded. "We'll keep an eye out for them."

You have to wonder why the UFOs so many people claim to see don't ever land in downtown LA, New York, or Chicago—places where millions of people could see them. It's hard to believe in aliens when they appear just to one or two people at a time in a remote cornfield.

Jesus wasn't that elusive after his resurrection. He didn't show up in his resurrected body only for a few folks—he appeared to hundreds! His victory over the grave wasn't intended to be a secret. He *wanted* his followers to see him alive. He *wanted* us to know that his resurrection was fact—not fiction, hearsay, or wishful thinking. He *wanted* to make it easy for you to believe that the resurrection life he promised you is real, so you can *know* beyond doubt that he rose from the dead to provide it for you.

REFLECT: Why did God make his plan to save the world so easy to see?

PRAY: Thank your Lord for making his plan to save you so out in the open—and pray for your friends who still haven't opened their eyes to the truth.

8 Whatever Happened to Easter?

Bible Reading: 1 Corinthians 15:12-20

If we have hope in Christ only for this life, we are the most miserable people in the world. 1 Corinthians 15:19

ALMOST ANY LITTLE KID with a couple years of Sunday school under his belt can explain the highlights of the New Testament's story of Easter: Jesus was crucified and then rose from the dead on the third day.

By the time that little kid reaches your age, he or she can grasp that the Easter story is more than just a nice Bible tale. God boldly foretold Christ's resurrection in Old Testament prophecy, Christ actually stepped out of the tomb alive as the prophets predicted, and the risen Christ was seen by so many people that no one has succeeded in refuting it. You might be one of these students who has no trouble accepting the reality of Christ's resurrection.

But have you ever wondered what your life would be like if Jesus *hadn't* been raised from the dead? Below are several statements describing some of the harsh realities of life in a world where Christ never came out of the tomb. Check (✔) the one statement that would make you the most miserable in a life with no Easter.

- ☐ There would be no Easter bunny—and likely no Energizer bunny.
- ☐ There would be no such thing as "Spring Break."
- ☐ Baskets of jelly beans wouldn't play hide-n-seek with you.
- ☐ Easter lilies would be free agents looking for another holiday sponsor.
- ☐ Easter Island, in the South Pacific, might cease to exist.
- ☐ Youth groups would have no sunrise services at which to serve donuts.
- ☐ You and your friends would have absolutely zero hope of having your sins forgiven and spending eternity in heaven with God.

Did the last one catch you off guard? If Jesus hadn't come back to life like he promised he would, people might stare at his mummified corpse in a museum somewhere—as a curiosity, not a cure for the world's sin. The Bible clearly explains that it took the Crucifixion *and* the Resurrection to provide our forgiveness. Christ's death paid the *penalty* for sin. But Christ's resurrection freed us from the *power* of sin. If Christ were not alive, we would face all the trials, struggles, and sacrifices of the Christian life—and then die with no hope of heaven. What a waste!

 REFLECT: Seriously—and personally: What would your life be like if Jesus had never come to save you from your sin?

PRAY: Tell Jesus about it in prayer.

9 It's a Matter of Life and Death—and Life!

Bible Reading: 1 Corinthians 15:21-23
All who are related to Christ . . . will be given new life.
1 Corinthians 15:22

TEX WAS A VERY WEALTHY man who was well-liked. When Tex died and his will was opened, the family found Tex's plans for his funeral. Topping his instructions was a request to be buried in his prized possession: a gold-plated, diamond-studded Rolls Royce convertible worth over a million dollars. Tex's family loved him dearly, so they followed his funeral plans to the letter.

The big day came, and the entire town turned out to view the funeral procession. It included marching bands and Cadillacs full of politicians. But the main attraction was the Rolls Royce convertible. Just like he wanted, Tex was propped up in the back seat wearing his most expensive suit. His eyes were glued open and a broad smile had been pasted on his face. As the chauffeur-driven car came into view, the crowds cheered.

Meanwhile, down by the railroad tracks, a stranger hopped off a slow-moving freight train hoping to find something to eat in town. Attracted by the commotion on Main Street, the stranger pushed through the crowd to find out what was happening. When the gold Rolls Royce came into view, the stranger's eyes bugged out. Focusing on the handsome, dignified passenger sitting in the expensive convertible and hearing the enthusiastic applause of the crowd, the stranger exclaimed to those around him, "Now that's what I call really living!"

Major cluelessness, huh? Tex had all the appearances of living high, but the guy riding in the Rolls Royce couldn't have been more dead. Tex and his beautiful car would soon be an earthworm playground six feet underground.

We might not like to think about it, but unless the Rapture happens first, each of us has an appointment with the undertaker. Your great-great-great . . . grandfather Adam had a nose, so you have a nose. He had armpits, so you have armpits. He died after 930 years, so we'll each die after 930 years—give or take a few centuries.

But we are also related to Jesus Christ, the conqueror of death. When we trusted him, Christ's resurrection power raised us to life *spiritually*. At the end of this world, his resurrection power will raise his followers to life *physically*.

He will locate the bones or ashes that were once you and change your remains into a glorious body like his own (see Philippians 3:21). Just as surely as Christ came out of his grave alive, you also will come out of your grave alive.

REFLECT: What do you really expect to happen to you when you die? How does the resurrection of Jesus reassure you that your own resurrection will be real?

PRAY: Tell God about your expectations of living with him for eternity.

10 Power Struggle

Bible Reading: 1 Corinthians 15:24–28

God, who gave his Son authority over all things, will be utterly supreme over everything everywhere. 1 Corinthians 15:28

THE POWERFUL KING of a tiny Polynesian island discovered that his enemies on a distant island were planning an invasion by war canoes. The king was determined not only to defend his life but to protect his most valuable possession: a huge, golden throne that sat in the middle of his grass hut. So the king recruited thousands of warriors and stationed them all around his hut.

But just to be on the safe side, the king decided to hide his golden throne. So he had his strongest warriors lift the thousand-pound throne into the wooden rafters of his grass hut and cover it with grass. With his army outside and his throne safely hidden above, the king lay down on his mat and went to sleep.

During the night, the king's warriors were awakened by a loud noise coming from the king's grass hut. They rushed in to find that the rafters had first weakened and then collapsed under the weight, and the throne had crashed to the floor where the king was sleeping. The king, who had planned his defense so well, was dead.

The moral of the story: People who live in grass houses shouldn't stow thrones. Ouch! What a silly twist on the old proverb that *people who live in glass houses shouldn't throw stones.* But this story reminds us that not everything goes right for even the most powerful people in the world. Think about it:

- Adolf Hitler swayed millions of people to his Nazi beliefs, but multiplied millions rejected him and his murderous philosophy.
- Bill Gates, the co-founder of Microsoft, is one of the richest men in the world, but that doesn't mean he can buy a cure for cancer or AIDS.
- Tiger Woods might become the winningest golfer of all time, but his success doesn't relieve him of sand traps and water hazards.
- Hillary Rodham Clinton might someday become the country's first woman president, but she can't keep wars from happening around the world.

There is only one undisputed, supreme authority: the God and Father of our living Lord, Jesus Christ. No thing or person is his equal in power, authority, capability, wisdom, or wealth. The Resurrection proved that God rules over both life and death. By trusting Christ and becoming a member of God's family, you're a child of the most powerful and influential person in heaven, earth, and hell!

REFLECT: Is there anything the God of life and death can't do? Do you have any problem he cannot help you overcome? No—the Resurrection proved it!

PRAY: Talk to God about the difficulties you are facing today. Invite him to exercise his resurrection power in you.

11 Does Love Make It Right?

Bible Reading: Romans 13:8-10
Love does no wrong to anyone, so love satisfies all of God's requirements. Romans 13:10

HERE'S A TOUGH question for you: Does love make "it" right?

You know what "it" is. When you're in a relationship, do you think that loving someone makes sexual involvement right?

This answer may shock you, but love *does* make it right.

You can't understand that answer, though, unless you know exactly what love is. Many couples get sexually involved and then say, "We love each other so much we got swept away." The truth is that they got involved because they love each other too little.

According to Romans 13:9-10, love is when the happiness, security, spiritual growth, and physical health of another person is as important to you as your own. Ephesians 5:29 explains how you are to love yourself and others: "For no one ever hated his own flesh, but *nourishes* and *cherishes* it, just as the Lord does the church" (NKJV, emphasis added). To nourish your own body means to bring it to maturity—big-time happiness, security, spiritual development, and physical health. To cherish your body literally means to protect it from anything negative and destructive.

If you truly love yourself the way God intended, you will nurture yourself to grow up in your body, your spirit, your brain, and your relationships. You will guard yourself from anything that gets in the way of those goals. And that love you learn to show yourself is the basis for loving someone else. If a guy or girl you date cares about your spiritual growth, your maturing, and your being nurtured, your date will be careful about where you go, what you do, and what you chat about. This person will want to be sure nothing thwarts your happiness, security, spiritual growth, and physical health. Could you trust someone like that? You bet.

If, on the other hand, a person tries to push your standards sexually, he or she doesn't really love you. Forget what that person says. He doesn't love you too much, he loves you too little. And if you love yourself too little you will let others push your standards outside of God's boundaries.

Love makes it right. Absolutely. Love sees the sexual boundaries God gave and honors them. Therefore, love makes it right to wait until your wedding night. Love makes it right to wait until commitment confirms and faithfulness seals the love in a relationship.

REFLECT: Is it your goal to nourish and cherish your boyfriend or girlfriend God's way? What are you really looking for in your guy-girl friendships?

PRAY: Pray today for God's purity in your relationships.

12 What You Do for Love

Bible Reading: 1 John 4:16-21
Perfect love expels all fear. 1 John 4:18

DO YOU REMEMBER being a newborn baby, still toasty from the bun warmer? Back then you wanted to sleep and gulp milk. But you also longed to be held and cuddled. It's as if you've always had a "love tank" inside you that needs to be filled. And if your capacity for love isn't met, you will experience hunger pangs.

As a little kid you reached out for hugs, kisses, and pats on the head. As you grew, you craved a love that accepted you for just being you—a love that squeezed you silly and said, "No matter what you do, I will always love you for just being you!" And you wanted that love to last and be so secure that no matter what happened, you could count on that love to be there.

Many kids grow up love-starved. And the more love-starved you are, the more fear you have—a fear that comes from all the conditions placed on love: *I'll be loved IF I get good grades; I'll be loved IF I'm popular; I'll be loved IF I make the cheerleading squad.* Or maybe it seems that being loved hangs on how you look or what you have, like a new car or cool clothes. See the problem? You started with a natural hunger for love. Now you have a fear that drives you to greater and greater lengths to get love. Many students try to succeed in a sport or get perfect grades or join a gang or take drugs—all in a quest for love and acceptance. For many, the gnawing hunger for love has led them to sex.

A tender kiss, a warm embrace, and all the passion that comes with sex—it seems to say, "I love you." You see it in movies, you hear it in songs, you read it in magazines and spot it on television.

But sex will never fill your love tank. Sex was never designed to *create* love; it was made to *express* love. Sex was made to reinforce and communicate a love that is *already* there—a love big enough to say, "I love you so much for who you are that I will nourish that love and protect that love within the context of a permanent commitment."

Sex, the way God designed it, is to be the result of a committed relationship, not the cause of it. For sex to be positive and do what it's supposed to do, love must be nourished and grow to maturity. And *then* sex can be explosive!

The first source for filling your love tank is the unconditional, perfect love that demolishes the fear that no one will ever love you just the way you are. And that's a love that comes from Jesus.

 REFLECT: If your love tank is on empty today, open your heart to God's love right now.

PRAY: *Lord God, I ask you to fill me now with your unconditional, perfect love.*

13 God on Patrol

Bible Reading: Psalm 16:1-11

You will show me the way of life, granting me the joy of your presence and the pleasures of living with you forever. Psalm 16:11

MANY PEOPLE THINK of God as a cosmic cop standing in the center of the universe—like a police officer gunning you down with his radar detector. "Hey, you!" he snarls. "Yeah, you! You look like you're having fun over there. Well, cut it out! And you with the video. What's it rated? PG-13? R? Hand it over, slow and easy. And who's lip-locked in that dark corner? Is that you, Kaitlin? And Jake—I should have known. We'll have no more of that. Not while I'm on patrol."

All I want to do is have a little fun. But God just wants to spoil it for me. Have you ever thought that way?

The same folks who see God as the ultimate party-pooper imagine the devil as a fun-loving guy aiming only to help people enjoy themselves. That's a lie. The devil doesn't care if you have fun. He hates your guts. He will eat you up. Peter says that the devil is always "looking for some victim to devour" (1 Peter 5:8).

A guide once told a group of tourists in Israel that they were probably used to seeing shepherds driving sheep through the fields and roads. "But in Palestine," he pointed out, "things are different. The shepherd always leads the way, going in front of the flock."

The tourists were amused when the first flock of sheep that happened along was being driven, not led as the guide had explained. Embarrassed, the guide asked the man, "How is it that you are driving these sheep? I've always thought that Eastern shepherds *lead* their sheep."

"Oh," replied the man, "that's true. The shepherd does lead his sheep. But I'm not a shepherd. I'm a butcher."

Satan is a butcher. He isn't interested in giving you pleasure or happiness. He only means to chew you up and spit you out. If you want to really see him at work, read Job 2:1-8 to see what he did to righteous Job. And that's just what he wants to do to you.

So don't think of the devil as an outrageously fun dude just waiting to pack your life with extreme excitement. Jesus dashed that myth when he said, "The thief's purpose is to steal and kill and destroy" (John 10:10). The devil doesn't care if you have fun. His only goal is to steal and kill and destroy you.

God's goal is the exact opposite. Jesus said, "My purpose is to give life in all its fullness" (John 10:10). God wants you to experience a jam-packed, joyful life.

REFLECT: Are you experiencing the full and joyful life Jesus promised, or are you just trying to keep God from getting mad at you?

PRAY: Talk that over with God today.

14 Getting Personal with "The Force"

Bible Reading: Proverbs 8:17-21
I love all who love me. Those who search for me will surely find me.
Proverbs 8:17

REMEMBER THE FIRST trilogy of the *Star Wars* movies? Luke Skywalker was the big hero in those three films.

In the first movie Skywalker, having just escaped from the Sandpeople, stands in the quarters of Obi-Wan Kenobi on the planet of Tatooine. Luke has just learned that Obi-Wan was the Jedi Knight who had fought in the Clone Wars with Luke's father. Obi-Wan gives Luke a light-saber that once belonged to Luke's father and, in the course of the conversation, mentions "the Force."

"The Force?" Luke says.

Obi-Wan responds, "Well, the Force is what gives the Jedi his power. It's an energy field created by all living things. It surrounds and penetrates us. It binds the galaxy together."

The idea of the Force sounds spookily familiar because the Force is what many people imagine God to be. They picture God as a faceless, formless energy, an impersonal force that mysteriously surrounds and guides the universe.

But that's a myth. Sure, God does surround and guide the universe. He is everywhere. He is Spirit. But he is not some mysterious, elusive energy force out there somewhere. He is not a *thing* or an *it*. The astounding thing about God is that he is a *person*. Read again Proverbs 8:17 at the top of this page. Notice the personal pronouns: "I . . . me . . ." Does that sound like cosmic energy talking?

God is referred to in the Bible as the God of Abraham, Isaac, and Jacob. He told his name to Moses. He revealed himself to the boy Samuel. He spoke to Isaiah in the temple. He told Jeremiah, "I knew you before I formed you in your mother's womb" (Jeremiah 1:5). King David called him a "Father to the fatherless, defender of widows" (Psalm 68:5). And all Christians have been "adopted into his family" so that we may call him "Father, dear Father" (Romans 8:15).

God, the true God, is *personally* interested in you. He knows your name. "See," he says to his people, "I have written your name on my hand" (Isaiah 49:16). "He cares about what happens to you," the apostle Peter says (1 Peter 5:7). Jesus says that "the very hairs on your head are all numbered" (Matthew 10:30). And God promises that "when you pray, I will listen. If you look for me in earnest, you will find me when you seek me. I will be found by you" (Jeremiah 29:12-14). Those are personal promises that could come only from a loving, personal God.

REFLECT: How would you explain to a friend why it matters that God is personal?

PRAY: Ask God to make these incredibly important truths clear to you.

15 This Machine Is Out of Order

Bible Reading: 1 John 3:21-24

If our conscience is clear, we can come to God with bold confidence. And we will receive whatever we request because we obey him and do the things that please him. 1 John 3:21-22

"OKAY, GOD, I'm going to give you a chance to prove yourself." Mark knelt beside his bed. He was nine years old and fiercely wanted to believe in God. So he bowed his head, folded his hands and kept praying.

"I really want to believe in you, God. So when I wake up in the morning, if there's a billion dollars under my bed, I'll know you're real."

Mark didn't get the billion dollars. Maybe God turned him down because a billion dollars—he told God he wanted it in one-dollar bills—wouldn't fit under the bed with the action figures, dirty clothes, and dust bunnies.

A more likely reason Mark didn't get the money was his goofed-up idea about God. He imagined God was a heavenly vending machine: Deposit a prayer, push the right button, and you get your wish. He thought God was a sort of Santa Claus figure waiting to fulfill kids' wish lists. If he only prayed and believed hard enough, God would plop down everything a nine-year-old heart desired.

It's not a surprise when a kid thinks that way. Unfortunately, lots of adults also think of God as the Divine Vending Machine. They never get a better understanding of God than this "Santa Claus myth."

God loves to answer prayer. He says, "Ask me and I will tell you some remarkable secrets" (Jeremiah 33:3). He even promises, "While they are still talking to me about their needs, I will go ahead and answer their prayers!" (Isaiah 65:24).

But prayer isn't a coin to plunk into a vending machine, and faith isn't a button you bang on. God doesn't cave in to human whims and wishes. God thinks bigger than petty human wishes. He's the Almighty, Love Incarnate, the God who longs for his children to return the love he has heaped on them. He wants us to love *him,* not stuff. He wants us to seek *him,* not answers to greedy prayers. He wants us to obey him, not because we hope it bags us a billion dollars, but because we love him and want to please him.

Here's the huge irony: When you quit thinking of God as a heavenly vending machine, you can be confident you will receive what you ask from him. It won't happen because you punch a button and expect God to produce, but because you obey his commands and do what pleases him (see 1 John 3:22).

REFLECT: How do your prayers sound? Do you treat God like a vending machine?

PRAY: Spend a few moments sharing your love with God. And in your prayer, don't ask him for anything.

16 Taking a Stand When You Would Rather Take a Seat

Bible Reading: Matthew 5:10-12

God blesses those who are persecuted because they live for God.
Matthew 5:10

YOU WALK DOWN the hallway wearing your new *Love God, Hate Sin* T-shirt. At lunchtime your friends let fly a flock of jokes about your T-shirt, your church, and your faith. Then you start to think you really messed up your social standing by letting your youth pastor talk you into wearing that shirt.

The next time you get mocked for being a Christian—even if you're not wearing a T-shirt that screams *Turn or Burn*—throw a party! The Bible says you're *blessed*.

You might wonder what there is to be happy about, which is what that word "blessed" actually means. After all, only a "sick-o" likes a big dish of pain with a heap of fried embarrassment on the side. But you can be happy because you're worthy to suffer for the name of Jesus Christ and because you're in good company. After being beaten for their testimony, the apostles rejoiced "that God had counted them worthy to suffer dishonor for the name of Jesus" (Acts 5:41).

Standing up for God and all that's good won't automatically make life easy. Some people will tease you. Others will pick you apart if you do the least little thing wrong. But you don't have to pretend you're perfect. When you blow it, admit it, get up, and move on. You are a *follower* of Jesus Christ, not Jesus Christ himself.

Fear of turning off your friends may keep you from standing up for your faith. The quickest way to turn off your peers is saying, "I'm a good Christian, and I don't do those things!" It's better to say, "I accept you as you are. Please accept me as I am." If you accept people, it's amazing how they respond. You have a decent chance of being well-liked even if you don't plunge into all their activities.

Acceptance or friendship isn't always what you get, however. Sometimes you do lose friends or slide into a season of loneliness. But be encouraged. You're in a transition. If it comes down to winning a popularity contest or winning the pleasure of Jesus Christ, shoot for the latter every time. If your friends reject you because of a stand you take, it's not really you they're rejecting. It's Christ.

As you stay sensitive to what the Holy Spirit's teaching you, you'll know when it's wisest to keep quiet and witness without words. You don't have to leap up on the lunch table and preach while kids eat. But there are times when the right thing to do is to stand up and speak up. Who knows what kind of spiritual fire your sparks might start?

REFLECT: Have you ever been made fun of or left out of an activity for following Jesus? How did you deal with it?

PRAY: *Give me your wisdom, God, so I'll know how to stand up for you.*

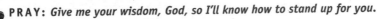

17 Finding the Road to Freedom

Bible Reading: 1 Corinthians 10:12-13
God is faithful. . . . When you are tempted, he will show you a way out so that you will not give in to it. 1 Corinthians 10:13

PICTURE YOURSELF WALKING down a road. The scenery is stunning, the weather is great. Then you see a fork in the road. Your map shows that the road to the right is the correct road. But that narrow road heads straight uphill and looks grueling. The road to the left is wide and runs downhill. So which do you pick?

If you want to honor your Lord, you'll choose the road to the right that leads away from evil. Walking this tougher road takes faith that says, "Regardless of what Satan tells me, regardless of how appealing sin seems, regardless of how easily I can keep my wrong quiet, I choose to follow the right road."

Take sex, for example. Left-hand road thinking says, "Any time, any place, any person available." Right-hand road thinking says, "I'm confident that if I don't compromise physically, God will build character into my life and provide the right person for me to marry."

As you walk the path of life, you will stand at many forks in the road. Each time you have to make a choice. The first choice is always the hardest. Each time after that it gets easier. It's like training for a marathon. The first run is a killer, but as a runner builds strength and endurance, runs become faster and farther. Only after months of training is a runner ready for a 26.2-mile race.

But what would happen if a marathon runner flopped on the couch, scarfed junk food, and hung out with friends who made fun of running? Spiritual laziness, spiritual junk food (like too much TV with no Bible reading), and unspiritual friends who mock godly things will all shrink your spiritual endurance. If you want to honor Jesus Christ to the last step of the race, first be a man or woman of faith. Second, stay spiritually fit so you will have the stamina to keep saying no.

One of the best ways to keep on God's road is to learn to walk away from situations you know will press you to compromise. Think about it: If you know you're in for a bad situation, why go there? Some parties are just asking for trouble. So are places like your girlfriend's or boyfriend's home when parents are away. And some possessions, like an R-rated video, can be killers in your walk with Christ.

Think hard when you reach a fork in the road. And pick God's path.

REFLECT: How determined are you to pick God's path? What makes choosing the right road hard?

PRAY: Talk to God now about some of the danger areas in your life. Ask him to build up your resistance to those temptations.

18 No Compromise

Bible Reading: 1 Peter 2:11-12
Be careful how you live among your unbelieving neighbors. 1 Peter 2:12

KYLE FEELS SICK as he rethinks how he and his friends snuck into an X-rated movie last night. What he saw was shockingly gross. He knew it was wrong, but he just couldn't say no to his friends.

Amber and her friends spent the whole evening bashing one of the girls at school. It was vicious. Amber later wished she had walked away when the gossip started, but she just couldn't. She regretted the ugly things she said.

Swimming against the current in a river for very long takes more strength than any of us can muster. It's easier just to relax and go with the flow. Problem is, the wrong flow can sweep you away from shore—forever. Friends, like that flow, can tire out even the strongest swimmer. That's what makes it so crucial that your closest friends pull you in the right direction, challenging you to live for Christ.

You can't claim to follow Christ and keep on compromising. Like 1 Peter 2:12 says, if you keep your behavior excellent, your friends might one day glorify God. If you compromise, though, your friends won't ever see a difference between your life and theirs. And if they see no difference, they will have no reason to become followers of Christ themselves.

How can you keep from compromising? By becoming a person of convictions. A conviction is a standard you commit to keep regardless of the cost. You might have a conviction, for example, that says, "Because my body is the temple of God, I will never take any illegal drugs."

Write down what your no-compromise convictions are. Then you'll have no doubt what your standards are and what actions you need to take. When you are in a tempting situation, you can recall what you decided while you still had your head—and you'll be more motivated to follow your convictions.

As you write your convictions, follow these guidelines:

- Put them in first person: "I will . . ." or "My goal is . . ." or "I plan to . . ."
- Make them action-oriented, something you will do or not do—instead of something you believe.
- Make them pointed and specific, not fuzzy and general.
- Base them on Scripture.

 REFLECT: What are your no-compromise convictions? Have you started to write them down?

PRAY: Spend some time today asking God to help you begin formulating your convictions.

19 Deal with It and Keep Moving On

Bible Reading: Psalm 32:3-7

I confessed all my sins to you and stopped trying to hide them.
Psalm 32:5

SUPPOSE THAT three months ago you chose to live totally for God. You pulled away from negative friendships and since that day have lived for Jesus in a no-compromise way. Then, after a basketball game, you drop in on a party you should have passed up. You throw down a cold one. One brewski leads to another and—*boom!*—you find yourself beyond buzzed.

By the time you get home, you feel rotten—not just from the beer but also from the Holy Spirit's kind yet no-kidding conviction. The moment you realize you've blown it, you confess your disobedience to God. Once you confess your sin—check out Psalm 32:3-5 and 1 John 1:9 to see how—you know that everything is right between you and God.

But that's the easy part. Monday morning at school is far harder. How you acted made a big joke of Christ and his followers. The only way to slow down the slander is to admit to your friends—Christian and non-Christian—that what you did was wrong. Tell them you're sorry. Ask them to forgive you.

And if you do that, congratulations. You've accomplished one of the hardest things you'll ever do in your entire life. It might also be one of the most stunning sermons your friends will ever hear. When they see a Christian blow it and admit it, they realize that Jesus really does have control of your life.

Now what do you do about changing your behavior? You won't make believers out of people by getting buzzed again, and it takes more than a resolution to break a bad habit. First, think through how you will respond when temptation hits again. Second, find someone to hold you accountable—to ask you daily or weekly, whichever works best, how the habit is doing. Third, replace the old negative habit with a new positive one.

But these practical steps are useless if you try to bust old habits through brute willpower. Spiritual power comes from the Holy Spirit, and to overcome your sinful tendencies you need the Spirit's help. Galatians 5:16 says, "Live according to your new life in the Holy Spirit. Then you won't be doing what your sinful nature craves." You walk by the Spirit when you listen up for what Christ wants, decide to do what he's shown you to do, and trust him to enable you to do it.

The Holy Spirit has power to alter every area of your life. Don't exclude anything. He can help you control your thoughts, your feelings, even the desire for alcohol, drugs, or sex outside God's boundaries. Ask him to do it, then let him!

REFLECT: Are there some patterns of behavior you need to talk to God about?

PRAY: Invite the Holy Spirit today to remake every area of your life.

20 Living on the Edge

Bible Reading: Romans 12:1-2

Don't copy the behavior and customs of this world, but let God transform you into a new person by changing the way you think. Romans 12:2

IN EIGHTEENTH-CENTURY ENGLAND, the king was interviewing drivers for the royal coach. He asked each one, "If you were driving on a winding mountain road, how close could you come to the edge of the road without going over?"

The first driver boasted, "I'm an excellent driver, Your Majesty. I could drive your coach to within eighteen inches of the edge at top speed and not go over."

The second driver bragged, "My skill and experience are unparalleled in the kingdom. I could drive your coach to within six inches of the edge."

But the third driver responded, "I wouldn't take any chances with your safety, Your Majesty. I would drive the coach as far away from the edge as possible."

The king chose the third driver, who was more interested in the king's welfare than in showing off how well he could drive.

Sometimes students are like the first two drivers: "I want to see how *close* to the edge I can get without getting into trouble." Their only question about sex is "How far can I go?" The one thing they want to know about school is "How little can I study?" And their one puzzle about getting along with parents is "How mouthy can I be?" Those who are useful to the King have the attitude of the third driver: "To honor my King, I will see how *far* from the edge I can stay."

You're driving sane when you not only let God change your *behavior* but also remake your *thoughts* from the inside out. According to Romans 12:2, there are two groups of people: those becoming more like everyone else in the world, and those being transformed into Christ's likeness. Your mind is the battlefield. Lose the war there, and you lose it in your actions.

If you always have lustful thoughts romping through your mind, for example, it's all too easy to give in to the least little pressure to play around physically or stare at pornography. And if you let the thoughts romp, you'll never see an end to the pressure you feel.

If you want to change, begin today to spend at least a few minutes every day reading, studying, and memorizing God's Word. Think about how the verses specifically apply to your life. Here's how the formula works:

Information		Meditation		Transformation
(The Bible)	+	(Applying it to your life)	=	(A new you)

If you haven't spent much time reading your Bible before, 1 John is a great place to start. Begin today and watch God's Word change your life.

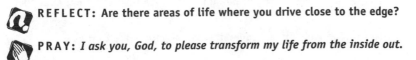

REFLECT: Are there areas of life where you drive close to the edge?

PRAY: *I ask you, God, to please transform my life from the inside out.*

21

The Higher the Price, the Greater the Value

Bible Reading: 1 Peter 1:13-20

God paid a ransom to save you from the empty life you inherited from your ancestors. And the ransom he paid was not mere gold or silver. He paid for you with the precious lifeblood of Christ, the sinless, spotless Lamb of God. 1 Peter 1:18-19

SEVERAL CENTURIES AGO, a Protestant scholar named Morena was forced into exile in Lombardy, Italy. Living in poverty, he fell seriously ill and was taken to a hospital for the poor. The doctors, assuming that Morena was uneducated, began speaking in Latin among themselves at his bedside. They said, "This worthless creature is going to die anyway, so let us try an experiment on him."

Morena, of course, knew Latin almost as well as his native language. Summoning his strength, he raised himself up and said to the surprised doctors, "How can you call 'worthless' someone for whom Christ died?" Touché.

Our society uses a multitude of methods to determine a person's value:

- A Major League Baseball team decides a player is worth tens of millions of dollars over his playing career.
- A soldier in combat discovers he is worth a human life when a comrade takes a bullet to save him.
- A mom on welfare finds she is worth the efforts of volunteers who spend days repainting her broken-down house.

But as Morena clearly understood, our biggest value as Christians comes from the fact that God the Father allowed Jesus Christ—his sinless Son—to die for our sins. In 1 Peter 1:18-19, the apostle Peter remarked that money can't compare to this sacrifice. Jesus declared the high value of giving one's life for another when he said, "The greatest love is shown when people lay down their lives for their friends" (John 15:13). Paul expanded that thought when he described the ultimate life-for-life sacrifice: "God showed his great love for us by sending Christ to die for us while we were still sinners" (Romans 5:8).

By God's estimation, you were worth the death of his Son. While you were stuck in your sin, there was nothing about you to attract God to you or to cause him to send his Son to die for you. You weren't righteous. You weren't moral. You were a sinner, the total opposite of the perfect Lamb. But God saw you as lovable, and your value skyrocketed when Jesus gave up his life for you.

No matter what your value is to others in earthly terms, you are eternally priceless because of the ransom the Father lovingly paid for you.

REFLECT: Why are all people worthy of being treated with respect? What does that have to do with respecting yourself?

PRAY: Ask God to flood you with an understanding of your value to him.

If You Were the Only One

Bible Reading: 1 Corinthians 6:19-20
You do not belong to yourself, for God bought you with a high price.
1 Corinthians 6:19-20

TERESE SHRUGGED whenever her youth pastor talked about how Jesus' death for her proved his love. She felt lost in a crowd. "Sure, Jesus died for my sins," she argued, "but he didn't die for me alone. He died for the whole world. I'm just one among bazillions of people who received God's gift of forgiveness in his salvation 'group plan.' "

The fact that you're only one believer among bazillions doesn't cheapen your value to God. If you were the only person on the planet, Christ still would have died for you! And the Bible proves that point: When God first issued his promise to rescue sinful humankind, there was only one couple on earth. After Adam and Eve sinned, God promised to crush Satan's head—cool, huh? (God was talking about the victory over sin that Christ's death on the cross would bring—see Genesis 3:15.) If, instead of Adam and Eve, you had been in the Garden of Eden, you too would have disobeyed God. And you too would have received God's great promise to save you.

If you want to transform your identity so it lines up with the stupendous way God sees you, catch this fresh vision of your worthiness to God. As a member of God's family, you are chosen to receive "the manifold grace of God" (1 Peter 4:10, KJV). That's part of the Crucifixion story we don't always think about.

Most Christian youth will tell you that the cross was about "sin and forgiveness." But look closer. *Why* did God deal with your sin and offer forgiveness at the cross? Because you are lovable to him, and the only way you could belong to his family was if Christ died for your sin. God loves you so much that you are worth the death of his Son. As you realize your value to God more clearly, it changes how you live and interact with others. You've got love to give. You don't treat anyone with less respect than God deems they deserve.

God says, "You are valuable." You can read in 1 Corinthians 6:19-20, "You do not belong to yourself, for God bought you with a high price." Now try that verse again, this time personalized. Read it aloud to yourself a few times to let it slap sense into you: "I am so valuable to God that he bought me at a high price."

So how does it feel to know that God loves you enough to have paid an enormous price for you—not because of anything you have done, but just because he finds you valuable? What are you worth?

REFLECT: Explain it to a friend: What does Christ's death for us say about our value?

PRAY: Spend a few minutes telling God you appreciate the value he gives you.

23 Who Gets into Your World?

Bible Reading: Philippians 2:5-11
[Christ Jesus] took the humble position of a slave and appeared in human form. Philippians 2:7

LUCAS WENT BONKERS when his favorite uncle came to visit. As soon as Uncle Miguel was in the door, he was on the floor with Lucas designing Lego skyscrapers. Uncle Miguel knew how to give superheroes even more super powers. Uncle Miguel could even make cool army guy noises and car noises and all sorts of other interesting noises. And Uncle Miguel never got tired of playing with Lucas.

Little kids need adults who ditch the world of jobs and responsibilities and enter the tiny-tyke world of toys, games, and pretend.

You're no little kid. But even adolescents need attention. You still need adults to get into your world and care about your activities and interests. And your requirement for attention is met when a loving adult leaves the grown-up world for a period of time and gets into your world.

A family in which you get that kind of attention showered on you might seem like a different planet from where you've grown up. If you haven't received attention from the adults around you, perhaps you wonder how you can matter to God or to others. You might see yourself as less than first quality because significant people in your life didn't care enough to spend time with you.

Let your heart grab hold of this fact: God left his world—heaven—in the person of Jesus Christ and entered your world—sinful earth—to demonstrate that you are the object of his love. That's the message of Philippians 2:5-8. God is the one who meets your ache for attention.

Besides that, God is still looking after you. He values you so highly that he sticks around in your world day by day in the person of the Holy Spirit (see John 14:16; Matthew 28:20). He has known every detail about you since before you were born (see Psalm 139:13-16). He knows all about your everyday hassles, inviting you to "give all your worries and cares to God, for he cares about what happens to you" (1 Peter 5:7). He couldn't be closer to you moment-by-moment, because he's right here with you. He's so close that one of Christ's names is " 'Immanuel'—which means 'God is with us' " (Matthew 1:23).

As you let this truth flood your mind and heart, you'll be awash in a new view of you. You'll begin to see yourself as you really are: a person of infinite value and worth.

REFLECT: How has Jesus showered incredible attention on you? What does that say about how much he loves you?

PRAY: Ask God for his help in seeing yourself as he sees you.

24 Forgive and Forget

Bible Reading: Psalm 103:8-13

[The Lord] has not punished us for all our sins, nor does he deal with us as we deserve. Psalm 103:10

JOSH, I'M WRITING to you because I'm alone and confused. I had sex with my boyfriend, thinking I owed it to him. About four months later I learned I was pregnant. Jeff left me, and my parents still don't know. About a month ago I became a Christian. But I have been feeling so guilty. How can God love me after what I have done? I feel that my life is not worth living anymore. I cry myself to sleep every night. Can God really love me and forgive me? Please write back.

Kaila is confused—with no idea how to resolve some huge issues. She's also clueless—with no idea of her immense value to God. The truth is that Jesus came into her world to die for her sins—*all* of them, including the wrong sexual relationship that left her pregnant. Yet Kaila thinks her sin is too enormous for God's love to cover, like a check that has bounced because of insufficient funds. Truth is, she can't empty God's account of forgiveness. Every sin we confess, he forgives. And that's what I told Kaila in my letter back to her.

If you want to gauge the grand size of God's forgiveness, look at King Manasseh, one of Judah's most wicked kings. Manasseh turned his back on God, worshiped false gods, and plunged the people into idolatry (see 2 Chronicles 33:1-9). When the Assyrians captured the nation of Judah, Manasseh humbled himself before God and prayed (verses 12-13). Despite Manasseh's evil past, God forgave him. The king no doubt returned home seeing himself worthy of being forgiven.

If God was able to forgive Manasseh's staggering sins, Kaila can surely count on God's ability to forgive the wrongs she has done.

Maybe you see yourself as being way beyond forgiveness. But what matters is how God sees you. King David sinned greatly. But he knew he was never beyond forgiveness. He wrote, "[The Lord] does not treat us as our sins deserve or repay us according to our iniquities. For as high as the heavens are above the earth, so great is his love for those who fear him; as far as the east is from the west, so far has he removed our transgressions from us" (Psalm 103:10-12, NIV). David held on to God's unlimited forgiveness and discovered the worthiness God saw in him.

One of the most awesome aspects of God's forgiveness is getting free to forgive *yourself.* The director of a mental hospital once said that half of his patients could go home if they only knew they were forgiven. If you don't get hold of forgiveness, you tip your whole life off kilter.

REFLECT: Feeling bad about sins is normal, but do you let bad feelings cloud the fact of your forgiveness? How are you going to grab hold of God's forgiveness?

PRAY: Thank God today for his forgiveness—past, present, and future.

April 25

A Safe Place for You

Bible Reading: Psalm 46:1-6

God is our refuge and strength, always ready to help in times of trouble. Psalm 46:1

YOU'RE SWIMMING in a sea of hurt. Know it or not, all around you are people drowning in disappointment, discouragement, or depression—family members, Christian peers, students in your youth group, non-Christians friends at school. You probably don't need more than an instant to think of someone who needs a friend who "is always loyal . . . born to help in time of need" (Proverbs 17:17). And to be that kind of friend means you must be *available*.

Check (✔) the phrases that tell what it means to be an available friend:

☐ Saying, "Call me when things get better for you."
☐ Taking the time to listen to what someone has to say.
☐ Saying, "Here's a quarter, call someone who cares."
☐ Saying, "I want you to know I'm going to be here for you, no matter what."

Here's the truth short and sweet: Being available means you are interested enough in people to take time to listen to them and actually care about what happens in their world.

Jesus is the ultimate example of an ever-present friend, and you see his availability best when he helps hurting people. The woman at the well in John 4 was a total outcast, but Jesus made himself available to talk with her about her life. The woman who was caught in adultery in John 8 was a nobody to everyone else, but Jesus was available to care for her. Lepers were despised by society, but when ten lepers came to him for healing (see Luke 17), Jesus was available to them.

So how does it make you feel to know that the God of the universe is available to you as a refuge or "safe place" in time of trouble? Check (✔) all that apply.

☐ Angry   ☐ Disappointed   ☐ Grateful
☐ Humbled   ☐ Important   ☐ Pleased
☐ Scared   ☐ Secure   ☐ Worried

God will always be there for you, and he will never fail you. He wants you to be that kind of friend to others too.

REFLECT: Write a prayer, thanking God for being available to you and telling him what that means to you.

PRAY: Ask God to help you be an available friend to someone this week.

26 Being There When Your Friends Are Down

Bible Reading: Galatians 6:1–5
Share each other's troubles and problems, and in this way obey the law of Christ. Galatians 6:2

"I'M REALLY FRUSTRATED with this friend of mine," Jamal fumed. "His parents are divorcing, but he hardly talks about it. I want to be there for him, but I'm never sure if I'm butting in."

That's a problem you face when you want to be an available friend. Figure on this: People seldom blurt, "I need help." But you can be sure it's time to be available when someone talks or acts in a way that shows any of these signs:

1. *Disappointment.* This happens when hopes or expectations aren't met. Most disappointments are pretty minor, but they still sting.
2. *Discouragement.* When disappointments pile up, they often lead to discouragement. You're seeing discouragement when your friend's hope and confidence shrink and he or she drifts through life half-heartedly.
3. *Depression.* A friend who is continually discouraged might slide into long periods of dejection, sadness, and withdrawal—signs of depression.

People weighed down with disappointment, discouragement, and depression might be all around you, yet you still might not see it. Why? Like Jamal's friend, they cover up and bottle up. But the more you become known as a caring person, the more those friends will open up and share their feelings.

You can always ask someone, "How are you—*really?*" You can spot those signs mentioned above. But it's also helpful to simply notice events that trigger disappointment, discouragement, and depression. People need an available friend when they have faced anything like the following:

- an unresolved conflict with someone
- separation from a loved one or a recent breakup of a relationship
- parents fighting, separated, or recently divorced
- failing classes, getting cut from a team, or struggling financially
- physical illness or injury

There's no doubt that God invites your hurting friends to tell him their cares and troubles (see 1 Peter 5:7). Because God cares about us, he says we can come to him, and he promises to help (see Hebrews 4:16). But God has another strategy to help: inserting *you* into the lives of struggling friends.

REFLECT: Who in your world needs you right now to be an available friend?

PRAY: Tell God today that you are available to minister his care and love this week to a hurting friend.

27 Be-Attitudes for Friends

Bible Reading: Ecclesiastes 4:9-12

A person standing alone can be attacked and defeated, but two can stand back-to-back and conquer. Ecclesiastes 4:12

"WHEN MY MOM had cancer," Trisha recalls, "my Sunday school teacher took a lot of time for me. I don't know how I would have gotten through everything without her help. My mom couldn't pay attention to me. Then Soo-Min took me walking or went out with me for fast food once or twice a week. And she listened. She made me feel like I mattered."

Feeling like you matter doesn't come so much from what friends *do* but from who they *are:* true friends. Friendship isn't so much about *doing* things as it is about *being* someone. Doing for your friends is important, but doing feels fakey unless it flows from who you are as a true friend. Here are three don't-leave-home-without-them qualities for being an available friend.

First, *be interested.* Being interested means genuinely caring about your friend and what he or she faces. It's about caring enough to put time into your friendship and get involved in your friend's world. An interested friend might:

- Schedule time to spend with someone at a time that works for him or her.
- Communicate, "I'm here for you, and with God's help we'll get through this together. I'll be calling you to see how you're doing."

Second, *be a listener.* Listening is one way you identify with what your friend is feeling. If you don't really listen, the time spent with your friend doesn't mean much. Here are a couple of practical ideas for being a good listener:

- Make sure you understand by asking something like, "What do you mean by that?" or "Why is that important to you?" to draw your friend out.
- Don't interrupt your friend or jump in to finish his or her sentences.

Third, *be a safe zone.* Your friend needs to feel that whatever he or she shares with you won't be blabbed all over school, church, or the community. Being a safe zone means you treat information with confidentiality, letting your friend feel safe about sharing his or her struggles. You demonstrate that you are a safe zone when you:

- Say something like, "I won't share what you tell me with anyone unless you want me to." Mean it. And keep your promise.
- Don't share what was told you in confidence with others even if you leave out your friend's name. People figure things out.

REFLECT: In what areas do you need to grow as an available friend?

PRAY: Ask God to help you grow!

28 Plugging In to the Power Source

Bible Reading: 2 Corinthians 12:8-10

My gracious favor is all you need. My power works best in your weakness. 2 Corinthians 12:9

SO YOU WANT to be an available friend. What's the first step?

Your first step is to believe with all your heart that you are completely, utterly, absolutely clueless how to be that kind of friend.

Really. The secret to being a good friend is admitting that on your own you can't be that kind of friend. It's not fun to own up to, but you don't have the strength and wisdom to be such a friend. Nobody does. That truth isn't meant to make you feel bad but to make you depend on Christ for the power and strength to be the kind of friend he is. Admitting that you are weak and needy is humbling. But plugging in to Christ's strength is empowering!

Think of all the times your brain is engaged with your own needs. Will you admit your need to depend on Christ to be more caring like him?

☐ Yes   ☐ I'll try

Think of all the times your attention drifts when other people talk. Then will you admit that you need to depend upon Christ to be a better listener like him?

☐ Yes   ☐ I'll try

Think of times you have told someone's secret—just to one person, of course. Then will you admit that *you* don't have what it takes to keep your friends' comments confidential? Will you depend on Christ to be a safe zone like him?

☐ Yes   ☐ I'll try

Whisper this verse to God: "I can do everything with the help of Christ who gives me the strength I need" (Philippians 4:13). Whisper the verse again. Then once again.

You *can* be more Christlike and a better loving friend to others—but only with Christ's help and Christ's strength! He will help you to admit your weakness and help you depend on his strength even more.

Your power source for being a more Christlike friend is the Holy Spirit living and working inside you. As a Christian, you are God's child, and his Spirit of love lives inside you. You grow into being a good friend as you live in God and he lives in you.

 REFLECT: In being a Christlike friend, what's the area in which you need to depend on him most?

PRAY: Ask God for help in that specific area.

29 The Super Superhero

Bible Reading: Mark 1:21-28

"What sort of new teaching is this?" they asked excitedly. "It has such authority! Even evil spirits obey his orders!" Mark 1:27

PLASTIC MAN is one cool-but-almost-forgotten comic book superhero from the past. He couldn't leap tall buildings with a single bound, but he could stretch, twist, and mold his body into any shape—from credit-card thin to slide under a locked door to brick-wall solid to block a bad guy's escape. He used his elastic body to rescue good guys and keep the world safe from evildoers.

Your childhood hero might have been Superman, Spiderman, a Pokemon character, or one of those Power Ranger dudes or dudettes. But in reality, there is only one true *super*-man: Jesus Christ. As God in human flesh, he had a special power that distinguished him from everyone around him: his authority. Though he looked like an ordinary guy, his authoritative action showed who he actually was—the Son of God.

First, *Jesus' teaching had authority.* When he taught, he blew worshipers right out of their pews! Jesus' teaching was authoritative because he knew God the Father personally. He not only taught what God's Word *said* but also what it *meant.* His authoritative presentation was a change of pace from teachers who merely repeated what other teachers had said.

Can you think of a time when a Bible passage seemed to flash at you like a strobe light? That was Jesus, making his written Word come alive for you, just like he did for those listening in the synagogue. He has the authority to pierce your mind with his Word, teach you what it means, and help you apply it to your life.

Second, *Jesus had authority over evil spirits.* The synagogue was still buzzing with surprise about his teaching when everyone heard a demon-possessed man's scream. The weak teaching of the scribes had left him undisturbed, but the authority of the Son of God terrified the evil spirit within him. Jesus showed his authority over the demon world by delivering the man from his demon captor.

You've gotta be glad that Jesus has authority over the spirit world, because God's archenemy Satan still works to suck in and slime people who let him into their lives—God lets Satan exert sizable power in the world, and people who play around with spiritism and satanism are prime candidates for satanic control. But people who submit to Jesus Christ as Savior and Lord are under the authority and protection of the one who has already smashed the devil and his God-opposing kingdom (see 1 John 3:8; 4:4).

REFLECT: Have you thanked Jesus any time in recent memory for exercising his authority on your behalf?

PRAY: Say thanks to Jesus for being stronger than any opposition you face.

30 Faith like a Hole in the Ceiling

Bible Reading: Mark 2:1-12

Seeing their faith, Jesus said to the paralyzed man, "My son, your sins are forgiven." Mark 2:5

"HEY, WHAT'S going on up there?" A scribe in a fancy flowing robe jumps to his feet, interrupting Jesus mid-sentence. He wags an angry finger at a wooden stick poking through the crowded home's clay ceiling. Other important-looking leaders rise indignantly to watch the stick break a gaping hole in the ceiling, spraying chips of clay and dust over the people below as they scurry for cover.

The onlookers stare through the hole as four pairs of hands break off roof tiles. Soon those hands lower into the room a stretcher bearing a motionless man. The man hurts in more ways than one. He's paralyzed. He utterly depends on help from family and friends. And his needs are even bigger, because he also hurts spiritually. He's a sinner needing forgiveness.

That's the scoop on the guy lowered to Jesus in Mark 2. But who in the world are the four guys who hacked through the roof to put their paralyzed friend in front of Jesus? The Bible doesn't give their names, but it's safe to assume that these guys were just ordinary people with a friend who needed Jesus. They were just like us—ordinary people who have needy friends.

These ordinary guys were able to tap into Christ's authority. How? They really believed that Jesus would do something for their hurting friend. Jesus, who has authority over sickness and sin, began ministering to the sick man when he saw their faith (see Mark 2:5). Their faith looked like chunks of clay covering the floor and four sweaty faces peering down at Jesus as he stood over the paralytic. Jesus always associated faith with doing something, not just mouthing sweet-sounding promises. And in response to the faith he saw, Jesus exercised his authority and healed the paralyzed man.

Think about it. One minute, a guy is flat on his back, unable to twitch even a toe. Then Jesus speaks: "Stand up, take your mat, and go on home, because you are healed!" (Mark 2:11). And suddenly the man is on his feet, moving around like anyone else in the room. What authority!

You don't have to worry that Jesus will crash into your life and muscle in on your activities. He's the only one in the universe who has the power and authority you need to meet and beat all of life's obstacles—physical, mental, social, or spiritual. But he won't force himself on you. He's patient. He stands ready. He's available to exercise his authority in your life. All you have to do is ask.

REFLECT: What obstacles do you face in life where you need Jesus to exercise his authority?

PRAY: Ask Jesus to act on your behalf.

1

Love and Hell Don't Mix, Do They?

Bible Reading: Luke 16:19-31

Anyone whose name was not found recorded in the Book of Life was thrown into the lake of fire. Revelation 20:15

IF GOD is a God of love, why did he create hell? And why does he send people there? Good question. The Bible says that Jesus—who loved the world enough to die for it—will one day bring "judgment on those who don't know God and on those who refuse to obey the Good News of our Lord Jesus. They will be punished with everlasting destruction, forever separated from the Lord and from his glorious power" (2 Thessalonians 1:8-9).

Isn't the existence of a place like hell more than a little bit incompatible with a loving God? No.

Actually, absolute love demands that the universe have some sort of a holding cell like hell. See, God won't *force* anyone to love him. You have to *choose* to love God. His plan for saving humankind is all about him doing everything within his loving power to invite all people to love him. But for those who totally refuse, God won't infringe on their freedom. Hell is the place built by a very patient God for those who refuse to go his way. He's tried to win them, but God ultimately says, "Okay, have it your way!"

So does this make God cruel or unloving? No.

Ponder this: If God did let unbelievers into heaven, it would be hell for them. How could people who hate prayer and praise to God stand to hang out in a palace of prayer and praise for the rest of eternity? If they squirm in church, how much worse would they wiggle in heaven? Heaven is where people bow to worship God. He won't force people to go who don't want to worship him—people who would rather hate him or ignore him like they have in this life.

Don't take that to mean that people who end up in hell will actually like being there. People don't want to go to hell. But by refusing Christ, that's the destination they pick. And the Bible leaves no doubt how bad it will be. It's a choice people will have to live with forever.

That's why God gives us the task of urging unbelieving family members, friends, and fellow students to trust God's love and submit to his reign. God can soften the hearts of people hardened against him by anger or apathy. He can teach them to love him as we do. And yet God won't force anyone into heaven who doesn't want to hang out with him for eternity.

REFLECT: How would you explain the fairness of hell to a non-Christian friend? Why doesn't hell disprove God's love?

PRAY: *Lord, don't let me miss an opportunity to share the love of Christ with my unbelieving friends, so they can enjoy heaven with me and escape hell.*

2 Too Late for Another Chance

Bible Reading: Hebrews 9:27-28

It is destined that each person dies only once and after that comes judgment. Hebrews 9:27

WHAT IF SOMEONE in hell changes his or her mind? Won't a loving God let a repentant person loose from hell and issue a transfer to heaven? Isn't believing in God like turning in a term paper—better late than never? No.

Sometimes people will get out of jail early for good behavior, but people are in hell only because God knows they won't flip-flop how they think about him. If a thousand more chances would have swayed them to choose his way, God would have provided those opportunities. But because he knows when people's minds are cast like concrete, God lets them go. God didn't fail to display his love to them. Instead, they sadly refused to recognize that love. It's like he offered up on a platter the opportunity to choose the best, even while allowing each person to choose the worst. Refusing God's love is like knocking the platter out of the server's hand and stomping on the choicest morsels.

When you understand God's love that way, his wrath isn't so puzzling. Wrath is the result of rejected love. Hell is where love no longer works. It's where love no longer pulls people to God—not because something is wrong with God's love, but because everyone there has chosen to refuse his love.

It's not that God no longer loves. His love still shines hot like the sun, but the result is wildly different when love is rejected. Like the old saying goes, "The same sun that melts wax also hardens clay." The difference isn't the source of the heat but the response of the thing heated.

If you've ever liked someone who took your love, crumpled it up, and shot it back to you as a spit-wad—and who hasn't?—you have had a small taste of the frustration God feels. And if you have stubbornly or pridefully rejected the love others have extended, you have experienced a little bit of what hell is like. It's miserable to need love and want love and yet not let someone love you.

Unbelievers are like buckets turned upside down under Niagara Falls. They wonder, "Where is the love of God and the God of love?" They moan, "My life is empty and meaningless." Yet they won't turn their lives right-side up and let the waterfall of God's infinite love fill their lives. God's love is a gushing torrent, but people set against God don't feel a drop. And hell is where people have decided they don't even *want* to feel God's love.

REFLECT: The better you know God, the more you will want to share his heart of love with people who don't know him. How are you expressing God's love to non-Christians?

PRAY: Ask God to help your non-Christian friends sense his love through you.

3 Bad Things Happen to Good People

Bible Reading: James 1:2-8

When your faith is tested, your endurance has a chance to grow.
James 1:3

WHEN A TORNADO tore through Justin's midwestern town, it lifted houses off foundations and blew some to bits. Justin felt as if God's harsh hand had reached down from heaven. He couldn't see how a loving God could allow earthquakes, hurricanes, and floods to destroy homes and kill thousands of people in a swipe.

The truth is that natural disasters are not the result of an angry God. A transformation occurred on earth after Adam and Eve disobeyed God in the Garden of Eden (see Genesis 3:17-18). The world is now stained by a physical evil that often puts pain and disaster in the lives of its inhabitants, even those who love God. But people who experience tragedy through natural disaster don't suffer because they are more wicked than those who escape (see Luke 13:3-5). This physical evil comes into our lives for a bunch of reasons.

1. *Some evil results from free choices.* If you go to the ocean and go for a swim in rip tides, it's not God's fault if you're sucked somewhere deadly.
2. *Some evil comes from choosing to do nothing.* Not pulling over to sleep when you're too tired to drive, for example, can cause a deadly crash.
3. *Some evil results from the free choices of others.* Child abuse, drive-by shootings, and drunk-driving deaths are a few ways innocent people suffer.
4. *Some evil is a by-product of good activities.* People driving to church sometimes die. Roller coasters sometimes fly off tracks.
5. *Some evil comes from evil spirits.* Job's sufferings were chalked up to Satan (see Job 1:6-12).
6. *Some physical evils prompt moral development.* Joseph's brothers sold him into slavery, but "God meant it for good" (Genesis 50:20, NASB).

So why doesn't your all-powerful God miraculously jam his hand into your world and keep physical evil from happening? God does sometimes intervene. But he couldn't do that all the time without overriding humans' free will—which he won't. Second, if he always prevented evil, you wouldn't learn anything from adversity because you wouldn't experience the consequences of bad choices.

God hasn't promised to shield you from everything evil. But he did say he would be with you through anything and everything (see Matthew 28:20).

REFLECT: Be able to explain it to a friend: How are natural disasters connected to human sin? Are individuals always to blame when bad things happen to them?

PRAY: Pray for clear understanding of this deep thought.

4 Can We Blame God for Bad Things That Happen?

Bible Reading: Galatians 6:7-10

Whenever we have the opportunity, we should do good to everyone, especially to our Christian brothers and sisters. Galatians 6:10

STUDENTS SHUFFLED nervously into the school assembly. They listened silently as their principal explained that yesterday after school a seventh-grade girl had been dragged into a boys' lavatory and raped. The students erupted with anger when the news sunk in. *How could their school have let this happen?*

That's the same question we toss at God: "Why do you allow people to mistreat each other? Why do you let people become murderers, rapists, child abusers, abortionists . . . ?"

At the heart of that deep question is why God would make creatures capable of choosing evil—sometimes big-time evil. As hard as it may be to accept when you howl with hurt, creating people with free will was God's perfect choice. While God's choices are always unlimited, let's think about just a few that he had:

- *God could have chosen NOT to create a world at all.* Besides being the least popular choice among four out of five people, the choice wasn't popular with God. He is love—and he wanted a family to share his love.
- *God could have made a world of robots that had to love him.* But "forced love" is a contradiction. Robots are simply programmed to respond.
- *God could have created a world where people were free to choose.* That's what he did. He gave Adam and Eve the capacity to obey or disobey, to love or not to love. They ultimately chose to rebel, and as a result sin entered our race.

It might seem like a mammoth contradiction that God is holy yet picked the only option where evil could occur. The result: Free human beings choose to reject him, mock him, and disobey him, and we jump at the chance to violate each other. Yet God allowed choices in order to show his love and allow us to love him.

In order to know God's love in its fullness, we live with pain and the occasional horrors of sin. But because love is a choice, we live in a world where love is all the more spectacular. When people choose to love in a world where they have total freedom to do evil, every act of love stomps on evil. And that kind of heroic love reminds us we were made by a loving God so we could love him.

 REFLECT: How could a loving God create a world where evil can take place?

PRAY: Ask God for an opportunity to share what you have learned with a friend who struggles with understanding evil.

5 Bringing Out the Big Gun

Bible Reading: Ephesians 6:10–20
Pray at all times and on every occasion in the power of the Holy Spirit.
Ephesians 6:18

MAYBE YOU BELIEVE that helping non-Christian friends get right with God starts with sharing the good news about Christ. Actually, it begins with prayer. When you share truth, you march into enemy territory. You can't do that without prayer any more than ground troops can take control of enemy territory without air support.

Prayer is simply talking to God in everyday language about your thoughts, feelings, and concerns. And you can be totally confident that God hears you when you pray. In fact, God eagerly waits for you to come to him in prayer. You are his child, and he values every minute you spend with him.

Why is prayer so great? Some important answers:

1. *Prayer helps you focus on God.* It helps you plug in to God's strength (Psalm 105:4). When you take time to pray, you unplug your mind from TV and CDs and plug in to God.
2. *Prayer is intimacy with God.* As you pray, God becomes a deep, personal friend. As you hang with God in prayer, you stay in tune with his heartbeat for you and the non-Christians he wants to reach through you.
3. *Prayer is a vital weapon in spiritual battle.* Spiritual conflict is real. And prayer is the biggest evil-blasting bomb in your arsenal. In Ephesians 6:10–20, the apostle Paul lists the armor you are to use to fight the spiritual battle. He says to wear your faith as a shield against Satan's flaming arrows, to put on salvation as your helmet, and to use God's Word as your sword (verses 16-17). Then Paul tells how prayer works in spiritual warfare (verses 18-20):
   • Pray at all times and on every occasion in the power of the Holy Spirit.
   • Stay alert and be persistent in your prayers for Christians everywhere.
   • Ask God to give you and other Christians the right words.
   • Pray that Christians will keep on speaking boldly for him, as we should.

When you pray, God acts! Your prayers for your non-Christian friends paralyze Satan as God works in their lives. God prepares your friends to receive the message—and he gives you strength to speak up.

God has his mind made up to do some astonishing things on your campus and in your community. When you pray, you get hold of God—and in sync with what he intends to accomplish.

REFLECT: Are you taking advantage of the powerful weapon of prayer? How could your experience of prayer be improved?

PRAY: Ask God to deepen your prayer life.

6 How Is Your Prayer Confidence?

Bible Reading: John 17:2-5

[God the Father has] given him [Christ the Son] authority over everyone in all the earth. He gives eternal life to each one you have given him. John 17:2

STUDENTS WHO PRAY with confidence for their schools are sure of this not-so-secret truth: God has a plan for reaching your friends at school.

God has some wild promises for you. Try this one: "Only ask, and I will give you the nations as your inheritance, the ends of the earth as your possession" (Psalm 2:8). To hear God's promise hit home even harder, put it like this: "Only ask, and I will give you your football team—or your Spanish class, your lab partners . . ."

God's promise is to give. Your responsibility is to ask in prayer. But you need to know how to ask confidently and take hold of what God has promised.

1. *Keep depending on Christ.* Jesus said, "If you stay joined to me and my words remain in you, you may ask any request you like, and it will be granted!" (John 15:7). What does it mean to "stay joined" to Christ? Try this: Remain in Christ by confessing sins God has pointed out to you and by inviting the Holy Spirit to fill your life. Allow Christ's words to stick in you by reading God's Word, studying it, memorizing it, discussing it, and doing what it says.
2. *Pray specifically.* Write down the names of people God wants you to witness to—parents, friends, classmates, teammates, etc. Ask God for exactly what you want him to do. One idea: Select a Bible verse about salvation and claim it for the people on your list. You might use John 17:2, praying, "Thank you, Lord, that you have authority over my lab partner, Vicki. I ask you to break Satan's grip on her. Get her ready to receive your Good News."
3. *Pray according to God's clear will.* There's no doubt about God's will for your friends: He doesn't want any of them to go up in smoke (see 2 Peter 3:9). When you pray that your friends will be saved and trust Christ, you can be sure you're asking for something God has announced as his will.
4. *Expect God to answer your prayers.* Jesus promised: "If you believe, you will receive whatever you ask for in prayer" (Matthew 21:22). As you pray for the non-Christians on your list, start to see them as people impacted by God through your prayers. Act on your belief by figuring out ahead of time how best to share the Good News with your friends. Expect that God is going to answer your prayers and liberate your friends—maybe through you.

REFLECT: How can your prayers better reflect God's goals for your world?

PRAY: Lift some non-Christian friends up to God in prayer today.

7 When Prayer Needs a Voice

Bible Reading: James 5:16-18

The earnest prayer of a righteous person has great power and wonderful results. James 5:16

HERB STOOD BACK, thumbs hooked in his armpits, admiring his baby-room paint job. His wife Beatrice spread Winnie-the-Pooh stick-ons all over the wall. They set up the crib, acquired an arsenal of diaper-changing supplies, and filled the dresser with baby clothes. They waited for the baby they were adopting to arrive, staring at each other blankly when none showed up on their doorstep.

And then they remembered—they hadn't called the adoption agency!

It works the same way with friends being reborn into God's kingdom. Wishes aren't prayer. You can think all you want about how fantastic it will be when your non-Christian friends trust Christ. But those wishes are ultimately as effective as waiting for Storks 'R Us to deliver the baby you plan to adopt. Until you *pray,* you haven't done the one thing that brings people to spiritual birth.

Prayer is more than a happy thought. It's an action. It's spilling your heart straight to God. And here are some ways you can become an active pray-er:

- Pray regularly—start by thanking God and praising him for his greatness.
- Pray alone over your personal list of non-Christian friends.
- Pray for non-Christians with a small group of friends. Meet with friends at church or on campus to pray about your witness to non-Christians.
- Pray with other Christians as you walk around your campus, but not in a showy parade of the holier-than-thou club. Just walk around the areas where kids clump and ask God to set your peers free to know him.

Prayer is the big gun, your ultimate spiritual weapon. And the biggest thing you can pray about for your non-Christian friends is that they hear and respond to the Good News. You can let God know you would like to be a part of that.

However, prayer is just your first job—it isn't your only job. At some point your friends who don't know Christ need to hear the truth about what it means to be a Christian and be challenged to trust Christ. They need to know what Christ has done to provide forgiveness for their sin. They need an invitation to accept God's gift of salvation—ditching the thought that they can save themselves and admitting that only what Christ has done will get them close to God and into heaven.

You can pray for your friends until you're hoarse—but you'll eventually need your voice to share the Good News with them. To become Christians, the people you're praying for must hear the Good News and respond to it by trusting Christ.

REFLECT: Why has God given you the privilege of praying for friends?

PRAY: Talk to God about your attitude about praying for non-Christians. Tell him if you are eager—or apathetic.

8 Brain Transplant

Bible Reading: Philippians 2:5-11
Don't copy the behavior and customs of this world, but let God transform you into a new person by changing the way you think. Romans 12:2

HOW WOULD YOU like to be smart—*really* smart? You wake up one morning and discover that your IQ has surpassed your weight. You go from working yourself to death just for average grades to computing logarithms in your head and learning German, Russian, and Japanese simultaneously.

This is what happens to Charlie Gordon in *Flowers for Algernon*, a story also told in an old movie called *Charly*. Thirty-two-year-old Charlie is a gentle, friendly guy who lives in a mental twilight zone. He can sort of read and write. But he knows he isn't as bright as people around him. In fact, a lab mouse named Algernon in some ways seems more intelligent than Charlie.

When Algernon undergoes an experimental operation, he becomes a genius among mice. Charlie, after a similar operation, rockets from moron to genius. He now absorbs knowledge like a sponge, but the results aren't all pleasant. Along with super-intelligence come self-centeredness, suspicion, and conflict with others—traits foreign to Charlie before the operation.

Then Algernon unexpectedly relapses, again becoming a run-of-the-mill rodent. When Charlie finds out, he's smart enough to realize he faces the same fate. His brain power indeed fades, and he slides back to his mentally handicapped state.

When Paul talks about God "changing the way you think" in Romans 12:2, he isn't asking you to go under the knife for a brain rearrangement. God isn't looking to spike your brain power and turn you into a rocket scientist either. What he wants is to transform you into a person who thinks more and more like Jesus.

So exactly how does Jesus think? In a word, *sacrificially*. In Philippians 2:5-11, Paul calls us to possess the same attitude as Jesus, who left heaven's glory, took on a human body, and sacrificed his life on the cross for us. Nobody forced Christ to live among us and die for us. He did it voluntarily. He set aside his rights as God in order to meet our need for forgiveness and reconciliation. That loving attitude of sacrifice motivated Christ throughout his visit to our planet. And it's the attitude God aims to cultivate in us.

You're not Jesus. So what would a sacrificial attitude look like in you? For one thing, it's so different from how the world acts that people would think you had your brain rewired. Human nature whines, "I want what I want when I want it!" But Christ's sacrificial attitude says, "I give what you need when you need it." Your generous, loving God will rearrange your brain as soon as you say "Yes!"

REFLECT: What will your brain look like when God gets done rearranging it?

PRAY: *Father, build in me a loving, sacrificial attitude like the one Jesus had.*

9 A Body in Need Is a Body Indeed

Bible Reading: Romans 12:3-8

Since we are all one body in Christ, we belong to each other, and each of us needs all the others. Romans 12:5

YOUR BODY PARTS are getting together for a meeting. The chairperson, your hand, gripping a gavel, calls the meeting to order. In a surprise first piece of business, your big toes step to the podium and say, "We quit."

"What are you talking about, Toes?" growls your belly.

"We're tired of getting stepped on," your big toes moan together.

"You *are* low guys on the totem pole," injects the funny bone. Hand raps the gavel. "Order, please!"

"Order? Cheeseburger, please!" the funny bone howls. Hand motions to the sergeant-at-arms, who promptly twists the distracting member behind your back.

"I don't like the sound of this, Toes," the ears say. "How do you think you can get along without the rest of us?"

"We'll run away," Toes reply. "We can wriggle to wherever we want."

"You won't be able to see where you're going," observe the eyes.

"We'll get by," one toe insists. "We might even take some of our other toe friends with us. In fact, the feet feel the same way we do. They'll probably hoof off with us too."

The forehead wrinkles. Then your mouth speaks up. "Maybe you can get along without us, Toes, but we won't make it without you. We count on you to keep us balanced."

"Because of you," say the hands, "we can put our best feet forward."

The toes wiggle at the outpouring of attention. "We do get a kick out of hanging out with the rest of you. Maybe we need each other more than we realized."

"And that's what I've been thinking all along," the brain concludes.

Twentieth-century songsters Paul Simon and Art Garfunkel sang these immortal words written by Simon: "I am a rock, I am an island." You probably have moments when that defiant strain of self-sufficiency wells to the surface. But seventeenth-century English poet John Donne wrote these wise words that better reflect reality: "No man is an island, entire of itself."

As much as you might try, you can never be completely independent. Even Jesus wanted fellowship, friendship, and prayer with his peers. Part of living sacrificially is admitting you need others and allowing others to need you.

REFLECT: Do your family members and friends know that you need them? Are you meeting their need for you?

PRAY: Talk to God about it.

10 The Thrill of Second Place

Bible Reading: Romans 12:9-13
Love each other with genuine affection, and take delight in honoring each other. Romans 12:10

SCENARIO #1: You're gabbing with your friends at a big party, and almost everybody beats you to the food. When you finally get to the table, there are only two choices left: (a) a gorgeous wedge of French Silk pie, and (b) two sad little vanilla wafers. Your choice is obvious—until you notice Chad, heavyweight captain of the wrestling team, ambling toward the dessert table. What will you do?

- ☐ Body check Chad into the next room, grab the pie, and run.
- ☐ Jab your finger into the middle of the pie, then say, "Sorry, Chad, this one is infected with my germs."
- ☐ Slide the pie toward the approaching hulk and say, "I'd like you to have this piece of pie, Chad. Enjoy!"

Scenario #2: The Stale Donuts have been your favorite Christian band forever, and their only concert in town all year is next week. Your youth leader snagged fifteen tickets, and they're going fast. You hand your money to her and she gives you the next-to-last ticket. As you walk away, you hear Lisa, another student, say, "Only one ticket left? But I need two. My friend from school isn't a Christian, and she promised to go hear the Stale Donuts with me if I could get tickets." What will you do?

- ☐ Ask Lisa, "What? You won't give up your ticket so your friend can go to the concert? What kind of Christian are you anyway?"
- ☐ Tell Chad he can have the French Silk pie if he will sell Lisa his ticket.
- ☐ Turn to Lisa and say, "It's great your friend wants to go with you. Here—have my ticket. I'll be praying for your friend."

Was the third choice in each scenario hard to swallow? Maybe those choices didn't bother you, but there are probably other times you've hesitated to give up something you wanted in order to put someone else first. There's a simple reason: Humans like to be at the head of the line.

But God desires to transform your thinking to be like Christ's, who put you first by sacrificing his life for you. God calls you to display the same attitude toward people around you. It's called *honoring* each other. God is pleased when you choose to honor others above yourself like Jesus did.

REFLECT: What stands in the way of your letting God transform your thinking?

PRAY: Tell God about your struggles now.

11 Hurting with Those in a World of Hurt

Bible Reading: Romans 12:14–16

When others are happy, be happy with them. If they are sad, share their sorrow. Romans 12:15

THE PHONE RINGING in the middle of the night jarred the young pastor awake. "Pastor, our daughter . . ." the voice on the phone choked. "She was in a bad car accident tonight. She's in surgery and . . . we're not sure . . . she'll make it."

The pastor dressed quickly and hurried to the hospital, praying all the way. When he arrived, tear-streaked faces told the story. The girl had died in surgery. He tried to say something to the parents, but he couldn't get the words out. He just sat and sobbed with the heartbroken mom and dad.

Not much later the girl's parents moved away, and the young pastor didn't see them for several years. When the pastor ran into them at a conference, he fumbled for words. "I have an apology to make," he finally said. "The night your daughter died, I failed you. I should have read Scripture to you and offered you words of hope. But I didn't. I just cried. I'm so sorry I let you down that night."

"You didn't let us down, Pastor," the girl's dad said. "What you did brought us great comfort. You felt our hurt and cried with us. You shared more than words with us; you shared your heart. And we will always be grateful."

Deep lesson: The pastor thought he failed. But what he actually did was show the kind of deep sympathy Jesus showed.

If people slam into sorrow or disappointment, the first thing they need is someone who feels their pain. When his friend Lazarus died (see John 11), Jesus cried with Lazarus's sisters, Mary and Martha. Why didn't Jesus just say, "Don't cry, ladies. Give me a few minutes and I'll have Lazarus back from the dead"? Because at that exact moment what they needed was someone to cry with them. So Jesus did. Later he performed the miracle that turned their sorrow to joy.

If you have family members and friends who hurt, the greatest gift you can give is to sorrow with them. Comfort isn't a pep talk nudging someone to "hang in there." Comfort isn't trying to explain why bad things happen. Comfort isn't just saying that God is in control and everything will be okay. Those things might be helpful later, but they don't deliver what people need most: comfort.

People walloped by hurt find comfort when they know they aren't suffering alone. So when a friend is crushed with sorrow or disappointment, feel crushed too. And it's okay to say something like, "I'm so sad for you" or, "I hurt for you" or, "I'm sorry you are hurting." It's what Jesus would do.

REFLECT: What does comfort look like when you show it to hurting friends?

PRAY: Pray for your friends who need God's help—and ask God to use you to comfort them.

12 It's Payback Time

Bible Reading: Romans 12:17-21
Never pay back evil for evil to anyone. Romans 12:17

EVER HAD ANY of the following—or something like them—happen to you? Check
(✔) either yes or no for each statement:

Yes No

☐ ☑ A careless brother or sister destroys something of yours.
☑ ☐ A "friend" spreads a nasty rumor about you.
☑ ☐ Somebody gets perturbed with you and pushes you around.
☐ ☑ You are *not* invited to the biggest party of the year.
☑ ☐ A sibling treats you like you're a nuisance.

Okay—somewhere, sometime, somehow you've probably been wronged. Check
(✔) any of the following you wanted to do in response—or actually did.

Thought Did

☑ ☐ Do unto him what he did unto you—only twice as bad.
☑ ☐ Pound his head in.
☑ ☐ Send her a note with "Dear Ex-Friend" as its opening line.
☒ ☐ Hack into the school computer and change all his grades.

Perhaps your brain seems to have come equipped with a sinister little "payback
chip." Whenever you're wronged, something inside you kicks into action and
strongly prompts you to do unto others just as they have done unto you. Since we're
all tempted this way at times, how should we respond?

Once again your sacrificing Savior shows you the way to go. If anybody
deserved to lash back at unfair treatment, it was God's sinless Son. Yet, "He did not
retaliate when he was insulted. When he suffered, he did not threaten to get even.
He left his case in the hands of God, who always judges fairly" (1 Peter 2:23). Jesus'
Father knew the treatment his Son received was rotten beyond belief. And he knew
exactly what kind of payback it required. God is your Father too, and he will justly
avenge—in his own way and time—any wrongs done to you.

REFLECT: When you are wronged, what's your usual reaction?

PRAY: Ask Jesus today to begin reprogramming that payback chip inside you—
to help you put down your weapons of retaliation and slowly back away.

13 Have I Died Yet Today?

Bible Reading: Romans 12:1

I plead with you to give your bodies to God. Let them be a living and holy sacrifice—the kind he will accept. Romans 12:1

MASKED ROBBERS enter a bank. Guns zip out a stream of bullets, and a security guard is hit twice as he shields an innocent customer in the line of fire. The customer escapes unharmed, but the guard dies on the way to the hospital.

A young child trying to cross a flood-swollen river falls in the swift current. A passing motorist plunges into the river and pulls the victim to safety. Exhausted from the ordeal, she is swept away and drowned.

It's "the ultimate sacrifice," laying down your life to let another live. These stories resemble the most heroic rescue of all time—the one that spared *you* from death. Because no one is holy like God, we all face judgment—death and eternal separation from our Creator. But Jesus became a man and died the death that all sinners deserve so we could live.

Here's the wild part. God turns around in Romans 12:1 and calls you to do the same thing: to sacrifice your body—with one key change. He's looking for a *living* sacrifice. Sounds like an oxymoron, doesn't it—one of those figures of speech that ties together contradictory terms, like "pretty ugly" or "virtual reality" or "long-sleeved T-shirt"? "Living" and "sacrifice" don't seem to fit together. After all, "sacrifice" usually means something *dies*.

Someday you might get the chance to be a hero. But in the meantime, God invites you to sacrifice your body and live to tell about it—and to do it again and again. One way to sacrifice your body without dying is by serving God and others with your abilities, time, and resources. It might look like this:

- helping an elderly neighbor by doing yard work
- giving some of your money to a missions project
- using your singing ability by serving on a worship team
- spending a couple hours each week visiting patients at a nursing home
- volunteering to help your parents clean the garage or attic
- spending the summer on a short-term missions trip, etc.

Sound like a lot of work? Paul must have anticipated his readers might think that way. In the second part of Romans 12:1, he wrote, "When you think of what [God] has done for you, is this too much to ask?" Your daily, living sacrifices are acts of worship to the one who sacrificed *everything* for you.

REFLECT: What changes do you want to make in order to offer your life as a living sacrifice?

PRAY: Spend some time right now praising Jesus for his sacrificial death for you.

14

He Just Keeps Loving and Loving and Loving You

Bible Reading: Jeremiah 31:1-6

Long ago the Lord said to Israel: "I have loved you, my people, with an everlasting love. With unfailing love I have drawn you to myself." Jeremiah 31:3

SHAY STORMS INTO the house, slamming the door behind him. He mouths off to his parents, then grinds his little brother's face into a bowl of ice cream. Grounded to his room for the rest of the day, Shay kicks the cat and beats his fist on the wall. Some very bad words just beg to pop out. As Shay cools down, it occurs to him that he's been a jerk. And that Jesus has been with him all day long. And that Jesus is still with him now. So he wonders, *Lord, why do you love me so much?*

Ever blown it big and asked God that question?

Well, he loves you because he created you.

Have you ever watched a mother and father *ooh* and *ah* over their newborn baby? Some newborns are the ugliest creatures on earth. But not to their parents. They think their baby is the cutest thing ever born. Why? Because they helped create the little critter. And because God created you, he loves you even when you're neither lovely nor lovable. He thinks you are the greatest. More than that, he loves you simply because he is a God of love. It's his character to love. And nothing you do can make him stop loving you.

You might wonder how God can keep loving you after you've sinned. Suppose it's the night after your school let out for vacation, and you get wild with your friends and wind up doing hundreds of dollars' worth of damage to school property. While some of your classmates might dance all over your destruction, it wouldn't thrill God. But would he quit loving you? No! He loves you—and the whole world—so much that he died for us to remove "our rebellious acts as far away from us as the east is from the west" (Psalm 103:12).

So what can cause God to change his mind and stop loving you? Nothing! Listen to what God has to say about it. Romans 5:8 tells you how much God loved you before you were even a Christian: "God showed his great love for us by sending Christ to die for us while we were still sinners." Romans 8:38-39 tells you what might try to separate you from God's love but can't: "I am convinced that nothing can ever separate us from his love. Death can't, and life can't. The angels can't, and the demons can't. Our fears for today, our worries about tomorrow, and even the powers of hell can't keep God's love away. Whether we are high above the sky or in the deepest ocean, nothing in all creation will ever be able to separate us from the love of God that is revealed in Christ Jesus our Lord."

Get it in your head: *God loves you!* You can't scare away his love.

REFLECT: Think again: What could you do that would separate you from God?

PRAY: Spend a few moments now telling God how great he is.

15 It's an Honor to Serve Him

Bible Reading: Psalm 8:1-9

What are mortals that you should think of us, mere humans that you should care for us? For you made us only a little lower than God, and you crowned us with glory and honor. Psalm 8:4-5

IF YOU COULD trail a superstar for a day, you would see everything people do for the fabulously famous. Fans honor them. Bodyguards protect them. And *everyone* makes special arrangements for them.

Before you feel wretchedly jealous because *you* never get that kind of treatment, listen up: God does those things for you, because you are important to him.

- He honors you with special attention, as Psalm 8:4-5 describes.
- He sends his angels to guard you. Psalm 91:11 says, "He orders his angels to protect you wherever you go."
- He is making special arrangements for you. John 14:2 says, "There are many rooms in my Father's home, and I am going to prepare a place for you. If this were not so, I would tell you plainly."

You're probably no superstar—not to the tabloids, anyway. So how can God be so good to you? God accepts and honors you because of what Jesus Christ did on your behalf. He died for your sins, taking away any and every offense that made you less-than-acceptable to God.

Instead of wondering, "How can God like me?" a better question might be, "How can God *not* like and accept me?" If you are a Christian, you are a child of God. John 1:12 says, "To all who believed him and accepted him, he gave the right to become children of God." God isn't like some earthly dads who can't fit you into their schedule or find anything nice to say about you. He's the perfect Father. Because you are his child, he will always accept you.

You still might figure that God sees you as a failure when you sin, shaking his head and wishing you would shape up. But God's love for you doesn't change when you sin. You can bet that your sin *grieves* God. He gets the same feeling you do when a friend hurts you—except that God doesn't pout like people do.

So how does a friend fix things up with you after hurting you? He or she comes back to apologize and ask your forgiveness. First John 1:9 says, "If we confess our sins to him, he is faithful and just to forgive us and to cleanse us from every wrong." When you blow it in your relationship with God, get things right with him ASAP. He loves you too much. Don't put it off.

REFLECT: Make a list of anything you have done or said in the last few days that grieved God. Confess your wrong to God and receive his forgiveness.

PRAY: Write your prayer of thanks for God's forgiveness.

16 Who's That Looking Back at You?

Bible Reading: Ephesians 1:3-8

How we praise God, the Father of our Lord Jesus Christ, who has blessed us with every spiritual blessing in the heavenly realms because we belong to Christ. Ephesians 1:3

YOU LOOK IN the mirror. How do you react to what you see? Check (✔) the statement which best describes your response.

- ☑ Sigh.
- ☐ Please be patient. God isn't finished with me yet.
- ☑ The mirror is twitching, but it hasn't cracked.
- ☐ I kiss myself!
- ☑ Pass me a full-body paper sack.
- ☐ What potential!

You can have all sorts of thoughts—good, bad, and ugly—about yourself. But how does God feel about what he sees in you? To see yourself as God sees you—as you really are—start by understanding your "position" in Christ. If you want a healthy self-image, you want to get God's view of you. And Ephesians 1 tells you these truths:

- You have been given "every spiritual blessing" in heavenly places (verse 3).
- You were chosen before the world was made "to be holy and without fault" in God's eyes (verse 4).
- You were picked for adoption as God's child (verse 5).
- Your freedom and forgiveness were purchased through Christ's blood, which was poured out for you on the cross (verse 7).
- You were identified as belonging to God through the Holy Spirit (verse 13).

Because of your position in Christ, those great things are true of you. Those are truths Paul wants you to count on. "I pray that your hearts will be flooded with light," he writes, "so that you can understand the wonderful future he has promised to those he called. I want you to realize what a rich and glorious inheritance he has given to his people. I pray that you will begin to understand the incredible greatness of his power for us who believe him" (verses 18-19).

God wants you to see yourself as he sees you. He wants to open wide the eyes of your heart so you see all the great things he sees in you.

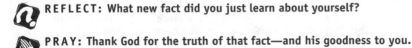

REFLECT: What new fact did you just learn about yourself?

PRAY: Thank God for the truth of that fact—and his goodness to you.

17 Move over, Mona Lisa

Bible Reading: Ephesians 2:4-10
For we are God's masterpiece. Ephesians 2:10

YOU DON'T HANG on the wall. You don't stand frozen like a carved-up rock. Yet you are God's masterpiece. More stunning than the most ornate sculpture or the most sublime painting, you are God's cherished, hand-crafted creation. Look at what Ephesians 2 says about your worth and value:

- You are alive together with Christ (verse 5).
- You were raised up with Christ (verse 6).
- You are now seated with Christ in heavenly realms (verse 6).
- You are one with Christ Jesus (verse 6).
- You have been saved by God's special favor (verse 8).

And that's only the beginning. If you have trusted Christ, every one of the following huge truths is a fact about you. Whenever you wonder if you matter to God or anyone else, read this list aloud to yourself:

- I have peace with God (Romans 5:1).
- I am loved and chosen by God (Ephesians 1:4).
- I am a child of God (John 1:12).
- God's Holy Spirit lives in me (1 Corinthians 3:16).
- I have access to God's wisdom (James 1:5).
- I am helped by God (Hebrews 4:16).
- I am reconciled to God (Romans 5:11).
- I am not condemned (Romans 8:1).
- I have been made right with God (Romans 5:1).
- I have Christ's righteousness (2 Corinthians 5:21).
- I am God's ambassador (2 Corinthians 5:20).
- I am completely forgiven (Colossians 1:14).
- God meets all my needs (Philippians 4:19).
- I am tenderly loved by God (Jeremiah 31:3).
- I am holy and blameless (Colossians 1:22).

Paul meant it when he said, "Those who become Christians become new persons. They are not the same anymore, for the old life is gone. A new life has begun!" (2 Corinthians 5:17). When God looks at you, he sees his flawless and awesome masterpiece.

REFLECT: Do you believe that you are God's masterpiece? Spend time chewing on any of those Bible facts about you that you have a hard time swallowing.

PRAY: Thank God for his great love for you.

18 The Spirit of the Matter

Bible Reading: Acts 1:4-8

When the Holy Spirit has come upon you, you will receive power and will tell people about me everywhere. Acts 1:8

"FINE!" MELISSA SPAT. "It might be true that God thinks I'm really worthwhile. I might even be his masterpiece. But right now I'm failing algebra—and I'm slipping in most of my other classes. I need a break from school, but if I fail they'll make me sit inside all summer and do all my work again."

Seeing yourself as God sees you isn't a mind game. It isn't telling yourself nice lies. It's realizing that God has made you *competent* in Christ.

Paul wasn't bragging when he said, "I can do everything with the help of Christ who gives me the strength I need" (Philippians 4:13). He just knew he was gifted and equipped to serve God. And that fact is true of you too.

Being gifted by God doesn't mean you'll be a clone of the apostle Paul or that you'll star at everything you do. It doesn't mean you'll never need to redo a class. Even so, God wants you to rest in the fact that he has equipped you to use the abilities he's given you. He has called you to help reach the world, the most significant task he could give you.

Your connection with the Holy Spirit is the key to grasping the truth that God sees you as competent and useful. The Bible has loads to say about that relationship:

- You are born again by the Spirit (John 3:3-5).
- The Spirit lives inside you and will be with you forever (John 14:16-17).
- The Spirit teaches you what you need to know (John 14:26).
- The Spirit testifies to you that you belong to God (Romans 8:16).
- The Spirit guides you (Romans 8:14).
- The Spirit equips you with talents, abilities, and spiritual gifts so you can live a focused life in service of God (1 Corinthians 12:4, 11).
- The Spirit prays for you when you're weak (Romans 8:26-27).
- The Spirit develops his fruit in you: love, joy, peace, patience, kindness, goodness, faithfulness, gentleness, and self-control (Galatians 5:22-23).

God reminds you through Paul in 1 Corinthians 1:7: "Now you have every spiritual gift you need as you eagerly wait for the return of our Lord Jesus Christ." God has given everything you need to serve him. What a wonderful Father! You have everything you need to succeed at doing exactly what God wants you to be doing!

REFLECT: What difference does it make to you that the Holy Spirit lives inside you?

PRAY: Thank God for valuing you enough to make you competent to serve him.

19 The Only Way to Go

Bible Reading: Ephesians 5:15-20
Let the Holy Spirit fill and control you. Ephesians 5:18

LET'S GRAB another look at how the Holy Spirit makes you competent—outfitted with the skills you need to live out your Christian life. Jesus described it like this: "You will receive power when the Holy Spirit comes on you," he told his disciples, "and you will be my witnesses in Jerusalem, and in all Judea and Samaria, and to the ends of the earth" (Acts 1:8, NIV). Without the Holy Spirit, it's impossible to become a Christian or produce the fruit of the Spirit or introduce others to Christ. Jesus was talking about the Spirit as well as himself when he explained, "Apart from me you can do nothing" (John 15:5).

Get this: From the moment you trust Christ, the Holy Spirit lives in you, giving to you everything you need to be capable and effective for him. You start to see that competence when you let the Holy Spirit fill you daily, putting to work everything he puts at your disposal. Paul conveys this in his command, "Let the Holy Spirit fill and control you" (Ephesians 5:18). Literally translated, the verse reads, "Keep on allowing yourself to be filled with the Spirit." If you want to be competent day by day as a Christian, you need to be filled day by day.

Being filled with the Spirit daily doesn't mean you need more of the Holy Spirit to enter you from the outside. It means allowing the Holy Spirit—who is already in you—to occupy more and more of your life from the inside, to *empower* you. Daily filling with the Spirit gives you renewed power to live committed to Christ, do his will, and be his witness.

Having the Holy Spirit get a grip on you each day is a gift from God you can count on. God commands you to be filled with his Spirit, so you can be sure he will fill you up when you open yourself to him. It's like getting money from the bank when you have plenty in your account. You don't approach the bank teller with panic, afraid that your account will come up empty. You don't need to beg the teller to give you the money. Instead, you go to the bank "in faith," fill out a withdrawal slip, and receive the money that's already yours. In the same way, receiving the Holy Spirit each day just means taking hold of something you already have. You are empowered with the Spirit by your faith in an all-powerful God who loves you.

Being filled with the Holy Spirit isn't an option. It's a command, but it has cool results. And God never issues a command without also giving you a way to obey (see 1 John 5:14-15). Just ask God to fill you. Because you know he hears you, be confident he will fill you.

REFLECT: Have you invited the Holy Spirit to fill you today?

PRAY: Give him that invitation first thing as you pray right now.

20 Are You Power-Packed?

Bible Reading: Job 42:1-5

Job replied to the Lord: "I know that you can do anything, and no one can stop you." Job 42:1-2

"EVEN IF IT'S TRUE that I need to be filled with the Holy Spirit every day," Matt complained, "I think maybe I have a leak. I don't feel him. I'm not sure if he comes and goes or what. I'm a little nervous that he'll just up and leave. Or maybe he was never in me to begin with. I'm confused."

Most of us need to know more about how the Holy Spirit works. Unlike your heart, which beats whether you ask it to or not, the Holy Spirit does his best work when you invite him to do his thing and make you more like your Lord.

So here's the scoop. When you ask to be filled with the Holy Spirit, you aren't asking the Holy Spirit *into* your life. He's *already there.* As a Christian you are *indwelled* by the Holy Spirit only once, at the time you first trust Christ. But you are to be *filled* repeatedly. You can ask the already-there Holy Spirit to control every part of your life, every hidden crack, corner, and crevice. As you do, you tap into his power. You let go of the frustration of trying to be a Christian using your own strength and instead rely on the Holy Spirit's strength to obey and serve God.

So do you want a life filled with the Spirit and his competence? You only need to ask the Father for it. Admit that you have been in control of your life—a sin against God, the rightful ruler of your life. Thank him for forgiving your sins through Christ's death on the cross for you. Invite Christ to take control of your life, and invite his Spirit to empower you so you can glorify Christ in all you do. Then thank him for doing what you have asked. (By the way, you aren't being arrogant to thank God before you actually experience the result of your request. Saying thanks is an act of faith that he will keep his promise to give you whatever you ask that fits his will. And since he commands you to be filled with the Holy Spirit, you know it's his will that you ask and receive.)

The apostle Paul cheered that he was competent because of the Holy Spirit's empowering. "I can do everything with the help of Christ who gives me the strength I need," he proclaimed (Philippians 4:13). The emphasis isn't on what *Paul* can do but on what *Christ*—the source of his strength—can do. Paul attempted great things *for* God because he expected great things *from* God. And so can you, because your competence comes from God (see 2 Corinthians 3:5).

When you are empowered with the Spirit, you are teamed up with the God who can do everything. Don't doubt that he's in you. If you believe in Jesus, he is. He will stick with you and do all that he has promised to do. No fooling. And no leaks!

REFLECT: Are you allowing God to do his great work through you?

PRAY: Invite God to change inside you whatever he sees that needs changing.

21 It's Not You, but What God Can Do through You

Bible Reading: Philippians 1:3-6

God, who began the good work within you, will continue his work until it is finally finished on that day when Christ Jesus comes back again. Philippians 1:6

CHANG WAS a high-powered investment accounts manager for a bank. People at his church figured he was a slam-dunk for the budget committee. "He knows how to manage money," they reasoned. Not much later Chang joined the committee.

Chang was a disaster. His smarts in money management turned out to be a gross weakness. Relying on his financial training, he saw every church expenditure in terms of "the bottom line." If a church program didn't show a profit—growth in numbers of people reached or dollars raised—he argued to ax it. After a blunt but kind discussion with his pastor, Chang left the committee.

As Chang grew in faith and let the Holy Spirit control his life, he had a new idea—that he'd like to volunteer in the junior-high ministry. He hadn't worked with kids and had no training in youth ministry. But he cared for kids who came from non-Christian homes. His wife, Nikki, felt the same burden.

Chang and Nikki prayed—a lot. Then they met with the youth pastor. "We don't know much about youth work," they confessed, "but we love these kids and want to learn. If you can use us, we're available." It turned out that kids flocked to Chang and Nikki because they felt genuinely loved and accepted by them. And that group has kept growing because of Chang and Nikki's willingness to let the Holy Spirit lead them someplace they never expected to go.

Big Holy Spirit lesson: When you allow the Spirit to empower your life and tell God you're willing to serve wherever he wants, you might be surprised where he plunks you. God knows best how to make you competent, and he knows best where you'll fit. Chang's story is a prime example of how to let God lead you.

Like everyone else, you have limitations. Chang and Nikki—and youth leaders you know—don't do ministry perfectly. But when you look at the people God uses, you notice that their real power comes from submitting to the Holy Spirit and asking God to equip them for ministry. Like Chang found out, being an "expert" in an area sometimes gets in the way.

God isn't limited by your age, your weaknesses, or your lack of experience. Whoever you are and wherever you are in your Christian growth, you're most useful to God if you let his Spirit empower you daily. Just watch what he can do through you when you give his Spirit control!

REFLECT: What bold new thing do you think God would like to do through you?

PRAY: Ask God to lead you wherever he wants you to go.

22 Potted Plants Can't Answer Prayer

Bible Reading: Acts 16:25-34

Believe on the Lord Jesus and you will be saved, along with your entire household. Acts 16:31

KELLY SAT ACROSS the kitchen table from her friend Angelica. "I think we each have the faith that's right for us," Kelly said. "Christianity isn't all there is, you know. The important thing is that *you believe.*"

Angelica scrunched up her brow. "I guess," she said. "After all, Christianity is all about being saved by faith. So I guess . . . it's not that big a deal what you believe, as long as you believe it enough."

Wrong! It *is* a big deal what you believe.

I was invited to debate the head of the philosophy department at a large university. We bantered back and forth about the Marxist theory of humans as economic creatures—one of the key ideas that drove communism. At one point I explained how crucial the resurrection of Jesus was to me. "Look, McDowell," my opponent interrupted, "it doesn't matter if the Resurrection happened or not. The important thing is—do you *believe* it happened?"

"Sir," I answered, "that's wrong. The truth of what I believe *does* matter, because if what I believe isn't true, then I have no right to my Christian faith."

After the debate, a Muslim student said to me, "I know some Muslims who have more faith in Muhammad than some Christians have in Christ."

"That might be true," I said, "but the issue isn't how much faith you have, but *who you have faith in.*"

The value of faith isn't in the one doing the believing, but in the one who is believed. You can have more faith than anyone on the planet. But suppose you put your faith in the potted plants in your house. Will this provide a saving relationship with God and forgiveness of sin? Why not—if believing big is what matters? *Because the object of your faith is a potted plant, and plants can't save.*

On the other hand, suppose you have faith the size of a freckle, but you put that faith in Jesus Christ. Will this give you a saving relationship with God and forgiveness of sin? Definitely! What made the difference? The object of your faith—the one you put your faith in. *Jesus made the difference.*

The Christian faith isn't fuzzy. It's objective. It's focused on the real truth of what Jesus did for you. Faith in anything else—no matter how hard you may believe—can't save you.

REFLECT: Is your faith in faith—or in Jesus?

PRAY: Pray for friends who put their faith in anything or anyone other than Jesus.

23 Is Elmer Gantry Alive and Well?

Bible Reading: 2 Peter 3:17-18
Grow in the special favor and knowledge of our Lord and Savior Jesus Christ. 2 Peter 3:18

ELMER GANTRY WAS the slimy lead character in Sinclair Lewis's novel by that name. Gantry—a greedy, lustful, hypocritical evangelist—preached one thing and lived another. His words, his sermons, and his life were all fake.

Elmer Gantry was a made-up man. But plenty of scandals have ruined real preachers. One televangelist was disgraced by revelations of extramarital sex and his subsequent coverups of the scandal. Another televangelist's condemnations of the first one crashed down around him when he was forced to confess his own addiction to pornography. With cameras and microphones snooping out every ugly detail of these and other scandals, more and more people have bought the "Elmer Gantry myth." That myth is the mistaken belief that Christian preachers, evangelists, and leaders are all crooked hypocrites.

The media coverage misses the many evangelists and preachers who continue to serve God with utter integrity and humility. Think of the evangelistic ministry career of Billy Graham. Over a span of sixty years, Dr. Graham's preaching has reached millions, and his life has never contradicted his preaching. Even so, Graham confesses that from the start of his ministry, "I was frightened—and still am—that I would do something to dishonor the Lord."

Billy Graham, Luis Palau, Charles Colson, Dawson McAllister, and Charles Swindoll are just some of the well-known Christian leaders whose lives are true to their teaching, proving that the Elmer Gantry myth isn't true.

Way back in the first century—before investigative reporters and worldwide media—Peter warned Christians, "There will be false teachers among you. . . . And because of them, Christ and his true way will be slandered" (2 Peter 2:1-2). That's why Satan works so hard to spread the Elmer Gantry myth. He wants the truth to be squashed by false accusations. He wants the preaching of godly men and women to be smeared by the sin and hypocrisy of others.

Christian leaders aren't the only ones who need to heed Peter's warning to guard against error and grow in the grace and knowledge of Christ. Each of us has the potential to bring disgrace down on other believers. But keep your focus on getting close to Jesus, and you won't make your faith or your fellow Christians look foolish. After all, God has the power to "keep you from stumbling," and he "will bring you into his glorious presence innocent of sin and with great joy" (Jude 24).

REFLECT: Have you been disappointed by a Christian leader? Who can you look up to as an example of living close to God?

PRAY: Pray that the Christian leaders in your life will stay faithful to God.

24 Never Believe a Snake in the Grass

Bible Reading: 1 Peter 3:18

For Christ died for sins once for all, the righteous for the unrighteous, to bring you to God. 1 Peter 3:18

WITH TOTAL SERIOUSNESS, a woman tells her friend in the grocery store checkout about the amazing healing powers of her mystical quartz crystals. "I haven't had a sniffle or a headache in over a year," she proclaims. She isn't the only one who claims unusual, miraculous powers:

- A quiet man says he can communicate with numerous species of animals—whales, dolphins, birds—with musical notes and patterns.
- A powerful executive uses ancient Chinese principles to make her business decisions.
- A seventy-one-year-old woman "remembers" being a Roman Catholic nun in the eleventh century.

Gurus, extraterrestrials, hypnotism, astral projection, eastern philosophy—the New Age movement is a smorgasbord of ideas and beliefs brought into the mainstream by actress Shirley MacLaine's books and television miniseries, *Out on a Limb*. What people call "New Age" isn't an organized religion or group. It's a trend, a way of thinking that takes many forms. However, New Age thought does have some core beliefs: that God is in everything, that we are all God, and that by transforming our consciousness we can discover the "god" within us.

That's a myth. An avalanche of New Age television miniseries, best-selling books, and business seminars doesn't make this mind-set something new. Parts of it date back to the Garden of Eden. Genesis tells how Satan, appearing as a serpent, promised Adam and Eve that they would be like God if they ate the forbidden fruit. But Satan—Chief Inventor of Half-Truths—lied. Eating the apple didn't make the first people like God.

The one-of-a-kind message of the Bible isn't that people can become gods, but that God became a human in the person of Christ and died for our sins so we can have eternal life. You don't have the power and potential in yourself to become a god, but you can hang tight with the risen Christ and his resurrection power.

REFLECT: What are some of the places where you see New Age thinking in your world? How do you respond to it?

PRAY: Ask God to guard the minds of your non-Christian friends so they don't put their trust in the false messages of the New Age movement.

Hey, I Don't Deserve This!

Bible Reading: John 16:31-33
Here on earth you will have many trials and sorrows. But take heart, because I have overcome the world. John 16:33

MEGAN, A SEVENTEEN-YEAR-OLD Christian, drives home late one Friday evening. A car from the other side of the highway suddenly crosses the center line and collides with hers. Megan dies on impact, killed by a drunk driver.

As two-year-old Tyler plays in his backyard, a bee stings him. Immediately his face swells. Before his mother can get him to the hospital, Tyler dies.

A baby is born to a lower-caste woman in India. He spends four months cradled in a cardboard box, then dies of starvation. His mother dies two months later.

Life isn't fair. Innocent babies die. Good people suffer. Christians hurt terribly. And good people who suffer often respond, "Why is this bad stuff slamming into *me?* I don't deserve this! It's not fair." People have asked forever where suffering comes from—and why good people suffer. And lurking in the back of our brains is the thought that good people—especially Christians—are entitled to lives free from big-time struggles, sorrows, and suffering.

Problem is, God never promised Christians an easy life. When Jesus' disciples saw a guy who had been born blind, they asked Jesus that ancient question about why people suffer. "Teacher," they said, "why was this man born blind? Was it a result of his own sins or those of his parents?" (John 9:2).

Jesus responded, "It was not because of his sins or his parents' sins" (verse 3). Then he healed the man.

Some people suffer because of *their own sin,* like a person who contracts AIDS from illicit sex. Others suffer because of *the sins of others,* like the deformed baby of a cocaine addict. But a lot of suffering comes from *neither their sins nor the sins of others.* When God made the world, he put in place natural laws, like the law of gravity and the laws of motion. Most of the time we benefit from those laws, but sometimes they make us victims. Gravity yanks a disabled airplane to the ground, and people die. The laws of motion cause out-of-control cars to hurl at each other. God doesn't suspend those laws for good people.

Life isn't fair. Accidents, disease, tragedy, death—all of them happen to Christians, too. That's one reason why Jesus promised us, "Be sure of this: I am with you always, even to the end of the age" (Matthew 28:20). Your loving Savior never promised you an escape from life's tough stuff, but he did promise to tromp through it with you. And since Christ got through his own suffering and death to rise triumphantly, he can certainly get you through whatever you suffer.

REFLECT: How would you explain to a friend why bad things happen to people? How does God bring hope to bad situations?

PRAY: Ask God for sensitivity as you share this message with hurting friends.

26 Telling What You Know

Bible Reading: Mark 5:1-20

Go home to your friends, and tell them what wonderful things the Lord has done for you and how merciful he has been. Mark 5:19

EVER HEARD stories like this?

"I was sitting in the airport waiting to board my plane when a guy sat down beside me. We started talking, and soon I asked him, 'Are you sure that you will go to heaven when you die?' He said he wasn't sure, so I explained how he could become a Christian. Within ten minutes he bowed his head and trusted Christ as Savior and Lord.

"And on the plane, a young woman sat beside me. When I told her I was a Christian, she said she had no idea what a Christian was. So I shared the gospel with her and she too trusted Christ before we landed.

"Then there was the taxi driver who took me to the hotel who . . ."

Do stories like that make your skin crawl with guilt because you haven't introduced hordes of people to Jesus? Do those reports make you feel like a flop as a Christian? Well, the spectacular deliverance of a demon-possessed man in Mark 5 has a message for you if you feel overwhelmed with incompetence as a one-on-one evangelist.

As Jesus and his disciples prepared to sail away, the guy Jesus had set free volunteered to join the disciples. But instead, Jesus gave him an assignment that makes a smart first step in telling people about Jesus: "Go home to your people" (verse 19, NASB). That seems like the scriptural pattern for all witnessing. The place to start is where you live—with your family, your friends, your neighbors. Acts 1:8 suggests the same thing—that witnessing starts at home and spreads from there.

The second part of Jesus' instructions was to "tell . . . what wonderful things the Lord has done for you" (verse19). Jesus didn't instruct this guy to cook up a batch of evangelistic sermons, memorize a bunch of spiritual principles, or even highlight all the salvation verses in his Bible. Instead, Jesus told him to tell about his own experience with God. That's your basic plan for one-on-one witnessing—what Jesus has done for you! Six-point sermons, underlined verses, and witnessing plans can all work, but the message you know best is the awesomeness of what Jesus has meant in *your* life. When you fumble everything else, you still know what God has done for you, and you can talk about that with authority.

Thank God for people who can win others to Christ on planes or buses, in grocery stores, and at parks. But God hasn't given most Christians that gift. Your first candidates for one-on-one sharing are people you see every day. And your first words should be about your own experience of Christ's love and power.

REFLECT: Where do you think God can use you to tell others about him?

PRAY: Ask Jesus to help you share him with the people right around you.

27 On the Outside Looking In

Bible Reading: Mark 6:1-6

A prophet is honored everywhere except in his own hometown and among his relatives and his own family. Mark 6:4

LOGAN AND HIS CLASSMATE Olivia were chubby, brainy, and homely. When year-book time rolled around, the two students were voted the most perfectly matched pair in their middle school, even though they hardly knew each other.

So when Logan and Olivia showed up hand in hand at the last dance of the school year, the kids snickered. And when the couple stepped into the dance area and awkwardly tried to move their uncoordinated bodies to the music, the crowd exploded. Finally Olivia grabbed her partner by the hand and snorted, "Come on, Logan!" The laughter should have ended there. Except Logan tripped and dragged Olivia to the ground with him. And they both bounced.

Unless you count yourself among the world's cruel elite, you probably wince when you see a pair like Logan and Olivia mocked. You might not have this pair's problems, but surely you know what it means to feel unwanted and unloved.

It's hard to believe that Jesus could have faced that kind of rejection. But the apostle John says it bluntly: "Even in his own land and among his own people, he was not accepted" (John 1:11). The residents of planet Earth have erected a kind of "You don't belong here" sign to their Creator, and if you check out Mark 6, you see that Jesus was even rejected by the people of Nazareth, the town where he grew up.

When you're a Christian, you have to get ready for some rejection. Jesus didn't leave any doubts that at times the world would snub—even hate—his followers: "I chose you to come out of the world, and so it hates you" (John 15:19). When a friend finds out that you won't cut class with him because you figure obeying Christ means showing up for school, he might cross you off his list of friends. When a group of girlfriends discovers you don't have any personal sexual adventures to brag about, they might kick you out in the cold. Your loyalty, purity, honesty, and dependability as a Christian will make you look as laughable to some people as Logan and Olivia looked to their peers.

There's better news, though. Jesus promised a special blessing and reward for his rejected followers (see Matthew 5:11-12). You can coast along as a camouflaged Christian, dodging confrontation and rejection. But if you take a stand for what's right—even if it means losing popularity, friends, or status—you're in line for eternally significant rewards.

REFLECT: As a Christian you are guaranteed to face rejection. What makes it worth it?

PRAY: Ask God to make you strong even in the face of rejection for your faith.

28 The Walking Dead

Bible Reading: Mark 6:14–29

If you want to be my follower you must love me . . . more than your own life. Luke 14:26

ON SUNDAY AFTERNOON, January 8, 1956, five young men stood on the bank of a shallow river, staring into the dense foliage of the jungle. They searched for the faces of the notorious Auca Indians of remote Ecuador. For weeks the missionaries had flown their single-engine plane over the primitive river settlement, dropping gifts in hopes of establishing friendly contact with the Aucas that would lead to an opportunity to share the Gospel. On the Friday before, an Auca man and two women had made a friendly visit to the missionaries' camp. Now the men waited for a second face-to-face meeting with the Aucas.

Suddenly there was a flurry of activity in the undergrowth. Several Auca warriors attacked the defenseless missionaries. Within minutes the spear-punctured bodies of five young men lay motionless at the river's edge.

The cruel death of Jim Elliot, Nate Saint, Ed McCully, Pete Fleming, and Roger Youderian in the Ecuadorian jungle was one of the most widely publicized news stories of the 1950s. Five selfless individuals—and the families they left behind—demonstrated that Christ's great commission (see Mark 16:15) mattered more to them than their own lives. They were examples of Jim Elliot's famous quotation, "He is no fool who gives what he cannot keep to gain what he cannot lose." The families of these men, by the way, continued working in Ecuador and eventually reached the Aucas for Christ.

Someone has said, "You're not ready to live until you're ready to die." Alter this saying a bit to fit the example of John the Baptist in Mark 6: "You're not ready to live for Christ unless you're ready to die for Christ." What if God asked you to put your life on the line by doing something like John the Baptist or the five missionaries did? How would you respond?

Whether you admit it or not, when you signed on as a follower of Jesus Christ, you signed on as a potential martyr. Living for Jesus means there's nothing more important than finding out what Jesus wants for you and then doing it. For Jim Elliot and his co-workers, that meant sharing Christ with the Aucas until their ministry was abruptly ended by Auca spears.

Even though following Christ is a life-and-death commitment, you won't likely be called on to experience death as a martyr. But you'll be ready for the possibility if you live every day as close to Christ as possible.

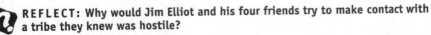

REFLECT: Why would Jim Elliot and his four friends try to make contact with a tribe they knew was hostile?

PRAY: Ask God for courage to obey him even when it costs you everything.

29 One of God's Great Gifts

Bible Reading: Proverbs 5:18-19
Give honor to marriage, and remain faithful to one another in marriage.
Hebrews 13:4

YOU MIGHT GET THE IDEA from listening to some Christians that sex is dirty. That it's wrong. That God goofed when he created our sex organs—or that sex comes from Satan.

Way wrong. When God created the world, he looked at it and pronounced everything good. Including sex! We know that God planned for sex to be a good, enjoyable part of human life. After all, he devised the idea in the first place. According to Hebrews 13:4, God designed the gift of sex to be enjoyed within marriage. There's nothing more beautiful than sex between two people committed to one another in marriage, and the Bible's healthy view of sex is clear in Proverbs 5:18-19.

The vast majority of church people—young and old—think the Bible has a negative view of sex. Yet there's not a single verse in the Bible that slams sex or makes sex look dirty or wrong.

Now don't misunderstand. There *are* many passages in the Bible that speak against the *misuse* of sex—sexual activity outside the loving commitment of marriage. It's not sex itself but the wrong use of sex that the Bible labels as immoral.

Two specific passages speak about the sin of sexual immorality, which means voluntary sex between people of the opposite sex who are not married to each other. In 1 Corinthians 7:2, the apostle Paul writes that one reason for marriage—certainly not the only reason, though—is to avoid sexual immorality. When a husband and wife meet each other's sexual needs, they're less vulnerable to temptation. Paul offers the same wise advice in 1 Thessalonians 4:3-5.

In both spots, Paul warns unmarried people that immorality is tempting. He's clear that marriage is God's great plan. And as long as a Christian is single, he or she is to abstain from sexual activity.

Maybe you read this and wonder, "What happens if I've already committed sexual immorality?" Here's the big question: Have you slipped just once, or is having sex a continuing pattern in your life? It's always possible for a Christian to sin, and God's forgiveness is available to us (see 1 John 1:9). But if sexual sin is habitual, it's time to seriously examine your life. First John 2:4 says that someone who claims to be a Christian but constantly lives like a non-Christian doesn't live in the truth.

REFLECT: Have you ever made the huge decision that you will live by God's standards of moral purity? Now is the time.

 PRAY: Talk to God today about your desire to keep yourself pure for marriage.

30 Where Do You Draw the Line?

Bible Reading: 2 Timothy 2:20-22
Run from anything that stimulates youthful lust. Follow anything that makes you want to do right. 2 Timothy 2:22

HAVE YOU EVER THOUGHT, *Why do I have such strong sexual feelings if premarital sex is wrong?* Maybe you've never asked that question out loud, but it might have danced through your mind. Don't you sometimes wonder why God made your desire for sex so potent if you can't do anything with it right now? Is God playing some kind of joke on you?

Not at all. Say thanks that you have that strong desire for sex—but also realize that you might have many years ahead of you to keep that desire under control until marriage. Your sex-saturated culture doesn't make it easy. But remember: God has given you all the power you need to keep your sexual desires in line. Follow his advice in 2 Timothy 2:22.

"So if sex before marriage is wrong," you might still wonder, "how far *can* you go? I mean, how far is too far?"

Most kids want someone to step up, draw a bold line, and say, "Okay, everything up to here is fine. But if you go past this point, you're out of God's will." It sounds nice and simple, but it doesn't work that way.

Actually, there are better questions to ask than, "How far is too far?" Try these: "What caring actions can I use to show my true feelings to my date?" "What actions best express how much I care about my date at this point in our relationship?" "What is honest, righteous, and best for where we are right now?" But at the same time, the Bible is clear about drawing a line when it says, "Never cheat a Christian brother" (1 Thessalonians 4:6). We "cheat" others by taking from them to fulfill our sexual desires. Here's how to avoid that.

First, realize when you start wanting what you can't have. It usually starts so slowly that you don't realize it's happening. But when you raise your own desires above what's right and spiritually healthy, you have crossed an important line.

Second, aim at applying the command to love one another. Learn to love the 1 Corinthians 13 way—selflessly seeking out God's best for the other person.

Third, recognize that physical affection between a guy and girl is exciting because God made it that way. And it's progressive—one stage naturally leads to the next. Setting your standards and drawing your "lines" ahead of time will enable you to stand up in a situation that requires serious resisting and keeps you from making a mistake you might later regret.

 REFLECT: What are you going to do to keep your sexual desires inside God's boundaries?

 PRAY: Ask God for wisdom and power to keep his great wedding present—sex—for the wedding.

31 Fire in the Eyes

Bible Reading: Proverbs 6:24-29

Anyone who even looks at a woman with lust in his eye has already committed adultery with her in his heart. Matthew 5:28

DEREK WAS SURFING TV channels when he saw her. Looking sweet in a bedroom scene, the actress was too sexy for words. Derek didn't have to watch long before he had mentally put himself in that love scene and in bed with her.

Cassie devoured the same paragraph in the novel over and over again. It described the handsome hero and his love for the heroine. Cassie could almost feel the hero's strong arms around her. She imagined what he would say, what he would do, and how much she would like it.

The Bible calls what Derek and Cassie are feeling *lust,* and Jesus didn't take it lightly. He said lust is adultery of the heart. The word he uses in the Greek is *epithumia. Epi* means "over" and *thumos* means "passion." So lust means passion that has gone over the top or out of bounds. Lust is a burning desire for the opposite sex beyond the boundaries God set for sexual relationships.

God has blessed you with your sexual desires. He has special plans for you to put them to good use within marriage. So when you look at a person and say, "Now there's a good-looking person," that's okay. But sexual desires that come from lust are not healthy. When you start to wonder what he or she looks like undressed, you're headed toward lust. From there your thoughts can run out of control—until you're imagining everything from sex-play fantasies to having sexual intercourse.

Proverbs 6:25-29 compares lust to fire. Imagine your eyeballs lit on fire, then the fire torching your mind, then incinerating your body. Fire begins with your eyes, which are constantly bombarded with lust-producing materials online, on TV, on CD covers, and in movies, magazines, advertisements, books, etc. Suggestive poses and attractive bodies are just a glance away.

If lust catches fire in your eyes, it can spread to your mind—and your mind is the most important sex organ in your body. If lust smolders there, it's only a matter of time until your body blazes. It's not because of what you have done but because of what has entered your mind through your eyes—and how you then thought about it.

You can stop the fire from ever catching hold in your mind by protecting your eyes. Job said, "I made a covenant with my eyes not to look with lust upon a young woman" (Job 31:1). Do you need to make a similar covenant—a serious promise—with your eyes? What will you look at? And what will you turn away from?

REFLECT: In what ways is lust going on in your life?

PRAY: Talk to God about it now.

1 Jury Duty

Bible Reading: Psalm 19:7-11
There is great reward for those who obey [the laws of the Lord].
Psalm 19:11

YOU CHECK the mail, and there it is: your official summons to jury duty. It's your pass to the jury box and the job of finding someone guilty or innocent.

You want to sit in on something huge—like an ax-murder case or an espionage trial or the slicing up of some monopolistic multinational computer corporation. But whatever you get, you want to be ready. You want to make a wise decision when it comes time to determine the verdict.

You plan to be the best juror the court has ever seen. More than anything, you don't want to stupidly set a guilty person free. You're going to put some people behind bars. With you on duty, if they did the crime, they'll do the time.

So you cram to learn all you can about the laws of the land. You dig through statutes and ordinances. You study every law book you can find. You're ready to bring down the hammer of justice on some bad guys.

But in your study, you make an amazing discovery. There's more to the law than catching people doing wrong and filleting felons. Surprisingly, you find that a huge hunk of the law has to do with great rewards for people who do right. Laws don't just punish bad people; they protect and provide for good people. By living within the boundaries of the law, people gain things like freedom, prosperity, safety, and other highly-prized outcomes. A light bulb blinks on in your brain and you realize that protecting victims is just as important as punishing the criminals.

In the same way, God's law isn't just a rule book loaded with reasons to send people to the slammer. Rules, regulations, and consequences aren't the only thing you need to know about God's law. The law isn't just about "you shall do this" and "you shall not do that." Sure, you have to know where God's boundaries are. Psalm 19:11 says that God's laws serve as "a warning to those who hear them." But the next phrase paints the rest of the picture: "There is great reward for those who obey them." Warnings, in other words, are there for a reason. They reward us with God's protection and provision—things like peace with God, healthy relationships with others, and eternal life.

God didn't give the Bible to hammer you but to heal you. The goal of God's Word isn't to grind you into dust but to grow you to maturity. God isn't out to catch you doing something wrong but to coach you in doing what's right. He loves you so much he wants you to enjoy the rewards of living within his law.

REFLECT: What good does "the law" do in your life?

PRAY: Tell God why you think the law is a pretty good idea.

2 Stick with the Game Plan

Bible Reading: Psalm 119:1-8

Happy are those who obey his decrees and search for him with all their hearts. Psalm 119:2

BRUISER BOOTKANSKI was the best. Hands down, no doubt, without question, he was the greatest quarterback ever in the NFL. Cheerleaders adored him, kids idolized him, and all the cereal companies wanted his picture on their boxes. Bruiser was a football icon. At least he used to be . . . before the big game.

All his life Bruiser had waited to play in the Super Bowl. Every football player's dream is to take home a championship, to wear the winner's ring. Not every player gets that chance, but Bruiser did. He was determined to make the most of it. Bruiser didn't just want to win. He wanted to be the Super Bowl superstar by scoring the winning touchdown.

The game was close because both teams were evenly matched. Every time Bruiser's team got the ball, he threw it with laserlike accuracy, and it usually paid off with a score. The coach's game plan was for Bruiser to throw, throw, throw—and it worked. Unfortunately, the other team had racked up just as many points.

So the game came down to the last few seconds. Bruiser dropped back to pass, and the final gun sounded. If he didn't throw for a touchdown now, the game was lost. With the goal line only a few yards away and his receiver in the clear in the end zone, all Bruiser had to do was to lob the ball to him. It was the game plan.

Bruiser, though, wanted to score the winning touchdown himself. So instead of passing the ball to the receiver, he ran for the end zone. He could hear his coach yelling, "Throw the ball, Bruiser!" But Bruiser wouldn't listen. He darted, he dodged defenders, and he dove for the line . . . but he came up one foot short.

Bruiser never became that Super Bowl hero. Instead of experiencing the thrill of victory, he dragged his team into the agony of defeat. His face lost the chance to be on a Wheaties box, and his family wasn't exactly going to DisneyWorld. If he had only stuck with the game plan . . .

You get the chance to make game-winning choices every day. When you make the right choice, you experience the happiness of success. If you make the wrong choice . . . well, at least once or twice you have no doubt had to live with the consequences of bad choices. Good outcomes result from good decisions, and good decisions result when you follow God's game plan—his Word. Psalm 119:2 promises happiness to all who obey God's decrees. That's right—God really wants you to be happy. He gave you his Word so you can get into the end zone.

REFLECT: How have good decisions led to good outcomes in your life?

PRAY: Talk to God about your commitment to study and follow his game plan.

3 The Driver's Instruction Manual

Bible Reading: Psalm 119:9-16
I have hidden your word in my heart, that I might not sin against you.
Psalm 119:11

TODAY IS THE DAY you've been dreaming about for sixteen years. The picture in your brain is so real you can feel the breeze blow through your hair—it's you and all your friends piled into your brand-new SUV as you cruise the town.

You enter your local DMV and take your spot in line, eager to pay your money and walk out with a driver's license. Finally Ms. Gearshift, the cheery clerk, hands you a sheet of paper. "Take a seat at the table, answer the questions, and return the sheet to me when you're done." *Sounds simple enough,* you think.

So you sit down and glance at the paper. *Wait a minute! This is a test!* You sweat as you read down the sheet. Question after question asks about speed limits, signaling, and traffic laws. You recall hearing about some sort of driver's test, but you never gave it much thought. Driving comes naturally, right? You get in the car, start the engine, and work the pedals. What's so hard about that?

You push your way back to Ms. Gearshift. "I've seen people drive, I've taken rides in cars, and I even sat behind the wheel of a car once. I know that green means go and red means stop. I'm sure I can drive, so I don't need to take your silly test. Just take my picture and give me my license."

Friendly Ms. Gearshift suddenly shifts gears and glares at you with beady eyes. "If you can't pass the test, you don't know the rules. And if you don't know the rules, you can't drive. Drivers who don't know the rules are dangerous." Then she shoves a driver's instruction manual at you. "It's your choice, kid. Learn the rules if you want to pass the test."

You swallow hard. "But these questions are pretty hard," you whine.

Ms. Gearshift taps the booklet. "That's the point. There's a lot to know. But the answers are right here for you. Get this stuff inside you and you won't have a problem with the test—either here or on the road."

Know what? God has given you an instruction manual. That's right, the Bible contains God's instructions for successfully getting through life's tests and temptations. If you don't study the instruction manual, you are likely to fail the test—and somebody, including you, might get hurt because of your carelessness. But as you study God's Word, stick it in your memory, ponder it, and live by its directions, you will find the strength to resist temptation, make right choices, and walk close to God.

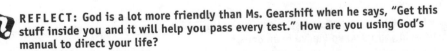

REFLECT: God is a lot more friendly than Ms. Gearshift when he says, "Get this stuff inside you and it will help you pass every test." How are you using God's manual to direct your life?

PRAY: Thank God for giving you rules meant to steer you toward good things.

4 Which Way Is Up When You're Down?

Bible Reading: Psalm 119:25-32

I lie in the dust, completely discouraged; revive me by your word.
Psalm 119:25

THREE YEARS AGO, Doug's parents were divorced. Dad promised to call when he could. "You're still my son. That will never change, I promise," his dad had assured him when he left. Now those words rattle painfully in Doug's head. Yesterday was Doug's birthday, and Dad didn't call.

Jessica hadn't planned to go all the way. But she had been going out with Brett for eleven months, and he said he wanted to spend his whole life with her. Jessica had intended to wait for sex until she was married, but this was love. This was something worth making a few sacrifices for. This was forever. At least that's what Brett told her, and she believed him. But forever ended last weekend.

Tatiana had been challenged when her best friend, Danielle, announced that God was calling her family to the mission field. Danielle had left with her parents to spread God's love in Indonesia. Tatiana worried about her, but Danielle had huge faith, saying, "God will protect me, because I'm doing his work." So Tatiana and Danielle had said good-bye seven months ago. Today Tatiana received an e-mail from the mission. Her best friend, Danielle, had just died of malaria.

No one escapes discouragement. Even if you have never been slammed by a bitter, hurtful event like Doug or Jessica or Tatiana was, you surely know about smaller discouragements firsthand. Somebody fails you, something goes wrong, a plan doesn't work, a friend says something unkind, a dream goes unrealized, you get a poor grade. You can't avoid it. Discouragement happens.

The question isn't whether you will be discouraged. The question is how you *respond* to discouragement when it comes. Do you get mad? Sulk? Throw things? Do you use food or drugs to escape? Do you drown yourself in music or TV to ease the pain? Do you boycott church?

God has an antidote for discouragement. It's not a pill. It's an exercise. Here's what you do. You sit down with your Bible, open it, and begin reading. Or you go for a walk and mull over a verse you have read or memorized.

The psalmist wrote, "I lie in the dust, completely discouraged; revive me by your word" (Psalm 119:25). Discouragement knocks you down—God's Word picks you up. Discouragement leaves you in the dark—God's Word shines new light. Discouragement yanks you away from God and others—God's Word helps you tighten relationships.

 REFLECT: How do you respond to discouragement? How have you used the Bible to help you up when you've been down?

PRAY: *God, I want to listen to your words of encouragement when I'm discouraged. Thanks for your Word.*

5 Read All about It

Bible Reading: Psalm 119:89-96
Forever, O Lord, your word stands firm in heaven. Psalm 119:89

YOU CAN'T ALWAYS BELIEVE what you read in the newspapers, especially the weird ones at the checkout line. The following headlines showed up in newspapers—real newspapers, in fact:

- Iraqi Head Seeks Arms
- Police Begin Campaign to Run Down Jaywalkers
- Teacher Strikes Idle Kids
- Drunks Get Nine Months in Violin Case
- Stolen Painting Found by Tree
- Local High School Dropouts Cut in Half
- Man Struck by Lightning Faces Battery Charge
- New Study of Obesity Looks for Larger Test Group
- Typhoon Rips through Cemetery; Hundreds Dead

You don't have to look far in a daily paper to find slip-ups, even slap-you-in-the-face mistakes like those. But a newspaper is produced in a rush and gets tossed into the recycling bin the day after you buy it. It's here today, gone tomorrow. It's not something you can build your life on.

But the Bible *is* something to trust your whole life to. It is "God-breathed." It isn't here today, gone tomorrow. It was here before you arrived and will be here after you make your exit. Why? Because it is God's Word. You can read the paper for daily information, but for error-free direction and inspiration, you need your nose in the Bible.

Dr. Henrietta Mears wrote, "Do you come to the Bible with such eagerness? Do you read with that purpose and persistence? The Bible is not a book of texts—it is a story—it is a revelation, to be begun and pursued and ended as we start and continue other books. Don't trifle with the Bible. . . . We must come to it in a commonsense fashion. Believe that every book is about something and read and reread until you find out what that something is."*

Behind and beneath the Bible, above and beyond the Bible, is the God of the Bible. Whenever you open your Bible to read, you find the eternal, loving God waiting for you. And what he shows you will be totally true.

 REFLECT: Why do you read the Bible? What are you looking for? Are you finding God?

 PRAY: Tell God you want to get hold of him in a deeper way each time you read his Word.

---

*Henrietta C. Mears, *What the Bible Is All About* (Ventura, Calif.: Regal Books, 1966), 10.

6 Love That Touches Your Heart

Bible Reading: Daniel 10:10-11, 19

Don't be afraid . . . for you are deeply loved by God. Daniel 10:19

WHEN YOU DIG down into your heart, you find that your deepest human need is to be loved and to sense you belong to someone.

You might know in your head that you're loved. After all, the Bible makes God's love for you stunningly clear. And someone very near to you—a parent, boyfriend or girlfriend, or close friend—has probably said those little magic words, "I love you." But hearing about love isn't enough. Do you *feel* loved? See, only when your understanding of love hits your brain *and* your heart do you feel you really belong.

John 1:12 refers to God's love by declaring that when you received Christ you became God's child. *Knowing* that fact isn't enough, though. You need to wrap yourself in its truth and *experience* it. Try on these truths too:

- The God who created the universe desires a close, family relationship with you. If you have trusted Christ, you are his child.
- The God who has existed for all eternity wants to call you his son or daughter—and he invites you to call him "Father, dear Father" (Romans 8:15).
- God didn't make you to meet his needs in any way. He loves you without a hidden list of things he needs fulfilled by you.
- Your becoming a Christian didn't barge in on God and force him to do something he didn't want to do.
- God loves you because he chooses to.
- God welcomes you into his arms as a dearly loved child simply because he wants you as his child.
- God knows all about your weaknesses, your faithlessness, and your past, present, and future sins—and he still wants you as his child.
- These things sound too good to be true, but because God is God, they *are* true!

You might be growing up around people who say they love you or who show their love by things they do. But that love might not convince you that you really are lovable, that you are wanted, that you belong.

God, with his unchanging love, wants to grip both heart and mind so you *feel* loved. You can personalize Daniel 10:19 by saying: "God loves me deeply. I don't have to be afraid or insecure. I'm lovable."

REFLECT: What does it mean to you that God loves you deeply and eternally? Do you sense God's care for you in surrounding you with his unchanging love?

PRAY: Take time to thank God for what he has shown about himself to you.

7 I Love You—Period!

Bible Reading: Ephesians 2:4-10

Salvation is not a reward for the good things we have done, so none of us can boast about it. Ephesians 2:9

AT THE END of a church retreat on friendships, people were hugging and crying. Besides the fact that the retreat was all about caring for each other, everyone knew this was their last big event together before the seniors graduated. Kyle walked over to his friend Shane, gulped, and said, "I've never told you that I'm glad you're my friend. But I am." Simple. Deep. Heartfelt. And nowhere near as slobbery as everything else in the room.

But instead of returning the kind words, Shane snapped. "Get away from me. What do you want?" Shocked, Kyle answered, "Want? I don't want anything. What are you talking about?" Shane didn't reply. He just walked away.

On the bus ride home, Shane sat down by Kyle and apologized. "I've been thinking about why I snapped," he explained. "I'm not used to someone caring about me without wanting something. My parents only tell me they love me when they want me to get better grades or do them a favor."

If all you have known is love with strings attached, if "I love you" always came with an "if" or a "because," it can be hard to receive unconditional love from God and others.

Some people respond to God the same way Shane responded to Kyle: "What do you want?" They get suspicious of any kind act because they wonder what the catch is. True, God wants you to love and obey him. But he loves you whether or not you do.

Other people think they need to bargain with God before he will love them. They think, *I need to straighten out my life before God can accept me.* But God says, "I already accept you just the way you are. I proved it by sending my Son to die for you while you were lost in your sin" (Romans 5:8).

And because God loves you unconditionally, you don't have to perform perfectly to get God to accept you. Paul wrote, "It is by grace you have been saved, through faith—and this not from yourselves, it is the gift of God—not by works, so that no one can boast" (Ephesians 2:8-9, NIV). Your acceptance by God isn't based on your good deeds or great attitudes or on anything cool you have done for him. He loves you unconditionally because of what *he* has done.

When God shows you his love, there's no catch. He really cares.

REFLECT: God loves you unconditionally. What does that mean in your everyday life?

PRAY: *Father, your love for me has no strings attached. Thanks.*

8 Wrong Way!

Bible Reading: Isaiah 43:1-4

Do not be afraid, for I have ransomed you. I have called you by name; you are mine. Isaiah 43:1

UNIVERSITY OF CALIFORNIA football player Roy Riegels made Rose Bowl history back in 1929. In the second quarter of the game, he scooped up a Georgia Tech fumble and headed for the end zone—the *wrong* end zone. He was tackled—by a teammate—just before crossing the goal line. Riegels's mistake would have earned Georgia Tech six points. Riegels's team had to punt from their own end zone. Georgia Tech blocked the kick, resulting in a two-point safety—points that eventually won the game for Georgia Tech.

During halftime, the California players filed glumly into the dressing room. Riegels slumped in a corner, buried his face in his hands, and sobbed uncontrollably. Coach Price offered no halftime pep talk. What could he say? As the team got ready to go out for the second half, his only comment was, "Men, the same team that played the first half will start the second."

The players started for the door, all but Roy Riegels. Coach Price walked to the corner where Riegels sat and said quietly, "Roy, didn't you hear me?"

"Coach, I can't do it," Roy said dejectedly. "I have ruined you, the university, and myself. I can't face that crowd again to save my life."

Coach Price put his hand on the player's shoulder. "Roy, get up and go back; the game is only half over." Inspired by his coach's confidence, Roy Riegels went out to play again. After the game, the Georgia Tech players commented that Riegels played harder in the second half than they had ever seen anyone play.

What you see in Coach Price is just a glimmer of God's accepting attitude toward us. We make mistakes. Once in a while we run the wrong way. And when we stumble and fall, we make the problem worse by shrinking from God in shame. But he comes to us and says, "Get up and keep going; the game is only half over." That's unconditional love. And as you receive and enjoy God's unconditional love, you see more clearly that you are unconditionally lovable!

In Isaiah 43:1, God commits to love and accept you. He says to you, "I have called you by name; you are mine." You can personalize the verse this way: "The God of the universe has called me by name. He says I belong to him."

God doesn't disown you when you go the wrong way. He never says, "You blew it, so you don't belong to me any longer." Sure, he wants you to turn around and go the right way, and he puts his Spirit inside you to get you going again. But he never says anything but, "You belong to me; you are mine."

REFLECT: Think of an area where you've blown it. What does God think of your not being perfect?

PRAY: Thank God that he still believes in you even when you blow it.

9 You're Accepted, Not an Exception

Bible Reading: Romans 15:5-7

Accept each other just as Christ has accepted you. Romans 15:7

YOU DON'T REMEMBER what happened to you when you were born. But think about what happened to you when you were born again (see John 3:3-5; 1 Peter 1:23)—when you trusted Christ as your Savior and when God accepted you as his child:

- You became an heir of God (see Ephesians 1:13-14; Romans 8:17).
- You were adopted into God's family (see Ephesians 1:5).
- God poured his love into your heart (see Romans 5:5).
- You became one with Christ in such a way that you won't ever be parted from him (see John 17:23; Galatians 2:20; Hebrews 13:5).
- Nothing will ever separate you from God's love (see Romans 8:38-39).
- You will spend eternity with God in a place he has prepared for you (see John 14:1-4).
- You were welcomed into a new family, and you are a member in good standing throughout all eternity (see 1 Corinthians 12:13, 27).

God has proven his unconditional love for you in many ways. If God loves you, you must be lovable. The fact that God loves you unconditionally in spite of your flaws and failures is a huge reason to accept yourself.

If you can't take yourself the way you are—weaknesses as well as strengths, shortcomings as well as abilities—you aren't likely to give anyone else the chance to accept you as you are. You will always put up a front to prevent people from knowing what you're really like. And if you think it's tough to be honest and open—and let others sometimes see you at your worst—it's even harder to live the life of a phony.

When Jesus took children into his arms and blessed them (see Mark 10:16), you can bet that those kids weren't perfect little angels. They were kids—disobedient, disagreeable, sometimes downright bad. Yet Jesus displayed his heavenly Father's unconditional love by blessing the imperfect little ones.

Here's a huge command—one that will change the world around you if you live it out: "Accept one another . . . just as Christ accepted you, in order to bring praise to God" (Romans 15:7, NIV). But you can love like God loves only when you see yourself as God sees you—totally acceptable and totally lovable.

REFLECT: In light of all God has done to prove his unconditional love, what keeps you from seeing yourself as lovable?

PRAY: Thank God today for his acceptance and ask him to help you see yourself and others with God's eyes.

10 Dad Really Loves Me

Bible Reading: Romans 8:14–17

His Holy Spirit speaks to us deep in our hearts and tells us that we are God's children. Romans 8:16

NO ONE SHOULD ENJOY a bigger sense of belonging than God's kids. You belong to God and his family. The apostle John wrote, "See how very much our heavenly Father loves us, for he allows us to be called his children, and we really are!" (1 John 3:1). Something to notice: As soon as John wrote the words "his children," he must have paused as that truth hit him, because he tops off the thought with an exclamation. If John were here today, he might say it this way: "Whoa! We really *are* God's children! That's incredible!"

Maybe you're thinking, *But we're only* adopted. *It's not like we're real children in God's family.* You might think that being adopted by God makes us second-class kids in his kingdom.

If that's what you're thinking, listen to how my longtime friend Dick Day views adoption. After having parented their five biological children, Dick and his wife, Charlotte, went to Korea and adopted a sixth child, Jimmy. Dick says, "That little guy Jimmy is my son. He has the same rights and privileges as our other five children. He has the same access to our inheritance, our time, and our love." And you know what? Jimmy sees himself just as much as Dick and Charlotte's child as do his siblings.

The way Dick talks makes me better appreciate our spot in God's family. We're adopted, but like Dick, God declares that "everything God gives to his Son, Christ, is ours, too" (Romans 8:17). We're equal inheritors of God's blessings. We get the same gifts Jesus does. In other words, God sees us just as my friend Dick sees Jimmy.

Some adopted young people doubt whether they truly belong to their earthly family. Others say they are specially loved because they were *chosen* to belong to a dad and mom. In God's family, all of us are wanted because we were chosen. No doubt about it.

Your adoption as God's child is a truth worth pausing over. You can say these words with enthusiasm and awe: "Whoa! I really am a child of God! I really belong!" It's a biblical insight that is key to transforming your sense of identity.

You may want to pull out a blank sheet of paper and write a letter to your Father—your *heavenly* Father. Write in your own words how you feel about belonging to him and receiving the same inheritance Christ receives.

 REFLECT: So does being adopted by God make you a second-class member of his family? Why or why not?

PRAY: If you wrote a letter to God, take time to pray your letter aloud. Or simply tell God how you feel about belonging to him.

No Longer an Island

Bible Reading: 1 Corinthians 12:13, 23-27
All the members care for each other equally. 1 Corinthians 12:25

KIMIKO'S MOM had to work long hours to keep the family afloat after she and Kimiko's dad separated. As the divorce was being finalized, bitterness overwhelmed her, and Mom cut herself off from fourteen-year-old Kimiko. Kimiko felt doubly rejected—first by her dad, then by her mom. When Kimiko accepted a friend's invitation to her youth group, she found people who understood her problems. "Finally," she says, "I feel like I belong again."

God knew we might have a hard time grasping two enormous facts: that he finds us lovable, and that we belong to him. So he built us a support system. He gave us his church as our spot to find love and acceptance.

Before Jesus died and returned to heaven, he proclaimed, "Believe me when I say that I am in the Father and the Father is in me" (John 14:11, NIV). He mentions two persons in that union: God the Father and God the Son. The next few verses talk about God sending a third person, the Holy Spirit. And then Christ said, "On that day [perhaps referring to Pentecost and the birth of the church] you will realize that I am in my Father, and you are in me, and I am in you" (verse 20, NIV).

What in the world did Jesus mean by that? Well, when you believed in Christ as your Savior and Lord, you were placed in Christ and Christ took up his residence in you. And since Jesus and his Father are in union, you are also in the Father and the Father is in you. Talk about belonging!

But there's more. If the Father is in you—and if you are in the Father—you and I have an incredibly close relationship. You might even say that our mutual relationship with God means I am in you and you are in me. As a Christian, you're not an island. Neither am I. We're in Christ, so we're in each other.

Besides that, you and I are just two small parts of Christ's body (1 Corinthians 12:13, 23-27). There's a whole world of members who are to show equal concern for one another. We're to get together regularly so we can show each other that we're lovable—and that we belong.

When you fumble or fail or feel rejected, someone in your church or Bible study group is there to remind you that you are loved and accepted no matter what. And when someone in your group goes the wrong way and feels ashamed, you get to come alongside with encouraging words (see 1 Thessalonians 5:11).

Hanging tight with other Christians is one way you transform a warped sense of identity into God's beautiful picture of you.

REFLECT: Have you planted yourself in a group of loving believers and let God's unconditional love touch you through them?

PRAY: Ask God to strengthen your relationships with your Christian sisters and brothers.

12 What's the Latitude of Your Dating Attitude?

Bible Reading: Philippians 2:1-4
Don't think only about your own affairs, but be interested in others, too, and what they are doing. Philippians 2:4

DID YOUNG NOAH ever take his future bride on a romantic boat ride?

Did Moses ever take his girlfriend to the Saturday night chariot races?

Did Jacob and Rachel go out for pizza and Cokes before they were married?

Did Solomon ever take any of his 700 wives and 300 concubines on a date?

You might never know the answers to those deep dating questions, because you can't find dating in the Bible—for the same reason you can't find Sunday school. Sunday school and dating weren't part of Bible-times society. Back then, most marriages were prearranged by parents (see Genesis 24 for an example).

Just think about how great ready-made marriages would be. No worries about finding a partner. No problem about locating a date for the prom. No more demands from your friends to go out with some loser. No more dateless weekends. Your biggest worry would be figuring out who to double with.

The arranged-marriage plan has drawbacks, however. Your parents might do a deal for you to marry the cutest baby on the block—but in high school he might still be sucking his thumb. Then there's that little thing called love—which most of us want to find *before* we marry. And your parents can't even pick out clothes you like, so how could they pick out a husband or wife you would like? Given those alternatives, you're probably glad for today's system of dating.

Although you can't find dating in the Bible, you can find plenty of Scripture verses that apply to your dating relationships. Most of them have to do with attitudes. Some people enter dating with an attitude of *ownership*. They think you belong to them and refuse to allow you to live your own life. They act as if you are their private property and want you to fulfill their every whim.

Then there are those who approach dating with an attitude of *relationship*. They put all the emphasis on being "in love." They major on the romantic and go ugly with insecurity and jealousy when you go out with another person.

Philippians 2:3-4 expresses the right attitude to have about dating: *friendship.* The purpose of dating isn't to meet *your* needs but the other person's needs. It isn't to "fall in love" but to grow in friendship. A relationship rooted in friendship is God's idea of the appropriate attitude for any two people to have. And that includes two people who are dating.

REFLECT: Are you aiming your affections at someone God would be pleased by? How are you approaching your relationship with an attitude of friendship?

PRAY: Spend some time praying for your attitude toward any future dates with him or her.

13 Staying within the Lines

Bible Reading: 2 Corinthians 6:14-18
*Don't team up with those who are unbelievers. How can goodness
be a partner with wickedness? 2 Corinthians 6:14*

"SO, WHAT'S WRONG with dating non-Christians?"

Wherever dating is part of the culture, Christian students ask this question. And whenever they ask this question, they probably get the same answer: "Second Corinthians 6:14 says not to be 'yoked' or teamed up with unbelievers."

That's a tough teaching to accept, especially if you haven't found dating material among the Christians in your world. So you start making excuses for wanting to go against God's plan:

"There aren't any Christians I want to date."

"Non-Christians have more fun than Christians."

"I'll go out with him (or her) only once or twice."

"My friends want me to go, and I'll disappoint them if I don't."

And the *big* one: "I might be able to lead him (or her) to Christ if we date."

But what if your date doesn't accept Christ and you get married? Ponder these possible outcomes:

Loneliness: Because the non-Christian is dead spiritually, he can't communicate about things that matter hugely to a Christian.

Disappointment: The non-Christian said she would change but didn't.

Mistrust: Because of lies and hurts, it's hard to trust the non-Christian spouse.

Pressure: The Christian desperately wants the spouse to change, so she begins to nag and preach.

Resentment: Because of the pressure to change, the spouse gets angry and goes farther in the opposite direction.

Guilt: The Christian feels he has let everyone down—himself, his family, and God.

Depression: All the joy is gone. All that's left are scars and heartaches.

Fear: The Christian realizes that she will have to start life all over again with nowhere to go. That frightens her. The future seems terribly bleak.

The Next Generation: Children suffer tremendously because of a decision to marry the wrong person.

God isn't out to spoil your fun. He wants to spare you the pain and heartache that can come from falling in love with a non-Christian. So hang in there and wait patiently for the right opportunities to come along.

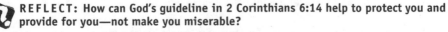

REFLECT: How can God's guideline in 2 Corinthians 6:14 help to protect you and provide for you—not make you miserable?

PRAY: Have a talk with God about your dating choices.

14 It's All about Character

Bible Reading: Galatians 5:19-23

When the Holy Spirit controls our lives, he will produce this kind of fruit in us: love, joy, peace, patience, kindness, goodness, faithfulness, gentleness, and self-control. Galatians 5:22-23

DATING IS no game. But pretend it is. Here are some rules—and tips for winning:

Object of the Game

Find a friend with whom you want to spend the rest of your life.

Rules of the Game

1. Character qualities—not popularity, good looks, possessions, or the opinions of friends—should decide who you go out with. Use Galatians 5:22-23 as a list of positive character qualities you are looking for.
2. Major on friendship. Romance may follow. But don't go looking for it.
3. You don't own the other person, so always give him or her the freedom to date other people.
4. Consider respect a key ingredient. Be respectful of your date's interests and wishes, and conduct yourself in a way that you keep his or her respect.

Tips for Playing the Game

1. Define what you are worth by who you are in Christ, not by who you date or what people think of your choice.
2. Treat your date as you want your future spouse to treat you.
3. Work on becoming the best person inwardly you possibly can be.
4. To really get to be close friends, avoid getting too physical.

The most significant part of dating is *who you go out with*. Why? News flash: Short of winning a bride or groom on a bizarre TV game show, you will end up marrying someone you date. If you date people who exhibit the character traits listed in Galatians 5:19-21, for example, you greatly increase your odds of marrying a loser. But if you date winners, it's likely you will marry a winner.

It's the stuff on the inside that makes someone a winner. Now, that doesn't mean you have to date people you don't like to look at. And it doesn't mean that you should stop trying to look your best. But if you're searching for someone to date, start by studying what kind of person a potential date is on the inside. Are his or her inner qualities consistent with yours? Do his or her standards match up with the Bible's standards? If you can say "yes!" then you've found a winner.

REFLECT: So, why be careful about the people you date?

PRAY: Ask God for a date—and a mate—who meets his standards.

15 Do You Have That Loving Feeling?

Bible Reading: 1 Corinthians 13:1-3

If I gave everything I have to the poor and even sacrificed my body, I could boast about it; but if I didn't love others, I would be of no value whatsoever. 1 Corinthians 13:3

TRY THIS "Christianity Reality Check" to diagnose your health as a Christian. First, check (✔) the statements you think are essential to your Christian belief system.

☐ God created the heavens and the earth.
☐ Jesus Christ is the Son of God, who died on the cross as the sacrifice for our sins and rose from the dead.
☐ The Bible is the Word of God.
☐ King James Bibles with black covers are more inspired than others.

If you checked the first three, your belief system is probably intact. Now let's look at actions. Check (✔) the statements you think a Christian must do regularly.

☐ A Christian should read the Bible, pray, and attend church.
☐ A Christian should share his or her faith with others.
☐ A Christian should obey the Bible and avoid sinful activities.
☐ A Christian should wear a long scratchy robe and chant in Latin.

Okay. Once again, if you checked the top three statements you have a good idea of some positive behaviors that can help you grow as a Christian.

Here's the problem. A lot of Christians stop there. They say, "Hey, I *believe* right and I *behave* right—most of the time. So I have the Christian life mastered. When I reach heaven, I'll get my solid gold crown for being a model believer."

Nice try. Unfortunately, God doesn't agree with you. Believing the right things is important. But it's not enough. Behaving in the right way is also important. But it's not enough. You still might be missing one vital element—and it just happens to be at the top of God's list.

It's called *loving* right. According to 1 Corinthians 13:1-3, all your right *believing* and right *behaving* is worthless if it's not accompanied by right *loving*. It matters just as much to God how you manage to get along with people as it does how you master doctrine and rules.

REFLECT: Have you ever focused more on *believing* and *behaving* right than on *loving* right? What did or could happen if you made that mistake?

 PRAY: *Lord, I want to believe right and behave right. But help me love right too.*

16 Who's Keeping Score?

Bible Reading: 1 Corinthians 13:4-7

Love . . . keeps no record of when it has been wronged. 1 Corinthians 13:5

DEAR GOD,

It has been three years since my parents' divorce. I have struggled to be patient with you on this one. I know you have a plan and that I just can't see it. Still, I wish things were different. I wish my parents were still together.

Last month I went to visit my dad. He hasn't changed much. Sure, he likes to buy me things. Doesn't he know that I'll love him no matter what he does? And then he goes off on Mom. He's very bitter, but none of the things he says about Mom are true. He used to tell me that true love could weather any storm. I guess true love couldn't weather his storms. I haven't heard from him since I got home, not even a quick phone call. Give me the strength to love my dad, God, even when he lets me down. I know he needs love as badly as anyone.

And you know that Mom is no easier for me to love. She doesn't give a rip about who I am or what's going on in my life. Last week she asked me how I was doing in Algebra. I finished Algebra last semester! Whenever I try to talk to her, she doesn't listen. She just keeps right on working. She says she's doing it for me. Yeah, right. If she wanted to do something for me, she would get back together with Dad and listen to me when I talk to her. Oh God, give me the strength to love my mom even when she disappoints me.

You see each time my parents let me down, Lord. Help me to stay faithful to you and help me to love my parents. I know it is what you want, so I want it too.

Love,
LeShona

You can see in those words the heart of a student who loves God and others more than herself. How can you tell? Because LeShona is obviously more concerned about loving her parents than about their failure to love her. That's the kind of love Jesus came to earth to demonstrate. He didn't keep score of the hurts he suffered. He loved everyone just where they were. He even asked his Father to forgive the people who crucified him (see Luke 23:34).

Your situation might not be as bad as LeShona's. On the other hand, it might be a lot worse. Either way, Christ calls you to love as he loves, focusing on loving others and not fixating on how others have failed to love you. If Jesus can love the people who murdered him, he can help you love people who fail you.

REFLECT: Who in your life do you pick apart—looking only at his or her faults? Are you keeping score of hurts you suffer?

PRAY: Talk to God today about people you have a hard time loving.

17 You Want Me to Build <u>What?</u>

Bible Reading: 1 Corinthians 13:8-12
Now we see things imperfectly as in a poor mirror, but then we will see everything with perfect clarity. 1 Corinthians 13:12

WHACK, WHACK, WHACK. The sound of hammers echoes across the valley. An old man's neighbors watch his progress with amusement. They have seen him do strange things before, but this is really weird. They can't help but laugh at him.

The old man and his grown sons pay no heed to the scoffers. Instead, they go about their work. A nail here, a board there. Piece by piece they see the creation take shape. The master builder has given them the blueprint, and they have to follow it precisely.

"Now what's going on?" somebody laughs. "That old fool has definitely lost it. Why is he filling his house with hay? Hasn't he heard of furniture?"

"That's no house," says another observer. "That's a boat. But why in the world would someone need a boat out here? There's no water for miles!"

"Hey! Anyone seen my two elephants?" someone interrupts. "I had a male and female right in my backyard, but now they're gone."

Just like the elephants, the rest of the animals came two by two. When the ark was full, Noah and his family went inside, and God slowly closed the door. The people outside were probably still laughing when the rain started.

Get the picture? Everyone thought Noah was nuts for obeying God.

God's instructions won't always make sense to you. God gave Noah an assignment: build an ark. But he was laughed at as the community idiot because no one had ever seen rain before, let alone a flood. Even though he had plenty of reasons to doubt, Noah did exactly what God told him to do. And only as floodwaters covered the earth did he start to understand God's plan.

Sometimes God sticks you in situations that don't fit, and you wonder what on earth he's thinking. He commands you to love people who seem unlovable, and to make friends with people who take from you more than they give. Why should you do the loving thing when it doesn't make sense? That's when you can remember Noah—you can read his story in Genesis 6-9.

Your assignment is clear: 1) love God; and 2) love people, even when they don't love you back. It's how Noah loved, and they laughed at him. It's the way Jesus loved, and they killed him for it. But God calls you to love anyway. Someday it will become perfectly clear to you. In the meantime, keep loving as God directs. It's a strategy that will float your boat for sure.

 REFLECT: How do you show love for God when his commands don't seem to make sense?

PRAY: Tell God that you trust him even when you don't understand everything about following him.

18 Love Lasts Longer than Ice-Cream Sandwiches

Bible Reading: 1 Corinthians 13:8, 13

There are three things that will endure—faith, hope, and love—and the greatest of these is love. 1 Corinthians 13:13

IN THE BLANK next to each statement, indicate how long you think that thing will last. You can use minutes, hours, days, months, or years.

_____ A million dollars in your pocket.

_____ The most recent pair to become a "couple" in your school.

_____ Your spiritual high after a youth retreat.

_____ Your best friendship.

_____ A box of ice-cream sandwiches in your freezer.

_____ Your brother or sister's latest promise to be nice to you.

_____ The impact of loving someone unconditionally.

Some things last a long time. Others don't seem to last at all. That box of ice-cream sandwiches in your freezer could vanish in an instant if you and your friends aim to inhale ice cream. On the other hand, a friendship could last for decades. It's tough to know what will last and what won't. Sometimes the thing you expect to be permanent is the first thing to fall apart when times get tough.

One thing that always keeps going and going is God's love—and the love you show others when you love like Christ loves you. That makes the last item on the list the most enduring.

There's never been—nor will there ever be—a greater demonstration of love than what Christ did on the cross. Romans 5:8 says, "But God showed his great love for us by sending Christ to die for us while we were still sinners." The world will feel the impact of what Jesus did on the cross for eternity.

Fortunately for the world, God's expression of love didn't end on the cross. When Jesus rose from the dead, he charged us all to spread his love throughout the world (see Matthew 28:18-20). When you love someone as Christ loves, the impact of your action can last as long as God's love. It's like knocking down dominoes. Your love changing one person can ripple through countless relationships.

So are you focusing your life on the only thing that will last—loving God and loving others as Jesus loves you? If anything else drives you, your efforts might disappear faster than that box of ice-cream sandwiches in the freezer.

REFLECT: What commitments are you making to things that will last?

PRAY: Talk to God today about where love fits in your priorities.

19 The Bad News Makes the Good News Even Better

Bible Reading: Romans 6:20-23

The wages of sin is death, but the free gift of God is eternal life through Christ Jesus our Lord. Romans 6:23

SOMEWHERE AMONG the people around you are those who picture God as a cosmic bogeyman just waiting for them to do something wrong so he can stomp on them. They figure God's biggest goal is to trap them, trick them, or rip on them.

But that's not the God you know. The core of the Bible's message is that God is love. He's not scheming to make us miserable. Here's what he's really up to: " 'I know the plans I have for you,' says the Lord. 'They are plans for good and not for disaster, to give you a future and a hope' " (Jeremiah 29:11). If you want to persuade your non-Christian friends to trust Christ, you first have to assure them that God actually loves them and wants to fill their lives with good things.

But there's a problem—something standing between your friends and God's love. It's called sin. Sin is the condition we're all in before we trust Christ (see Romans 3:23). Sin is an attitude of independence from God. It doesn't matter if your friends are violently anti-God or just indifferent toward him. Their self-sufficient attitudes and actions keep them from knowing God and experiencing his awesome love.

The righteous, loving God of the universe can't stand to be around sin (see Psalm 5:4), so sin separates sinners from him. But wait—it gets worse. Since your unbelieving friends are cut off from the God who made them and loves them, their lives are totally controlled by themselves and their circumstances. They might think that makes them independent, but it doesn't. They're in a serious mess, slaves to their own sinful nature (see John 8:34; Romans 6:16). Ultimately, they face the consequence of eternal separation from God (see Romans 6:23).

To try to soothe the emptiness they feel, unbelieving friends might do really good things—like saving the environment or doing charity work. Or they might get into really bad things—like taking drugs or breaking the law. But they are powerless to bridge the gap (see Romans 5:6). Unless they realize the serious weight of their sin, they won't get why Christ died on the cross. And minus an understanding of Christ's death and resurrection, they have no reason to trust him.

So you have both bad news and good news to share with your non-Christian friends. The bad news is utterly bad—that their sin separates them from a loving God. But the good news is utterly fantastic—that Christ died and rose again to deal with the sin that cuts them off from their loving Creator.

 REFLECT: How can you explain to your non-Christian friends that God isn't out to get them?

PRAY: Ask God to help you share the whole truth with your friends in a way that encourages them to trust Christ.

20 A Personal Invitation

Bible Reading: John 1:1-13

To all who believed him and accepted him, he gave the right to become children of God. John 1:12

GOOD NEWS doesn't get any better than this. While we human beings were still blinded by Satan *and* trapped in darkness *and* separated from God because of our unforgiven sin—no small set of problems—Jesus Christ stepped forward and paid the penalty for our sin. He bridged the gap between us and God (see Romans 5:8; 1 Timothy 2:5). God, the righteous Judge, had seen that our enormous sin problem left us with no way to pay the penalty ourselves. The price, after all, is eternal death! So he paid the penalty for us through the death of his Son. Then Jesus rose from the dead, guaranteeing eternal life and making it possible for him to live in us by the Holy Spirit. That's how we experience the fulfilling, powerful life he planned for us in the first place.

But as fantastic as it is, the gospel really won't be good news to your friends until they respond to it. The gospel is more than information about God's provision in Christ. It's an invitation to trust Christ by faith and welcome him as Savior and Lord.

The apostle John says that responding to Jesus is the whole reason he wrote down his account in a Gospel: "These [facts about Christ] are written so that you may believe that Jesus is the Messiah, the Son of God, and that by believing in him you will have life" (John 20:31). As you spread the good news, your presentation becomes complete only when you ask your friends to admit they need Christ's forgiveness.

Listen to what needs to happen: "To all who believed him and accepted him," John 1:12 states, "he gave the right to become children of God." Jesus says, "Look! Here I stand at the door and knock. If you hear me calling and open the door, I will come in, and we will share a meal as friends" (Revelation 3:20). Spot the response required in these verses? Your friends won't become Christians simply by osmosis—by hanging around you. Coming to Jesus takes a response of trusting their lives to him. If you're not ready to ask them to make a decision, you're not fully prepared to share the Good News.

Remember: Your job is to explain the gospel and invite people to respond. You can't control how people will respond. That's why you share Christ—asking the Holy Spirit to use you—and then leave the results to him. He's the one who takes your words and uses them to convince people they need Christ.

REFLECT: Are you ready to share with your friends not only the information of the Good News but also the invitation to trust Christ? The Holy Spirit can help you do both.

PRAY: Tell God you want his power for witnessing.

21 Building Bridges

Bible Reading: John 17:14-19

As you sent me into the world, I am sending them into the world.
John 17:18

YOU'RE PRAYING for a list of people who need to know Christ. You're taking some leaps of bold faith toward sharing the gospel with them. And you're chomping at the bit to get started—passing out tracts at the mall, dangling fish symbols from your book bag, and wearing your "Turn or Burn" witnessing T-shirt to school.

There might be nothing wrong with any of those strategies for telling people about Jesus. But if you want to get good at sharing the gospel with friends and family, you can practice some key relational and communication skills. Your hottest witnessing opportunities are with the people you know well—people with whom you already have a growing, positive relationship. There are inescapably good reasons for building bridges of communication with non-Christians:

1. *God fills you so you can serve people.* When God tops you off with his Holy Spirit, he reproduces his supernatural qualities in you—like love, joy, peace, patience, kindness, goodness, faithfulness, gentleness, and self-control (see Galatians 5:22-23). But he doesn't jam you full of good fruit just to satisfy you. He builds these qualities in you so you're equipped to get along with and minister to people.

2. *God planted you among unbelievers.* If God's only purpose for your existence was to save you, he would have yanked you out of your world the moment you trusted Christ. And if he wanted you to spend your life only with other believers, you'd find Bible verses instructing Christians to huddle together in isolation. But after you trusted Christ, God left you plunk in the middle of a school and community full of non-Christians. He planted you there so you can influence them—and invite them to a personal relationship with Christ.

3. *Your unbelieving friends really want to know God.* They might not act like it, but your non-Christian friends have a mighty inner desire to know their Maker. God wired that desire into their hearts when he created them. Study your friends long enough and you'll realize that many of their activities are frantic attempts to fill their inner emptiness. And as you get to know your friends better, you'll spot their inner needs.

You might be tempted at times to pull away from your non-Christian friends because you don't want to be associated with some of their choices. But how can you reach people if you're never with them?

REFLECT: How does God help you with the task of telling people about him?

PRAY: Ask God today to help you begin to build bridges of relationship to those around you who need to know him.

22 Blend with Your Non-Christian Friend

Bible Reading: Acts 2:43-47

Each day the Lord added to their group those who were being saved.
Acts 2:47

YOU WOULDN'T WRESTLE an alligator without first getting some helpful hints. So here are some helpful hints about witnessing. These practical strategies won't take the bite out of every nonbeliever, but they might keep you from getting eaten alive:

1. *Meet non-Christians on their turf.* Learn what your non-Christian friends like to do. You can get involved in your friends' interests without ditching your personal standards. (Example: "I'll go to the basketball game with you, but I won't go drinking with you afterward.")

2. *Arouse spiritual curiosity.* How you act, talk, and think tells your non-Christian friends, "I've found something you really want and need." The way you handle conflicts with parents and friends, the way you respond to problems with grades and teachers, and the way you defuse the pressure to join your non-Christian friends in doing something wrong will make them wonder what's different about you. You arouse curiosity, of course, only if you are walking in the Spirit daily.

   Another way to stir up curiosity is by tossing out thought-provoking questions like, "What do you think happens after you die?" "What do you think God is like?" "What's your greatest fear?" If you show interest in what your friends think and feel—without pouncing on them in judgment—you're more likely to get receptive ears when you share Christ with them.

3. *Pray for opportunities and confidence to share Christ.* Remember: Just being a friend to unbelievers won't turn them into Christians. They need to understand the gospel and respond to it personally by trusting Christ. Your big prayer should be, "Lord, get my friends' hearts ready to hear and respond to the gospel. Give me confidence to talk with them about you."

   It's likely you'll have to begin the conversation. You can start with, "Do you ever think about God? I do. I think about him a lot."

Make no mistake: Your ultimate goal in your friendships with non-Christians is to share Christ with them and persuade them to trust him as Savior and Lord. You might get a great chance to communicate the Good News to a friend after only a few days or weeks of being friends. If not, be faithful in your friendship and trust the Holy Spirit to help you wisely time when to dive in.

REFLECT: What do you think your best strategy is for sharing Christ?

PRAY: Pray about that!

23 Dead and Alive

Bible Reading: 1 Corinthians 15:1-9

Christ died for our sins, just as the Scriptures said. He was buried, and he was raised from the dead on the third day, as the Scriptures said.
1 Corinthians 15:3-4

AS A YOUNG MAN, I set out to prove Christianity was a joke. That didn't happen, of course, for one simple reason: I couldn't explain away an event in history—the resurrection of Jesus Christ.

The Resurrection is central to Christianity. As Michael Green stated in his book *Man Alive,* "Christianity does not hold the resurrection to be one among many tenets of belief. Without faith in the resurrection there would be no Christianity at all. The Christian church would never have begun. . . . Christianity stands or falls with the truth of the resurrection. Once you disprove it, you have disposed of Christianity."

That's why so many people have attacked the Resurrection and set out to disprove it like I attempted to do.

Dr. Hugh Schonfield's book *The Passover Plot* caused a volcanic controversy in the mid-1960s. This book caused such a fuss because it brought back an old explanation for the resurrection of Jesus Christ called the "swoon theory." This theory—made popular by Venturini several centuries ago—says that Jesus merely fainted (or "swooned") from exhaustion and loss of blood, later recovering.

Schonfield cooked up a clever variation of the swoon theory, concluding that Jesus planned his arrest, trial, and crucifixion, arranging for himself to be drugged on the cross so that he could fake his death. Then he supposedly recovered from the beatings, exposure, trauma, and loss of blood from the spear wound in his side and the bloody holes in his hands and feet where spikes that supported his weight on the cross had ripped his flesh and bones.

But the swoon theory is a myth. Jesus had suffered a vicious beating with a flagellum, which had cut and ripped him to shreds. Prisoners often missed their own execution because they couldn't survive the flagellum. Then Jesus journeyed to the place of his death. But Simon of Cyrene was forced to carry the cross after Jesus collapsed. Jesus was placed on the cross and removed from it only after a Roman centurion had certified to the Roman governor that Jesus was dead.

To imagine that any human could survive that experience to appear to more than five hundred people requires a huge willingness to rewrite history and ignore the simple truth that Christ died for our sins, was buried, and was raised on the third day (see 1 Corinthians 15:3-4).

REFLECT: Why is the swoon theory so unbelievable?

PRAY: Ask God to help you make the Resurrection understandable to your non-Christian friends.

There's Plenty of Room in the Tomb

Bible Reading: Matthew 28:1-10

I know you are looking for Jesus, who was crucified. He isn't here!
He has been raised from the dead, just as he said would happen.
Matthew 28:5-6

"I'M TELLING YOU, Lizzie, it was the strangest thing! It was me and the other Mary and . . . let's see . . . Salome and . . . give me a minute, I'll remember. . . ."

"Will you get on with it!" Elizabeth urged.

"All right, all right," Mary said. "As I was saying, we went and found an empty tomb where just two nights before we had laid Jesus. Did you hear what I said, Lizzie? It was empty! Nothing there. *Nothing.*"

Elizabeth stared at her friend. "Are you sure it was the right tomb?"

"Am I sure? What kind of question is that? Give me a little credit, will you? It's not like I was the only one there. We went together, and Mary and I had been there just two nights before. If we were at the wrong tomb, don't you think one of us might have figured it out? How stupid do you think we are?

"And angels were at the empty tomb too, shining like lightning! They told us not to be afraid—Jesus was risen, just like he had said. I suppose you think the angels showed up at the wrong tomb too, huh?

"And you might as well call Peter and John stupid too. After all, I ran to tell them, and they ran *straight* to the empty tomb! And what's more, how many tombs in Jerusalem do you think had the remnants of a broken seal?"

"Well, I . . . I—"

"And what about the chief priests and the guard? Don't you think they knew which tomb was the right one? If we went to the wrong tomb, wouldn't they just have pointed to the right one and said, 'Ha! Proved you wrong! Here's the body!'?"

Elizabeth threw up her hands. "I'm sorry, okay? I didn't mean to suggest anything so stupid."

Unfortunately, Elizabeth isn't the only one to make such a suggestion. Kirsopp Lake theorized that the women who reported the missing body of Jesus actually went to the wrong tomb. But, as Mary so strongly protested to Elizabeth in our "might-have-been-said" conversation above, a fifteen-minute stroll from the palace of the high priest or the Roman fortress in Jerusalem down to the right tomb could have quickly shut up for all time any rumors of a resurrection.

But that didn't happen, of course. That's because it *was* Jesus' tomb the women had found. And they found it empty.

REFLECT: What do you think about the theory that the disciples couldn't find the tomb where Jesus was buried?

PRAY: Jesus stepped out of that tomb so he could step into your life with resurrection life and power. Give him thanks today for his life in you.

25 Hide-and-Seek

Bible Reading: Matthew 28:11-15

They told the soldiers, "You must say, 'Jesus' disciples came during the night while we were sleeping, and they stole his body.' " Matthew 28:13

WANT TO HEAR another fairy tale? How about the one where Christ's body was stolen from the tomb? The Bible itself contains the first mention of the Stolen Body myth. After the Resurrection, some of the soldiers who had been guarding the tomb reported to the chief priests what had happened. The chief priests bribed them to say the body had been stolen while they slept (see Matthew 28:11-15).

Some people today still imagine that the disciples played a game of hide-and-seek with Jesus' body. But a load of facts make that fairy tale impossible to believe. The stone, for example, that sealed the tomb wasn't the kind of stone you skip across a pond. According to textual information and the calculations of two Georgia Tech engineering professors, it might have been a five-foot-high circular stone weighing around *two tons*. When the tomb was first prepared, a team of laborers likely would have set the stone in place, using a wedge to keep the stone from rolling down a trench that sloped down to the opening of the tomb. When Jesus was buried, the wedge was removed and gravity did the rest, sealing the tomb so it could only be re-opened with much noisy grunting by a gang of strong men. That's why the women, on their way to the tomb Easter Sunday morning, wondered who could roll the stone away (see Mark 16:3).

Besides that, the chief priests requested a detachment of soldiers from Pilate, the Roman governor, to guard the tomb. The Roman guard unit could have numbered as many as sixteen highly trained soldiers. Those who entertain the Stolen Body myth suppose that a scared little group of disciples confronted a guard of heavily armed, battle-trained soldiers. The disciples either overpowered the soldiers or snuck past them in their sleep to heave a two-ton stone up an incline without waking a single man. Then, so the theory goes, the disciples carted off Jesus' body, hid it, and—over the next several decades—endured ridicule, torture, and martyrdom to spread what they knew to be a lie!

That's staggeringly ridiculous! Harvard law professor Simon Greenleaf lectured for years on how to break down testimony and determine if a witness was lying. He says, "It was . . . impossible that [the disciples] could have persisted in affirming the truths they narrated, had not Jesus actually risen from the dead, and had they not known this fact as certainly as they knew any other fact."

Like the first Christians, you can have complete confidence that the Christian faith is based on the solid historical fact of the empty tomb and the risen Christ!

REFLECT: Why is it impossible that Jesus' disciples stole his body?

PRAY: *Thank you, God, for helping me know that Jesus really rose from the dead.*

26 Have a Heart

Bible Reading: Mark 6:30-44

He had compassion on them because they were like sheep without a shepherd. Mark 6:34

JESUS' DISCIPLES had just returned from a preaching mission—and they were exhausted. Jesus felt their fatigue and kindly suggested that they jump in a boat for a while and get away from it all.

But the crowds chased Jesus and the disciples, running along the shore and waiting when the boat pulled in. Again Jesus acted kindly. He gathered the crowds around and taught them. But late in the afternoon the disciples interrupted Jesus to tell him the people needed to leave—and go find supper. But Jesus in his kindness also heard their stomachs growling. He wowed his disciples by feeding the multitude with a snack of five biscuits and a couple of fish.

If you look closely, you see that Jesus' compassion moved him to do three huge things in this scene: (1) he gave his *time* to the worn-out disciples when they needed to pull back with their Master; (2) he gave his *teaching* to the crowd when they wandered shepherdless; and (3) he gave his *help* by meeting the material needs of thousands when they were hungry.

Being a Christian means tuning in to Christ's compassionate heart and letting his kindness propel you into doing something for people whose hurts you feel. Tuning in and doing are both hard. Christians need to keep growing toward mature selflessness. Most of the time others' needs have to be downright tragic to crash through our selfishness and command our attention.

Like Jesus, you can act on your compassion in at least three ways:

First way: Give time to hurting people. It's great to congratulate people who made the cheerleading squad. But do you ever pay attention to the people who weren't picked?

Second way: Give advice, instructions, or insight to someone in a world of hurt. After you comfort a person slammed by a tough circumstance, ask your all-wise God for insight on how to make the situation easier.

Third way: Give something solid to a needy person. Buy lunch for a classmate who's short on lunch money. Take magazines or flowers to a person in the hospital. Do whatever you can to act on your feelings of compassion.

If you're anything like every other human being, your own interests often dull your sensitivity to others' needs. But there may be times when you notice that people around you are hurting. Does that sometimes hurt you too? Well, that's the compassion of Jesus rising in you. So don't let that feeling die. Take a clue from the compassionate Savior and act as compassionately as you feel.

REFLECT: How do you plan to fan the flame of compassion inside of you?

PRAY: Ask God to show you opportunities to give like Jesus gave.

27 Time Out

Bible Reading: Mark 6:45-56
He went up into the hills by himself to pray. Mark 6:46

YOUR YOUTH PASTOR might rant. Your parents may hand you a Bible and this devotional book! You might even have been hit with, "If Jesus needed to spend time alone with his Father, how much more do *you* need to spend time with God?"

Guess what? That's the truth! See, there's a definite link between Jesus' powerful miracles and the hours he spent alone in prayer recharging his spiritual batteries. You might never walk on water, but you still need spiritual jolts.

Here is a simple plan for spending quality time with God:

1. *Get alone with God.* Our noisy, pushy, in-your-face culture doesn't make it easy to find a place to be alone with God. But if you think hard enough, you can discover a place where no one will disturb you. If you have a bedroom with privacy, use it to get alone with God. If you share a room with a brother or sister, look for another place—a storage room, attic, garage, or basement.

   When you get alone with God, get comfortable so you can concentrate. If you fall asleep when you pray lying down, walk around the room. If you're uptight when you sit, lie down and relax. Kneeling might put you in the right frame of mind when you need to talk to God about something serious.
2. *Talk to God.* Just talk to him as if he were sitting alongside you. Tell him about your anger, frustration, happiness, thankfulness, anything, everything. You can even say, "Lord, I don't feel like talking to you today, but I will because I know it's good for me." How you talk isn't as important as how honest you are. If talking to God bores you, it's time to find a different way to communicate with him. You can write God a letter, sing him a song, or read Scripture to him. Use your imagination.
3. *Let God talk to you.* If you give God the chance, he will talk to you. Not out loud, perhaps, but through the Bible and through your thoughts and ideas. The Bible is the main way God talks to you today. Make a point to tell God that you want to hear what he has to say to you. Then read a few verses during your quiet time and mull over them for a while. Listen to some Christian music, read a solid Christian book or magazine, or just ponder what God has done.

God probably won't ask you to heal crowds like Jesus did. But God has plans for you, and you will be ready for those plans each day after some quiet time with God.

REFLECT: What changes might give you better times alone with God?

PRAY: *God, use the times we talk together to get me ready for the cool things you have for me to do.*

28 Lending a Hand

Bible Reading: Galatians 6:1-6

Carry each other's burdens, and in this way you will fulfill the law of Christ. Galatians 6:2, NIV

YOUR FRIEND CAL asks you to head to the mall with him after school. "Sure," you say, "but I promised Coach I would move some benches in the gym first."

Cal says, "Fine, I'll go with you and help out." At the gym, he parks himself in a chair with his hand-held video game while you sweat out your chore.

The benches you are to move out of the storage room to the gym floor are eight feet long, and the doorway to the storage room is narrow. "Lift the front end up higher," Cal calls out as he watches you struggle with the first bench. "Now turn the bench on its side. . . . No, the other way." You bang the bench against the wall. Then a corner of the bench cracks into the door molding, leaving a big dent. You still haven't moved one bench out of the storage room.

Cal continues to instruct from his perch on the chair. "Now pick up the back end and move it to the left." You catch your finger between the bench and the door jamb and yelp. The pain causes you to drop the bench. You can't believe how *un*helpful your helpful friend is.

Cal looks up from his video game. "C'mon, hurry up," he barks. You limp out of the storage room holding your throbbing finger.

Check (✔) the statement below that best represents what you might say to Cal:

☐ "Will you find me a Band-Aid and a cup of water, please?"
☐ "This is taking longer than I thought. I'll meet you at the mall later."
☐ "Where did you learn so much about moving benches?"
☐ "Please stop *telling me* what to do and *help me!*"

Cal probably thought he was being supportive by barking out instructions, but that's a kind of help you really didn't need. Support means coming alongside to lift up a friend in need. Galatians 6:2 doesn't say, *"Tell others how to carry their burdens"* or *"Pray for someone to help others carry their burdens."* It says *"Carry each other's burdens"* (NIV).

Being a supportive, helping friend is a cool way to express Christ's command to love others. When your friends need support, you have an opportunity to showcase Christ's love in concrete ways. Try hard to spot those opportunities this week.

REFLECT: Who do you know who needs your help right now?

PRAY: Pray for that friend who needs a burden lifted.

29 A Supportive Attitude

Bible Reading: Galatians 6:3

If you think you are too important to help someone in need, you are only fooling yourself. You are really a nobody. Galatians 6:3

YOU NEED HELP studying for a big exam. Or you need a friend to go with you to resolve a conflict. Or you just need someone to hang with because you're feeling a little low. So what kind of a response are you looking for from a friend?

One friend says, "Not now. I have stuff to do." No support there, just mixed-up priorities.

Another friend responds, "Sorry, I can't spare any of my precious time." You won't get help from someone that stingy.

One friend explains, "I can't help right now. I have my own problems." Sounds too self-centered to be much help.

Another friend rudely retorts, "Help you? Why would I want to help a dork like you?" Hmmm. With friends like that. . . .

Real friends aren't usually blunt or unkind. Neither are you. Yet all of us easily slide into self-centeredness—unless we continually cultivate an "other focus" attitude, that is. Here are three biblical attitudes to aim for:

Be caring and not self-absorbed. Being a supportive friend means caring. Like Galatians 6:3 says, "If you think you are too important to help someone in need, you are only fooling yourself. You are really a nobody." It's not possible to get so important or so busy that you're above helping others. So how hot is your caring attitude toward your friends? Do you need to heat it up?

Be humble and unselfish. Philippians 2:3-4 bans selfishness and thinking that always puts yourself first. That means carving out time to check in with your friends, see how they are doing, and offer help when they need it. It also means actually telling your friends you care about them and want to be there for them. So how would you—or someone else—rate your humble attitude toward others?

Be generous and giving. Jesus said, "Give, and it will be given to you; good measure, pressed down, shaken together, running over, they will pour into your lap. For by your standard of measure it will be measured to you in return" (Luke 6:38, NASB). There are huge benefits to being a caring giver. For starters, God says you never have to worry about your own needs being met, because the more you give to others, the more you will receive from others. That's God's promise.

REFLECT: So do you have a giving attitude? How much do you need to grow a giving attitude?

PRAY: Ask God today to help you become more caring, unselfish, and generous in your loving support of your friends.

30 Guess Who You Are Really Supporting

Bible Reading: Matthew 25:35-40

When you did it to one of the least of these my brothers and sisters, you were doing it to me! Matthew 25:40

EVERY MORNING you leap out of bed and excitedly ask yourself who needs your support today. Once you sprained your arm at school from waving it so hard to volunteer to help your teacher. And you're so eager to lend a hand that your parents have put a lid on your constant offer to carry out the garbage—for the whole block. That's you, right?

Actually, most of us need a kick of motivation and compassion to support others. The apostle James must have run into some people who were lacking in the compassion department, because he wrote: "Suppose you see a brother or sister who needs food or clothing, and you say, 'Well, good-bye and God bless you; stay warm and eat well'—but then you don't give that person any food or clothing. What good does that do?" (James 2:15-16).

So how do you get enthused to support the needy people around you?

Well, how would you feel if the friend who needed your support was Jesus himself? Would that spark your motivation? Imagine leaving the home of a friend you have just helped. Someone taps you on the shoulder. You turn around and see Jesus. He says, "Hey—thanks for taking the time to help me. Your compassion and support mean a lot to me." Would that make your mind explode? And—get this—what if you knew you would get that same awe-inspiring response every time? Would you be more swiftly motivated to support your friends?

According to Matthew 25:35-40, Jesus is looking for his followers to provide loving service to others. He could have said something like, "I was behind on my homework, and you helped me catch up. My parents told me to clean out the attic, and you helped me get the job done. I had to baby-sit all day Saturday, and you came over for the afternoon just to keep me company during the kids' naps." Whenever you serve a friend, Jesus applauds as if it were done to him.

But when you ignore an opportunity to support someone in need, it's like you failed to help Jesus. In Matthew 25:42-45, Jesus could have said something like, "I needed help decorating for the youth group party, but you said you couldn't be bothered. I asked you to help support me financially on a short-term missions project, but you said you were saving up for a new sound system. I needed a ride to church on Sunday, but you wanted to sleep in."

Whatever you do or don't do, you do to Jesus. Or not.

REFLECT: When you realize your actions will directly affect Jesus, does that rev up your desire to help others?

PRAY: Ask God today to give you a greater heart of compassion for those who need your help and support.

1
Busted by Jesus!

Bible Reading: Romans 13:1-5
Obey the government, for God is the one who put it there. Romans 13:1

YOU'RE JOGGING down the sidewalk to meet your friends at a fast-food place for a frenzied burger feed. But you're a little late, so you dart across a busy street in the middle of the block. Faster than you can say the word "jaywalk," a motorcycle officer roars up beside you with his lights flashing. You freeze in your tracks. Busted!

You're watching the officer approach when your eyes suddenly bug out. The cop is wearing the standard uniform, but the bearded, kind face looks familiar. It's uncanny. He looks just like the picture of Jesus in your old childhood Bible!

He speaks, and his voice sounds just like you figured Christ's voice would sound. "Believe it or not, lots of people are killed every year right here because they tried to cross the street outside of the crosswalk. I don't want that to happen to you. That's why there's a law against jaywalking." Then he quickly fills out a citation and hands it to you.

You scan the sheet for the officer's signature. When you see the letters "J. C." initialed at the bottom, your jaw drops to the ground in amazement. You look up and the officer winks, like he knows exactly what you're thinking. Then he says, "Have a safe day," hops on his motorcycle, and roars away.

Now, Jesus doesn't have a badge that shows he belongs to the police force in your town or state, but he's definitely interested in what they do. You might be a little surprised to get this news: "Those who refuse to obey the laws of the land are refusing to obey God, and punishment will follow" (Romans 13:2). Sounds a little like Christ in a police officer's uniform, doesn't it?

In reality, whenever you spot someone tasked to uphold the law and protect the public, you're looking at God's representative. Public servants might not *know* they are God's representatives, and some might go off at you for even suggesting such a thing. But they truly are God's instruments, because God is the one who puts authorities in place to protect and defend you. God cares for you through the laws of the land and those who uphold them.

You might never get busted by a police officer who reminds you of Jesus, but you can still spot God providing for you and protecting you through police, government, and laws. When you obey the authorities he put in place, you aren't just being a good citizen—you're honoring God.

 REFLECT: When you obey the authorities in your life, you are obeying God. How does that fact help you do what is right?

PRAY: Talk to God today about your relationships with the people who have authority in your life.

2 Do IOU?

Bible Reading: Romans 13:6-7
Give to everyone what you owe them. Romans 13:7

CHECK (✔) any of the statements that sound like something you've said:

- ☑ "Hey, can I borrow a buck? I'll pay you back tomorrow."
- ☑ "Thanks for the favor. I owe you one."
- ☑ "If you help me clean my room, I'll help you next week."
- ☐ "Sure, Dad, I'll pay you back $10 every month until it's paid off."
- ☐ "I'm going to miss you when you move away. But I'll write every week."
- ☑ "Mom, I'll clean up the kitchen as soon as this program is over."

When you make a promise, it's like using a credit card. It's painless to plop a credit card on the counter, scribble your name, and walk away with something you want. No money leaves your pocket, and you take home something of value—like a new CD, for example. But in a few weeks, a statement shows up from the credit card company, and it's time to pay up. At that point, you might wish you had never whipped out the plastic. And if you don't pay your bill on time, that $15 for the CD grows to $17, $20, $24, or more as interest racks up.

One secret to getting along well in this world is to pay people what you owe them. Paying your financial debts is important. But so is taking care of other commitments you make to friends, siblings, parents, or strangers. Some promises are easy to make—and even easier to regret you ever made. But here's the big question: Do you pay what you owe, or just blow off your promises?

Here's a great thing: Jesus always keeps his commitments to you. He promised, "My purpose is to give life in all its fullness" (John 10:10), and hasn't he filled your life with good things? He said, "I . . . have come to seek and save those . . . who are lost" (Luke 19:10), and that's exactly what he did when he died on the cross. He promised, "I am with you always, even to the end of the age" (Matthew 28:20), and haven't you sensed he's really there for you? And your biggest hope in life is seeing him show up to fulfill this promise: "I will come and get you, so that you will always be with me where I am" (John 14:3).

So when God says to pay what you owe by making good on your promises, he's asking you to do something he's already done. And is still doing. And will always do.

REFLECT: Why bother to keep your commitments? What does it have to do with following Jesus?

PRAY: *Jesus, help me be faithful in keeping the promises I make.*

3 Love Is Always Right

Bible Reading: Romans 13:8-10
"Love your neighbor as yourself." . . . Love satisfies all of God's requirements. Romans 13:9-10

WHAT IS the most right thing you could ever do—the best, most righteous, most applaudable task you could cross off your to-do list? Put a check (✔) next to the statement that sounds to you like the biggest good thing:

- ☐ Read your Bible and pray every day.
- ☐ Actually give your mother a Mother's Day present right on Mother's Day.
- ☐ Finish all your homework before playing computer games.
- ☐ Never wear plaid socks with striped pants and a checked shirt.
- ☐ Eat something from the four basic food groups every day.
- ☑ Love others as you love yourself.

Yep, there are loads of likable things you can do every day. But if you have to choose the one most right thing, you're smart to stick with the one Jesus selected and modeled for us: loving others selflessly. Paul explained why when he wrote, "Love satisfies all of God's requirements" (Romans 13:10). Ponder that: Loving others like Christ did checks off every item on God's list of right things to do. Love is the ultimate moral absolute, the most right thing anybody can ever do.

Your own life experiences prove that fact. You surely want to be loved by others. You certainly want to be treated with fairness, respect, courtesy, and honesty. And you likely hope for kind, loving treatment in all your relationships and encounters with others. If you don't want those things, then you're absolutely abnormal. People universally act as if they deserve the respect and dignity of being loved by others.

And what happens when you don't get that loving treatment you hope for? Don't you feel slammed when you are abused, slandered, lied to, cheated, ignored, made fun of, or otherwise treated with anything less than love? Don't you go bonkers when you don't get the treatment you expect? Examples: You expect your parents to compliment you for doing things right—and you're disappointed when they take you for granted. You expect your friends to be interested in what you want to do—and you get angry when all they want to do is what *they* want to do.

You expect to be loved, so love others. Love is the basic moral absolute. It's always the right thing to do. It's how God treats us every day.

REFLECT: Why should you love like God loves?

PRAY: Ask God to help you treat others the way he treats you.

4 What's the Difference?

Bible Reading: Romans 13:13-14

We should be decent and true in everything we do, so that everyone can approve of our behavior. Romans 13:13

COREY, 17, parties on weekends, sometimes blacking out from drinking too much beer. He smokes a little weed now and then, and he and his girlfriend have been sexually involved for months.

Jamie, 16, is paranoid about getting good grades, so she hangs out with a group of kids known to cheat on exams. Jamie has offered to pay other students to slip her correct answers during an exam.

Tyrone, 14, has a raging temper. He settles arguments by swinging his fists around. At least twice a semester he gets suspended from school for fighting.

Leah, 15, has made enemies out of most of her friends. She's known as "The Blab" because she tells the nastiest stories about people. She likes nothing better than spreading—and creating—juicy rumors.

So from what you just read, how many of these students are Christians? None of them? Some of them? Most of them? All of them? Can you tell?

Here's another important piece of information to help you answer this question: All of these students attend church and belong to a youth group.

So which of them are Christians?

In reality, all of them trusted Christ at some point in their lives.

Are you surprised? Shocked?

True, how each student is acting doesn't fit how the Bible says a Christian should live. But a person's standing with God is based on faith in Christ, not behavior. Still, you have to wonder about these students. As Christ's representatives on earth, they don't look much like Christ, do they?

That's Paul's point in today's Bible passage. Even though salvation is an issue of faith—not behavior—there *should* be a difference in how a believer acts. Just as Christ lived according to a different standard when he walked this earth, his followers are to live by a different standard. If you want to become more like Christ in your behavior, you need to give him control. That's when you'll look like him—instead of looking like you don't know him or follow him.

Jesus came to earth in human flesh to show you how to live and to die for your sin. That's called the *Incarnation*—God alive in human form. Having risen from the dead and returned to heaven, he now wants to live through you. That's another kind of incarnation—God alive in *your* human form. He wants to show the world the mind-blowing difference he can make through you.

REFLECT: Will you let Jesus live through you? Is anything stopping you?

PRAY: Talk to God about your answer to that question.

5 Time's Up

Bible Reading: Romans 13:11-12
Another reason for right living is that you know how late it is; time is running out. Romans 13:11

BROTHER WILLIAM stopped by the log cabin of Brother Frederick so the two of them could walk to church together. There had been reports of wolves roaming the woods, so Brother William didn't want to walk to church alone.

When Brother Frederick stepped out of the log cabin, he was carrying a loaded musket. Brother William was shocked because their church didn't believe in weapons, war, or killing animals. As they started into the woods, William said, "Brother Frederick, I see that you have a musket with you today."

"That's right, Brother," Frederick said.

William stopped his traveling companion and turned to face him. "Brother Frederick," he said sternly, "don't you realize that when your time is up, the Good Lord is going to take you whether you have a musket to defend yourself against the wolves or not?"

"Yes, I realize that, Brother."

"Then why are you carrying a musket today?" William pressed.

Frederick smiled. "Just in case I meet a wolf whose time is up."

You probably don't want to think about it, but some day your stroll on planet Earth will stop. You might buckle up in the car religiously, avoid dancing on downed powerlines, and just say no to all invitations to run with the bulls in Pamplona. You may do a zillion things to prolong your life, but you can't keep it from ending. Unless Christ comes back first, some day someone will write a nice little bitty blurb in the newspaper telling everybody what a wonderful person you were. That's *were*, not *are*, because you'll be gone. Like it or not, the clock is ticking. The days of your life are slipping away.

And since you can't peek at God's giant calendar in the sky, you don't know when your time will be up. It could be eighty years from now, eighty days from now, or eighty minutes from now. All you can say is what Paul said: "Time is running out." There's no time to waste. Now is the time to start living the way he wants you to live in front of your friends. They need to see Christ alive in your life. How come? Time is running out for them too.

The sinless Son of God became incarnate to live the light before us. Let him become incarnate in you so you can show others what he looks like—for however long you have left.

REFLECT: How do you want to spend the rest of your time on earth—however long it is? Who do you want to live for?

PRAY: Ask God to live through you and help you use your time wisely.

6 Family Feud

Bible Reading: Romans 15:1-6
*May God . . . help you live in complete harmony with each other—
each with the attitude of Christ Jesus toward the other. Romans 15:5*

"SIT UP! I've told you fifty times you look like a caveman when you eat like that."

It's a typical evening meal at the Nelson house. Dad is usually engrossed in his own world, but occasionally he looks up long enough to bark at Bryce.

"Dad, for once couldn't you stop picking at me about something?" Bryce answers disgustedly. "Just once I'd like to eat a meal without being yelled at for something I'm doing wrong."

"Honey," Mrs. Nelson breaks in, "I think Bryce is right. You do criticize him a lot."

"There you go again," Dad says with an angry edge to his voice, "taking sides with the kids. If you can't support me, then keep your mouth shut."

Thirteen-year-old Lara doesn't like family arguments and tries to calm things down. "Dad, Mom means well. Please don't get mad at her."

"I've worked hard all day," he replies. "When I come home I want peace and quiet, not criticism!"

"We'd all have peace and quiet if you weren't always jumping on Lara and me," Bryce says, his voice rising. "You yell about our music being too loud; you yell if we haven't finished our homework; all you do is yell, yell, yell!"

"I don't appreciate your attitude," Dad snaps, his voice rising sharply.

Bryce abruptly pushes back from the table, knocking his chair to the floor. "Well, I'm sick of *your* attitude," he yells through gritted teeth. "I'm going over to Luke's. At least *his* dad isn't always yelling at me!"

Maybe you've noticed: Parents, brothers, and sisters aren't always easy to live with. But let's be honest—*you* aren't always easy to live with either. "Okay," one student admits, "so sometimes, especially when I have a bad day at school, I get so mad I lash out at Mom. I know it's not her fault, but she's just there and I guess I have to scream at somebody."

So are you able to accept the truth about your problems, stresses, and emotional blowups? Can you be admit that living with you isn't always a barrel of laughs for your family? Can you go to your parents and admit when you blow it? Can you say, "I know I've been cranky lately and I'm sorry about that. I appreciate your patience. I'm working on it"? In lots of situations, that kind of honesty between family members builds the closeness you all seek. And you never know—they might admit they aren't perfect either.

REFLECT: Which of your faults do you like to blame on other people? Is there anything you need to own up to when it comes to getting along with your family?

PRAY: Ask God to give you a heart that is honest about your less-than-best side.

7 Home Is Where He Is

Bible Reading: Psalm 46:1-3
Lord, through all the generations you have been our home! Psalm 90:1

LIKE EVERYONE else alive, you have a need to belong. God meant that need to be met first in your family. No matter how ugly the world gets, the idea is that you can always come home and say, "I can be myself here." It's an unbeatable feeling when home is safe, relaxing, and friendly. Unfortunately, lots of students don't get that when they go home. For them, home is lonely—or worse.

Jesus knew what it was like not to have a home. His brothers and sisters weren't exactly excited about his public ministry. They may have even labeled him the family laughingstock. Besides that, he was homeless as he traveled throughout Israel for the last three years of his earthly life (see Matthew 8:20). Given all that, where did he get his sense of belonging? Or, better yet, *who* gave it to him?

Jesus leaned on the undeniable fact that he belonged to his Father. He couldn't see the Father any more than you can. But he knew his Father was with him, and that knowledge gave him a peace and security that kept him going.

Because Jesus is so secure in his Father's love, he has strength to live in a less-than-perfect situation. In other words, Jesus *can* live in your home, even if he finds your family members tough to get along with. And that's a clue for you to succeed in less-than-swell circumstances. Jesus wants you to take him into your home and to be at home with him. If you check the first four books of the New Testament—the ones that tell about Jesus when he was here on earth—you find him constantly hanging out in people's homes and working wonders even in weird situations.

At the very end of the Bible, Jesus says in the book of Revelation 3:20, "Look! Here I stand at the door and knock. If you hear me calling and open the door, I will come in, and we will share a meal as friends." He means those words for you. When you're at home, he wants you to know that he is actually and perpetually there with you. When he says he wants to eat a meal with you, he's saying he wants to talk to you and have you talk to him—like two close friends sitting across the table, chatting and visiting.

The more you enjoy Jesus' friendship at home, the less lonely home becomes. You're less aggravated and unsettled inside yourself because Christ makes you more at ease, more okay with your circumstances, whatever they are. The other people in your home might not change, but you have a close personal friend changing you and helping you to cope.

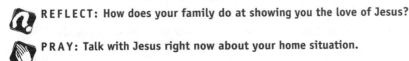

REFLECT: How does your family do at showing you the love of Jesus?

PRAY: Talk with Jesus right now about your home situation.

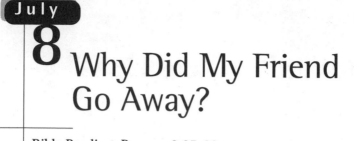

8 Why Did My Friend Go Away?

Bible Reading: Romans 8:35-39

Nothing in all creation will ever be able to separate us from the love of God that is revealed in Christ Jesus our Lord. Romans 8:39

FOURTEEN-YEAR-OLD Holly lived in a foster home for several years. She was active in the youth group at her church and had a bunch of friends there. One summer, Holly went away for a week of church youth camp. When she got home, her foster parents told her she had to leave *the next day* to live in a group home in another state. The authorities had made the decision without talking to Holly or her foster parents.

Holly felt ripped from her friends and family, tossed into a strange new environment. Over the next weeks and months she felt wrenching loneliness.

You might never face a situation as severe as Holly's, but sooner or later everyone faces a loss or separation that ends in inward hurt.

Loneliness and sadness can hit you from many directions:

1. *Life changes.* As you grow up, your interests and values change. That affects who you spend time with—and who spends time with you.
2. *Friends move away.* Career moves and other reasons lead adults to uproot families and move away, sometimes yanking friends from your life.
3. *Families sometimes split up.* If your own parents separate or divorce, your relationships almost always change. That can cause deep loneliness.
4. *Love sometimes leaves.* When a boyfriend or girlfriend torpedoes a relationship, you feel hurt. Unloved. Devastated. You might figure that no one will ever love you again.
5. *Loved ones die.* There's nothing as painful as the ache of losing a parent, grandparent, sibling, or friend to death. Losing a pet can hit hard too.

What makes these painful situations even harder is that the loss might be completely beyond your control. But here's a great truth: Jesus is the one friend you can never lose. Every other relationship you have will someday change through moves, divorce, or death. But Jesus will always be there for you. He won't move away or die. He won't change how he feels about you or dash your heart to pieces. He won't ever say, "That's the last straw! I'm leaving!" And he goes with you when you go through the loss of your earthly friends.

 REFLECT: What in your life is making you lonely right now?

PRAY: *Jesus, I'm grateful that you stick with me even when my other friends aren't around.*

9 Turning Losses into Gains

Bible Reading: Romans 8:26-30
We know that God causes everything to work together for the good of those who love God and are called according to his purpose.
Romans 8:28

PEOPLE SAY love stinks. Well, loneliness stinks worse.

You might wonder if anything good can come from losing a relationship. Sure, you get reminded that Jesus never leaves you. But is there anything else to learn? Try hard to think about these four pluses when your life seems like a pile of minuses:

1. *You learn that losses are a fact of life you have to deal with.* When you realize you can't escape change, you learn how to cope in a positive way. If you don't, your next loss will further bang up your unhealed heart. And you find out that God truly can use your losses to help you grow.
2. *You learn that grief is a normal feeling when you lose a family member or friend.* You might think you only grieve when someone dies—and grief sure fits there. But grief also happens when separation slices off a special friend. It's still a painful loss. Grief is natural. You just need to learn how to let the grieving process happen in a healthy way.

   Sometimes grief will throw you into such an emotional spin that you can't think straight. Sometimes you might come to warped conclusions like "God is punishing me!" or "I must be a bad person for this to happen to me." One way to kick that wrong thinking out of your head is to find someone to offer you support and advice while you're hurting and uncertain. Look for someone compassionate, wise, and patient—a church leader, a family member, or an older Christian friend.
3. *You learn the wisdom of having several Christian friends, not just one or two.* If you only have one friend, you're left alone and lonely if that relationship ends. Having more friends means you have others who can fill that gap. Making friends outside your age group—like having solid friendships with a couple of older adults—means you gain support and input from people who see things from a different perspective.
4. *You learn that God can turn each loss into a gain.* It's possible that a painful situation will take you somewhere better. Some questions to ponder: Do you depend too much on that one friend? Have you been looking to that person to meet needs only God can meet? Is there someone new that you need to reach out to?

REFLECT: What can you learn from any of the changing friendships in your life?

PRAY: Ask God to help you look on the positive side of each negative situation.

10 Who Will Be Your Everything?

Bible Reading: 2 Thessalonians 2:13-17

May our Lord Jesus Christ and God our Father, who loved us . . . , comfort your hearts and give you strength in every good thing you do and say. 2 Thessalonians 2:16-17

YOU WANT to date. Why?

That's not such a dumb question. There are plenty of bad reasons to date. But the right reason for getting to know someone of the opposite sex—in God's way, in God's time—is to answer the desire God built into you to have a special friendship with someone. You're probably not breathing if you don't need an intimate, affectionate, transparent relationship with someone.

And ponder this: *Filling that need starts with Jesus.* It's not trite or tacky to say that he has everything you could ever want in a special, intimate friend.

Jesus seeks your friendship. Revelation 3:20 is Jesus' way of saying he wants a tight, personal relationship with you.

You are special to Jesus. To Jesus, you're not ordinary. Or unappealing. Or ugly. You're amazing to him. No matter what you or others see as your personality quirks or physical flaws, he likes you. He's reserved a place in your heart that no one else can ever fill. And his love isn't fickle—he won't ditch you because you bore him.

Jesus has affectionate feelings for you. When you feel down, Jesus cares. When your life is a thrill and you're filled with joy, Jesus celebrates with you. Because he is a God who feels, you can be sure he shares your happiness and sadness. He's involved in every aspect of your life.

You can be intimate with Jesus. No one knows your most locked-tight thoughts and feelings like this companion. He's glad when you share your most private thoughts with him. You can let him in on your dreams and longings and know that he understands what you mean. When your relationship with your parents is under stress, Jesus is available to listen.

Dating didn't happen until the twentieth century. Until then, there was no youth culture, so no dating like you face today. If a young Christian man or woman was lonely, he didn't look to his boyfriend or girlfriend for comfort and companionship. He or she sought out a family member or friend—or learned to make Jesus his most intimate friend.

Instead of expecting a special guy or girl to give you identity and security, start by looking to Jesus Christ as the one friend who will *always* be there for you. Choose to make him the most special person in your life.

REFLECT: When you look for identity and security, where do you start? Whom do you expect to provide that for you?

 PRAY: Talk to God about his being your unfailing friend and the most important person in your life.

Mirror, Mirror on the Wall

Bible Reading: Psalm 139:13-14

Thank you for making me so wonderfully complex! Your workmanship is marvelous—and how well I know it. Psalm 139:14

EVER STOOD in front of the mirror and thought something like, "God, you messed up when you made me"?

Is it possible for God to make a mistake on one of his creations?

You're lucky if you've never looked in the mirror and gagged. Maybe you noticed a creepy resemblance of your backside to a rhino's back end. Or you suddenly discover why you have to run around in the shower to get wet—you're so skinny the water spray misses you. Or you're missing the bulked-up muscles of a professional bodybuilder.

And even people with perfect complexions have had the experience of heading out the door for school and grabbing one last glance in the mirror, only to find a Godzilla-like pimple is holding the end of their nose hostage.

You yell, "Why me, God? Did you have to blow it on me? Wouldn't my little brother have made a better victim if you had to make a mistake?"

Listen carefully. You aren't alone. All of us have felt that way—even your school's homecoming queen and starting quarterback. But the truth is that God doesn't make mistakes. He didn't goof on you or anyone else. Whether you feel too tall, too short, too big, too little, or even too ugly, God made you just as you are. He thinks you are perfect.

God loves variety. That's why no two flowers are exactly the same, no two snowflakes are the same, and no two people are the same. He didn't want you to be just like everybody else because to him, you're a stand-out. He made you different because you deserve to be different. You deserve to be interesting and unique.

You do, of course, have some options in how you look. You can't change how tall you are, but you can somewhat control how much of you there is filling up that height. How you eat (several slabs of pizza every day for lunch do impact how you look—duh!) and how you exercise (sitting in front of the TV doesn't really count) will make a difference. And a doctor can help you solve some appearance problems with your skin, weight, and overall wellness.

But the basic genetic formula that stares back at you in the mirror is God's masterpiece. You are special because God made you special, different because God made you different. If you looked like everyone else, you wouldn't be you.

REFLECT: What do you think when you look in the mirror? How are you different from other people?

PRAY: Use David's prayer in Psalm 139:14 today to start your own prayer of appreciation for who and what you are.

Are You Looking to the Media or the Master?

Bible Reading: Psalm 139:15-18

How precious are your thoughts about me, O God! They are innumerable! Psalm 139:17

ONE DAY Adam walks in from a hard day of tilling the soil. When he sees Eve, he drops his hoe in surprise. "What's with the tiger fur? You always wear goat skins. I like you in goat skins."

"Adam, darling," Eve says with a little laugh, "goat skins are so out this year. Everyone's wearing tiger fur. Haven't you noticed on TV? Haven't you seen the fashion magazines? And by the way, I'd get rid of that cowhide outfit of yours if I were you. Sheepskin is all the rage with the guys these days."

Okay—so maybe Adam and Eve figured out what to wear without the help of TV, magazines, movies, and commercials. But nowadays it seems we can't get dressed without someone telling us what's hot and what's not.

The media screams that you have to look a certain way to be acceptable. Guys have to be tall, dark, and handsome. Women beat themselves up if they don't have measurements in perfect proportion. If you want people to consider you good-looking, you'd better not have a bad complexion or wear the wrong clothes.

So the media has made up its own standard for what it considers to be a good-looking person. Maybe you have bought that standard as the ultimate standard. And if you don't look like that, then you probably don't like the way you look.

Does that make it wrong to try to look the way the media says you should? Not usually—at least when it comes to clothes and other easy-to-swap styles. But if you're physically trying to match the media's ideal of a perfect body, look out. You are in for some frustration. Why? Two reasons. First, the media's standard is constantly changing. Don't whittle yourself down to ninety-five pounds if the media says skinny is in, because next year skinny will probably be out.

Second, *you* are constantly changing. Sure, you might look like a movie star today, but in a few years you will probably look more like how your father or mother looks today. That's just how it works. If you base your self-worth on the way you look, you are going to be frustrated.

You need to base your self-worth on a value system better than the media's—God's. He was the master designer, chief architect, and construction supervisor when you were put together in your mother's womb. He watched it all happen to make sure you came out just right. And he still thinks you're just right. Your basic design and appearance is his masterpiece.

REFLECT: How much do you try to keep up with trends? When does that get in the way of appreciating the way God made you?

PRAY: Thank God for making you uniquely you.

13 Image Is Everything

Bible Reading: Genesis 1:26-28
Then God said, "Let us make people in our image, to be like ourselves."
Genesis 1:26

IMAGE IS supposedly everything. So what's a self-image?

Your self-image is the mental picture you have of yourself. It started being formed the moment you were born, and by the time you were five or six the person you think you are was so locked into your brain that you madly resist efforts to change it. That doesn't mean you *can't* change it. Lots of people have moved from a negative to a positive self-image—or from a positive to a negative self-image. The point is this: Once you get a fix on who you think you are, you don't change easily. And since your self-image impacts every responsibility and relationship you have, it's crucial to acquire a healthy self-image *now*.

If you have a negative self-image, you don't think highly of yourself. You're often pessimistic, lacking in confidence, extremely sensitive to the opinions of others, self-conscious about how you look or perform, constantly wondering what people think of you, clingy in relationships, unsure of how to receive another's love, looking for possessions to make you happy, and speaking negatively about yourself or others. That's not a happy way to be.

If you have a positive self-image, you think highly of yourself. You might think you're the greatest because of the way you look or how smart you are or some other outstanding ability. That's not a good way to be, either. A quick car accident could change all three of those in a flash.

A healthy self-image is seeing yourself as God sees you—no more, no less. If you have a healthy self-image, you *do* think highly of yourself—but that's because God thinks highly of you. You accept the reality that God created you in his own image as someone with infinite value and worth.

When you see who you are in Jesus Christ, nothing can ever change that. You gain a positive and a healthy view of yourself. And you can get ready for God to do things through you. Why? Research shows that people act in ways that fit the mental picture they have of themselves. If you see yourself as a failure, you will act like a failure. You'll also find it hard to believe God wants the best for you.

A healthy self-image bulks you up with the strength to meet not only your own needs but also others' needs. It empowers you to be the kind of friend and Christian God calls you to be.

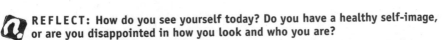

REFLECT: How do you see yourself today? Do you have a healthy self-image, or are you disappointed in how you look and who you are?

PRAY: Spend some time today asking God to give you a healthy self-image— by helping you see yourself as he sees you.

14 Who Told You Who You Are?

Bible Reading: Romans 12:1-3

Be honest in your estimate of yourselves, measuring your value by how much faith God has given you. Romans 12:3

YOU GET your self-image the same way you got food when you were little: You eat what people put in front of you.

If kind people gave you healthy meals and good sleep, you thrived. If all your body ever inhaled was junk food, sooner or later you're going to have grief. And if all you ever ate was garbage, your body likely needs some serious repair.

Your self-image also comes from what people dish up for you. As you grew up you listened to what people—parents, teachers, youth leaders, friends—said about you. You saw yourself in light of how they talked, thought, and acted toward you. Maybe you were fed nutritious, accurate information about yourself. Maybe you lived on junk food—being told you could do no wrong. And maybe you got leftovers or worse. All of these formed your self-image.

So answer this: Do you remember getting fed negative statements like these, even in fun? Check (✔) any that sound like something you remember:

- ☐ "You'll never amount to anything."
- ☐ "You're so much trouble. I wish you'd never been born."
- ☐ "You are so ugly you'll never have a boyfriend/girlfriend."
- ☐ "Why can't you get A's and B's like your sister does?"
- ☐ "What are you growing on that face of yours, a zit farm?"

What happens when you hear statements like that about yourself? A subtle chain reaction takes place inside you.

First, you hear it: "You're stupid."

Next, you think about it: *Is he right? Am I really stupid?*

Then an experience reinforces it. You make a big mistake and someone laughs at you and says, "That was a stupid thing to do."

Then you begin to feel it: *That was so dumb. I really feel stupid.*

Finally, you believe it: *I am told that I'm stupid, I act stupid, and I feel stupid. It must be true. I am stupid.*

See why it's so important to know what God says about you? As you read the Bible, you find out how God values you. The more you see yourself as God sees you, the more you get a *true* view of you.

REFLECT: How have other people shaped how you see yourself?

PRAY: Ask God today to let his Word fill you with his view of you. Welcome that view as the truth—that's exactly what it is.

15 Is There a Way to God's Will?

Bible Reading: Jeremiah 29:11-14

If you look for me in earnest, you will find me when you seek me.
Jeremiah 29:13

JASON JUST started his senior year of high school. Since he was eight, he was sure he wanted to study biology—until he actually took biology, that is, and found he had to do dissections with one hand on the knife and the other holding his nose.

Besides that discouraging experience, Jason keeps hearing about the poor job outlook for biologists and the high educational requirements to succeed in the field. When his older sister lands a high-paying computer job straight out of technical school, Jason thinks about bypassing college altogether. And on top of everything else, Jason wonders what God thinks of any of his plans for his life.

Jason faces some of the same choices you might face soon. And he's asking the biggest question about his future: Where does God want me to head in life?

"How can I know God's will?" is a question Christian leaders often hear from students. Some talk about it. Others worry about it. Some even lose sleep over it. These students burst with sincere, serious questions about God's will.

Why is God's will such a big deal for people your age? Because you face the three most important decisions of your life:

1. You're deciding who will guide your life—your *master*. If you've trusted Jesus Christ as Savior and Lord and intend to live your life according to his Word, you're headed in the right direction.
2. You're deciding if you will marry and whom you will marry—your *mate*. A marriage decision is doubly difficult because it takes two to tie the knot. You both have to see God's will the same way.
3. You're deciding what you will do with your life—your *mission*—and what preparation you need to accomplish your goals.

God loves you and has a great plan for your life. Jeremiah 29:11 declares, " 'For I know the plans I have for you,' says the Lord. 'They are plans for good and not for disaster, to give you a future and a hope.' " God also promises, "I will instruct you and teach you in the way you should go; I will counsel you and watch over you" (Psalm 32:8, NIV).

Even if you aren't yet wallowing in confusion about God's will, you can plan on facing some questions about how to spend your life. You can also plan that God will be with you to figure out the answers.

REFLECT: What kind of plans does God have for your life?

PRAY: Have you ever told God you want to do his will before you even know what it is? Now would be a great time to do that.

16 Finding God's Will Is an Attitude Issue

Bible Reading: Jeremiah 33:3
Ask me and I will tell you some remarkable secrets about what is going to happen here. Jeremiah 33:3

PSSST . . . here's a hot secret to living a meaningful life. All you have to do is *figure out God's will for your life*. Then all your worries are over.

Easier said than done, you say? You might know God has a plan for your life, but do you have a clue how to find out what it is?

God *wants* to show you what he wants. But it's easy to get stuck in several wrong attitudes about God's will. Get mired in any of these, and you won't escape your confusion about God's will for the important decisions in your life:

God's will is hidden and I have to find it. Some students think that discovering God's will is like hunting for Easter eggs. God hides his answers to your questions—and if you can't find them, too bad! That attitude isn't what the Bible shows about God. He eagerly reveals his will to you if you're willing to receive it.

I don't really want to know God's will because I might not like it. Some students are afraid God will tell them to marry someone they don't love or spend their lives doing something they don't want to do—like being a missionary in a remote jungle. But is God looking to make you miserable? No. According to Romans 8:32, he wants to graciously give you all things that will fulfill your deepest desires.

I only want to do part of God's will. Students with this attitude might never know God's will. It's like trying to drive a car by stepping on the gas and the brake at the same time. One moment you're saying, "Lord, show me your will," and the next moment, "I don't want to do *that* part of your will." If you don't follow through with what God shows you to do today, why should he show you what to do tomorrow? Commit to do the total will of God.

I want to know God's will so I can decide whether or not I want to do it. Seeking God's will isn't like shopping for a new car. You can't test-drive his will and then decide if you want to buy it. You either want God's will or you don't. You will never really know God's will until you desire it more than your own.

Put those faulty attitudes side-by-side with the appropriate attitude: *I am willing to do God's will, whatever it is.* The only attitude God will reward is a willingness to accept God's will even before you know it. It's the attitude expressed by the psalmist who wrote, "I take joy in doing your will, my God, for your law is written on my heart" (Psalm 40:8). God is eager to share his plans and counsel with you—*if* you are eager to obey.

REFLECT: Do you need to confess to God one or more of those less-than-appropriate attitudes toward finding his will?

PRAY: Spend a few moments telling God that you want his will for your life.

God's Will on Two Levels

Bible Reading: Proverbs 3:1-6
Seek his will in all you do, and he will direct your paths. Proverbs 3:6

CARLOS WALKS into his pastor's office feeling a little nervous. But Pastor Keene tries to put him at ease. "Welcome, Carlos, I'm glad you came. Please sit down. How can I help you?"

Carlos gets right to the point. "I'm confused about where God wants me to go to college. How am I supposed to find out what he wants me to do?"

"Well, let me start by asking you a few questions," the pastor begins. "Have you trusted Christ as your Savior?"

"Yes sir, four years ago at church summer camp."

"Good. Are you obeying your parents?"

"Well, er, yeah—most of the time, Pastor," Carlos says, "but that isn't what I came here to talk about. I want to find God's will for my education."

"I understand, Carlos," the pastor says patiently, "but I want to know if you're already following God's will. If you're not committed to obeying God's will in the obvious, right-here-right-now decisions of life, there's no point looking for what he wants about college."

When you want to find God's will for your life, you have to look for it at two distinct levels. The first is God's will for everyone—what some people call God's *universal* will. The second is God's will for each individual—his *specific* will. Here's the problem: A lot of people try to know God's specific will for their individual lives, all the while ignoring God's universal will.

God's universal will is the clear, unmistakable will for all people you find in the Bible. You know from Scripture, for example, that God's will is for everyone to trust Christ for salvation. Or think about 1 Thessalonians 5:17, which says, "Pray continually" (NIV). You can be sure it's God's will that everyone grow in a consistent attitude of prayer and closeness with him. God makes other pieces of his universal will equally clear—like loving God and people, obeying parents, sharing your faith with others, remaining sexually pure, etc. You will have a hard time finding God's specific will about things like marriage, college, and career if you waffle on obeying God's universal will.

That doesn't mean you have to be perfectly obedient before God will show you his specific will. Nobody is. But when you set your heart on obeying God's will for everybody in Scripture, you are in the right place to find God's will for your own future.

REFLECT: Answer this question in your own words: Why does God want you to be doing his universal will before he shows you his specific will?

PRAY: Talk to God about your desire to do his will.

18 First Things First

Bible Reading: Romans 12:1-2

Let God transform you into a new person by changing the way you think. Then you will know what God wants you to do. Romans 12:2

GOD'S UNIVERSAL will is the big part of his expectations that you can't miss. It's clear. It's indisputable. It's spelled out in his Word. And understanding and yielding to that universal will is the first step in finding God's more detailed will specific to your life. So here's where you start:

Trust Christ. The most important part of God's will is for everyone to be saved—to trust Christ as Savior and Lord. It's pointless to look for any other aspects of God's will until you walk in his will regarding your salvation.

Submit totally to Christ. Once you trust Christ, God's will for you is to submit your life and future to Christ. Paul wrote, "I plead with you to give your bodies to God. Let them be a living and holy sacrifice—the kind he will accept. When you think of what he has done for you, is this too much to ask?" (Romans 12:1).

Be filled with the Spirit. Ephesians 5:17-18 says, "Don't act thoughtlessly, but try to understand what the Lord wants you to do. . . . Let the Holy Spirit fill and control you." God wants to permeate your life through the Spirit he put in you. It's God's will that you ask him to fill you day by day.

Obey your parents. God's no-doubt-about-it will for every student is that he or she live in obedience to parents (see Ephesians 6:1). One reason: God might choose to reveal his specific will to you through the advice and example of your dad or mom.

Stay sexually pure. You don't ever have to wonder if it's God's will for you to become sexually involved with your boyfriend or girlfriend. God has already shown his don't-miss-it will: "It is God's will that you should . . . avoid sexual immorality" (1 Thessalonians 4:3, NIV). If you have never been sexually active, stay that way until marriage. If you have been sexually active in the past or if you are sexually active now, determine to obey God's will in this area from now on.

Share your faith. You don't need to ask God, "Should I share my faith with others?" God has already revealed what he wants—for all believers. Jesus commanded, "Go and make disciples of all the nations" (Matthew 28:19). God's will is for you to share your faith with *all* nations—not just across the ocean but with those across the hall and the lunch table at school.

Whatever questions you face, by committing yourself to follow God's universal will you open the door for God to reveal his specific will for your life.

REFLECT: How are you doing in obeying God's universal will? Are you ready to start looking for his specific will?

PRAY: Talk to God about anything that gets in the way of doing his will.

19 God's Will, Your Desires—
They Fit

Bible Reading: Psalm 37:1-7
Take delight in the Lord, and he will give you your heart's desires.
Psalm 37:4

"I'M DOING all that universal-will stuff," Natalie says. "But I have to decide what school to attend and what major to declare and what classes to take. And I have my eye on this guy. Where does he fit into God's plans?"

If you're committed to following God's clear, universal will, it's time to dig in and discover God's specific will day by day. You can seek his plans for you through a four-step process:

1. *Seek God's will in the Bible.* Knowing Scripture is basic to looking for God's will. If your idea of God's specific will for you doesn't square with Scripture, then it's your will—not God's.
2. *Seek God's will in prayer.* Jesus taught his disciples to pray, "Our Father in heaven, . . . may your will be done here on earth, just as it is in heaven" (Matthew 6:9-10). God is willing to give you the direction you seek. Ask him for it daily—or as often as you need to!
3. *Seek God's will in the counsel of others.* God has put wise, mature Christians in your life to help you discern God's specific will. Your parents, other family members, youth leaders, or your pastor might fill that role. Mature believers can speak from a background of experiences you might lack—and their objectivity can keep you from being swayed by your emotions.
4. *Seek God's will in your circumstances.* God often directs you through outside circumstances beyond your control. If you have musical talents, being offered a scholarship to a top music school might give you a hint that you should pursue a career in music. But keep in mind that circumstances alone don't always clearly indicate God's will. The circumstances you see in your life must be balanced by Scripture, prayer, and the wise counsel of others.

Let's say you're living God's universal will—and you have sought his specific will in Scripture, prayer, counsel, and circumstances. So how do you decide what to do? It's simple. *Do what you want to do.* If you put God first in your life, he promises to give you the desires of your heart (see Psalm 37:4). And guess what? If what you want somehow doesn't line up with God's will, he will kindly make that clear to you.

REFLECT: Which steps to finding God's specific will do you have a handle on? Which do you need to put into practice?

PRAY: Spend a few moments now talking to God about his will in your life.

20 Love without Strings

Bible Reading: John 15:9-17
I command you to love each other in the same way that I love you.
John 15:12

THE SCRATCH MARK across Alondra's face was too big to cover up—but it made a great conversation starter. For her spring break, Alondra baby-sat and taught inner-city children. While her friends lounged on the beach, she cleaned up after babies. And when they came back to school to show off their tans, Alondra wondered if the scratch dug into her cheek by an angry five-year-old would leave a scar.

Have you heard of *agape* love? Agape (rhymes with "uh-SLOP-pay") is a Greek word in the New Testament that English Bibles translate simply as "love." Agape is love that's *of* God and *from* God. It's the love that gives without demanding anything in return. It's the love that makes the health, happiness, and growth of others as important to you as your own. And it's the kind of love that motivates students like Alondra to sacrifice time to take part in short-term mission projects—or to pull off countless other kind deeds every day.

C. S. Lewis calls agape "gift-love." God's gift of his Son supremely demonstrated his gift-love. John wrote, "This is real love. It is not that we loved God, but that he loved us and sent his Son as a sacrifice to take away our sins" (1 John 4:10).

You can exercise gift-love in two ways. Human-powered gift-love is generous and centered on others. But it always has strings attached to it. It loves those you find lovable and deserving—or whose needs tug hardest on your heart.

But you can also love with a God-powered gift-love. That's when God works in and through you to protect and provide for others. Only God's potent love can empower you to love anyone and everyone without strings—even people you don't find lovable, like enemies, social misfits, and grimy little kids. That's the level of love Jesus called us to when he said, "Love your enemies!" (Matthew 5:44); "Love your neighbor as yourself" (Matthew 22:39); and "Love each other in the same way that I love you" (John 15:12).

This is the kind of love that shouts all through Scripture. Paul was talking about God's gift-love when he instructed, "Live a life filled with love for others, following the example of Christ, who loved you and gave himself as a sacrifice to take away your sins" (Ephesians 5:2).

And John tells you how to keep loving even when it hurts: "Let us continue to love one another, for love comes from God," he wrote. "Since God loved us that much, we surely ought to love each other" (1 John 4:7, 11).

REFLECT: Are you learning to love others without strings as God exercises his divine gift-love through you?

PRAY: Talk to God today about the agape factor in your life.

You Don't Have to Be a Doormat

Bible Reading: John 2:13-17

The Lord disciplines those he loves, and he punishes those he accepts as his children. Hebrews 12:6

CHECK (✔) ANY statements that say what true agape love looks like:

☐ Lie down in the doorway at school on a rainy day so people can clean their shoes on you.

☐ Invite the clod who dings one door on your car to ding the other.

☐ Offer your former best friend your computer and printer so she can make posters that spread ugly rumors about you.

Those weren't too tough. Agape love doesn't obligate you to do any of those things. But you might still think agape love—God's gift-love—makes you into someone people can abuse. If that's what you think, you're missing a clear picture of love. Here are a few more points you need to know about agape.

First, *love involves discipline.* God is the flawlessly loving Father, yet he "disciplines those he loves, and he punishes those he accepts as his children" (Hebrews 12:6). In the same way, love confronts people who are out of line—like Christian friends involved in obvious sin—because confrontational love ultimately spares them the painful consequences of their misbehavior.

Second, *love can be tough.* Jesus—God's love in human form—unleashed anger at his opponents (see Mark 3:5), verbally blasted hypocrites (see Matthew 23), and physically chased greedy merchants out of the temple (see John 2). Love for your boss might require you to risk your job by confronting him or her about illegal business practices. Divine love is patient and kind, but it's anything but spineless.

Third, *love can fail.* You may remember from some wedding sermon the 1 Corinthians 13:8 phrase "Love never fails" (NIV). Actually, the right translation is "Love will last forever." The sad truth is this: Not everyone is won over by love. God loves unbelievers unendingly, but the reality of hell says untold numbers choose to spend eternity there.

God's perfect love working through you protects and provides for others, but the truth is your best efforts might fail to make a difference in their lives. You might empty yourself of time, energy, and resources protecting and providing for someone only to find she isn't interested. Then it's time to remind yourself that God has been in the same spot: Jesus loved his apostles, but one betrayed him (see John 17:12). And God loves the world (see John 3:16), but many run from him (see Matthew 7:13-14).

Don't give up doing love God's way.

REFLECT: What does agape love really mean?

PRAY: Ask God to help you love wisely.

22 Please Help Me; I'm Falling

Bible Reading: 1 Thessalonians 4:3-8
God has called us to be holy, not to live impure lives.
1 Thessalonians 4:7

KRISTIN SOUNDED feisty. "Some Christians make it sound like romance shouldn't exist," she fumed. "I've been going out with my boyfriend for six months. We're staying pure physically, my parents love him and his parents love me, we try hard not to let our relationship get in the way of school or other friends, and he's the best thing that's ever happened to my spiritual life. I admit it: I'm 'in love.' How can that be such a horrible thing?"

Physical attraction and sexual desire between guys and girls are natural. It's how God designed us. Solomon's poem, Song of Songs, celebrates the physical delights of marriage. The love story of Jacob and Rachel also puts physical love in a positive light, even in a culture where marriages were usually arranged by parents: "Rachel was beautiful in every way, with a lovely face and shapely figure. . . . Jacob was in love with Rachel" (Genesis 29:17-18).

Proverbs 5:18-19 is blunt: "Let your wife be a fountain of blessing for you. Rejoice in the wife of your youth. . . . Let her breasts satisfy you always. May you always be captivated by her love." The writer of Hebrews declares, "Marriage should be honored by all, and the marriage bed kept pure" (13:4, NIV). Make no mistake: In the Bible, falling in love, being in love, and enjoying the sexual dimension of love within marriage are gifts from God.

Physical love only becomes a problem when it is *misused*. Physical desire was designed to work best within God's boundaries. Even though a dating couple feels a huge pull of physical attraction, sexual activity is meant to be saved until marriage. Desire for someone other than a person's spouse must be turned away and not acted upon, and sex outside of marriage is sin (see 1 Thessalonians 4:3-8).

Here's why: Physical attraction and sexual desire aren't a sufficient foundation for a lasting, healthy relationship between a man and a woman. Sexual attraction can fade over time, and even the ability to perform sexually can quit because of illness or injury. A marriage dependent on erotic feelings and good sex is bound to fail. If a relationship is to succeed as a Christian marriage, it has to grow to include friendship and unselfish agape love.

"Hey, I'm not exactly thinking about marriage right now," you might say. That's fine. But if you're relating to people of the opposite sex, the same principles apply. In fact, if you put agape into action in your guy-girl relationships now, you'll be ready when marriage rockets to the top of your agenda.

REFLECT: When is romance wrong? When is it right?

PRAY: Tell God what you think of his gift of romance.

23 What the World Needs Is Love, God's Love

Bible Reading: Luke 19:1-10

I, the Son of Man, have come to seek and save those like him who are lost. Luke 19:10

PAUL EXITED the movie theater with some friends from the ski team and almost crashed into a group of guys from church. When Paul said hi to his church friends, they hit him with a look of disgust. Paul shrugged and kept walking, puzzling over the weird looks. *They must have been upset with me because of who I was with.*

Have you bumped into Christians who think it's wrong to have good friends who are unbelievers? Or do you feel that way? Where should you draw the line when it comes to having non-Christian friends?

When it comes to showing agape love, the Bible says, "If you love your neighbor, you will fulfill all the requirements of God's law" (Romans 13:8). As a Christian you are to make the health, happiness, and growth of *anyone* and *everyone* within your reach as important to you as your own.

Christians who think it's wrong to have good friends among unbelievers often quote James 4:4: "Don't you realize that friendship with this world makes you an enemy of God?" But that verse warns against buying into the world's *system* of believing and behaving, not befriending the world's *people*. Jesus spent so much time among unbelievers that he was mocked as a friend of sinners (see Luke 15:2). His openness to "sinners" like Zacchaeus was all part of his mission to "seek and save those like him who are lost" (Luke 19:10).

That mission of Jesus to save unbelievers gives you a huge clue about how to act in the world. If you can be friends with a non-Christian and keep up a positive influence for Christ, the relationship might be right. But if you are sucked into evil—if you are compromising Christian beliefs and behaviors—the friendship is most likely unhealthy.

There's more to think about with guy-girl relationships. The Scriptures are very clear: "Don't team up with those who are unbelievers. How can goodness be a partner with wickedness? How can light live with darkness?" (2 Corinthians 6:14). If you're a Christian and you date a non-Christian, the physical and sexual attraction can lead to an "unequal" partnership. You might think you can "missionary date" someone into God's kingdom. Don't fool yourself. If you are emotionally attached, you will do way better to remain single and pray for the salvation of that guy or girl than to risk a close relationship that may damage your faith.

REFLECT: Is there anything in your attitude toward having non-Christian friends that needs to change? What is it?

PRAY: *Dear Lord, I pray that my love for the non-Christians in my life will lead them to a loving relationship with you.*

24 Putting On a Show

Bible Reading: Luke 12:1-3
Beware of the yeast of the Pharisees—beware of their hypocrisy.
Luke 12:1

SARAH WAS an incredible actress—the darling of her eighth-grade drama class. She was an extrovert with a bubbly personality. Sarah's rise to stardom continued in high school, not just in drama but as the center attraction in everything she did. During her senior year, she was class president and prom queen.

Funny thing about Sarah, though. Hardly anyone knew her as a real person. She was an actress. From her flashy personality to her flamboyant signature in the yearbook, Sarah's classmates saw only Sarah the performer. Sarah the real person was camouflaged from their view.

All of us are like Sarah—to some extent, anyway. You probably learned early on to put on masks and disguise flaws you didn't want anyone to see. When we were little, most of us broke into the cookie jar—and then acted like an angel so mom wouldn't bust us. When we got older we maybe figured out how to turn on the charm and manipulate facts to get what we wanted.

Jesus calls that kind of behavior the "yeast of the Pharisees" or "hypocrisy." It's all about pretending to be something you're not—putting up a front to conceal your true identity. The Greek word actually means "play-acting," and first referred to Greek dramatists, who were famous for their masks. The Pharisees were the Bible's Oscar-winning hypocrites. Jesus said about them, "These people honor me with their lips, but their hearts are far away" (Mark 7:7). They put all their energy into looking religious in front of people, but they were only play-acting. Their relationship with God was fake.

So God doesn't want his people lurking behind masks. What is he looking for? He wants the opposite of a mask. He wants you to be see-through—transparent. A transparent person shows a completely honest face to himself, to others, and to God. You can see right through him because he's missing the mask.

Being transparent is especially indispensable for a Christian. You likely blow it on occasion—angry words, hateful deeds, failure, sin. The key to recovery from a bad situation isn't hypocrisy—hiding behind a mask. It's transparency—admitting to God and your Christian brothers and sisters that you're less than perfect and that you need forgiveness.

Easier said than done? Yes. But being transparent is the only way people can get to know and love the real you.

REFLECT: When have you been hidden behind a mask? Why does God not like that brand of hypocrisy?

PRAY: Ask God to help you become transparent.

25 Mountaintop High

Bible Reading: Mark 9:2-13
This is my beloved Son. Listen to him. Mark 9:7

THE KNOT in Jacki's stomach tied tighter and tighter during the long ride back from her youth group's winter retreat. "I want to stay up there," she moaned. "It's so easy to be a Christian. The teaching is great. Everyone tries to get along. And there's none of the hassles of living at home. Jesus is so real up there."

After a week of fun where Bible study, quiet times, and Christian friendships happen so easily, who would ever want to go back home to the tests, trials, and temptations of real life? It's so much easier to live on the mountaintop.

In Mark 9, Peter, James, and John got a taste of the "church-camp high" in a big way. As the Master's three disciples stared in amazement, Jesus' appearance changed drastically. Then Elijah and Moses showed up. Peter, a guy who never lacked something to say, stepped forward and awkwardly suggested they build three shrines to commemorate the glorious event. Then God spoke from the clouds, and the mountaintop experience stopped.

Isn't that the way it is when you get away with your Christian friends? Great music, a God-charged atmosphere—Christianity couldn't be easier. Everything is rosy and bright. But then, *thud!* Monday morning. Your alarm nags you out of bed, the clothes you want to wear are still dirty from camp, and your mom serves you oatmeal. The thrill is gone! Camp is over! Life with all its disgusting realities and conflicts is back.

It's a brutal fact of life that the only people who get to stay on the mountaintop are camp staff. For everyone else, it's back to the here-and-now.

But wait a minute! Take a look back at the mountain in Mark 9:9. There are *four* figures winding their way back to the valley from that peak experience. Peter, James, John—and Jesus! That's the truth you might forget when you slide down from camp, Bible study, or any other spiritual rush. Jesus isn't chained to a mountaintop lodge, chapel, or sanctuary. He journeys with you into everyday life to help you with nagging alarms, grungy clothes, and gloppy oatmeal.

The disciples were no doubt glad to climb to a mountaintop and glimpse a gloriously glowing Jesus. Those rare experiences can help charge your spiritual batteries and even permanently change you. But everyday life is lived in the trenches, not on the mountaintop. And if you just look around, that's where you find Jesus—hanging out in valleys, helping you live out the mountaintop glow.

REFLECT: What can you and your Christian friends do to make everyday life at home a little more like heaven?

PRAY: Tell Jesus thanks for being with you at home—and invite him to hang out with you in your valleys.

26 I Believe—Kind Of

Bible Reading: Mark 9:14-29

Anything is possible if a person believes. Mark 9:23

"WHY CAN'T you do something for the boy?" The scribe screams a taunt at the nine disciples. "You say the Rabbi has given you power to deliver the demon-possessed, but there you stand powerless while a boy suffers. Let's see some action here—or stop all this talk about being followers of the Son of God!"

In the shadows stands a sorrowful-looking man with his arms wrapped around a pale, thin boy with dark eyes and unkempt hair. Tears streak the father's weathered face. The boy rests his head on the father's chest—a blank stare in his shadowy eyes and saliva dripping from his chin.

Suddenly the argument stops. The crowd hushes as it turns in the direction of four approaching men—Peter, James, John, and Jesus. Recognizing Jesus, the father half-carries, half-drags his son forward and tells him the story behind the argument. As Jesus draws near, the boy stiffens and moans, and the evil spirit within him wrenches him into violent convulsions.

"Have mercy on us and help us," the father cries helplessly (Mark 9:22). Jesus encourages the man to have faith. But the confused father sobs piercing words: "I do believe, but help me not to doubt!" (verse 24).

Is that dad delirious? How can he say he believes and doesn't believe at the same time?

If you have followed Jesus for more than a few feet, you probably know the feeling: "Lord, I really believe in you and your power. But I'm having trouble trusting you in this mess." The statement isn't contradictory—it's reality! And Jesus responded to the dad's statement by healing the boy.

Faith is the ability to see and act on what God can do in a certain situation. Kim can "see" her friend Robin coming to Christ in the future, so she prays for Robin and invites her often to campus Bible study. Ian can "see" God work in his life as a result of quiet time alone with God, so he spends 10-15 minutes each morning reading his Bible and talking to God in prayer.

Faith looks ahead to see what God wants to do and then acts on what it sees. But how do you sharpen your vision to see what God wants to do? You start by soaking in Scripture. Romans 10:17 says, "Faith comes from listening to this message of good news—the Good News about Christ." The more of God's Word you get into you, the more clearly you will see where he's going and what he's doing. And your faith will grow as a result.

REFLECT: When have you felt torn between believing—and knowing you needed to believe more?

PRAY: Pray these words to God: "I do believe, but help me in my doubt!"

27 The Faith Factor

Bible Reading: Hebrews 11:1-6

What is faith? It is the confident assurance that what we hope for is going to happen. Hebrews 11:1

THE SAME Kim who can see her friend Robin becoming a Christian has a hard time seeing what God has to do with her schoolwork, so she worries about grades constantly. The Ian who sees God at work as a result of his quiet time sometimes thinks he alone is responsible for his financial needs, so he seldom gives any of his hard-earned cash to God in the church offering.

What kind of faith is that?

Faith is like the pitcher on a baseball team—you can't have much of a game without one. The Bible uses strong words to describe the role of faith in the Christian life: "It is impossible to please God without faith" (Hebrews 11:6); "It is through faith that a righteous person has life" (Romans 1:17); "Everything that does not come from faith is sin" (Romans 14:23, NIV). The apostle Paul said faith was one of the three great qualities in the Christian life—along with hope and love (see 1 Corinthians 13:13). You can't get along without faith.

But at times faith can be slippery. Sometimes your faith can peer into a situation and see God at work. Other times the eyelids of doubt, worry, or spiritual ignorance droop across the eyes of faith, blinding you to what God wants to do. Sometimes you can say, "I do believe!" But other times you beg God to help you trust that he really wants—and will do—what is good for you. If you ever feel stuck between belief and unbelief, you're normal.

God's Word flashes two pieces of encouragement as brightly as neon signs for us. First, God is the one who deals out faith to begin with (see Romans 12:3). You don't have to earn it or buy it. God gives it. Second, faith grows when you dig into the Word of God (see Romans 10:17). As you bury yourself in God's Word through reading, studying, memorizing, and sharing the Bible, you can expect your faith to have more "I do believe" and less "Help me in my unbelief."

Rest assured: Jesus' disciples—even though they watched him up close and personal for three years—were often short on faith. Can you imagine? With their own eyes they saw Jesus raise the dead, heal the sick, calm the storm, and cast out demons—and they still struggled with faith.

When you wish you had bigger trust in God, pray these words straight from the mouths of Jesus' closest disciples, and be confident God will grow your faith in him: "We need more faith; tell us how to get it" (Luke 17:5).

REFLECT: How are you going to grow in faith? What is God's plan to help?

PRAY: Say thanks to God for providing the Bible to build your faith.

28 Serving God Hands Down

Bible Reading: Mark 9:43-50

If your hand causes you to sin, cut it off. Mark 9:43

THIS NEXT story actually happened. Really.

Two police officers spotted a young man staggering along the roadside carrying a Bible under one arm. The other arm was tucked tightly under the Bible in an attempt to stem the flow of heavy bleeding—where the man had chopped off his own hand!

Yes, you read that right. The guy had cut off his own hand. He said he lopped it off to obey Mark 9:43: "If your hand causes you to sin, cut it off." Apparently his hand had touched something or taken something it shouldn't have, so he took Jesus' words literally and whacked off the offending member. Fortunately the police officers were able to retrieve the severed hand from a trash can, and doctors sewed it back on.

The point? You had better know what the Bible *means,* not just what it *says.* If you took Jesus' commands in this section literally, you and I and every believer alive would need to get in line for several amputations! Who hasn't ever sinned with their eyes (lusting, coveting), hands (stealing, hitting), or feet (walking where they shouldn't)? If you did exactly what the Bible said in this spot, you would need artificial limbs.

Jesus was exaggerating for effect and emphasis. People do this all the time: "I've told you a million times." "I was so embarrassed I could have died." "I could eat a horse." The statements aren't literally true but overstated to drive home the point that we were really, *really* annoyed, embarrassed, hungry, defensive, etc.

The real point Jesus was driving home wasn't that you should whack off body parts left and right. It was that you have two ways to use your physical body—*for* God's purposes or *against* God's purposes. If your goal is to serve God, and you let your body do things that don't please him, your body has become your enemy. Jesus wants you, his follower, to give to him not just your soul but your eyes, hands, feet, and every other part of you.

Paul put it this way: "I plead with you to give your bodies to God" (Romans 12:1). God isn't interested in watching you chop yourself to sinlessness, but rather he wants you to discipline your physical body to match your spiritual commitment. It's not a lot easier, but it's a lot less bloody!

REFLECT: How are you using your body to serve God?

PRAY: *God, I want to honor you with my body. Help me discipline my physical body to match my spiritual commitment.*

July

29 The Dating Game

Bible Reading: Galatians 5:16-18
> *Live according to your new life in the Holy Spirit. Then you won't*
> *be doing what your sinful nature craves. Galatians 5:16*

JOSHUA AND KAYLA were masters at hiding their relationship from their parents. They snuck around and built a relationship on high-pressure lip locks. Joshua thought it was true love. When the parents of this high school sophomore found out he was going steady with Kayla—and communicated their disapproval—he pouted. "If we ever break up," he hollered, "it will be your fault!" But a month later when Kayla dumped Joshua, he wondered if he had just wasted half a year on a girl who drained his wallet and then ditched him.

Do you want to come out a winner in your experience with love? If so, here are five massively important questions to ask yourself about dating.

1. Am I mature enough to date? A person isn't ready to date until she has developed the character—spiritual, emotional, and physical—to look a person who is pressuring her straight in the eyes, say "No," and put off immediate gratification. Sex is fun, especially in God's timing and context. But it takes maturity to say "no" now so you can say "yes" to something better later in life.

2. What kind of person will I not date? Will you date—even once—someone whose moral convictions and choices are significantly different from yours? If you will, you're headed for situations where you might face great pressure to compromise your own standards.

3. What are my standards for physical affection? Here's where maturity—or immaturity—shines through. It's easy to tell yourself, "Hey, I'm not going to do anything stupid. But I can at least enjoy myself." There's nothing particularly wrong with that, but in a world that often promotes warped sexual values, it's tough to think straight. If you think enjoying yourself means lots of physical affection, and if getting physical is a high priority in dating, you might not be ready.

4. How will I control my passions? To be ready to date, you have to be prepared to control the sexual passions God means for you to unleash only in marriage. That can get tough for some people. The best thing you can do is set your standards long before you head out on your first date. Decide now to avoid any situation or event that will get you sexually heated.

5. If I blow it, what will I do? Admit that you blew it, be restored through honest repentance and forgiveness, and commit yourself to standards of purity.

 REFLECT: What are you doing to win at love God's way?

PRAY: Tell God what is going on in your love life—and how you would like him to guide and guard you.

30 Your Route of Escape

Bible Reading: Proverbs 7:21-27

Don't let your hearts stray away toward [an immoral woman]. Don't wander down her wayward path. Proverbs 7:25

IT'S NO SECRET that sexual desires are potent. And like a young guy named Mitch found out, they can blow up on you if you aren't careful. That's just as true for girls as it is for guys.

Mitch's first mistake was deciding to satisfy his growing curiosity about sex in the same ways most of his friends were—by staring at all the sex magazines and videos he could get his hands on. He told himself it was okay because he would find out everything he wanted to know about women and sexuality, and his curiosity would then be satisfied. Since he wasn't fooling around himself, he thought he could become wise about sex without sinning.

But the only thing Mitch accomplished was filling his mind with twisted ideas about sex. When he dated, he could hardly help imagining trying out what he had read about and seen. Instead of satisfying his curiosity, the "information" he stored in his brain from magazines and movies produced huge battles with guilt.

There's hardly anyone who can claim to be out of reach of the temptations Mitch faced. How can you avoid getting snagged in the same snare?

First, promise yourself that no matter what you ever feel or do sexually, you will find someone—like a parent or a mature friend—to talk to when you need information or just need to talk. Big hint: Find someone other than your friends, who are going through the same pains you are.

Second, get out your Bible and concordance—or a Bible software program—and search under all the headings like "lust," "passions," and "sexual immorality." Write out what you learn on note cards and read through these cards at least once a week—more often if your feelings about sex are out of line with how God sees the subject.

Third, write a private note to yourself. On the left half of the page, spell out the specific standards and commitments you want to keep and why. On the right side, write down the best plan you can think of for escaping when you are tempted to sin sexually. You can't count on having clear, creative thinking when you're in the middle of intense temptation. That's nearly impossible. But it's amazing how God will remind you of what you wrote down earlier as a way of escape.

Guys and girls choose all kinds of ways to quench their curiosity about sex. Friends may pressure you to join them in actions that mess up your mind—and your body. But by choosing your *own*, better way to handle sexual pressure, you gain genuine independence. You grab hold of your God-given freedom to choose.

REFLECT: What are you going to do to avoid being hooked by sexual snares?

PRAY: Ask God to help you set biblical sexual standards—and keep them.

31 Good Reasons to Wait

Bible Reading: 1 John 2:15-17
The world offers only the lust for physical pleasure, the lust for everything we see, and pride in our possessions. These are not from the Father. 1 John 2:16

YOU HAVE NO doubt figured out that waiting until marriage to have sex keeps you free of sexually transmitted diseases—and keeps you close to Jesus.

But are there any other reasons to wait? Absolutely!

1. Premarital sex can make the rest of a relationship disappear. When your dates focus on the physical, you miss out on the rest of the relationship—discovering who each person is, what each personality is like, and what a really caring friendship can be.

2. Premarital sex can take away the specialness of sex in marriage. That's especially true when one partner enters marriage as a virgin and the other doesn't.

3. Premarital sex can decrease self-esteem. At first a sexual relationship can give you a false sense of feeling accepted and special. But when you realize that's a lie, you feel let down—a feeling that can take years to overcome.

4. Premarital sex can leave deep scars. Sex always gives some special part of yourself. And when a couple breaks up, it leaves an emotional scar tough to erase.

5. Premarital sex can lead to unwanted pregnancies and abortions. No method of birth control is 100 percent effective. So the pregnancy that you think only happens to other people could happen to you.

6. Premarital sex can lead to comparisons in marriage. Sex is supposed to get better and better as a marriage matures. But if one partner enters marriage with "experience," he or she usually has flashbacks. It's almost impossible not to draw comparisons to previous experiences—and that can lead to serious difficulties.

7. Premarital sex can tear down trust. Marriage partners who know their spouse didn't save sex for marriage often wonder whether their partner is being faithful.

8. Premarital sex can lead to sexual addiction. Sexual addiction might sound like a joke—but it produces pain and personal destruction.

9. Premarital sex can destroy freedom. The big lie is that freedom means doing what you want, when you want, with whomever you want. In reality, that's lawlessness, not freedom. True freedom is having the capacity to do right, which means saving sex for yourself and your spouse until marriage.

It's worth it to wait, don't you think?

REFLECT: Why is it worth keeping sex until marriage?

PRAY: Thank God for his great gift of sex and invite him to keep these reasons to wait fresh in your mind.

1 Call Them "The Ten Freedoms"

Bible Reading: Exodus 20:1-17
I lavish my love on those who love me and obey my commands.
Exodus 20:6

HERMAN THE CRAB stormed across the ocean floor and under the family rock. "I want to be free!" he screamed at his father. "I don't see how you can expect me to wear this stupid shell twenty-four hours a day. It's confining. It's cramped."

His father, Fred, placed a claw on Herman's shoulder. "Son," he said, "let me tell you a story about Harold the human."

"Dad, not another—"

"Harold wanted to go barefoot to school," Fred continued. "He complained that his shoes were too confining. He longed to be free to run barefoot through the grass. Finally, his mother gave in to him. He skipped out of the house—and stepped on the pieces of a broken soda bottle. His foot required twenty stitches."

"That's a dumb story, Dad," Herman said.

"Maybe, Son, but the point is this: Every crab has felt life would be a lot better if he could be free of the shell. Well, your time will come soon." The young crab looked surprised. "It's called molting, and all crabs do it as they grow up. But when that happens, you will be more vulnerable than at any other time in your life. Until your new shell hardens like this one"—he tapped his son's armored back—"you have to be more careful and more watchful than usual. Without this shell, you'll be less free—not more."

"That's weird, Dad," Herman said. "Some things seem to limit freedom, but really they make greater freedom possible, right?"

Fred draped his claw over Herman's back. "How did you get so smart, Son?"

Some people think the Ten Commandments and the teachings of Jesus rob them of freedom. They see God's rules as restrictions on their freedom, like Herman viewed his shell. Actually, though, God's directions release true freedom in the lives of those who follow them. For example, obeying the sixth commandment, "Do not commit adultery" (Exodus 20:14), provides freedom from sexually transmitted diseases.

Because of the benefits God provides, you could just as easily call the Ten Commandments the Ten Freedoms. And Jesus' teaching in Matthew 5:1-12 provides incredible freedom if you respond to it. Obeying his words in Matthew 5:4, "God blesses those who mourn, for they will be comforted," assures you freedom from being alone when you are hurt. Or Matthew 5:8, "God blesses those whose hearts are pure, for they will see God," tells you that when you stick close to God, you will learn even more from him.

REFLECT: Do you sometimes feel a little confined and restricted as a Christian?

PRAY: Thank God today for the freedoms he provides for you in his Word.

2 It Sure Feels like Love

Bible Reading: Ephesians 5:25-33

You husbands must love your wives with the same love Christ showed the church. Ephesians 5:25

"THERE I WAS in a crowd of guys down in the school commons on the first day of school, talking about, well, you know, what guys talk about. Then all of a sudden she walks in. I knew the second she glided into school that she was the girl for me. She was perfect. Blonde hair to her shoulders, a tan like she just walked off the beach, and a figure that made any seventeen-year-old guy like me a stammering fool.

"I fell in love. Love at first sight. Well, it was for me, anyway. It took a while, but I finally got a date with her. Things just kind of happened after that. Eventually we were married, had kids, and lived happily ever after."

Ahhh—that's how it happens. True love. Love at first sight. Bitten by the love bug. Sometimes you can look at a girl or a guy and just *know* you have found your love, your life's mate.

Dream on. Sure, it happens that way once in a while. But it can be dangerous to think those exceptions are typical of true love. You might think of love first and foremost as a feeling: a rush of emotion, butterflies in your stomach, stars in your eyes. But the Bible talks about love as an action—not simply something you *feel* but something you *do.*

Loads of people imagine love is like the New World was to Columbus: You're not looking for it, but all of a sudden you smash into it! Actually, love is more like a fragrant flower: You plant a seed, water it, nurture it, and weed out the things that threaten it—and if you care for that seed for days, weeks, and months, then later it blossoms. It keeps growing and blooming as long as you feed and water it.

Missing that truth might be why so many relationships fail: Nobody is prepared to *work* at love. Nobody thinks you need to water the seed. Nobody expects storms that threaten to uproot the seedling. Nobody tends the soil. And so few people ever enjoy love in full flower.

Paul couldn't have made the active quality of love any more obvious when he told husbands to love their wives just as Christ loved the church. Exactly how did Christ love the church? He gave his life for her.

You might still feel a rush of attraction when a tall blonde walks by. You might feel woozy when the captain of the football team notices you. But that's not love. It's exciting, but it's not the same as actually loving someone and watching that love grow and blossom into a sweet-scented flower. That's the kind of love God has for you, and it's the kind he wants to nurture in you for others.

REFLECT: What does "love at first sight" have to do with real love?

PRAY: Ask God for patience as you wait for—and work at—true love.

3 The Human Solution

Bible Reading: Acts 4:11-12
> *There is salvation in no one else! There is no other name in all of heaven for people to call on to save them. Acts 4:12*

ZACHARY AND CHRIS stopped in front of a half-price book table in the mall. A man at the cash register smiled at the guys. "Let me know if I can help you with anything," he said.

"Look at this." Zachary held a thick book titled *Isaac Asimov's Guide to the Bible.* "I've heard of this guy," he said.

The bookseller leaned over the table. "That's an excellent book. It's full of facts about the Flood and the parting of the Red Sea, and it also says a lot about what the Bible *doesn't* tell you. It shows how biblical myth and history fit into the larger picture of human history."

"Uh-huh," Chris said, nodding at the guy. Then he took the book from Zachary and laid it on the table. "Let's go," he said.

"What's with you?" Zachary asked when they had walked a few steps. "Why did you drop the book and run? It *was* about the Bible."

Chris shrugged. "I don't know. Something just wasn't right."

Chris's reaction was wise. He had bumped head-on into secular humanism, a philosophy that is often hard to spot. It's a way of seeing the world that stands against the Bible, Christians, and the church. Humanists believe that the world can only be saved by humankind. God cannot save people, they reason, because God does not exist. Religion can't save people, they say, because religion is a lie. Humanity shouldn't look to heaven for salvation, peace, and fulfillment, but to itself.

Humanists believe that the only hope for personal fulfillment and a better world is in putting faith in human ingenuity. They think humans need none of God's help to save themselves and their world from evil.

But humanists live in a dream world. Human history illustrates that, for all our technological progress, the human race isn't exactly becoming increasingly good and kind. Humanity is not perfecting peace or eliminating war. One look at the last century—two world wars, Hitler, Stalin, the Khmer Rouge, Idi Amin, the KKK, the proliferation of nuclear weapons, famine, and oppression—shows that hope placed in humankind alone is hope misplaced.

Of course, humans need to strive to erase war and famine, to fight disease and injustice. But we can't rescue ourselves. Humanity's only hope for salvation is the Savior, Jesus Christ.

REFLECT: Be able to explain it to a friend: What is secular humanism? What's wrong with that belief system?

PRAY: Invite God to guard your mind by teaching you to discern truth from lies.

4 Make Sure You Have the Basic Equipment

Bible Reading: 2 Timothy 3:10-17

All Scripture is inspired by God and is useful to teach us what is true and to make us realize what is wrong in our lives. It straightens us out and teaches us to do what is right. 2 Timothy 3:16

YOU WAKE UP on the morning of your sixteenth birthday and stumble into the kitchen for breakfast. Your mom greets you with a kiss and a cheery "Happy Birthday!" Then she adds, "There's something out in the driveway for you!"

You race outside with your mom right behind you. You stop a few feet from the driveway and stare. "It's not new," Mom says, nodding to the car in the driveway, "but it has a CD player that works, just like you wanted."

You look at your mom and then back at the car. "But where are the wheels?"

You get closer to the car. "And there's no steering wheel either!"

"But look at that CD player," Mom announces proudly. "Pretty neat, huh?"

You pop the hood to take a look. "There's no engine!" you bellow.

"You didn't say you wanted all those things," she says in a huff. "You just said you wanted a car with a CD player that works."

"Mom!" You're trying not to shout. "It has to have 'all those things.' If it doesn't, it's not a car. It's just . . . it's just a piece of junk!"

No one expects a car to work without tires, a steering wheel, and an engine. Without that basic equipment you really *are* the owner of a piece of junk.

It's the same with finding a trustworthy way to help you decide issues of right and wrong. You need a standard. And a true standard requires some basic equipment, or it's no standard at all—just a piece of junk.

First, a true standard of right and wrong has to be *objective,* meaning it exists independently of what you or any other person thinks or feels. You might consider stealing wrong, but your neighbor might not. Without an objective standard, how can you tell your neighbor not to swipe your big-screen TV?

Second, a true standard of right and wrong must be *universal,* applying to all people in all places. You may consider it wrong to abuse children, but if another culture in the world disagrees, who is to say that culture is wrong?

Third, a true standard of right and wrong is *constant,* meaning it doesn't change. If standards change, you never know what the rules are. What is right in one generation may be wrong in the next.

Someone uniquely loving and smart knew that you would need an objective, universal, and constant standard to teach you the truth and help you tell right from wrong. God didn't plop you on this planet without a reliable guide for making right choices. He gave you the Bible as your flawless map to life.

REFLECT: Why does God give you these flawless standards of right and wrong?

PRAY: Thank God today for loving you enough to teach you right from wrong.

5 I Love Your Book! May I Have Your Autograph?

Bible Reading: John 1:1-5, 14

The Word became human and lived here on earth among us. John 1:14

SIXTEEN-YEAR-OLD soccer fanatic Lucy Chavez had dominated her age group every year in the park league. Now she was dreaming that some day she would play soccer in the Olympics. But the competition kept getting tougher, and Lucy knew she had to play smarter just to stay ahead.

Then she discovered that her idol, Olympic soccer star Erin Dupree, had just published a book about soccer. In a snap Lucy ordered the book online for overnight delivery. It was the most comprehensive approach to soccer Lucy had ever seen. It was so complicated that Lucy sometimes gave up in frustration when she tried to read it. The information was there, but she wasn't getting it.

One day during soccer practice, her coach called out to her from the sideline. "Lucy," she hollered, "you need to plant your foot more ahead of the ball." When Lucy turned to acknowledge her coach, she saw another woman standing beside her—Erin Dupree. "Erin and I grew up together," Coach explained. "She's in town on a book-signing tour this week and wanted to check out the team. Erin suggested the correction I just gave you."

"Your coach has told me a lot about you," the former Olympian said, "and I like what I see. I would love to talk with you about your game. Can we get together after practice a few days this week?"

Can you imagine Lucy saying something like, "Thanks for the offer, but I have to hurry home from practice every day to study your book"? Not likely.

Unless Lucy has taken one too many headers, that girl will jump at the chance to get to know the author. What better way to understand a book than to have the author right there to explain it?

Understanding the Bible and having its truth really come alive to you happens the same way. You need a personal relationship with the author, the one John calls "the Word." That's right—the Bible you read *and* Jesus Christ its author are *both* called the Word of God. In Revelation, John describes Christ this way: "His name is the Word of God" (19:13, NIV).

Whenever you open your Bible, you are getting involved with God's *written* Word and his *living* Word. You are sitting down with the one who embodies the words you are reading, one who is eager to help you understand and put into action what he wrote.

REFLECT: Are you taking advantage of God's offer to teach you from his Word?

PRAY: Spend some time thanking God for getting so personally involved in sharing his Word with you.

6 There'll Be Some Changes Made

Bible Reading: John 17:9-21

*Make them pure and holy by teaching them your words of truth.
John 17:17*

PA AND MA had spent their whole lives raising five sons in the backwoods, completely out of touch with modern culture and its technological advances. But now Pa reckoned it was time to see what city life was like. So he hitched their old, tired horse, Nellie, to the buggy, loaded the family in, and headed for the bright lights and skyscrapers of the big city.

Arriving in the heart of downtown, Pa and Ma and the boys wandered the streets, mouths dropped at the modern conveniences of the twenty-first century. Eventually they stepped into the lobby of a posh hotel to look around.

Pa's attention was immediately drawn to a tiny little room with shiny brass doors. He watched with interest as a frumpy old lady walked up to the doors and pushed a button. Soon the brass doors slid open, the old lady stepped in, and the doors closed again. Pa watched curiously as lighted numbers flashed above. Then the doors opened and a gorgeous young woman in a tailored suit stepped out.

Pa's eyes bugged with astonishment. "Boys," he said to his sons excitedly, "go and get Nellie."

Don't you wish transformation was that easy—step into a little room, push a few buttons, and step out completely changed? Most Christians wish their sinful thought patterns and habits would magically disappear, making them pure and holy. You read verses like 1 Thessalonians 4:3, "God wants you to be holy," and God's command in 1 Peter 1:16, "You must be holy because I am holy." You ache to follow God's instructions, but by the end of practically every day your actions and attitudes slap you in the face, reminding you how unholy and impure you are. *If getting pure and holy is up to me,* you might think, *it's never going to happen.*

Do you realize that Jesus prayed about your struggle only hours before he was crucified? He asked his Father to make you pure and holy. How? Look again at his prayer in John 17:17: "Make them pure and holy by teaching them your words of truth." David understood this principle, writing, "How can a young person stay pure? By obeying your word and following its rules" (Psalm 119:9).

Every time you dig into and digest God's words of truth, Christ's prayer for purity is being answered in you. Purity happens when you daily welcome God's Word into your life. The transformation might not be as quick and dramatic as the wonder Pa thought that little room with the shiny brass doors could work. But you *are* being changed, because that's what Jesus prayed for.

REFLECT: How does it make you feel that Jesus would pray for your purity— and that God would send his Word so it could happen?

PRAY: Tell God how you feel about his support.

7 No Pain, No Gain

Bible Reading: Hebrews 4:12-13

The word of God is full of living power. It is sharper than the sharpest knife, cutting deep into our innermost thoughts and desires. Hebrews 4:12

"HOW BAD is it, Doc?" the patient asks. "Tell me the truth."

"I'm afraid it's bad—very bad," the doctor replies. "If I don't perform major surgery and remove the tumor, you will die in a matter of weeks."

"I don't want surgery, Doc. It will hurt."

The doctor smiles. "You won't feel a thing during the surgery."

"But there will be pain after the surgery, maybe for weeks, right?"

"We have medications to reduce the pain."

"But the incision will still hurt a little and the shots will hurt."

"Well, yes, there is always some pain involved in a major—"

The patient interrupts. "No surgery then. I don't like owies."

"Owies? You're whining like a three-year-old! Get a hold of yourself, man! Nobody likes pain, but I'm afraid it's unavoidable."

The patient shakes his head. "It *is* avoidable, because I won't have surgery."

"I don't think you understand," the surgeon says with a look of shock. "You have a choice: Four to five weeks of *minor* pain and discomfort followed by many years of pain-free life, or four to five weeks of pain-free life followed by *major* pain, as in death. Are you telling me that you would cut short your own life to avoid a little pain?"

"I'm saying I hate pain, and surgery is painful, so I'm not having surgery."

If you're normal, you make it a rule in your life to avoid pain whenever possible. But no sane person shies away from the surgeon's life-saving knife because he's scared it will cause an owie. You know that sometimes pain produces something good, whether it's the pain of a must-do medical procedure, the effort of a sweaty fitness workout, or the agony of attending your little brother's tuba recital when you would rather be hanging with your friends.

God's Word can hurt too. The writer of Hebrews pictures God's Word as a surgeon's scalpel. God, the master surgeon, knows exactly where cancers of wrong thoughts and desires lurk. And he knows that those diseases will destroy you if they aren't sliced out. His Word is the instrument he uses to cut you open, bring those issues to light, and show you how to get rid of them.

So whenever you read the Bible and feel the pain of God's scalpel digging in to convict or correct you, don't pull away. The Great Physician only allows the hurt because he loves you and wants to help you to spiritual health.

REFLECT: How is God using his Word like a scalpel in your life? Are you pulling away or letting him do his healing work?

PRAY: Thank your Lord today for sending his Word to heal you.

8 Make Yourself at Home

Bible Reading: Colossians 3:12–17
Let the words of Christ, in all their richness, live in your hearts and make you wise. Colossians 3:16

BACK IN 1909, nineteen-year-old Robert F. Stroud, a laborer with no formal education, shot and killed a man in Juneau, Alaska. He was sentenced to twelve years in prison. Two years later he assaulted a fellow inmate with a knife, adding another six months to his term. Five years later he killed a prison guard in the dining room with an ice pick. Altogether, Robert Stroud spent more than fifty years of his life in prison for his crimes, forty-three of them in solitary confinement or isolation. He died at age seventy-three.

Yet people don't remember Robert Stroud as a murderer. Early in his prison career, Stroud became interested in birds, supposedly when a stray canary flitted into his prison cell. With the prison's permission, he began raising birds in his tiny living space. When birds became sick, he requested books on bird diseases and doctored them back to health. As the years passed, he continued to study birds and bird diseases and eventually became one of the world's biggest authorities on the subject— all while serving a life sentence for murder.

Robert Stroud's life story was dramatized in a 1962 film starring actor Burt Lancaster. Since part of Stroud's sentence was served in the infamous Alcatraz Prison in San Francisco Bay, the film was titled *Birdman of Alcatraz*.

How did the murderer from Alaska become the Birdman of Alcatraz? It all began when he turned his prison cell into a home for little birds. As he cared about these creatures and devoted himself to curing them, he changed. And even though he spent most of his life in prison paying for his crimes, he is most famous as a birdman, not a murderer.

Get this: Whatever you make a home for in your life will influence you big-time. If you constantly entertain yourself with music, videos, and Web sites that glorify the nastier sides of your culture, you are giving that stuff a home in your life. And like it or not, whatever you welcome into your life as a roommate eventually starts bossing you around. An old proverb states, "You can't keep the birds from flying over your head, but you can keep them from making a nest in your hair." You have control over the things you allow to live inside you.

According to Colossians 3:16, the Word of God is a good choice to let nest in you. When you let God's Word into your life as a permanent resident, it changes you. God's Word will make you more like him.

REFLECT: What sorts of things are you letting nest in your heart?

PRAY: Talk to God today about your desire to let his words live in you and change your life.

9 Yesterday, Today, and Forever

Bible Reading: 1 Peter 1:21-25

The grass withers, and the flowers fall away. But the word of the Lord will last forever. 1 Peter 1:24-25

YOU'RE A contestant on TV's newest game show, *Answer These Dumb Questions and Win a Dumb Prize.* Answer this question right and you win something really big. Well, not really. But can you number the following items in order of newest to oldest (1 being *newest,* 9 being *oldest*)? Ready? Go!

a. The pyramids of Gaza
b. Your grandfather's first car
c. Your math teacher
d. Mount Everest
e. The first Star Wars movie
f. Noah's ark
g. Your mom's hair style
h. God's Word
i. Sputnik, the first orbiting satellite

If you picked God's Word for anything but number nine—oldest of the old—kiss your prize bye-bye. The Bible says, "In the beginning the Word already existed" (John 1:1). God's Word was here before anything. True, God's *written* Word as we know it has only been around since the Bible appeared on scrolls several millennia ago. But God's *living* Word has always existed, because Jesus Christ—"the Word"— has always existed. Nothing comes before God and his Word, because they have no beginning.

Now look at the list of nine items again and circle the one you think will be here the longest. Sure, Mount Everest should hang tight for a long time. But if you didn't circle God's Word, you probably skipped over today's verse: "The word of the Lord will last forever" (1 Peter 1:25). Like God himself, his Word is eternal. It has no beginning and no end. You might pass your Bible on to your grandchildren some day. That book will eventually fall apart and turn to dust, but the Good News about Christ written in those pages will stick around beyond the end of time.

Bottom line: God's Word was changing lives and healing hearts for thousands of years before you were born, and it will be here long after you leave planet Earth. It's the right answer for all the big questions of life.

REFLECT: God loves you so much that he made sure you would have his Word. How should you respond to that?

PRAY: Thank God now that his Word lasts forever.

10 The Jesus Question

Bible Reading: 1 Timothy 2:1-6

*There is only one God and one Mediator who can reconcile God
and people. He is the man Christ Jesus. 1 Timothy 2:5*

SO WHO IS Jesus Christ?

People through the ages have fought over that question—often with words,
sometimes even with weapons. Why so much conflict over one individual? Why is it
that his name, more than the name of any other religious leader, causes irritation?
Why is it that you can talk about "God" and nobody minds, but as soon as you say
"Jesus," people often want to stop the conversation or get defensive?

How is Jesus different from the other religious leaders? Why don't the names of
Buddha, Muhammad, or Confucius upset people? Because the others didn't claim to
be God, but Jesus did.

It didn't take long for people who knew Jesus to realize that he was making some
astounding claims about himself. He claimed to be more than just a prophet or
teacher—he obviously claimed to be God himself. He presented himself as the only
way to a relationship with God the Father, the only source of forgiveness for sins,
and the only way of salvation.

For many people, that's too exclusive and too narrow to believe. Yet the issue
isn't what we think or believe, but rather who Jesus claimed to be. What does the
New Testament tell us?

Jesus Christ is actually a name and a title. The name *Jesus* comes from the Greek
form of the name *Jeshua* or Joshua, meaning "Jehovah-Savior" or "the Lord saves."
The title *Christ* is derived from the Greek word for Messiah and means "anointed
one." The title *Christ* captures two offices—king and priest—affirming Jesus as the
promised priest and king of the Old Testament prophecies. That declaration is crucial
to understanding Jesus and Christianity.

Jesus received honor and worship that only God should receive. In a confrontation with Satan, Jesus said, "You must worship the Lord your God; serve only him"
(Matthew 4:10). Yet Jesus received worship as God (see Matthew 14:33; 28:9) and
sometimes even demanded to be worshiped as God (see John 5:23; also Hebrews 1:6;
Revelation 5:8-14).

Maybe you've heard the phrase "the deity of Christ." That phrase means he's divine. He's the Creator and Sustainer of the universe come to earth as a person, Jesus
of Nazareth. He's the God who created you. Jesus is your best friend, but he's even
more than a good friend. He's God.

REFLECT: Explain it to a non-Christian friend: Who is Jesus?

PRAY: You can enjoy Jesus, relate to Jesus, learn from Jesus—but don't forget
to worship Jesus as God. Do that now as you pray.

11 Those Who Knew Him Best

Bible Reading: John 11:25-27

I have always believed you are the Messiah, the Son of God, the one who has come into the world from God. John 11:27

YOU CAN GET a huge clue about who Jesus is by checking what his followers thought of him. Even though most of the people close to him were devout Jews—worshipers of the one true God—they recognized Jesus as God in human form.

The apostle Paul had been trained as a rabbi, making it absolutely unlikely he would worship a guy from Nazareth and call him Lord and God. But Paul acknowledged Jesus—the Lamb of God—as God when he said, "Be sure that you feed and shepherd God's flock—his church, purchased with his blood—over whom the Holy Spirit has appointed you as elders" (Acts 20:28).

When Christ said to Peter, "Who do you say I am?" Peter said this: "You are the Messiah, the Son of the living God" (Matthew 16:15-16). Jesus answered Peter's confession not by correcting his conclusion but by acknowledging its truth—and its source: "You are blessed, Simon son of John, because my Father in heaven has revealed this to you" (verse 17).

Jesus' close friend Martha said to him, "I have always believed you are the Messiah, the Son of God, the one who has come into the world from God" (John 11:27). Then there was Nathanael, who thought nothing good could come out of Nazareth. He acknowledged that Jesus was "the Son of God—the King of Israel" (John 1:49).

While Stephen was being stoned, he prayed, "Lord Jesus, receive my spirit" (Acts 7:59), acknowledging Jesus as God. The writer of Hebrews called Christ God when he wrote, "But to his Son he says, 'Your throne, O God, endures forever and ever'" (Hebrews 1:8). John the Baptist announced the coming of Jesus by saying that "the Holy Spirit descended on him in the form of a dove. And a voice from heaven said, 'You are my beloved Son, and I am fully pleased with you'" (Luke 3:22).

Then of course there's the confession of Thomas, a.k.a. "Doubting Thomas." After seeing the risen Christ and touching his wounds, he said, "My Lord and my God!" (John 20:28). Jesus accepted Thomas's acknowledgment of him as God. He rebuked Thomas for his unbelief—but not for his worship.

Those who knew Jesus best realized he was more than just a man. They accepted him as Messiah, God come to earth as a man just as the Old Testament Scriptures foretold. Were they sure? Well, they worshiped him. They obeyed him. And like Stephen, many of them died for the One who had died for them.

REFLECT: There's an old saying that Christ isn't Lord at all unless he's Lord of all. Is he Lord in your life today?

PRAY: Talk to Jesus about letting him take control as Lord of your life.

12 He Is Who He Says He Is

Bible Reading: John 10:22-33
The Father and I are one. John 10:30

"JESUS DIDN'T really claim to be God," Alexis argued across the table. "So what if people around him said he was God? His followers just made up what they wanted to believe about him. Jesus himself never said anything about being God."

Despite the arguments of people like Alexis, it isn't hard to spot places in the New Testament where Jesus claimed his own deity. One businessman who scrutinized the Scriptures to see whether or not Christ claimed to be God put it this way: "For anyone to read the New Testament and not conclude that Jesus claimed to be divine, he would have to be as blind as a man standing outdoors on a clear day saying he can't see the sun."

One example: In the Gospel of John you see a conflict between Jesus and some Jews—a confrontation triggered by Jesus' curing a lame man on the Sabbath and then telling him to go for a celebration hike with his bedroll. "So the Jewish leaders began harassing Jesus for breaking the Sabbath rules. But Jesus replied, 'My Father never stops working, so why should I?' So the Jewish leaders tried all the more to kill him. In addition to disobeying the Sabbath rules, he had spoken of God as his Father, thereby making himself equal with God" (John 5:16-18).

You would think that a healing would cause everyone to throw a party and live happily ever after. So why did the leaders blow up about Jesus' words? Because he said "*my* Father," not "*our* Father," and then added, "never stops working, so why should I?" Jesus' use of these two phrases made himself equal with God—on par with God's activity. The Jews never referred to God as "my Father," only as "our Father." That sounds subtle to us, but it was astounding to the Jews. By claiming that God was his Father, Jesus identified himself as one with God. And by saying that he was working just as the Father was working, Jesus boldly implied that he was God's Son.

Jesus didn't just claim *equality* with God as his Father. He also asserted he was *one* with the Father. Another example: Once when Jesus was approached by some Jewish leaders asking about his being the Christ, he ended his answer to them by saying, "The Father and I are one" (John 10:30). The leaders started rock collecting right then and there. They were ready to stone him—all because, as they said, "You, a mere man, have made yourself God" (verse 33). What Jesus stated clearly as truth, the Jewish leaders took as blasphemy.'

Jesus didn't hide the fact that he was God. His enemies just didn't believe him. But his claim was clear. He was no ordinary man. He was God's Son.

REFLECT: What did Jesus claim about himself? Are you clear on that?

PRAY: *Jesus, you are more than a human being. You are the Son of God.*

13 Guilty Because of Who He Is

Bible Reading: Mark 14:53-65

Jesus said, "I am [the Messiah], and you will see me, the Son of Man, sitting at God's right hand in the place of power and coming back on the clouds of heaven." Mark 14:62

LIKE A TRIAL meant to root out the truth, the whole truth, and nothing but the truth, the trial of Jesus lays out for all to see—beyond a shadow of a doubt—some of the Bible's clearest statements of Jesus' deity. Anybody wondering if Jesus claimed to be God needs to take a hard look at his trial, recorded in Mark 14:53-65.

The high priest put the question to him point blank: "Are you the Messiah, the Son of the blessed God?" (verse 61). Jesus said, "I am, and you will see me, the Son of Man, sitting at God's right hand in the place of power and coming back on the clouds of heaven" (verse 62).

The Jewish officials didn't miss Jesus' point, and the high priest responded by tearing his garments—publicly demonstrating the horror of blasphemy. Then he said, "Why do we need other witnesses?" (verse 63). Everything Christ said affirmed his clear claim to be the Messiah promised in the Old Testament. They had finally heard it from him for themselves. The words of his own mouth convicted him.

Now the leaders had only two alternatives: (1) to accept Christ's claim as true or (2) to convict him of blasphemy, which of course they did.

You start to see that this was no ordinary trial. Christ's identity—not any criminal action—was the issue. In most trials, people are tried for what they have done. But that wasn't true of Christ's trial. Jesus was tried for who he was.

The trial of Jesus should be enough to show convincingly that he claimed to be God. His judges witness to that. But on the day of his crucifixion, his enemies also acknowledged that he claimed to be God come in the flesh. "The leading priests, the teachers of religious law, and the other leaders also mocked Jesus. 'He saved others,' they scoffed, 'but he can't save himself! So he is the king of Israel, is he? Let him come down from the cross, and we will believe in him! He trusted God—let God show his approval by delivering him! For he said, "I am the Son of God" ' " (Matthew 27:41-43).

Christ's judges and enemies denied the truth about who he is.

So who do you say Jesus is?

 REFLECT: Are you convinced by the case that Jesus is God? What persuades you? What do you need to learn more about?

PRAY: *Jesus, I understand your claim to be the Son of God. I believe you. You are God come in the flesh. I welcome you as Lord in my life.*

14 Plant Yourself Where the Truth about You Flourishes

Bible Reading: 1 Thessalonians 3:9-13
May the Lord make your love grow and overflow to each other and to everyone else. 1 Thessalonians 3:12

JUST AS you're ready to burst out the door from school, your volleyball coach swoops down and not-so-gently breaks the news that you weren't elected team captain. Sure, you know it's not the end of the world. But it *is* your last chance before you graduate. You feel bad enough that you contemplate skipping your Bible study group and numbing your pain with a gallon of ice cream. But you drag yourself to Bible study anyway.

When you tell your friends at Bible study what a loser you are, they not only make you stop trashing yourself but remind you how talented and helpful you are both at school and in the group. You leave the group knowing that you are loved, appreciated, and needed. You go away with a better picture of who you are.

Sound mushy? Maybe. But having friends who boost you when you're down sure beats getting bludgeoned with insults and sarcasm.

The Bible informs you that God sees you as lovable, valuable, and competent. But that doesn't mean that seeing yourself as God sees you is easy. Lots of young Christians look at themselves as defective specimens of God's creation. They have difficulty accepting that God or anyone else really thinks they are worthwhile.

Getting around the right people is a great way to get God's view of you. Here's how:

Spend time with people who already know they are loved, valued, and useful to God and others. They're good role models of your true identity—and they're comfortable to be around because they are sure about their identity.

Get in a place where the people in charge clearly teach from the Bible the truth about your identity in Christ. You need to be around mature Christians who walk and talk your scriptural acceptance and worth in God's eyes.

The coolest group you can be part of is one where consistent, loving care reinforces the truth of who God says you are. It may be a youth group, a Sunday school class, a Bible study group, or just a group of Christian friends who care about each other deeply. Wherever you find it, that's an environment that can help you transform a self-image you don't want to wallow in.

 REFLECT: Are you part of a network of caring Christian relationships where people express love to one another, value one another, and serve one another in practical ways?

 PRAY: Ask God to direct you to relationships where your true identity is modeled, taught, and experienced—and ask him to help you be that kind of influence for other believers.

15 Hanging Out with a Helpful Crowd

Bible Reading: Acts 2:41-47

They joined with the other believers and devoted themselves to the apostles' teaching and fellowship, sharing in the Lord's Supper and in prayer. Acts 2:42

WANT AN EASY, electrifying way to a new you—one that singes your unhealthy self-image and makes you feel loved, valued, and useful? Well, you just bolt two powerful electrodes to your scalp, turn on the 30,000-volt transformer, and—

Just kidding.

You can spot the real program God designed to help you transform your sense of identity in the goings-on of the early church. The whole New Testament conveys three experiences you need in your life:

1. *You need a vital teaching experience.* Devotion to the teaching of God's Word was the first task of the first-century church. You study the Bible first not to learn what to do as a Christian but to get God's view of who you are and what you are becoming. Then the "doing" part of your faith practically takes care of itself. If you aren't part of an ongoing Bible study where you are taught God's Word by mature, wise Christians, you will continue to struggle to know who you really are.

2. *You need a vital relational experience.* The Jerusalem believers were as devoted to the fellowship—being together, praying together, eating together—as they were to studying the Word. Getting together was how they experienced the Word day by day. It's how they learned to treat each other as lovable, valuable, competent members of God's family. Spending time with other believers—living out what you learn—is where you learn the same stuff.

3. *You need a vital witnessing relationship.* The news that God loves and values the humans he has made is a message he wants spread to people who aren't Christians. The New Testament pictures witnessing as living the truth of who you are in Christ and talking about it whenever possible. That's how the early church grew every day. Modeling your identity as a valued child of God is how you share God's good news of salvation with others.

First Thessalonians 2:1-12 pictures how the apostle Paul intensely put this process into action among believers. He treated the Thessalonian believers with the tenderness of a nursing mother (see verse 7) and taught and encouraged them as a father (see verse 11). Got it? Paul *taught* the new converts the truth about how God sees them. He *related* to them in love and understanding. And then he *witnessed* to them—*modeled* for them—what it meant to see himself like God does.

REFLECT: Are you in an environment—your church, youth group, or Bible study—that provides you with these necessities for growth?

PRAY: Ask God to help you take full advantage of opportunities to grow in your biblical understanding of who you are.

16 Seeing Yourself with 20/20 Vision

Bible Reading: Ephesians 4:11-16

Instead, we will hold to the truth in love, becoming more and more in every way like Christ. Ephesians 4:15

WHENEVER ELIZABETH heard her youth pastor talk about "seeing yourself like God sees you," she knew that was exactly what she wanted—and needed. But she didn't want to work at getting God's vision of herself.

She wasn't willing to do the main thing she needed to do—spend time with her Bible, studying and soaking in God's truth. And even though she went to church, she wasn't nuts about letting those people too close.

Elizabeth sounds like someone with bad eyes who wants to see more clearly but won't wear glasses.

Fact is, you can't change how you see yourself without diving into God's Word. It's how you bring into focus the fact that you are lovable, valuable, and useful to God and others. Peter wrote, "You must crave pure spiritual milk so that you can grow into the fullness of your salvation. Cry out for this nourishment as a baby cries for milk, now that you have had a taste of the Lord's kindness" (1 Peter 2:2-3). God's Word is the number one agent in renewing your minds to think like he thinks and see as he sees (see Romans 12:2).

But you also can't change how you see yourself without connecting with God's people. Through his Word, God shows you what he is like—huge things like his attributes, character, and personality. Then through the church, God puts skin on those qualities. He makes them real to you.

It's like what Jesus did to demonstrate who God is. He revealed God in a way human beings could understand. Jesus told his disciples, "Anyone who has seen me has seen the Father. . . . Don't you believe that I am in the Father, and that the Father is in me? The words I say to you are not just my own. Rather, it is the Father, living in me, who is doing his work" (John 14:9-10, NIV).

God wants to use his Word and the Christians around you to make you doubly sure you are loved, valued, and useful. There's no better way to discover how God sees you than to dig into God's Word. And there's no better way to pound home that you are loved by God than to have caring believers remind you of and reflect to you what God sees. It's one thing to read about God's view of you in the Scriptures or hear about it in a sermon or Bible study. It's even more real when you experience God through the members of his church.

 REFLECT: How are you letting God's Word and his people into your life?

PRAY: Ask God to help you make God's Word and interaction with his people the priority it needs to be in your life.

17 Getting a Clear Picture Step by Step

Bible Reading: Deuteronomy 4:16-20

Remember that the Lord rescued you . . . to become his own people and special possession; that is what you are today. Deuteronomy 4:20

NO SOONER had Samantha jumped into the beautician's chair than she started to rattle off the major wonders she wanted worked upon her appearance—eyebrows raised, ears shrunk, teeth whitened, slouch straightened. As Sam inhaled before launching into the second half of all the imperfections she wanted fixed, Sam's beautician jumped in to set the record straight. "Look, girl," she said, "there's three things you gotta know. Betty only works from the neck up. Betty only does hair and makeup. And Betty is a beautician—not a magician."

You don't have to pluck your eyebrows or lop off the point at the top of your ears to accomplish an important change. The biggest alteration you could ever do to *yourself* is to realize your true identity as God's wildly loved, highly valued child. Here are a few simple steps to transform your inner portrait of yourself:

1. Pinpoint your specific need. Start by figuring out which fact you find hardest to accept: (a) God loves you just as you are and wants you for his child—you are lovable; (b) God would have sent Jesus to die for you even if you were the only person on earth—you are valuable; or (c) God trusts you to reach out and minister to others—you are useful. Do you have a big problem buying any one of those truths? That might tell you your first area to work on. It's also a great idea to ask God to show you which part of your inner portrait he wants to redo to match how he sees you.

2. Find help in Scripture. Start to study the Bible with your self-portrait in mind. Whenever you sit down to read, ask God to help you see yourself as he does. As you study, you will discover verses and phrases that seem just right for your situation.

3. Find help from other believers. Let members of Christ's body be part of the transformation the Holy Spirit is working in you. Scripture says we are to help each other get a clearer picture of who we really are (see Galatians 6:2). But if you want others to help, you have to be willing to let them into your life. It takes transparency to talk about your struggles, but you need to allow others to love and care for you just like you love and care for them.

Important note: If you have bad memories from the past that make even a short glance at your self-image painful, that's when you especially want to ask a parent, a trusted Christian friend, a youth leader, or a pastor to pray with you and ask God to transform your inner view of you.

REFLECT: What are you doing to allow God to change your inner portrait of yourself?

PRAY: Tell God where you need his help.

18 Putting In a Good Word

Bible Reading: 1 Peter 2:9-12

You are a chosen people, . . . that you may declare the praises of him who called you out of darkness into his wonderful light. 1 Peter 2:9, NIV

YOU KNOW God expects you to pray that he would use you to tell your non-Christian friends about him. But what if God answers your prayer?

God won't leave you dangling. When he opens up opportunities to share the Good News, here are a some helpful tips:

1. *Seize the opportunity confidently.* Don't be afraid. God has prepared you and your friends for this moment. They need what you have to share.
2. *Be friendly but firm.* Share what Christ has done in your life and explain what he can do in their lives. Tell it the way it is, but with care and respect.
3. *Talk their language.* Don't switch into Christian jargon. Put the gospel in language your friends understand—without losing anything in the translation.
4. *Use a simple step-by-step approach.* How much of the gospel do your friends need to know before they can make a decision to trust Christ? Not very much, since the gospel is simple. One good way to present the basic gospel message and ask for a response is in the booklet "Would You Like to Know God Personally?" (Campus Crusade for Christ), which you can purchase at your local Christian bookstore.

At some point when you present the Good News, you should briefly tell the story of your own relationship with Christ. Think through your story ahead of time. An effective personal story—or "testimony"—has three parts:

1. *What you were like before you trusted Christ.* Briefly describe your life before you trusted Christ. What was the focus of your life?
2. *How you trusted Christ.* Briefly tell what led you to trust Christ. When did you first understand the Good News? Why did you decide to trust Christ?
3. *What you have been like after trusting Christ.* What difference has Christ made in your life? What does Christ mean to you now?

As you prepare your testimony, don't juice up the facts or glorify a gory, sinful past to make your story more exciting. Scrap the Christian jargon. And make your focus your personal relationship with Christ—not your church or youth group.

REFLECT: Write a first draft of your testimony. Share it with a Christian friend and have him or her suggest how you could make it clearer and more relevant.

PRAY: Ask God to guide you as you prepare a testimony for your friends.

19 Tell It Like It Is

Bible Reading: 1 Peter 3:13-17

> *If you are asked about your Christian hope, always be ready to explain it. 1 Peter 3:15*

IT FINALLY happened. You find yourself sharing your testimony with a non-Christian friend, and you know God has opened a choice opportunity. But where do you go from here? Here are some things to keep in mind:

1. *Make the message personal wherever you can.* If you use a step-by-step presentation like the booklet "Would You Like to Know God Personally?" (see Appendix), keep the focus on your friend. But don't forget to add your own comments and personal examples where they fit best.
2. *Postpone questions whenever possible.* Your friend might have a million questions. If an issue fits where you are in your presentation, try to work it in right away. If not, ask your friend to hold off until you finish.
3. *Invite a response.* When you finish your presentation, ask your friend if he or she is ready to trust Christ. If yes, ask the person to pray and express trust in Christ. If no, don't be discouraged. Keep praying for your friend, and plan to get together again and offer another opportunity to trust Christ.

Your friend might have questions or objections during or after your presentation. Some questions are sincere—based in real concerns and needs. Other questions are insincere—asked just to stall you or get you off the point. And still other questions are like mini-tests—asked to check your sincerity or knowledge. The toughest part of answering any question is often your attitude. Some thoughts on how you can respond best:

1. *Get ready as best you can.* You don't need a doctorate in the Bible for God to use you to answer your friend's questions. Just keep learning and preparing to reply to others. If you can't answer a question, tell your friend you will find out more and share it at another time.
2. *Don't feel threatened.* You are Christ's ambassador, and when you discuss the gospel with your friends, God's power is at work in you (see Romans 1:16). Be confident without being pushy or proud.
3. *Don't argue.* You can't argue someone into trusting Christ. Just share the gospel with your friend in the power of the Holy Spirit, and let your loving attitude be your most persuasive argument.

REFLECT: How are you preparing yourself to share Christ when he gives you the opportunity?

PRAY: Pray for opportunities to share Christ with your friends.

20 Are You on Target?

Bible Reading: 1 Corinthians 9:24-27
You also must run in such a way that you will win. 1 Corinthians 9:24

OKAY. Pretend that you have a super-huge telephoto lens zoomed up close on you as you sit in rapt attention in your favorite class. Now widen that shot. Exactly how many students sit in your row? Now focus really wide. How many people make up your grade? And how many students are in your whole school?

God's goal for evangelism is to reach everyone he can squeeze into a wide-angle shot of the whole world. But you could easily get discouraged by the hugeness of that task. Your evangelistic efforts really need to focus first on your inner circle—your friends, your teammates, your immediate classmates, etc.

In 1 Corinthians 9:24-27, the apostle Paul compares the Christian life to the work of a runner training for a race. He says we are to run so we win the prize (verse 24). Evangelism isn't a fun run; it's going for the gold. We're out to rescue as many people as possible to the glory of God. We give it all we've got.

And anyone who wants to be a winner runs "straight to the goal with purpose in every step" (verse 26). If you hope to win this race, you need a clear goal. And if you want to maximize your effectiveness in your evangelizing, you need a strategy for reaching and discipling your family, school, and community. Try these steps:

1. *Define your target.* Ask God to impress on you the names of several individuals within your reach. Write down the names and commit yourself to sharing the gospel with each person.
2. *Pray for your target.* Post your list of names where you are sure to see it often and pray for these people daily.
3. *Surround your target with love.* Build bridges to people by becoming their servants. Spend time with them and meet their needs for friendship.
4. *Present the gospel to your target.* Pray for, watch for, and create opportunities to share Christ and call for a commitment.
5. *Stay connected to those who trust Christ.* Your task of sharing the gospel with your non-Christian friends doesn't end when they trust Christ. They need to be discipled to become disciplers of others.
6. *Let the Holy Spirit lead you.* Stay closely tuned to the Holy Spirit in case he wants to change your plans and lead you in another direction.

You won't be very successful at sharing Christ with your non-Christian friends unless you define your target and plan how to hit it.

REFLECT: What's your target for sharing your faith today?

PRAY: Ask God who should be at the center of your witnessing efforts.

21 Helping Babies Grow Up

Bible Reading: 1 Thessalonians 2:8-12

We loved you so much that we gave you not only God's Good News but our own lives, too. 1 Thessalonians 2:8

IF NEWBORNS don't have someone to feed and care for them twenty-four hours a day, they don't survive.

New believers are like newborns. Freshly born into God's family, they need a spiritual parent's care and protection—especially in the first weeks and months of their budding Christian life. And if you were the one who helped bring people to spiritual birth in Christ, it's natural that you fill the role of spiritual parent for them (see 1 Thessalonians 2:8-12). So what does a spiritual parent do?

First, *check their vital signs.* In the critical first few days of being a Christian, spiritual babes might be tempted to doubt they are truly different. The feelings that might have swelled when they trusted Christ might subside, making them wonder if Christ actually came into their life. Remind new believers that you care about them and their new life in Christ—and let them know you're available to talk whenever they need you.

Second, *supply nourishment.* Like a baby needs food to survive, a new Christian needs God's Word to mature (see 1 Peter 2:2). One of the first things new believers need is assurance about what happened to them when they trusted Christ. Go over the facts about their new life in Christ on your first visit together:

- When you trusted Christ, you became a child of God (John 1:12).
- Your sins were forgiven (1 John 1:9).
- Jesus Christ is in your life (Revelation 3:20).
- He will never leave you (Hebrews 13:5-8).
- Your old life is gone. You are a new creation in Christ (2 Corinthians 5:17).
- You have received eternal life (John 5:24; 1 John 5:12-13).

Third, *build in some bonding time.* Newborns need to bond with their caregivers, and new Christians need to get involved with other believers. Introduce them right away to Christian friends and your youth leader or pastor. Invite them to church with you. Welcome them into your Bible study or prayer group. To help them develop their faith, they need fellowship with good Christian friends.

When God lets you be part of reaching someone for Christ, that's just the start of his using you to nurture that new Christian.

REFLECT: How do you feel about becoming a spiritual parent to new believers?

PRAY: Share your feelings and concerns with God today.

22 Helping New Christians Get a Good Start

Bible Reading: 1 Peter 5:2-9
Care for the flock of God entrusted to you. 1 Peter 5:2

"THE APOSO-WHAT?" stammers a kid in the front row of the Sunday school class.

"That's 'apostle,' stupid," Austin corrects. "As in 'the apostle Paul.' An apostle is an official representative sent by God to preach the gospel and often to teach churches in more than one location."

The kid in the front row squirms. Austin shakes his head at the raw dumbness of the rest of the class. They're spiritually clueless, he figures, and after thirteen years as a Sunday school regular, he's too cool for Sunday school.

Of the non-Christian kids you might lead to Christ, fewer and fewer will come from a religious background or understand any Bible basics. Learning the nitty-gritty of the faith from a kind, patient teacher is one of their greatest needs. Believe it or not, *you* can be a teacher to friends you bring to Christ.

One of the best ways to teach others is to meet with new Christians, with three goals for being together—study, fellowship, and prayer. Invite your new Christian friends to join a small group with other young Christians. Or ask your youth pastor how you can meet and teach them one-on-one at least once a week. Whatever you do, don't miss these four key pieces of a weekly get-together:

1. *Share.* Talk about what's going on in your lives. Focus on what you see God doing and how you are growing in him.
2. *Study.* Put a significant part of your time into Bible study. You can pick a prepared study that will help your friends with their basic growth as Christians. You can also teach them how to study the Bible on their own.
3. *Ask and answer.* Your friends might have loads of questions. Give them plenty of time, and don't feel you have to be able to answer everything. It's okay to say, "I don't know; let's figure it out together," or "I don't know, but I'll do some studying so we can talk about it next time."
4. *Pray.* When you pray together each week, it's a chance to show firsthand *how* to pray. Teach that prayer is simply talking to God about your thoughts, feelings, and needs.

New Christians desperately need Christian friends. Instead of bashing them for not knowing much about God, be there for them.

 REFLECT: Do you feel inadequate to teach people the basics of the faith?

PRAY: Say thanks that the Holy Spirit is present in you to empower you and touch others through you.

The Christian's No-Brainer

Bible Reading: Matthew 25:34-40
When you did it to one of the least of these my brothers and sisters,
you were doing it to me! Matthew 25:40

I ONCE SPENT a summer teaching at Arrowhead Springs, Campus Crusade's former headquarters down in the foothills of the San Bernardino Mountains in Southern California. During that summer, my family and I lived in Blue Jay, a little town up in the mountains beside beautiful Lake Arrowhead. So every day I drove down the mountain twice—once in the morning and then again after lunch.

It's hot in the San Bernardino Valley during the summer, with temperatures often breaking the 100-degree mark. During my trips up and down the mountain, I often saw cars pulled over to the side of the steep, winding road to the summit—hoods open, steam belching from their radiators. It was soon apparent to me that my teaching ministry for God was pretty hollow if I didn't do something to help the poor stranded motorists. All my talk about loving God was meaningless if I didn't show love for these people in need.

So I came up with a plan. I kept four large water jugs filled and stowed them in my trunk. Whenever I came across an overheated car on my daily drive on the mountain, I pulled over and offered to fill the radiator with water. People were overjoyed at the offer and grateful for the help. Once the radiator was full, I offered a copy of my book *More Than a Carpenter* and talked to the motorists about Christ. It was one of the best summers of ministry I have ever experienced.

Love isn't an option for Christians. It's a command. God is love, and people born of God must express his love. Jesus said, "Your love for one another will prove to the world that you are my disciples" (John 13:35).

Love always goes two directions at once. When you love people in Christ's name, you are also loving God. Jesus taught that when you minister to anyone in need of love and care, you are ministering to *him* (see Matthew 25:34-40). And when you truly love God, you will also inevitably love people. Like John wrote, "If someone says, 'I love God,' but hates a Christian brother or sister, that person is a liar; for if we don't love people we can see, how can we love God, whom we have not seen? And God himself has commanded that we must love not only him but our Christian brothers and sisters, too" (1 John 4:20-21).

You can't get around it: Love is part of your life as a Christian. Anyone who doesn't love both God and people dares not take the name *Christian*.

REFLECT: What obvious, practical thing can you do to share God's love with people? What is right within your reach?

PRAY: Sometimes you might be blind to clear opportunities to show love. Ask God to open your eyes.

24 Taking Your Love in Two Directions

Bible Reading: Exodus 20:1-17

I am the Lord your God. . . . Do not worship any other gods besides me.
Exodus 20:2-3

FOR YEARS, Mrs. Jenson had had a nasty suspicion that her daughter was up to no good. So when her daughter became pregnant at age seventeen, Mrs. Jenson did what she thought Jesus would do: She kicked her daughter and her new grandson out of the house—and out of her family. Years later, her daughter had become a magnificent Christian mother, and her grandson loved Jesus with his whole heart. But Mrs. Jenson still saw her daughter as a dirty unwed mom.

Maybe you've met Christians who have forgotten that God put love smack in the center of what it means to follow him. If you are a Christian, you are called to love. But your love must be put into action on two different levels: love for God and love for people. Jesus taught, "'You must love the Lord your God with all your heart, all your soul, and all your mind.' This is the first and greatest commandment. A second is equally important: 'Love your neighbor as yourself'" (Matthew 22:37-39). You love God with your whole self—that's "vertical love." And you love others as you love yourself—that's "horizontal love."

The Ten Commandments in Exodus 20 are organized into the two directions of love. The first four commandments show what vertical love for God looks like:

You shall have no other gods before me.
You shall not worship idols.
You shall not misuse the name of the Lord your God.
Remember the Sabbath day by keeping it holy.

Then the next six commandments paint a picture of horizontal love for others:

Honor your father and your mother.
You shall not murder.
You shall not commit adultery.
You shall not steal.
You shall not give false testimony.
You shall not covet.

Loving God means you acknowledge his ultimate and supreme worth in all you think, say, and do. And to love people means you recognize their value as persons created in God's image—and you treat them accordingly.

 REFLECT: God calls you to love in two directions—to love him and love others. How are you doing at each?

PRAY: Invite God to increase both love for God and love for people in your life.

25 Whom Should I Love More?

Bible Reading: Luke 14:25-30

If you want to be my follower you must love me more than your own father and mother, wife and children, brothers and sisters—yes, more than your own life. Luke 14:26

BECAUSE OF an ugly run-in with the church, the parents of one well-known Christian teacher were so down on Christianity that when sixteen-year-old Norm announced to them that he had become a Christian, his mom and dad blew up. Norm's mother even threatened to kill him unless he gave up his faith.

Norm was nose-to-nose with a crisis: Should he obey his parents and turn his back on God? Or should he put God first and disobey his parents? With God's help, Norm chose God. Norm faced ridicule from his parents for years—years he spent praying for them. He eventually saw both of them trust Christ as their Savior.

God commands you to love God and love people. But what do you do when those two loves collide? When your love for *God* seems to say you should withhold love from a *person,* how should you respond? Or when your love for *family* or a *friend* demands you withhold love from *God,* what should you do?

Sometimes love for God has to win over love for others. Look at the example of Abraham. God told him, "Take now your son, your only son, whom you love, Isaac, and ... offer him ... as a burnt offering" (Genesis 22:2, NASB). Abraham loved his son deeply. But Abraham loved God supremely and would have sacrificed his son had God not seen Abraham's display of obedience and stopped him from harming Isaac.

Jesus said, "If anyone comes to Me, and does not hate his own father and mother and wife and children and brothers and sisters, yes, and even his own life, he cannot be My disciple" (Luke 14:26, NASB). Jesus isn't saying you should hate your family members. He's using hyperbole—exaggerated language. Your love for God must be so much greater than your love for any person—including those closest to you—that your love for people seems like hatred in comparison.

Make sure, though, that any issue that prompts you *not* to show love to a fellow human being is a clear violation of scriptural commands. Example: You might not like it if your parents said "no way" to you dating a non-Christian you really like. But their order doesn't violate any of God's commands—so you need to obey. On the other hand, if your parents tell you to fake information on a college application to get more financial aid, you have scriptural grounds not to obey.

Jesus said, "If any of you wants to be my follower, you must put aside your selfish ambition, shoulder your cross, and follow me" (Matthew 16:24). Your love for God has to be bigger than your love for *anyone* else.

REFLECT: Do you want to put obeying God before every other priority of life?

PRAY: Ask God for courage to obey him first, fast, and always.

26 When Authorities Clash

Bible Reading: Titus 3:1-2

Remind your people to submit to the government and its officers.
Titus 3:1

CHECK OUT these statements. Do they slip out of your mouth easily?

"I wish the principal would give me detention more often."

"I'm really happy I got caught copying answers off the math whiz who sits next to me in algebra."

If you're like most people, you squirm when someone in charge of your life lays down a rule you're forced to follow or catches you when you're doing what you shouldn't. But most days you probably also recognize that authorities usually act for your good. The Bible challenges you as a Christian to show love for leaders—from the head of your home to the head of your country—by submitting to their authority. Peter writes, "For the Lord's sake, accept all authority—the king as head of state, and the officials he has appointed" (1 Peter 2:13-14). Submission clearly means obedience.

Still, even when you build a habit of respectfully obeying civil authorities, you might face situations where your loyalty and obedience to authorities clashes with your bigger love and allegiance to God. Back in the New Testament, the apostles found they had to disobey Jewish authorities and declare, "We must obey God rather than human authority" (Acts 5:29).

Whenever you have to choose between love for God and love for people, love for God always wins. Your only right choice is to love and obey God *rather* than government. But here's the tough news: Doing the right thing won't always spare you from negative consequences, a fact you can learn from even a quick glance at Scripture and church history. "Some were mocked, and their backs were cut open with whips," the author of Hebrews reports. "Others were chained in dungeons. Some died by stoning, and some were sawed in half; others were killed with the sword" (Hebrews 11:36-37). Countless first-century Christians were fed to the lions because they loved God more than they loved the Roman emperor.

You likely won't face a choice with life-and-death consequences, but your love for God might cost you a job when you won't lie for your boss. Or a friend, parent, or teacher might reject you for putting God first. When you have to make those hard choices and face tough consequences, you can cling to the Bible promise that "God causes everything to work together for the good of those who love God and are called according to his purpose for them" (Romans 8:28).

REFLECT: Are you facing any situations right now where love for God and love for people are in conflict?

 PRAY: Ask God to strengthen you to make the right choice.

27 Levels of Love

Bible Reading: Acts 5:26-29
We must obey God rather than human authority. Acts 5:29

JEN IS A Christian, but her parents aren't. When Jen's dad tells her to lie about her age so she qualifies for a cheaper preteen fee for a summer soccer camp, Jen refuses.

Big question: Isn't she supposed to obey her parents no matter what? Isn't she shattering the fifth commandment, the one that says, "Honor your father and mother" (Exodus 20:12)?

Not really.

Look at it this way: Jen doesn't suppose that "honor your father and mother" wasn't meant for her. She doesn't say, "Forget you! My dad wants me to be a liar. He's a cheat. I don't ever have to listen to my parents again!" Because of the bad spot her dad placed her in, she's making an exception, *suspending* the law of obeying parents in order to follow God's higher law of truthfulness.

Jen's situation is just like when a jumbo jet takes off. As the plane lifts off, it doesn't *break* the law of gravity, it merely overrides it for a while. Gravity is still at work. It comes back into play when the pilot throttles down and gets ready to land, just like Jen works hard to obey her parents every time she can—all the times their demands *don't* conflict with God's commands.

Loving God *more* than people doesn't mean that you love God *instead* of people. Sometimes loving God means you love a human authority in your life with a tough love—a love that takes a firm stand against evil. Love doesn't mean you cave in to someone's sinful wishes. Love means you act for that person's best, and sometimes the best you can do for someone is to resist his or her sin.

An example: When you were small, your parents knew it would be nuts to give you everything you wanted. You begged for cake and ice cream at every meal. Or you insisted on playing with steak knives. Your parents didn't love you any less by saying "No!" to all those requests and requiring that you bend to their wishes. Whether you understood it or not, they knew they had your best interests at heart. Sometimes you might have to get tough with people to truly love them. Think about this: Loving God the most helps you love others the best.

Love has two levels—love for God and love for people. Those two levels of love might conflict, but they never contradict. And when they conflict, the lower law to love people always yields to the higher law to love God.

 REFLECT: When has someone you're supposed to obey asked you to do something you knew you shouldn't do? How did you solve the conflict?

PRAY: *Lord, help me love the people in my life completely—and love you supremely.*

28 The Oil of Relationships

Bible Reading: Luke 7:36-50
A person who is forgiven little shows only little love. Luke 7:47

"I DON'T think I can ever forgive him after what he said. He doesn't deserve it."
"She asked me to forgive her, and I said I would. But I can't."
"She's dead now. She can't apologize—so I won't forgive her."
You live in a culture saturated with stored-up grudges, resentments, bitterness, and broken hearts. When people don't take time to confront and mend those hurts—when they cling to attitudes like the ones you see in those sad statements above—they rip apart relationships. They break up the closeness God intends between Christians. They dull the cutting edge of the Holy Spirit in the lives of individuals. And they split families, friends, youth groups, and churches.

Forgiveness works like oil in relationships. It reduces friction and allows people to get close to each other without overheating.

If you don't sense a forgiving heart in someone, you won't ever be truly open and vulnerable to him or her. You know that an unforgiving person won't give you half a chance to develop a deep, lasting, and close relationship. And if *you* aren't a forgiving person—no matter how smart, talented, or downright good-looking you might be—you won't develop the close relationships you want. When you aren't able to forgive, even little conflicts blow your friendships to bits.

But once you learn to forgive others who wrong you, your relationships grow strong. You can talk openly and meaningfully. If someone can love you despite your faults and accept you even when you have wronged them, you can't help but become even better friends.

Your know-how in handling this one skill—forgiveness—largely determines how you handle conflicts in your relationships. Ask yourself:

Do I accept each situation where forgiveness is necessary as an opportunity to strengthen relationships and develop my own character?

Do I study the needs of people who hurt me and try to understand them?

Do I know that God will deal fairly with my offender if that person needs punishment—and that it's not my job to punish him or her?

Do I choose to thank God for each difficult experience and allow his love and grace to grow in me as a result?

When you want to learn how to forgive, Christ is your model. His forgiveness was absolute and immediate. Think about it: He even forgave the men who crucified him! So when you feel tempted to rip someone's head off, be like Christ: *Forgive.*

REFLECT: How skilled are you at forgiving—and receiving forgiveness?

PRAY: Ask God to help you learn the crucial habit of forgiveness.

29 Not Getting What We Deserve

Bible Reading: Psalm 103:8–14

[The Lord] has not punished us for all our sins, nor does he deal with us as we deserve. Psalm 103:10

HALF OF understanding forgiveness is knowing what it *isn't*. More on that next time. The other half is knowing exactly what it *is*. Check out these definitions—at least one of them will make sense to you:

Forgiveness means "to erase, to forego what is due" . . . "to give up resentment" . . . "to wipe the slate clean, to release from a debt, to cancel punishment" . . . "to personally accept the price of reconciliation" . . . "to give up all claims on the one who has hurt you and let go of the emotional consequences of that hurt." Forgiveness not only means you say the words "I forgive you" but that you also let go of your wounded emotions.

Forgiving is an action. It doesn't allow you to sit around and wait for the person who walloped you to say, "I was wrong; will you forgive me?" Just as Jesus died for you while you were still a sinner (see Romans 5:8), forgiving means you take the first step in healing a relationship.

Forgiving also means you "give up or give away." It means you give up the right to get even—no matter how good revenge would feel. Forgiving means you give mercy instead of demanding justice.

If you don't like that approach to life, ponder this: It wouldn't be smart to pray for justice in your relationship with God, because his justice would wipe you out. What you want to ask for is his mercy, the stuff that allows you to be forgiven in spite of your sin.

It works the same way in your human relationships. The world tells you to hate. God says to love. The world says you are entitled to revenge. God says to forgive.

Why? Because God wants you to forgive in the same way he forgives you—completely and continually. To the Colossians, Paul wrote, "God has purchased our freedom with his blood and has forgiven all our sins" (verse 1:14). In Hebrews 10, we discover that Christ's forgiveness was "once for all time" (verse 10). Once he had offered himself as the sacrifice for sin, "he sat down at the place of highest honor at God's right hand" (verse 12).

God doesn't forgive you because of something you've done but because of who Jesus Christ is and what he accomplished for you through the cross. That's your model for forgiving others. You don't forgive because the person who hurt you has changed or begged for your forgiveness, but because you have a Christlike readiness to simply forgive.

REFLECT: Are you a forgiving person?

PRAY: Ask Christ to share his heart of forgiveness with you today.

30 Sundown Is Coming

Bible Reading: Matthew 6:9-15
If you forgive those who sin against you, your heavenly Father will forgive you. Matthew 6:14

GOLDIE BRISTOL didn't learn of the rape and brutal murder of her twenty-one-year-old daughter until she received a blunt telegram from the coroner. It read: "Your daughter Diane—we have her body. How do you want it disposed of?" After the funeral, God led the family to pray for Diane's killer. He was caught, and Goldie received permission to go to the federal prison. There she looked the man square in the face and said, "I forgive you."

What makes someone like Goldie Bristol forgive a man who brutally raped and killed her daughter? Goldie knows that forgiveness isn't just for people you feel like forgiving. God says to forgive *everyone who hurts you.*

Say that again? Yes, God calls you to forgive anyone who has angered you, hurt you, abused you, or offended you. That covers anyone and everyone, but he wants you to start with those closest to you—your parents and your siblings. You might carry bitter feelings toward parents because of divorce, abuse, alcoholism, or abandonment—physical or emotional. But no matter how bad a situation was or is, God can still use it for your good. And you need to forgive your parents.

Knowing God's command to forgive doesn't make forgiveness easy, especially when someone has severely wronged you. But God means forgiveness to be given, extended, or received *immediately.* Paul exhorts us in Ephesians 4:26, "Don't let the sun go down while you are still angry." The Bible, notice, doesn't forbid you to get angry. It says, rather, to control your anger. The length of time between the hurt and the extending of your forgiveness often indicates the strength of your walk with God.

One wise caution: When you deal with others, you need to forgive them or ask forgiveness of them whenever it can help, bless, or encourage the other person. Sometimes, however, an immediate confession doesn't exactly encourage the other person—he or she isn't emotionally ready for it. You might put the issue on hold in your own life for few days and then deal with the other person.

Remember this: Forgiveness cuts both ways. You might be able to think of a pile of people who have wronged you. But you wrong others, too. Tape this phrase inside your locker: "When I refuse to forgive, I am burning a bridge that someday I will need to cross." More often than you can imagine, you are going to need forgiveness from someone else.

REFLECT: Is there someone you need to forgive today? Do you need to ask someone to forgive you? Take care of it before sundown.

PRAY: Talk to God about people you need to forgive—or people you need to ask for forgiveness.

31 Phony Forgiveness

Bible Reading: Matthew 5:23-26

If you are . . . offering a sacrifice to God, and you suddenly remember that someone has something against you, . . . go and be reconciled to that person. Matthew 5:23-24

"ALLISON *SAID* she was sorry for talking behind my back," Brooke fumed. "But she laughed like she thought the whole thing was stupid. And then she turned around that afternoon and did the same thing again. What am I supposed to do with that?"

Let's clarify. If you want to understand what forgiveness *is,* you also need to know what forgiveness *isn't.* Check these facts:

Forgiveness isn't conditional or earned. You can't say, "If you clean up your life, I'll forgive you." If you attach strings, you aren't showing true forgiveness.

Forgiveness doesn't wait around for the person who hurt you to say "sorry." Forgiveness takes the initiative. If God had waited for you to repent and ask his forgiveness, you would still be lost. And if you won't forgive until a person first asks for your forgiveness, you are letting that person control your life.

Forgiveness isn't a feeling. Sometimes you don't feel like forgiving, but when you forgive someone in faith—knowing you have done what God wants you to do—you often feel better afterward. But forgiveness starts with an act of the will.

Forgiveness isn't pretending a situation never happened. Some people just go on with life, acting like there was never a problem. If that's how you deal with a hurtful situation, don't be surprised if it happens again.

Forgiveness isn't pretending wrong is right. Forgiving someone doesn't mean you think that what happened is right. You can forgive the offender and still challenge him or her to quit hurting you.

Forgiveness isn't saying, "Let's forget about it." Face it: You don't forget about it. Instead, the hurt turns into resentment. Forgetting doesn't result in forgiveness. It works the other way around: Forgiveness results in forgetting.

Forgiveness doesn't erase consequences. Someone who does wrong could still face a loss of reputation, financial loss, emotional loss, loss of sleep, or any number of consequences. A person who does wrong has a *personal* responsibility and a *legal* responsibility and a responsibility toward *God.* If you forgive someone, that means you have dealt with it on a personal level, but that person still has to answer to God and to human authorities.

You might fear that forgiving and seeking forgiveness will make you weak. But ignoring a hurt is the weakling's way out. Trying to heal a relationship through forgiveness is a real sign of your strong character.

REFLECT: In what ways have you misunderstood forgiveness?

 PRAY: Talk to God about anyone you need to forgive but haven't because you misunderstood what forgiveness is and isn't.

1 Chasing the Wind

Bible Reading: Ecclesiastes 2:17-26
God gives wisdom, knowledge, and joy to those who please him.
Ecclesiastes 2:26

IT PROBABLY happens to you every year before finals. Little by little, subject by subject and assignment by assignment, you fall behind until you almost collapse under the load. "I can't take it anymore," you whine. "I'll never be ready for finals. I can't wait till school's out. I'm going to sleep for a week!"

But a day or two into your vacation, the words are out of your mouth before you can choke them back. "I'm bored. There's nothing to do around here."

All people need something to be part of, something to look forward to, or someone with whom to share their life. If those are missing, life loses its thrill.

You might be surprised to know that the worst known case of boredom in the history of humankind is recorded in the Bible. Solomon—the wisest guy on earth—wrote the book of Ecclesiastes to chronicle what he discovered about life. His opening words tightly, pointedly overview the whole rest of the book. He says, "Everything is meaningless . . . utterly meaningless!" (1:2).

Solomon then goes on to detail his own adventure in finding meaning in life. Soon after he became king, he asked God for wisdom. God granted his request. Then Solomon set out to apply this wisdom to his life. He read, studied, looked around, and asked questions to find out what life was all about. His conclusion? "Everything under the sun is meaningless, like chasing the wind" (1:14).

So the king changed his tactics. He decided to live for pleasure by surrounding himself with wealth, women, and wild living. But that was meaningless too. So he tried another route. Thinking productivity might bring meaning to life, he undertook massive building projects. But he still found that life was unfulfilling. Prosperity and success don't guarantee happiness.

"Oh, great," you might say. "If the wisest man who ever lived can't find his way out of boredom, what hope do I have?"

Thankfully, Solomon learned a few things during his journey. He also wrote, "God gives wisdom, knowledge, and joy to those who please him" (Ecclesiastes 2:26). Meaning, purpose, and fulfillment in life begin when you look to God—because he's the author of meaning, purpose, and fulfillment. So it's up to you. You can chase the wind and live in permanent boredom, or run straight to the one who holds your life and your exhilarating future in his hands.

 REFLECT: Where do you expect to find meaning in life? Are you trying to stuff yourself with things that won't satisfy?

PRAY: *God, I want the best out of life. I want to find my ultimate meaning, purpose, and fulfillment in you.*

2 The Basics of Avoiding Boredom

Bible Reading: John 10:6-10

My purpose is to give life in all its fullness. John 10:10

EVERYONE WANTS to have the fullness Jesus promises in John 10:10. But you only find that kind of excitement when you apply principles that let that full life happen. Here are six to consider:

1. *Have the right focus.* The Bible consistently says it's better to give than to receive. Check this basic life principle: The most fulfilled people in the world are those more concerned with giving than with getting. Yet a root of selfishness still lives inside most of us. It says, "Just take care of yourself." Listen to that lie, and life loses its zing.

2. *Climb out of the same old rut.* People who escape a life of boredom do it by seeking new interests and opportunities. They're not afraid to try something unusual, or even something scary.

3. *Make the most of your alone times.* Are you afraid to be alone? Are you comfortable with silence? Some people can't live without a constant buzz of people around—it keeps them from facing the emptiness inside. They fill their lives with a blur of activity—all to avoid facing themselves. Learn to use potentially boring "alone times" to read, pray, and ponder your life.

4. *Take personal responsibility for your life.* You're in the middle of an opportunity to mature. It's easy to want independence while continuing to resist responsibility and blame Mom and Dad for whatever unhappiness, loneliness, and boredom you experience. Face it: You are responsible for your own life.

5. *Seek God's will for your life.* Some students' lives are boring and empty because they aren't listening to the Lord. He might be trying to get your attention through your youth leader, Christian friend, Bible reading, or the quiet voice of the Holy Spirit. Got ears?

6. *Adjust your attitude.* God can't lead you into good things if you don't have a teachable, positive attitude he can work with. Are you looking for his opportunities to expand your vision and lead you to radical new challenges?

And one huge last thing: Jesus is the ultimate answer for loneliness rooted in lack of purpose. If you're missing fullness in life, Jesus, your friend, wants to grab you by the hand and lead you into some better-than-bungee-jumping life experiences.

REFLECT: Are you ready to follow Jesus in these steps to full life in him?

PRAY: Talk to him about filling your life today.

3 When You Want to Disappear

Bible Reading: Hebrews 5:11–6:1
Let us go on instead and become mature in our understanding.
Hebrews 6:1

"THAT'S IT!" Will bellowed, slamming the front door behind him and throwing his book bag on the hall table. "I'm never going back to Driver's Ed class again!"

"What's this all about?" Will's dad asked.

"Oh, nothing," Will answered sarcastically, "except that my life is over. I'll never get my driver's license, that's for sure.

"I felt like a total dork, Dad," Will continued. "First, I started the car. I was so nervous. I put my seat belt on and adjusted the mirror. Then I forgot the car was already running. I grabbed the key and turned it again, and it sounded like the engine was about to blow up. The guys wouldn't stop razzing me about it. It's just so much to think about, you know? I'll never learn how to drive."

Did Will learn to drive? Of course. And over the next weeks he figured out that the other guys were just as nervous as he was and felt just as incompetent.

If you don't have moments when you feel incompetent, then you're not human. What you might not know is that other kids have to cope with the same kinds of limitations, hardships, and lessons. Realizing that keeps you out of a trap—thinking you're worse than everybody else, labeling yourself a loser, and pulling away from people.

The best thing you can be is yourself. You don't have to play the people-pleasing game of trying to be like the classmate who starts at quarterback, plays first-chair violin, and has the highest GPA in the grade. You're not grown up until you outgrow the tendency to imitate others and try to match their behavior and attitudes. This dilemma led one college student to write:

All my life I've tried to please others.
All my life I've put on an act for others.
I will not do this.
For if I spend my time trying to be someone else,
Who will spend time being me?

Next time you feel a flash of incompetence, imagine Jesus sitting next to you. Is he razzing you? Hardly. He accepts you right where you are. He knows you are still growing.

REFLECT: Since Jesus accepts you, don't you think it's okay to accept yourself? How are you going to work at that?

PRAY: *Jesus, thanks for your acceptance. Help me to like myself as much as you like me.*

4 The Gift That Keeps On Giving

Bible Reading: John 14:15-18

He is the Holy Spirit, who leads into all truth. John 14:17

IT'S FINALLY finished! Your new invention is ready for its final test phase. It could be the greatest invention ever for Christians.

It looks a lot like a Walkman, so you call your machine "Truthman." You clip the control box to your belt and slip the headphones over your ears. *This is no CD player,* you think proudly. *This is one rockin' righteousness machine. It senses what I'm thinking and doing and then transmits the truth through my headphones.* You can't wait to crank it up.

On your way to school you're about to cross the street against the "Don't Walk" sign when you hear a voice in your headphones: "Romans 13:1-2 says we should obey the laws of the land. This is God's way of protecting us from getting hurt." *Truthman works!* You stop in your tracks and wait for the "Walk" sign.

Hustling through the crowded hall, you bump into another student. "Leper!" he snarls at you. Before you can even feel sorry for yourself, Truthman reminds you, "You're no loser. John 1:12 says you are a beloved child of God."

In third period, your geography teacher drops a surprise quiz on you. But you happen to sit next to geography genius Lynn Brazil. As you casually glance toward Lynn's paper, Truthman says, "One of the Ten Commandments in Exodus 20 is 'Do not steal,' and that applies to quiz answers." You snap your eyes back to your paper and glue them there.

Things don't work so well after lunch. You accidentally drop Truthman on the cement, and when a lustful thought toward another student comes along, all you hear through the headphones is "Bleeble . . . zok . . . snork." And when your mom asks if you have finished your homework, Truthman's batteries are totally dead, so you say "Almost, Mom!" when you haven't even started. So much for your great invention.

Having something like Truthman would be great—if it worked perfectly, that is. But actually, you have something way better! It's the Holy Spirit. He helps you grasp and apply God's truth to your life in everyday situations. In fact, Jesus often calls the Holy Spirit the "Spirit of truth" (see John 15:26; 16:13).

Unlike your fictional Truthman, however, the Holy Spirit can't get lost or broken or run out of batteries. He lives inside every believer—including you (see John 14:17, 20). And you don't have to leave the Holy Spirit in your locker. Jesus said his gift "will never leave you" (John 14:16). Moment by moment, day by day, the Holy Spirit is closer than your next breath, ready to share God's truth with you.

REFLECT: How do you respond when the Holy Spirit tries to teach you truth?

PRAY: Spend a few minutes thanking Christ for his great gift, the Holy Spirit.

5 An Inside Job

Bible Reading: John 14:19-21

When I am raised to life again, you will know that I am in my Father,
and you are in me, and I am in you. John 14:20

SIXTEEN-YEAR-OLD Sasha wakes up in a great mood and dresses quickly. She and her boyfriend, Nicholas, are going to spend the day at Dizzyland, her favorite amusement park. Bounding down the stairs to the kitchen, she chirps, "Hi, Mom. Beautiful day, isn't it?" Mom turns from scrambling eggs on the stove, and Sasha notices a strange green glow in her eyes. "Mom, are you all right?"

Her mother begins to twitch. "It might not be as beautiful as you think," she says in a voice that sounds like a fork grinding in the garbage disposal. Then Sasha's mother grabs at her own neck and pulls away her face as if it were a latex mask. Underneath is a throbbing purple head with one big eye and yellow slime oozing from a mouth jammed with fangs. Sasha screams in horror and sprints to Nicholas's house.

"Nicholas, the most awful things are happening to me," sobs Sasha in Nicholas's arms. She explains her terrifying experiences, and Nicholas holds her. "It's okay, Sasha," he assures. "You'll be safe with me."

Suddenly, Sasha pulls away. "Sorry I can't say the same for you, bucko," she hisses. Then she unzips her body from head to toe, and as the fleshy costume falls away, a giant squid-like creature emerges. Paralyzed with fear, Nicholas is quickly enveloped in the squid's slimy tentacles. Just before blacking out, he thinks, *I really should date other girls.*

You have something living inside you, but it's a not a monster from a B-minus horror flick. It's something as awesome as an alien is ugly.

Jesus told his disciples that he would be in them—not just *with* them, not just *beside* them, but *in* them (see John 14:20). Paul confirmed it. He wrote, "Christ lives in you" (Colossians 1:27). "Hey, time out," you may say. "Yesterday you said it was the Holy Spirit living inside me. Now you say it's Christ. Who is really in there: the Holy Spirit or Christ?"

If you are a Christian, Jesus Christ and his Holy Spirit *both* live inside you. They are one and the same. The Bible explains that the Spirit of God is the Spirit of Christ (see Romans 8:9), and the same Holy Spirit who lived inside Jesus lives in you to teach you, comfort you, and make you strong.

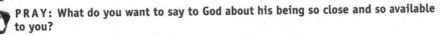

REFLECT: How do you feel knowing that God is so near to you?

PRAY: What do you want to say to God about his being so close and so available to you?

6 Taking Your Spiritual Vitamins

Bible Reading: John 14:22-26

The Holy Spirit . . . will teach you everything and will remind you of everything I myself have told you. John 14:26

IT'S YOUR first day of baby-sitting two-year-old Justin Miller, so his mom is giving you instructions just before she leaves.

"Justin isn't a very good eater," she explains. "So when you feed him lunch and dinner, it doesn't matter if he finishes. Just serve him a good meal and let him eat as much as he wants. Then give him one of my homemade cookies."

"Are you serious?" you ask, amazed. You can't believe it. Your mom never gave you dessert unless every single pea and carrot and brussels sprout disappeared from your plate. You silently wish Mrs. Miller would adopt you.

At lunchtime you serve Justin chicken noodle soup and carrot sticks. He has three slurps of soup and half a carrot stick. You give him a cookie, and he eats the whole thing. The same thing happens at every other meal that week. You hope the kid doesn't die of malnutrition while you're watching him.

By Friday night—after Justin's mom has paid you for the week, of course—you find the courage to say, "Mrs. Miller, I don't think Justin should get a cookie if he doesn't eat his lunch or dinner. He's not getting enough nutrition."

Mrs. Miller smiles a knowing smile. "That's why he always gets dessert," she says. "I put his vitamins in every cookie."

The Holy Spirit, the Spirit of Christ who lives inside you, is like that wise mom. His ministry is to keep you spiritually healthy by getting spiritual vitamins into you. Or in the words of Jesus, the Holy Spirit "will teach you everything and will remind you of everything I myself have told you" (John 14:26). He takes the truth you need to understand today and serves it to you in a form you can digest.

It might happen like this. You are studying your Bible and it's whooshing way over your head. Then you read a verse and—*wham!* —something is suddenly clear to you. It's like God is right there saying, "Here's what this means in your life." Or you are listening to a Christian CD and one line of the lyrics moves you to make a much-needed change in your behavior. Or you are in a Bible study, and something your leader says helps you make an important decision. Or you are singing a worship song, and suddenly you are moved to tears by seeing a side of God you never saw before.

God knows how to get you the "vitamins" you need to keep you spiritually strong.

REFLECT: Are you surprised that God is so committed to your growth? What do you think about that?

PRAY: Tell him about it in prayer.

7 Rest in His Peace

Bible Reading: John 14:27-31

I am leaving you with a gift—peace of mind and heart. John 14:27

IT'S NIGHTTIME, only a few hours after Jesus was crucified and buried. The disciples are sitting around together, still in shock from the brutal execution of their beloved Master. The following conversation isn't in the Bible, but something like it might have happened.

"I can't believe we were just eating dinner with the Master," Bartholomew says, shaking his head. "It seems like only yesterday."

"That's because it *was* yesterday, Bart," Peter snorts impatiently.

"Oh yeah, I knew that," Bartholomew snaps.

Thaddaeus scratches his head. "The Master told us so many things last night during dinner. I wish I had listened better."

"Me too," Andrew agrees. "Maybe we can piece together what he said. What do you guys remember from last night around the table?"

Thomas looks up. "What did the Master mean when he said he was going to send some kind of 'Holy Spirit'? I don't get it."

Philip speaks next. "He said this Holy Spirit would lead us into all truth. I'd sure like to know the truth about everything that has happened lately."

"The thing I remember most," Matthew puts in, "is the Master saying this Holy Spirit is *his* Spirit, and that he's going to be in us. Is that freaky, or what?"

James says, "And the Master said that his Spirit in us—this Spirit of truth—is going to teach us everything and remind us of what he said."

"Hey, guys, what if it's all true?" Simon wonders aloud. "What if the Master is really going to be inside us to show us what is true, teach us about the Father, and remind us of all the things he said to us? What could that mean to us?"

For several moments, the men don't breathe. Then one of them says what they are all thinking: "Wow. We would have his peace."

Peter brightens up. "Hey, the Master talked about peace last night too."

"Right, he said he's leaving his peace with us," John remembers, "just like he is sending his Spirit to us."

"He said his peace was a gift," James interrupts, "just like the Spirit he is giving."

"Maybe they're connected," Bartholomew tries. "Maybe the Master's peace comes with the Master's Spirit."

"Bart," Peter says with a smile, "maybe you do have a brain."

REFLECT: Do you sense God's peace as you consider the Holy Spirit's presence and power in your life?

PRAY: Tell him right now how much you appreciate his gift of the Spirit.

8 Who's Number One?

Bible Reading: Matthew 20:20-28
Whoever wants to be a leader among you must be your servant.
Matthew 20:26

RACHEL SLAMMED down the telephone and yelled for her secretary. The plush office attested to Rachel's importance. She had risen rapidly through the company by loudly promoting herself and viciously eliminating anyone who got in her way.

Her secretary entered the office, and Rachel began spouting orders as usual. "Get that stupid jerk Patterson in here. And tell Allison to—" She suddenly stopped at the pained expression on her secretary's face.

"It's your daughter," the secretary said. "Your baby-sitter called. Danielle has disappeared from her backyard."

Rachel raced out of the office, flung herself into the driver's seat of her BMW, and squealed out onto the street. Darting, dodging, and blaring the horn, she sped toward the sitter's house, thinking, *If anything happens to Danielle, I'll kill myself.* She ran a red light. Almost to the sitter's house, she saw the crossing guard in the intersection just in time to slam on her brakes. Fury erupted in her like a volcano. The old crossing guard had been on the corner for years, ushering children across the street. He had always seemed to Rachel to be a doddering, insignificant old man. And now he had forced her to stop, wasting her valuable time.

She opened her mouth to curse at him, then noticed the child in his arms—Danielle! Suddenly it was clear. The old crossing guard had found Danielle at the park and was bringing her back to the sitter.

Rachel swung open the door and ran hysterically to the man. She swept her three-year-old into her arms and hugged her, overcome with gratitude. Rachel, the corporate executive, suddenly felt very small. And the old man she once thought little of was very important.

Rachel is a prime example of an "egoist," a person who thinks he or she is the center of the universe. Egoists put themselves before everyone else, thinking, *Forget everybody else. As long as I get what I want out of life, I'll be happy.*

But it doesn't work that way. People who follow that course can end up wealthy or powerful, but they also reap a harvest of loneliness and bitterness. Jesus taught that each human being is immensely important to God. Recognizing the value of those around you doesn't get in the way of your happiness. It's part of what makes your happiness happen.

REFLECT: What do you suppose displeases God about the way an egoist looks at the world?

PRAY: Ask for God's help in treating others with importance today.

9 It's What's Inside That Counts

Bible Reading: 1 Samuel 16:7

People judge by outward appearance, but the Lord looks at a person's thoughts and intentions. 1 Samuel 16:7

CATHERINE'S cover-girl beauty qualifies her for the pages of *Vogue* or *Mademoiselle.* Her slim figure slides perfectly into a black evening gown. Her elegance and charm would grace the elite parties of the super-rich.

So what is she doing in a sewer?

In the old hit television series *Beauty and the Beast,* Catherine hangs around Vincent the man-beast. The whole plot of the series revolves around one gigantic question: *What does she see in him?* A gorgeous woman in love with a half-man, half-lion who lives in abandoned subway tunnels—what's up with that?

That puzzle, of course, is part of why the show works. Catherine is attracted to Vincent not *because* of his appearance, but *in spite* of it. She is in love with the guy under the lion's mane. She loves him for his sensitivity and compassion. And part of the show's appeal is that love like that is rare.

Lots of people buy into the idea that looks are everything. Our culture tells you that girls or guys who lack the looks of supermodels are, well, unattractive. That's ridiculous. Television, magazines, movies, and videos constantly drum into us a prepackaged image of what is beautiful and what is not. The media machine also pushes the idea that being beautiful means instant, unending happiness.

As a Christian, you aren't obligated to be ugly. But you're not obligated to look like a commercial for cosmetics or a body-building machine either. There's a lot more to beauty than clear skin, bulging biceps, and piercing blue eyes. The biggest beauty more often comes from a person's attitude and disposition. God chose David to be king of Israel not because of David's appearance or physical attributes but because of the attitude of his heart.

Beauty as the world defines it often isn't a blessing. Believe it or not, beauty sometimes is the beast that drives a girl to depression or robs a guy of his self-esteem. There are many outwardly stunning people who happen to be inwardly lonely, insecure, and unfulfilled.

Truth is, if you seek happiness in the color of your hair or the cut of your clothes, you're sure to be disappointed. Clothes can be cool, but they aren't as important as what lies beyond the reflection in the mirror. Whether you are pleased with the person you see has more to do with what you *can't* see than with what you *can.*

REFLECT: How are you trying to spot in yourself—and in others—a beauty that is more than skin deep?

PRAY: *Lord, develop in me the attitudes and intentions that you find beautiful.*

10 "Everybody" Isn't Always Everybody

Bible Reading: Daniel 1:6-15
Daniel made up his mind not to defile himself by eating the food and wine given to them by the king. Daniel 1:8

"COME ON, Mom, be reasonable," pleaded Kirsten. "There aren't going to be drugs or anything. It's just a party."

"You're not going to a party at Brad's house—or anywhere else," her mom argued, "unless there are some adults around to chaperone."

"I can't believe you're doing this to me," Kirsten whined. "Everybody else is going to be there. I'll be the only one whose mother won't let her go."

Kirsten didn't speak to her mother for the rest of the weekend. *Everybody goes to those kinds of parties these days,* she reasoned.

Kirsten got a surprise when she found out on Monday that Julia and Christopher hadn't gone to Brad's party either. Kirsten had bought the common belief that "everybody's doing it." What a lie! Everybody is *not* doing it, whatever *it* is. Sometimes it seems that way, but an aware teen will eventually spot a lot fewer people "doing it" than the crowd would have him or her believe.

Everybody is *not* having premarital sex. Recent research indicates that more than 50 percent of Christian kids are *not* doing it. That's a significant number.

Everybody is *not* using tobacco. Some surveys indicate that as many as 80 percent of today's youth don't smoke.

Everybody is *not* using alcohol. Surveys reveal that around 30 percent of high school students do not use alcohol and nearly 10 percent have never tried it.

Everybody is *not* doing drugs. The Institute of Social Research at the University of Michigan reported a sharp drop in the use of cocaine and other drugs by teenagers. Over 40 percent of all American young people have refused illicit drugs all the way through to high school graduation.

Everybody is *not* losing or outgrowing their faith in God. A survey of two thousand youth shows that 61 percent regard religion as the most important part of their lives.

Students often use the lie that everybody's doing it to manipulate their friends, parents, and peers into conforming to the crowd. Don't believe the myth. Everybody is *not* doing it. And even if everybody *is* doing it, you don't have to. Daniel and his three friends didn't yield to the pressure to conform, and God blessed them as a result. A hefty percentage of youth today know how to say no. And more and more, that's just what they're doing.

REFLECT: How strong is your resolve against this subtle pressure to conform?

PRAY: Ask God to build your courage to resist the line, "Everyone's doing it."

11 Sex Isn't a Dirty Word

Bible Reading: Song of Songs 4:8-11

*You have ravished my heart, my treasure, my bride. I am overcome
by one glance of your eyes. Song of Songs 4:9*

RERUNS OF the TV show *Saturday Night Live* show comedian Dana Carvey playing a comically prudish character called the Church Lady. The attitude of this old lady in her long dress and pulled-back hair is a perfect picture of how some people see Christians. They think the followers of Jesus believe in a God who condemns sex and sexuality. Not true.

Sex isn't a dirty word to God. Or even to ladies at church. It's not wrong, sinful, or shameful. God doesn't hate sex. He's the one who invented it! He started the whole thing. Sex has been a part of God's plan from the beginning (see Genesis 1:27-31). When he told humans, "Multiply and fill the earth" (verse 28), he meant for them to obey him through the activity of procreation, or sex.

The Bible contains some frank accounts of sexuality. The Song of Songs, of course, is a love poem with language that would shock the Church Lady. The apostle Paul offered down-to-earth advice on sexual behavior to married couples in the church at Corinth. And Scripture doesn't try to hide the fact that sex is to be enjoyed between husband and wife (see Hebrews 13:4).

God created sex. It is *humans* who have taken it outside the marriage covenant and dirtied it. God meant sex to be a fulfilling, exciting, satisfying experience between a man and woman totally surrendered to each other in the enjoyment of each other's sexuality. It is *people* who have perverted God's gift.

When God tells you not to commit adultery or not to have anything to do with sexual immorality, he doesn't do it to wreck your life.

God wants to protect you from distrust or suspicion and provide for you one of the most important factors for a fulfilled marriage and sexual relationship: trust.

God wants to shield you from the fear of sexually transmitted diseases and to provide peace of mind when you enter into marriage.

God wants to shelter you from bad relationships that are artificially sustained by sexual involvement—the kind that often lead to tragic marriages.

God wants to protect your virginity, one of the greatest gifts a person can present to a mate on his or her wedding night.

Can you believe God loves you that much? It's true. He's not trying to spoil your fun. He's trying to show you the way to real fun.

REFLECT: Do you think God sees sex as dirty? Why or why not?

PRAY: Talk to him today about your desire to receive the benefits of his loving provision and protection.

12 Loving the Person in the Mirror

Bible Reading: Ephesians 5:25-30
No one hates his own body but lovingly cares for it, just as Christ cares for his body, which is the church. Ephesians 5:29

TODAY'S VOCABULARY word: *Narcissism.* Can you pick the correct definition from the three choices below?

a. a plant with smooth leaves and white, yellow, or orange flowers
b. a new religion practiced by devoted narks
c. excessive interest in one's own appearance, importance, abilities, etc.

If you picked *c*, you either know your Greek mythology or you're a good guesser. Narcissism describes someone in love with himself. A lot of people think that's what Jesus' words in Matthew 22:39 are all about: "Love your neighbor as yourself."

"Wait a minute!" some people always say. "That's not right. We're not supposed to love ourselves. The Bible commands us to deny self and take up our cross. Jesus said if I love my life, I will lose it. It's like that acrostic J-O-Y: Jesus first, Others second, Yourself last. Self-love is narcissism—right up there with pride and conceit, things we are to avoid."

Wrong. Proper self-love is right for at least three big biblical reasons.

First, *it's right to love ourselves because we are made in God's image* (see Genesis 1:26). We love others for the same reason—particularly people who seem lovable for no other reason. An unborn fetus, a seriously brain-damaged person, an unrepentant mass murderer, or a dying AIDS patient might not seem to contribute much to society. But we don't love people because of what they can give us; we love them because God made them. We love ourselves for the same reason—even when we don't feel like we are worth loving.

Second, *it's right to love ourselves because self-love is the basis for loving others.* Had Jesus said, "Love others *instead* of loving yourself," we might agree that any kind of self-love is wrong. Rather, it's as if Jesus said, "You already love yourself, and doing that properly is good. Now love others the same way."

Third, *it's right to love ourselves because God loves us* (see 1 John 4:10). If we don't love ourselves, then we don't love what God loves.

The Christian's most basic earthly love obligation is to care for himself or herself. It's normal—and necessary—for believers to nourish themselves to maturity mentally, physically, spiritually, and socially, and to protect themselves from harm. And that loving regard for ourselves shows us how to love others.

REFLECT: How do you feel about yourself today? Do you love and accept yourself in a healthy way, or do you have trouble with this concept?

PRAY: Talk to God about ways you can learn to love yourself as he loves you.

13 Looking Out for Number One

Bible Reading: Mark 12:28-34

I know it is important to love [God] with all my heart and all my understanding and all my strength, and to love my neighbors as myself.
Mark 12:33

A GROSSLY overweight and out-of-shape mall security guard receives an emergency call on his radio. A girl is being assaulted at the other end of the mall. The guard runs as fast as he can to help her out, but his body rebels against such a strenuous workout. Halfway to the emergency, the guard drops dead of a heart attack. The girl he might have saved is beaten to death.

Obvious lesson: The guard's neglect of his own physical health cost him his life *and* resulted in another life lost. Had he cared about himself more, he might have lived to save the girl.

Jesus told us to love others as we love ourselves (see Matthew 22:39), revealing that proper self-love equips us to love others. The security guard is a simple illustration of why self-love is important.

Self-love means—as flight attendants remind you before every flight—that you put on your own oxygen mask first before you help a child with his or her mask. If you don't first put on your mask, you might keel over, leaving the child without any help. Self-love means eating and exercising properly in order to extend your life for the sake of people you serve. Self-love means investing time and effort in your own spiritual growth so you are prepared to minister to others. Only as you love and care for yourself are you equipped to love and care for others as Christ commanded you.

Self-love also means protecting yourself physically, mentally, spiritually, and socially from anything that might undo you.

Physically, you buckle up in the car, look both ways when you cross the street, refuse to abuse substances, and keep your kitchen free of crawly things.

Mentally, you guard your mind when you turn away from negative reading material, TV programs, videos, music, and movies.

Spiritually, you build yourself up by filling your heart with Scripture, holding yourself accountable to others for spiritual growth, and standing against Satan's attempts to discourage you from serving Christ.

Socially, you stay out of situations where your ability to be a good influence crumbles under pressure to do wrong.

Anything less than cautiously, wisely caring for yourself in areas like these is less than the healthy love God expects you to show yourself. And remember: You can love and accept yourself because that's how God relates to you.

REFLECT: What are you doing to love yourself wisely?

PRAY: Tell God you're glad he thinks you're worth taking care of.

14 Don't Overdo It or Underdo It

Bible Reading: 1 Corinthians 12:14-27
All of you together are Christ's body, and each one of you is a separate and necessary part of it. 1 Corinthians 12:27

TWO BIG dangers with loving yourself like Christ commanded: You can skimp on loving yourself until you wither away, or you can love yourself so much there's no room in your world for anyone else.

In 1 Corinthians 12, Paul says that everyone is gifted by the Holy Spirit for ministry (verse 7) and that God has created each Christian just as he wants him or her to be (verse 18). He compares the body of Christ to a human body and each member to a body part—an eye, ear, foot, and so on. The gist of this passage is that each of us is to accept the abilities God has given us and exercise them for the good of the body. That's the kind of healthy self-love that leads to healthy love of others.

Paul shows what the wrong attitude of *underloving* yourself looks like. It's like body parts that say, "Because I am not a hand, I am not a part of the body" (1 Corinthians 12:15, NASB). If you're like that, you don't love yourself enough. You whine, "I shouldn't be in the spotlight. I'm not important." You will have difficulty following Christ's command to love others because you let an inferiority complex or a false sense of self-denial get in the way of loving yourself.

Some clues that you probably love yourself too little: You are praised for doing something well, but instead of saying thanks you point out the flaws in your work. You don't give your opinion in an important discussion because you don't think it will make a difference. You are over-committed at church and stressed out at school because you feel guilty whenever you say no.

You're just as bad off if you *overlove* yourself. You overestimate your importance to God and to others. Pride and self-centeredness hinder you in trying to fulfill Christ's command to love others. Paul wrote of such people, "The eye can never say to the hand, 'I don't need you'" (1 Corinthians 12:21).

Some signs you probably love yourself too much: You can't pull yourself away from the TV to help a neighbor search for a runaway dog. You dominate discussions because you are convinced no one else knows as much as you do. You break commitments at home, school, or church when you become bored.

Failing to love yourself leaves you running on fumes when it comes to loving others—you will burn out fast and often. But you will also run out of gas in loving others if you direct most of your energy to yourself.

Think about it: When you love yourself for the sake of loving others, you can keep going and going and . . .

REFLECT: Do you love yourself too much—or too little?

PRAY: Talk to God about your desire to love yourself like he does.

15 How Can Anyone Love a Mess like This?

Bible Reading: 1 John 2:1-6

If you do sin, there is someone to plead for you before the Father. He is Jesus Christ, the one who pleases God completely. 1 John 2:1

"I KNOW I'm supposed to love others like I love myself," Sydney says with a pained look on her face, "but I have a hard time seeing anything about me worth loving. If I have an inferiority complex, it's only because I really *am* inferior."

The straightest route to good self-love is seeing yourself through the eyes of the God who loves you. Saturate yourself with scriptural truth about your identity in Christ. For example:

- God loves you and gave his Son for you (1 John 4:10).
- You are a child of God (John 1:12; Romans 8:14-15).
- Christ calls you his friend (John 15:15).
- God's Spirit lives in you (1 Corinthians 3:16; 6:19).
- You are brand-new in Christ (2 Corinthians 5:17).
- God has made you righteous in Christ (Ephesians 4:24).
- You are God's workmanship (Ephesians 2:10).

The more thoroughly you get into your head the truth about who you are in Christ, the more you will be able to love yourself as God does.

"But I don't get it," Sydney argues, sounding defeated. "How can I love myself when I keep sinning? It makes me hate myself."

Pretending you're perfect isn't what healthy self-love is about. You don't have to give up on yourself and say, "I'm never going to get it together spiritually." You aren't called to sin—but when you do, Christ represents you before the Father to help you make things right and go on (1 John 2:1). You can continue working to build your faith and fix patterns that lead to sin. As you press on toward maturity, you are in the process of becoming what God wants you to be.

So when you sin—and no, God isn't shocked when you do—don't make things worse by giving up on yourself. Confess your sin, receive God's forgiveness, and keep growing. Perfection is your ultimate goal, but you won't get there until you get to heaven. Don't get down on yourself every time your imperfections smack you upside the head. Your goal for now is maturity, not perfection—and you can succeed at that in some way every day.

 REFLECT: How can knowing your identity in Christ affect the way you think about yourself?

PRAY: Bring your failures and sins to God today in prayer and receive his forgiveness.

16 One-Sided Friendships

Bible Reading: Romans 15:1-4
We should please others. If we do what helps them, we will build them up in the Lord. Romans 15:2

GOOD FRIENDS are like diamonds. They're very precious; they arrive in the rough; they don't magically appear at your feet, you have to dig for them; and some people who should be gems turn out to be lumps of coal.

It's easy to spot at least four kinds of friendship that disappoint and frustrate. Maybe you're in the middle of one of these friendships right now.

1. *Part-time friends.* Some friends are great buddies when you're one-on-one. But they ignore you or worse when you're with the crowd. Others are just the opposite. When they're with a bunch of kids, they act plenty nice. But when you get them alone, they act like you don't exist. Some part-time friends are warm and cozy if you spend money on them. When the money cools off, so does the friendship.
2. *Conditional friends.* These are people who treat friendship like bait, dangling a relationship in front of you to get you to do what they want. As long as you cough up what they want, you are friends. But as soon as you choke, the friendship sputters.
3. *Undependable friends.* From the careless way they hurt their friends, these people seem to lack the tiniest sense of responsibility or integrity. They betray confidences, gossip, or break their word. Because you never know where you stand with them, a meaningful friendship can't thrive.
4. *Superficial friends.* A superficial friend can't ever get serious. You need to talk through something personal or meaningful, and your friend changes the subject to something trite or non-threatening or makes a joke about it. Chances are that relationship won't ever go beyond small talk.

It's discouraging to figure out that your friends fall into one of these categories. Sometimes you feel like you give a lot more than you get in these relationships, and you might come to the point where you don't have any energy left to inject into the friendship. You wind up discouraged, hurt, and lonely. You might not want to admit it, but you're not in a healthy relationship.

Here's a scary question: Can you spot any of these patterns in yourself? Do you show any signs of being a part-time, conditional, undependable, or superficial friend in any of your relationships?

REFLECT: Are you a diamond? Or a hunk of coal?

PRAY: Ask God to help you change any destructive patterns you might be living out with others.

17 Talking Deep

Bible Reading: Ephesians 4:25-29
> *Let everything you say be good and helpful, so that your words will*
> *be an encouragement to those who hear them. Ephesians 4:29*

WHEN AARON'S youth pastor divided his mission team into twosomes for what he called "Care and Share," Aaron revolted. He wanted nothing to do with anything called "Care and Share," and he didn't try to hide his disgust. "Girls talk," he argued. "Guys don't. Can I go now? When will this be over?"

If you think you can make solid friendships without ever talking about solid stuff, then you might as well try to make friends with a wall. Friendships need talk-time to grow. The deeper you go into your life—feelings, joys, fears—the deeper your friendship grows. Someone has categorized communication into five levels. If you want to cultivate close friendships, here's where you head:

Level 1: Surface topics. Conversation never gets beyond social courtesy. It sounds like, "Hi, how's it going?" "Fine, how about you?" "Good weather, huh?" "Yeah. Better than snow." You might touch the surface of someone's life at this level, but you will never really get to know him or her.

Level 2: Factual matters. You swap information about common interests—basketball, clothing styles, school subjects, music groups, etc. But conversation is still impersonal. You're talking about stuff, not how you feel about it.

Level 3: Opinions. You reach this level by sharing your thoughts and ideas about factual matters. If you discuss the scores, you talk about your favorite play of the game. If you discuss music groups, you share what you think about the lyrics on a particular CD. Opinions help friends start to know how the other views life. This level moves closer to more personal issues, but it's still basically safe conversation.

Level 4: Emotions. At this level, you are talking about how you *feel* about factual matters. "When that happened, I was really scared!" "This has been the loneliest week of my life." "Since Noah broke up with me, I've been totally sad." Here's where you begin to get insights into personal life. You can see what goes on inside each other.

Level 5: Intimacy. This is complete, intimate openness about your life. You aren't likely to practice this level of communication with anyone but trusted family members and close, special friends. You trust them so completely that you can be totally open about yourself. That kind of friend lets you cut through surface conversation and get down to honest, transparent talk.

REFLECT: Do you have friends you feel safe sharing your feelings with? Do you have at least one intimate friend—someone you can share almost anything with?

PRAY: If you have found some of those rare friends, thank God right now. If not, ask God to guide you to those special people.

18 Who Are You Hanging With?

Bible Reading: Proverbs 4:4-9
Learn to be wise, and develop good judgment. Proverbs 4:5

"IF A LOT of your friends are having premarital sex and talking about it," one girl explained, "your conscience kind of goes to sleep, and it's tough to keep feeling sex before marriage is wrong. After a while you begin to feel the pressure. The girls make you feel you aren't very attractive and aren't worth much, and the guys make you feel like a wimp because you're not experienced like the others. After so much of that from the crowd, you say, 'What the heck,' and do it!"

That's sharp insight—and it shows why you need to be careful who you hang out with. It's no huge news that the wrong kind of friends can pull you into wrong behavior that can alienate you from your parents and Christian friends. And alienation leads to painful loneliness.

Many students today want nothing more than approval from someone. If they don't get it from their parents, they seek it from their peers. It takes wisdom to choose friends who will exert good pressure—a push to help you grow rather than rip you up.

Believe it or not, the apostle Paul recognized the crush of peers a couple thousand years ago. He said to the Christians in Corinth, "I wrote you in my letter not to associate with immoral people" (1 Corinthians 5:9, NASB). When you hang out with immoral people, you often become immoral yourself.

Of course, peer pressure doesn't always have to be negative. If people in the group want to do what is right, you can get great help living a righteous life. As one guy said, "I know my friends have a great influence on who I am and also on what my values are."

It all comes down to what friends you choose. Those words you read from the Old Testament book of Proverbs contain timeless wisdom on the worth of being with like-minded people and the danger of being caught in the wrong crowd.

You can spot two vital guidelines to help you choose your friends:

First, purposely avoid close contact with people who don't share your basic values about how to live, regardless of how appealing those people are.

Second, don't ever let yourself forget the importance of selecting the right people to be with. Keep on aiming at friendships with people who share your values and convictions.

Like it or not, you tend to become like the people you hang out with. So ask God for the wisdom to hang out with the kind of people you want to be like.

REFLECT: Who do you turn to for approval? How are they shaping the person you are becoming?

PRAY: Ask God for wisdom as you choose your friends.

19 Super Friend

Bible Reading: Proverbs 18:24

There are "friends" who destroy each other, but a real friend sticks closer than a brother. Proverbs 18:24

FRIENDSHIPS ARE as different as flowers. Some are beautiful yet delicate, needing special care. Others grow anywhere in practically any conditions, even in the blistering desert. And you find out quickly which ones wilt when the temperature starts to rise.

As great as some of your other friendships are, you have only one totally unique friendship that stands apart from all others. It's your friendship with Jesus Christ. He is an all-weather, all-circumstance friend.

First, Jesus is a *full-time* friend. He will always be there for you. He doesn't treat you one way when you're alone and another way when others are around. You can count on him to be consistent, loving, warm, and open at all times.

Second, he is the one *unconditional* friend who will always forgive you when you fail him. He will stick with you through whatever circumstances occur in your life. When the going gets tough, Jesus will be by your side. David, the writer of the Twenty-third Psalm, said, "Even when I walk through the dark valley of death, I will not be afraid, for you are close beside me" (verse 4).

Third, Jesus is a fully *dependable* friend. You don't need to fear him making fun of you, turning his back on you, or betraying your confidence. And he keeps his word. You can count on his promises.

Fourth, Jesus, the ultimate friend, is never superficial or trite. He wants a *significant* relationship with you. He treats you with compassion and tenderness when you open your heart to him. You can hardly count the examples in the Bible of his compassion toward people who were physically disabled, socially outcast, or suffering emotional grief. And he cares for you in that same intense, personal way.

Jesus was no stiff, formal person. Common people didn't cringe in his presence. You don't have to put on a super-spiritual act to attract his attention. Just be yourself with him, and he will be himself with you.

You have one great, faithful, unconditional friend in Jesus. Take him at his word. Cultivate your friendship with him every day. Learn to take your disappointments, loneliness, and hurts to him—along with your excitement, happiness, and joy—and experience the friendship that lasts for eternity.

 REFLECT: Have you made Jesus your best friend? How do you see that in your daily life?

PRAY: *Jesus, make my friendship with you my best, most important friendship of all.*

20 How to Break Out of Loneliness

Bible Reading: Colossians 3:12-15
You must clothe yourselves with tenderhearted mercy, kindness, humility, gentleness, and patience. Colossians 3:12

LOADS OF STUDENTS figure loneliness is a lifetime sentence. They have decided they'll never have any real friends or they don't deserve for someone to like them. But that's not true.

You don't have be trapped in a friendless prison cell of boredom, loneliness, and depression. You can break out into a world of rich, close friendships. But busting loose takes personal honesty and seven sometimes-scary steps toward better friendships:

1. *Take an honest look at your life.* Be truthful—but not negative—about your social weaknesses. Recognize where you need to grow, then set realistic goals to make progress in those areas.
2. *Find someone who can mentor you.* A mentor is usually someone older who can show you the way. You can get unbiased feedback on your strengths and weaknesses—feedback offered in a kind, helpful way. A mentor can give you ideas about how to be a better friend.
3. *Have realistic expectations.* Some people keep trying to break into the popular crowd to bolster their own self-image. In the end, that crowd usually rejects them, which just feeds the defeat cycle. Make up your mind: Do you want a friend or a status symbol?
4. *Take a long-term approach.* Changes don't often occur quickly. Instead, small steps may take place over a longer time. A mentor can suggest some small, specific steps that will start you on the road to worthwhile friendships.
5. *Watch your attitude.* Attitudes determine actions. Guard against thinking things like, "I'm a jerk," "No one likes me," or "I'll never have any friends." If you treat yourself in a friendly way, you're more likely to present yourself in a positive way to others.
6. *Focus on being a friend, not on getting a friend.* You will find greater success and less loneliness when you focus on befriending others instead of trying to convince others to like you. Make it your goal to be a good listener, encourage others to talk about themselves, and show you care when others feel down.
7. *Cultivate a quality relationship with Jesus Christ.* The more you experience friendship with Jesus, the more relaxed you will be with others. A great friendship with him opens the door to great friendships with others.

 REFLECT: How are you doing in your search for friends? What needs to change?

PRAY: Share with Jesus your desire to be the kind of friend to others that he has been to you.

21 Laying Down the Law about Love

Bible Reading: Deuteronomy 28:1-6

If you fully obey the Lord your God by keeping all the commands
I am giving you today, . . . you will be blessed wherever you go,
both in coming and in going. Deuteronomy 28:1, 6

SOME PEOPLE think that love and law don't mix. They think that a God who loves you wouldn't hold you to any rules.

Some people say that believers in the Old Testament were "under law" while people from the New Testament on—including Christians today—are "under grace" or love. They quote John 1:17, "The law was given through Moses; God's unfailing love and faithfulness came through Jesus Christ," and Romans 6:14, "You are no longer subject to the law, which enslaves you to sin. Instead, you are free by God's grace."

But it's not a matter of living under law *or* love; you live out the *law of love.* Yes, it's true that you are not under the ceremonies or curses of the law of Moses in the Old Testament (see Hebrews 8–10; Galatians 3:13). But the ethical principles embodied in the law still apply to Christians today. In the two greatest commandments— love God and love people (see Matthew 22:37-40)—God tells you to do the loving thing. In the Ten Commandments and other instructions in the Bible, God shows you what the loving thing is and warns you against doing the unloving thing.

Love is at the heart of the Old Testament law. The introduction to the second commandment emphasizes God's love: "I, the Lord your God . . . lavish my love on those who love me and obey my commands" (Exodus 20:5-6). Descriptive words for God, such as mercy, kindness, goodness, and favor, are everywhere in the Old Testament. Anybody who thinks that love is only a New Testament teaching isn't reading the Old Testament!

The law itself, in fact, is one of the biggest expressions of God's love you could ever find. You see in the Ten Commandments God's commitment to provide for us and protect us from harm. In his farewell speeches to Israel, Moses urged, "Obey the terms of this covenant." Why? "So that you will prosper in everything you do" (Deuteronomy 29:9).

When God gave the law, he said it was "for your own good" (Deuteronomy 10:13)—to provide for and protect his children. God's purpose in giving his law was to provide for our prosperity and joy and to protect us from heartache and hurt.

You can't mistake this fact: God is incredibly loving to give us plenty of advance warning in hopes of sparing us from the consequences of sin!

REFLECT: How do God's laws spell out how to love him and others?

PRAY: How will you express your thanks to God today for his love?

22 Which Testament Is Number One?

Bible Reading: 1 John 2:7-11

I am not writing a new commandment, for it is an old one you have always had . . . to love one another. 1 John 2:7

TRUE OR FALSE: When Jesus came to earth, he tossed all the commands of the Old Testament on the back burner. He made them no longer important.

If you answered true, sorry. Jesus said, "I did not come to abolish the law of Moses or the writings of the prophets. No, I came to fulfill them" (Matthew 5:17).

The New Testament command to love God and people *summarizes* the Ten Commandments. It isn't a *substitute* for them. In God's Old Testament laws you find practical guidance for fulfilling God's command to love. Each of the Ten Commandments teaches you the loving thing to do—and the unloving thing to avoid—in your relationship with God and others.

1. *Do not worship any other gods besides me* says your devotion to God should be *pure*—unrivaled by any person, thing, or idea.
2. *Do not make idols of any kind* says that you should focus your loving dedication to God on *him*—not on religious practices, props, or substitutes.
3. *Do not misuse the name of the Lord your God* says your loyalty to God should include respect and reverence for his person and his name.
4. *Remember to observe the Sabbath day by keeping it holy* says your commitment to God should include honoring him by spending time each week in worship and rest.
5. *Honor your father and mother* says you should express love for your parents by respecting and obeying them.
6. *Do not murder* says you should express your love for others through huge regard for human life.
7. *Do not commit adultery* says you should demonstrate love for your spouse or future spouse through sexual purity and faithfulness.
8. *Do not steal* says you should express love for others through respect for their property and possessions.
9. *Do not testify falsely against your neighbor* says you should show love for others through honesty and truthfulness in all your dealings.
10. *Do not covet* says that your love for others should focus on what you can *give* others instead of how you can *get* what belongs to them.

In his commands to "do this" and "don't do that," God wisely and clearly spelled out what love looks like. You have an incredibly caring God!

REFLECT: Say it in your own words: What good do Old Testament laws do you?

PRAY: Ask God to teach you right and wrong through his unchanging commands.

23 So Are We under Grace or Not?

Bible Reading: Hebrews 13:8-16
Jesus Christ is the same yesterday, today, and forever. Hebrews 13:8

"I DON'T get it," Lauren said. "If Christians today are still supposed to obey the Ten Commandments, what does Paul mean when he says in Romans 6:14 that we are 'no longer subject to the law'?"

Confusing, isn't it? As Christians who trust in Jesus as God's provision for our sins, we no longer fear God's wrath. And understanding how grace and law fit together is the core of what it means to be a Christian.

You know that when Jesus died, he paid for our sins and opened the way for us to relate to God. We can know God because of *grace*—the unmerited, unearned favor of God expressed in Christ's work on the cross.

Christ's death on the cross removed the need for us to please God by acting perfectly—or die for our failings. Galatians 3:13 says, "Christ redeemed us from the curse of the law, having become a curse for us" (NASB). To be no longer under "the curse" of the moral law of the Old Testament means we are no longer subject to its penalty—an eternal death sentence—because Christ paid the penalty for all lawbreaking. That's good news!

But here's where you have to think hard. Taking away the penalty of the law and doing away with its moral principles are two different things. Since the Ten Commandments are restated in the New Testament, these moral principles of the law—the things they teach us about right and wrong—still apply to Christians.

See, love didn't change from the Old Testament to the New Testament. When Christ came to earth, God did remove *the ceremonial requirements* of Old Testament faith—more on that next time. And by dying on the cross, Christ removed *the penalty* we faced. There is no longer a death penalty for adultery, for example. That's why Paul said we are no longer under the law's curse.

But get this: God's definition of what is right, good, and healthy for us hasn't changed. Nor have the consequences of sin been removed. If you're sexually active outside of marriage, for example, you might have to live with an unplanned child or a sexually transmitted disease as a result of your disobedience.

God hasn't changed (see Hebrews 6:18; 13:8). In the New Testament, he's still the God of love you meet in the Old Testament. And the moral principles that express his love to us and show us how to express it to God and others are still the same. You can't escape that fact!

REFLECT: Why does God still expect you to heed Old Testament commands that tell you right from wrong?

PRAY: *God, I'm grateful that your definition of love doesn't change. Thanks that you have always made clear the best way to live.*

24 Tough Questions about the Law and Love

Bible Reading: Matthew 6:19-24
You cannot serve both God and money. Matthew 6:24

"A CHRISTIAN friend and I had a big blowup about the fourth commandment—the one about 'keeping the Sabbath holy,' " Kalli said. "Does it mean that I'm sinning if I work on Sunday or cause somebody else to work because I eat out or shop or watch Sunday afternoon football? My friend said the Bible forbids us to work or even do homework on Sundays."

Christians today aren't under the Old Testament Sabbath law. Following that law would mean halting all work between sundown on Friday and sundown Saturday. That's the Jewish Sabbath.

But don't miss this point: The *moral principle* behind the Sabbath law was kept by the early Christians who reserved the first day of the week—Sunday—for rest and worship (see Acts 20:7; 1 Corinthians 16:2; Revelation 1:10).

You don't have to obey the Old Testament Sabbath law, but you should reserve one day each week for rest and worship (see Hebrews 10:25). For most of us, Sunday works because Christian congregations mostly meet on Sunday. Christians who can't escape work on Sunday—such as doctors and nurses and dairy farmers—should take part of Sunday or another day for worship and rest.

And there are other issues. At this point in your life, school is your job. So you need to figure out how to keep homework from crowding out the time for worship and rest God wants to give you.

You need to be honest with yourself about how badly you need a job that fills up your Sundays and takes you away from what might be your optimum time to concentrate on worship and connect with Christian friends. Most bosses will give you Sundays off if you are a reliable worker and are bold enough to ask—and if you are willing to make some adjustments elsewhere in your week.

What about those professional football players forced to work on Sundays because you want to watch a good game? Well, you aren't necessarily sinning by watching ball or eating in a restaurant or going shopping on Sunday. The responsibility lies with the individuals serving you. If they are intent on obeying God from their hearts, they will choose another day of the week for rest, relaxation, and worship. If they don't, that's their choice, not yours.

REFLECT: Are you obeying God and taking time to rest and worship each week? Remember: It's his loving gift to you.

PRAY: Ask God to show you how to use your downtime well.

25 Up Close and Personal

Bible Reading: James 4:7-10
Draw close to God, and God will draw close to you. James 4:8

SO HOW do you get even closer to God than you are now? Try these ideas:

- Ride an elevator to the top floor of a skyscraper.
- Work hard and become an astronaut.
- Climb Mount Everest.
- Walk around on stilts.

Just kidding. Getting close to God isn't about getting physically closer to the heavens. You want to get closer *relationally*. Here are a few steps you might want to consider:

First, think of God as someone who wants to be your incredibly close friend. If you ever think that God isn't interested in you or doesn't have time for you, whack those thoughts right out of your head. They aren't from God. He loves you and wants to get as close to you as you let him.

Second, spend time with God. That translates into the nitty gritty activities of reading his Word and talking to him in prayer. When you pray, tell God about your fears and hopes. Thank him for loving you and wanting to be your friend. Confess your sin and ask him to help you get closer to him by doing the things that please him.

Third, make it your habit to attend church services. You pull close to God through worship. Worship is a whole host of activities: singing praises to God with other Christians, talking to him, thinking about him, remembering how much he loves you and what Christ did for you, and learning from his Word. Okay, so your church's worship services might not be the most appealing to your student tastes. You might gag at the music, and the service might seem planned only for adults. But focus on Scripture, the main point of the message, the words of the songs, and fellowship with your Christian friends. If you skip worship services, you miss one of your greatest opportunities to get closer to God.

Your key is found in James' simple words: "Draw close to God, and God will draw close to you" (James 4:8). With every step you take toward God, he takes a giant stride toward you. You can't get closer to God just by fitting a few "Christian" things into your life. But you can get closer to him by asking him to help you get to know him better.

REFLECT: How are you trying to get close to God? Does anything need to change?

PRAY: Celebrate the fact that God wants to be your incredibly close friend.

26 No Lie

Bible Reading: Ephesians 4:25
> *Put away all falsehood and "tell your neighbor the truth."*
> *Ephesians 4:25*

DO YOU ever wonder if it's okay to tell a little white lie sometimes?

You could just as easily ask, "Is it okay to put your hand on a red-hot burner sometimes?" or "Is it okay to step in front of a roaring freight train sometimes?"

Truth is one of those absolute, always-right kind of things. Your job is to always tell the truth, because God always tells the truth. It's never right or good to lie, not even sometimes, not even a little. Lying gets you into trouble because one lie usually leads to another. Lying also makes it difficult for others to trust you.

But what if you're embarrassed or scared? Is it okay to lie then?

No. Lying is wrong because God is truth and because he has told us not to lie. Telling the truth can be tough at times—especially if you get embarrassed or punished for speaking truth. But it's always better to do what is right, even when it isn't easy. In the long run, doing life God's way is better for you and everybody.

Even though lying is common in our culture, the people around you really want you to be truthful with them. If you tell the truth even when it's hard, people will think, *Wow!* They will really respect you. They will trust you and consider you dependable. They might even look to you for advice and leadership. Few people, in fact, will stop being your friend just because you tell the truth. Your friends, classmates, relatives, and neighbors want to be able to trust what you say.

"Yeah, but do I have to tell the truth even when someone asks me to spill what I got him for his birthday?" God wants you to be truthful. But that doesn't mean you have to answer every question people ask you, and it doesn't mean you have to tell them everything you know. If someone asks you, "So did you get me a new CD for my birthday?" and you did, you aren't obligated to say so. It's time to say something like, "You'll just have to wait and see" or "You'll know the answer when you unwrap it."

And you can be truthful without being brutally honest. For example, if your girlfriend asks, "Do you like my new summer top?" and you hate the color, you don't have to say, "That's the ugliest color I have ever seen." Instead, try something truthful but kind like, "It looks really comfortable."

Make it a personal rule always to speak the truth, but always speak the truth in love (see Ephesians 4:15). And there's a good chance that your commitment to truth-telling will spark honesty in others around you.

REFLECT: Are you a truth-teller?

PRAY: Ask God to help you tell the truth, even when it will get you in trouble or make your life difficult.

27 Can the Garbage

Bible Reading: Philippians 4:8
> *Fix your thoughts on what is true and honorable and right.*
> *Philippians 4:8*

BORIS, a big black horsefly, was starving. He buzzed around the outside of the house, banging up against the windows, looking for a hole to get in. He wanted to get inside so he could feast on scraps and crumbs lying around in the kitchen. But the house was locked up tight, and the famished horsefly was getting desperate.

As Boris circled the house again, he spied the garbage can in the backyard. Flying closer, his eyes bugged out with delight. On the grass next to the garbage can was a big hunk of moldy lunch meat that had been thrown away earlier in the day. Boris swooped down and started eating. It was delicious, so he stuffed himself. Even when he thought he couldn't eat any more, he still kept munching away.

When Boris tried to fly away, he was too bloated to get off the ground. He cranked his wings up to full speed, but he was still too heavy to get airborne. He needed some kind of a head start to launch him into the air. Looking around the yard, he spotted a lawn mower sitting on the sidewalk. He dragged himself heavily to the lawn mower and started climbing up the wheel to the engine. He trudged heavily up the long arm of the mower to the handle. He thought, *Now I can jump off and my wings can take over and fly me home.*

Boris got his wings buzzing as fast as he could and then stepped off into space. But he was still too heavy, and the chubby horsefly plummeted to the cement and exploded with a splat. Boris's final thought before impact was *I should never fly off the handle when I'm full of baloney.*

Whoops. As Boris proved, nothing good ever comes from filling up on garbage.

That's especially true of some of the garbage you might be tempted to put in your head. It's not wrong to watch television or videos, or listen to hit music. But God wants you to be wise about just what you put into your mind through the media. There's a lot of garbage served up by TV programs, videos, and music that are popular in our culture. And what you put into your head can cause you to crash and burn just like Boris did.

You wouldn't dine on a plate of garbage; be just as discriminating about what you watch and listen to. You don't want to cram your mind full of suggestive lyrics and sinful activities any more than you want to put rotten meat or moldy bread into your mouth. The bad stuff you let in through your eyes and ears can make you sick just as certainly as eating garbage can.

 REFLECT: What are you putting into your head these days? Is it good for you?

PRAY: *God, give me your wisdom as I think about the videos, TV, and music I watch and listen to. Help me guard my mind.*

28 Going One-on-One with Sexual Curiosity

Bible Reading: James 1:12-16
Temptation comes from the lure of our own evil desires. James 1:14

CURIOSITY doesn't just kill cats. Sometimes it also clobbers young people.

Sexual temptation is a battle you can win, but you have to know how to prevail. If you survive with a healthy sort of sexual curiosity, it will be a fantastic gift when you someday marry the man or woman you want to love for a lifetime.

There's nothing wrong with sexual curiosity—wondering what's under the wrapping of someone you love. It's natural. Healthy. Normal. The problem comes in how you satisfy that curiosity. You might be committed to saving sex for marriage, but curiosity can still catch you off guard and clobber you big-time.

So here are some tips on managing sexual curiosity as the pressure on you increases to be sexually active:

First, *deal with your curiosity immediately—before it has a chance to dig in*. Often when your guard is down, the thought will dart through your mind that "just one look" or "just one touch" won't hurt. If that lie has a familiar ring to it, think back to the deceit of the old serpent in the Garden of Eden. God made sexual desire so that one thing leads to another. Once you light a sexual fire, stopping it is almost impossible. So your best defense is to stop it before it gets started.

Second, *find a few friends who share your values*. Talk seriously with them about sexual pressure. When you have friends who share your beliefs and with whom you can talk honestly, you gain amazing moral strength. You can support each other when you're feeling weak and your resistance is down. And low resistance happens to everyone.

You get amazing moral weakness, by the way, when you have friends who don't support your values. The Bible makes a lot of sense here when it says, "Bad company corrupts good morals" (1 Corinthians 15:33, NASB).

Third, *the most important sex organ God created is your mind—not your body*. It's control of your mind that shows your maturity. Being able to manage and control your sexual desires proves a whole lot more about your readiness than anything you could "prove" by letting those desires run wild. It takes guts to guard sex like a valuable diamond.

The sexual pressure you face will be great. The battle to stay pure will likely be furious. But the rewards of toughing it out are beyond description.

 REFLECT: What are you doing to effectively resist sexual temptation? What are you doing to deal with your curiosity?

PRAY: Thank God for giving you a marvelous body worth keeping for the one you marry.

29 X-Rated Scenes on the Brain

Bible Reading: 2 Timothy 2:20-22
Run from anything that stimulates youthful lust. 2 Timothy 2:22

MOST PEOPLE today have grown so comfortable with lustful thoughts and feelings that they don't even see them as a problem. Your world basically says, "Sex is a natural appetite. So when you feel hungry, feed it!" And you and your Christian friends probably don't talk much about dealing with lustful thoughts. It's rather refreshing to discover that the Bible talks a whole lot about it.

Paul says, "Run from anything that stimulates youthful lust" (2 Timothy 2:22). Lust is any sexual thought or action that might lead you to disobey God's laws or possibly hurt other people.

But why would a loving God give you the ability to feel such a powerful force as lust and then command you to ditch it—and *fast?* First, lust isn't something God gave you. It's actually taking God's beautiful gift of sexual love and distorting it. Love is *giving*—fulfilling and building up the other person. Lust is the opposite. It's *using*—taking the other person for your own sexual desires.

Second, God tells you to flee because lust is like a thief. It tries to steal your heart away from what God wants to be your first love—himself. When you give in to lust, your feelings toward God fade. You don't feel his presence as strongly as you did before. And it's hard to regain that closeness to God as long as you keep excusing your lustful thoughts or actions.

Sexual lust—plotting and planning to have sex outside of marriage—*blinds* you to God's purposes for you and *binds* you like a slave to your own sexual feelings.

When you struggle with lust and give in regularly to temptation, honesty will gradually disappear from your spiritual relationship with God. You might still read your Bible. You might even keep praying or going to church or youth group. But real, genuine honesty in your prayers . . . or a serious desire to apply God's Word to your life . . . or a true sense of worship when you go to church—those things are just plain missing. You are only going through the motions.

When you renew the honesty of your relationship with God, you will start winning the battle with lust. Here's why that works: Genuinely feeling love for God *always* leads to wanting to please him. And that *always* leads to obedience—even though it may be tough. But renewing your relationship with God takes a deliberate decision on your part—a decision to be honest with God in your prayers and to respond obediently to what you discover when you read the Bible.

REFLECT: How are you fanning the flame of your friendship with God?

PRAY: Ask God to help you please him and be honest with him rather than giving in to lust.

30 Taking Control

Bible Reading: Proverbs 6:24-29
Don't lust for her beauty. Don't let her coyness seduce you.
Proverbs 6:25

"BEFORE I became a Christian, I messed around sexually," Tyler admitted. "I expected trusting Christ would make all my wrong desires vanish. So far it hasn't worked that way. I'm reading my Bible, praying, and getting close to new Christian friends. But what else can I do?"

Just keeping in step with God won't automatically guarantee your bouts with lust will disappear. The important point is how you deal with them.

Here are some practical principles to help you handle sexual temptations:

1. *Your body is a spiritual battlefield.* Get used to the idea that the war will continue until Christ returns. There will always be a struggle.
2. *Take responsibility for your actions.* What might trip you up is the rampant idea that sexual urges are beyond your control. God created you in his image with infinite value and dignity—and with the ability to make moral, righteous decisions and abide by them. Most of the time people land in bad situations because they dive into them.
3. *Control your thought life, because that is where lust begins.* There's no way to put a lid on sinful thoughts outside of filling your mind with God's Word. Here are some Scriptures that can help: Psalm 51; Proverbs 6:27-28; Romans 6:12-14; 1 Corinthians 6:9-11 and 10:13; James 1:12 and 4:7; and 1 John 4:4.
4. *Choose your friends carefully.* Make sure your closest chums are people who help you, not who make it harder for you to handle temptation. Right friends can help you make right choices.
5. *Don't get overconfident about lust.* But don't get overly fearful either. You put yourself in danger at either extreme.
6. *Admit your struggles and sins to God as well as to another Christian you trust.* Talking openly can protect you from fooling yourself.
7. *When you see or meet someone who brings lustful thoughts to mind, force yourself to look in that person's face and eyes.* Changing where you aim your eyes sounds trite, but it helps you recognize and respond to the real person that is there and not just to the body that person is living in.

These truths have been used by thousands of students like you. Combining these weapons with a steady stream of prayer will keep your mind and body safe.

REFLECT: What steps will you take to guard your heart from lust?

PRAY: Tell God about your desire to stay pure in body and in heart.

A Lifetime Commitment

Bible Reading: Mark 16:15-18
> *Go into all the world and preach the Good News to everyone,*
> *everywhere. Mark 16:15*

THINK ABOUT THIS: Of all the commitments you will make in your lifetime, probably only a handful will be for life. As a Christian, you have committed yourself for life to be a disciple of Jesus Christ. And someday you may say "I do" to one marriage partner for life. But these days it's highly unlikely you'll stay in one career for life. You might even live in different cities, states, or countries over the years. And you'll be lucky if you have one or two friends who last a lifetime.

But if you are serious about serving Christ from here on out, you need to understand one critical lifetime commitment he has called you to make. Everyone Christ has rescued and called to be his disciple is *also* called to be a rescuer and discipler of others. And just as he intends for you to be a *disciple* for life, he also calls you to be a *discipler* for life. Praying for others, building bridges of love and concern to others, and sharing the gospel with others is a lifetime commitment.

God's Word makes your lifetime call to disciple others totally clear. Mark 16:15 and Matthew 28:18-20 describe what is called Christ's great commission. What's the great commission all about? It's the last, the clearest, and one of the most important commands Jesus ever gave his disciples. It means that everyone everywhere—whether at your school or on the other side of the planet—should have the opportunity to say yes to Jesus. Do you wonder how important that is to God? The great commission is a true expression of God's heart (see John 3:16), and when the great commission is completed, Christ will return (see Matthew 24:14).

You can be absolutely sure that God plans for you and for every Christian to be involved in helping fulfill the great commission. Why? First, because *it is a command.* The Bible says that if we love Christ we will obey his commands (see John 14:23). Second, because *the need is clear.* You will always have people around who need to hear the gospel and be discipled. And you're on the receiving end of an amazing promise as you get involved in helping fulfill the great commission: Christ promises to be with you always, because you need him always in your lifetime ministry of reaching others.

So does that mean God wants you to ditch your dreams of a career so you can become a full-time evangelist, campus worker, pastor, or missionary? Not necessarily. What you do for a career isn't the big issue. Your real task is to keep seeking God's will for your life—and no matter what he calls you to do, plan on using your career to help fulfill the great commission.

REFLECT: God has called you to help him fulfill the great commission. Can you sense his deep confidence in you?

PRAY: Talk to him today about your response to his call.

2 Commissioned 110 Percent

Bible Reading: 1 Corinthians 9:16

*Preaching the Good News is not something I can boast about. I am
compelled by God to do it. How terrible for me if I didn't do it!*
1 Corinthians 9:16

JASMINE DIDN'T LIKE Missions Fest, an annual conference at her church reminding
the congregation of its assignment to reach the world. Every year one or two speak-
ers always made her feel like spiritual slime. They were the ones who had a table at
the back of the room for sign-ups to go to Timbuktu—*today*.

You might wonder what it really means to commit yourself for life to fulfilling
the great commission as a rescuer and discipler of non-Christians. It doesn't mean
God drags you screaming to the other side of the world. It simply means:

- You always have a list of non-Christians you are praying for—family
  members, friends, classmates, neighbors, people you work with, etc.
- You are always making time to relate to and build bridges of
  communication with the non-Christians God is calling you to reach.
- You are always prepared to share a clear presentation of the gospel.
- You are always ready to disciple those who trust Christ.

If you're tempted to think that being a rescuer is a chore, remember several
things:

- *You are privileged to join with God in his mission to liberate people living
  in darkness.* Sharing him with others is one way you worship him and
  thank him for rescuing you.
- *You are empowered for what you are called to do.* The Holy Spirit within
  you makes you totally adequate for the task.
- *You will prevail.* As you let the Holy Spirit lead and empower you, you will
  see non-Christians rescued from the dominion of darkness and transferred
  into the kingdom of God.

Being a lifetime rescuer and discipler isn't a job, it's a lifestyle. So whether
you're at school, at work, in a restaurant, at a game, at a party, or wherever, you're
on duty. And you don't get to retire. God has two ways to let you know when to stop:
RIP or Rapture. Until then, you're still on active duty as a rescuer.

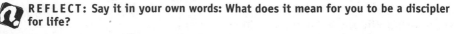 **REFLECT:** Say it in your own words: What does it mean for you to be a discipler
for life?

 PRAY: Ask God to guide you in the ministry of discipling that best fits the gifts he
has given you.

3 Do the Math

Bible Reading: 2 Timothy 2:1-7

You have heard me teach many things that have been confirmed by many reliable witnesses. Teach these great truths to trustworthy people who are able to pass them on to others. 2 Timothy 2:2

"JESUS TOLD US to go into all the world and make disciples," Jake said to four friends as they sipped milkshakes after youth group.

"Right," agreed Molly. "That's the great commission, God's strategy for reaching the world for Christ."

"But," Jake went on with a concerned look, "do the math. Even if all five of us won twenty-five people to Christ every day for the next twenty-five years—"

"Twenty-five people a *day?*" Blaine cut in. "Not going to happen."

"But if we *could* do that," Jake explained, "I mean, hypothetically, that would still only be a million people."

"But there are about six billion people in the world," Jenna said.

Carl said what they were all thinking. "What we can do is only a drop in the bucket. How is the world ever going to be won?"

There are two ways to look at the ministry of a lifetime rescuer and discipler. First, there is the strategy of *spiritual addition*—you share the gospel with unbelievers, they trust Christ, and the total increases with each new believer. If you were able to win a million people to Christ in your lifetime—or even a fraction of that—it would be great. But your efforts wouldn't come close to reaching the world.

The second strategy—the biblical strategy, by the way—is *spiritual multiplication*. Suppose you and four friends each win three people to Christ. In the next year you train those fifteen people to be rescuers also. In the second year, the five of you and your fifteen "disciples" each win and train three more, and you continue the process year after year. In ten years there would be over half a million in your multiplication network. And in fifteen years you could reach the whole world!

Multiplying is God's strategy for populating the earth physically (see Genesis 1:28) and for populating the kingdom of God spiritually (see 2 Timothy 2:2). God's plan is that you and your friends not only bring others to Christ, but that you equip the ones you win to rescue others. You might not trigger a network that reaches the world's population with the gospel in fifteen years. But you will have the joy of knowing you were part of the rescue of hundreds—maybe thousands—from Satan's kingdom. And that's really what it's all about.

REFLECT: Are you ready to accept Christ's commission to be a lifetime rescuer and discipler?

PRAY: If you are, pray a prayer of commitment right now.

4 After God Made You, He Broke the Mold

Bible Reading: Psalm 139:13-18
Thank you for making me so wonderfully complex! Psalm 139:14

GOD IS into wild variety. Have you ever thought about God's creativity? Every species of plants and animals is unique. Among the countless varieties of fish, for example, he designed some with spectacular coloring, some huge, others tiny. Marlin and manta ray, swordfish, shark, eel, and anglerfish all contribute to God's rich, colorful world of water life.

People love a world filled with variety too. Nikki paints striking watercolors, constantly searching for new subjects. Not satisfied with the garden in her backyard, she drives into the city for urban scenes or to a state park for forest images. Neal can sing every syllable of every song the classic Christian group Petra has ever recorded. But he also enjoys new groups.

Jesus, too, showed he liked a mix of people. He chose twelve disciples to live with him for three years, and they were radically different from each other. Some of them couldn't scrub away the smell of the fish they handled for a living. Matthew, on the other hand, probably reeked of expensive perfume when Jesus called him. One disciple probably had family connections in the high priest's administration. John seemed tenderhearted. Peter was often hard-nosed.

If God and Jesus, his Son, find variety and contrast appealing, and if we crave variety ourselves, then there's no way we should expect that God would make all of us alike. And all those stereotypes we create of who is "beautiful" or who is "better"—they're a lie!

You are unique. Of the six billion people alive right now on this planet, there's *no one* just like you. If there's only one you—out of all those billions and billions of people—why would you want to be like someone else? Multitudes go through life envying the build, hair, talents, or abilities of other people. So start fixing your thoughts on the fact that God made you one of a kind and, as one child put it, "God don't make no junk."

Maybe you're a jock and wish you were brainy. Or maybe you're quiet and introspective and would prefer to be the life of the party. Every quality has something valuable about it, and you're more likely to be at peace with yourself when you genuinely value the special personality qualities and skills God has given you—things that make you *you!* And when you appreciate those traits, you can work to develop them to the full.

REFLECT: Why did God make you the way you are?

PRAY: *Lord, thank you for making me just the way I am. Help me to appreciate the unique things about me.*

5 Specially Equipped

Bible Reading: 1 Corinthians 12:1-7

A spiritual gift is given to each of us as a means of helping the entire church. 1 Corinthians 12:7

ERIN FIGURED that all the popular girls at school were cheerleaders, and she was starved for that kind of recognition. She practiced all the routines and tried hard to improve her coordination. But she still failed in the tryouts.

"I worked so hard, Mom," she said. "I really wanted to make it. But I knew when I watched the others that they had the skills and I didn't. I finished the tryout, though, because I was still determined to make the squad."

Erin's mom didn't laugh off her daughter's hurt. "You know, Erin," she said, "you could probably make it next year if you want to. But what you said makes me think you might do better concentrating on something else. You learned from watching the other girls, and you were determined to stay in there even after you felt you couldn't win. Those are all good things, Erin, and there's someplace you can put those abilities to work." After a while her mom asked if she had thought of student council, thinking that might be a good fit.

Erin gave it a try. She started attending student council meetings and volunteered to help with schoolwide activities. She found she liked influencing student-body life.

Erin didn't make a mistake when she tried to be a cheerleader. She might have been miserable, though, if she'd kept trying to be something she wasn't. And she found her best fit when she decided to be herself. She's in a place where God can use her in meaningful ways as she seeks to befriend others.

God has equipped each of us with a special ability to serve others in a unique way. If you are a Christian, the Holy Spirit has a unique way he wants to express the love of God through you. It's your "spiritual gift." And that spiritual gift God gives you goes even beyond other talents and skills you have to offer others. It helps others at a deeper level.

That's a truth you accept by faith—in other words, God said it, so you believe it's true even if you can't see right now exactly what your gift is. You can anticipate God bringing it out as you learn how to share your life with others.

Your gifts make you significant not only to God but also to each other. Whether you realize it or not, you are a vital part of God's plan. No one else can do what God has planned for you to do.

REFLECT: How are you trying to fit in? Are you looking for *your* best fit—or someone else's?

PRAY: Ask God to show you the gifts you have to offer your world.

6 More Love than You Can Handle

Bible Reading: Jeremiah 31:1-6

I have loved you, my people, with an everlasting love. With unfailing love I have drawn you to myself. Jeremiah 31:3

WITHIN THE FIRST week at his new school, David realized his wardrobe was all wrong. "When we moved here, my parents said, 'Only girls have to worry about what they wear,' " he said in frustration. "But it's like there's a school uniform, even for the guys—clothes bought at one stupidly expensive store. If you aren't dressed from head to toe in those clothes, you don't exist."

Jesus is a unique friend. There's not one thing you have to do to gain his acceptance and friendship. That's sometimes hard to believe, because in every other human relationship, people expect you to measure up to their expectations. You have to earn, beg, or buy their respect. Different people have different kinds of expectations, but everyone has some expectations.

Jesus is a purely loving person. Love is a part of his very being, so it doesn't waver depending on what you do. He goes on being a friend in spite of your failures, sins, or setbacks.

Love can't be separated from Jesus. He can't stop loving you, because love is part of who he is. He doesn't love you because you behave or look good or wear the right brands—he loves you because he is love to the very core of his being.

You might not know that God loved you even before you became a Christian. Romans 5 says that even when you were God's enemy, he loved you—even while you were a sinner. If he loved you in that condition, how much more does he love you now as his adopted child? The bottomless depth of this love is revealed in John 15:9 where Jesus says, "I have loved you even as the Father has loved me. Remain in my love."

Jesus will always be your companion. You will always be significant to him. It can never be otherwise. Jesus will never dole out his friendship with you according to your performance; he pours it on according to his love. No one can be the friend Jesus is. When you know Jesus as a companion who affirms you, loves you, and drenches you with significance, then you are free to be who he made you to be. Even the devil's attacks can't keep you down for long, because you will bounce back through the encouragement, strength, and love of your compassionate, powerful friend, Jesus Christ.

You are accepted and significant to Jesus. Enjoy!

REFLECT: How is the way Jesus cares for you different from how people often treat you?

PRAY: *God, I want to be who you created me to be. I don't want to be like someone else. I just want to be myself in all that you intended for me.*

7 Is the Holy Bible Holey?

Bible Reading: Matthew 4:1-11

People need more than bread for their life; they must feed on every word of God. Matthew 4:4

"THE BIBLE is like Swiss cheese," Brianna argued. "It's tasty in some spots, but it's got a lot of holes in it too."

Some people praise the Bible for its help and inspiration. "I especially like Psalm 23," they might say. "It's so beautiful." But if you press them far enough, they eventually admit they don't think much of the Bible at all. "Of course, there are problems in the Bible," they say. "I mean, mistakes and all. But that doesn't bother me. After all, it wasn't written to be a history textbook. It's accurate where it needs to be, like in matters of faith and doctrine."

The *holey* Bible theory is a myth. Much of the time people who make that claim have only vague ideas what "mistakes" they're talking about. The Bible isn't full of holes. It's the inspired Word of God, written over a period of about sixteen hundred years by about forty different authors. It has been remarkably preserved from the original manuscripts by painstaking copyists and careful scholars. The Old and New Testaments are the most accurately preserved and widely attested documents of the ancient world.

The followers of Jesus can't ignore the fact that the Lord himself believed in the accuracy of the Scriptures. He said, "The Scriptures cannot be altered" (John 10:35). He related the experience of Jonah as fact, not fiction. He quoted Scripture in his desert battle with Satan. He regarded the teachings, historical details, and events of the Old Testament as accurate.

The New Testament writers likewise confirmed the reliability of Scripture. The apostle Paul wrote, "All Scripture is inspired by God and is useful to teach us what is true and to make us realize what is wrong in our lives. It straightens us out and teaches us to do what is right" (2 Timothy 3:16). And Paul also acknowledged the inspiration of the New Testament writings with statements like, "What I am saying is a command from the Lord himself" (1 Corinthians 14:37).

In the Bible you can find different perspectives of the same event—different emphases in retelling incidents, in other words—and other *apparent* discrepancies. Still, when you open the Bible, you are reading the inspired, preserved, reliable Word of God. It's reliable because the loving, powerful God who gave it to you is reliable.

REFLECT: How would you answer a non-Christian friend who thinks the Bible is full of holes?

PRAY: Pray for your friends who think the way Brianna thinks.

8 Fully Fact or Fanciful Fiction?

Bible Reading: John 19:35

This report . . . is presented so that you also can believe. John 19:35

ANNA GOT slammed when she mentioned in class that she believed the Bible was true. "You can't be serious!" someone said. "The Bible?" Another responded, "You can't tell me that you believe in that Jonah-in-the-whale stuff? And walking on water? Come on, get real!"

"Let's be reasonable," came another response. "The Bible may have its place in religion, but that's where it belongs. Don't ask me to take it seriously."

In the past few years some people—even some Bible scholars—have decided the Bible is best understood as a compilation of religious folklore and legends.

Admittedly, there's no missing the fact that the Bible does tell some pretty extraordinary stories. But no matter how incredible some Bible stories may seem, the people who reported these things clearly meant their accounts to be understood not as myth or legend but as fact.

Not only that, but the New Testament writers knew that relating such astonishing facts might cost them their lives. How many people do you know who would gladly go to prison or die for a lie?

The New Testament writers certainly knew that telling stories about a rabbi raising himself from the dead or feeding five thousand people from five loaves of bread and two fish was a sure ticket to the funny farm—unless there were other witnesses. Contrary to the myths, legends, and mystery religions of the ancient world, the events recorded in the Bible "were not done in a corner" (Acts 26:26). A whole bunch of people saw them as they happened. Reliable people testified—in writing—to the authenticity of those events and signed their testimony in blood. And those writings, far from being effectively refuted and discredited, stood the test of time and were recognized as authoritative.

Peter himself answered the myths and legends myth when he wrote, "We were not making up clever stories when we told you about the power of our Lord Jesus Christ and his coming again. We have seen his majestic splendor with our own eyes" (2 Peter 1:16).

Read John 19:35. Who is the writer? Was he an eyewitness to the things he wrote about? Do you think he intended what he wrote to be understood as fact—or as fiction?

REFLECT: Say it in your own words: How do we know the Bible isn't a pack of myths?

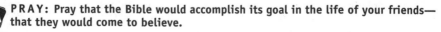

PRAY: Pray that the Bible would accomplish its goal in the life of your friends— that they would come to believe.

9 Details, Details, Details

Bible Reading: 2 Peter 1:16–21

It was the Holy Spirit who moved the prophets to speak from God.
2 Peter 1:21

NATHAN BURST through the door of his youth pastor's office. "Caleb, you've gotta see this book I got from Todd. It's a bunch of predictions by some old guy named Nostradamus. He predicted lots of things before they happened, like Hitler and World War II and Kennedy's assassination."

"Did you *see* the so-called prophecies he made?" Caleb probed.

"Yeah. Well, Todd pointed them out to me."

"Didn't they seem kind of vague? Like they might apply to any number of situations or interpretations?"

Nathan thought, then shrugged. "I guess."

"It's amazing to me that people get so wrapped up in Nostradamus's doubtful prophecies—but they completely ignore the prophecies of Scripture. Those are prophecies you can see are divinely inspired and clearly fulfilled."

Nathan was interested. He put the Nostradamus book down. "Like what?"

"Like Jesus being born in Bethlehem. Micah predicted that. And Zechariah predicted that the Messiah would ride into Jerusalem on a donkey."

"Oh yeah," Nathan said, "and that he would be betrayed too, right?"

"Right. Betrayed by a friend, for thirty pieces of silver; that his hands and feet would be pierced; that his bones would not be broken—*details*, not vague generalizations or lucky guesses, but dozens of specific predictions that came true with 100 percent accuracy. And that's just the prophecies about the Messiah. The same is true of prophecies about cities and nations all through the Bible."

Nathan's youth pastor is right. Biblical prophecy reveals with startling force the unique character and reliability of the Hebrew and Christian Scriptures. Awareness of the prophecies about the Messiah can convince all but the most biased reader of the truth of the Bible.

Some imaginative critics think that the fulfillment of biblical prophecy is due to coincidence. But could you find the forty-eight major prophecies that concern the Messiah fulfilled in any one man? The chances of that happening by coincidence, says Peter Stoner in *Science Speaks,* are 1 in 10 to the power of 157, or the number 10 followed by 157 zeroes!

God didn't want there to be any doubt in your mind that his Word is true and reliable. He made the proof undeniable, and the many detailed and fulfilled prophecies of Scripture are just one way he removes any shadow of doubt.

REFLECT: How does the reliability of Bible prophecies compare to those by folks like Nostradamus? Explain.

PRAY: Praise God for giving you his reliable Word.

10 A Life Worth Watching

Bible Reading: 1 Peter 1:13-19

He paid for you with the precious lifeblood of Christ, the sinless, spotless Lamb of God. 1 Peter 1:19

QUIZ TIME: Who is the most right-living person you know, the person who is a great example of obedience to God?

    a. One or both of your parents?
    b. A grandparent or another relative?
    c. Your pastor or youth leader?
    d. A well-known Christian figure?
    e. A friend?

When it comes to knowing and doing right, there is no substitute for a living, breathing, right-under-your-nose example. You can't beat having someone you know modeling a pattern of godliness in front of you.

But Jesus Christ does one better. No, you can't see him in person. But through the Bible you can spot him in action and witness his awesome acts as the ultimate example of doing right. His life and ministry on earth made all the moral precepts in the Old Testament up close and personal. Jesus not only taught the moral law of God, but unlike any other human being in your life, he also lived it to perfection.

The life of Jesus shouts God's love for his human creation. Like John observed, "God showed how much he loved us by sending his only Son into the world so that we might have eternal life through him" (1 John 4:9). Christ was God's love gift to us wrapped in human flesh. His coming in the flesh—his "incarnation"—was the expression of God's love in human life.

The Bible leaves no doubt about the perfection of Christ's life. Peter said, "He never sinned, and he never deceived anyone" (1 Peter 2:22). He was "the sinless, spotless Lamb of God" (1:19). He "faced all of the same temptations we do, yet he did not sin" (Hebrews 4:15).

John's first letter lays out several references to Christ's sinlessness: "There is no darkness in him at all" (1 John 1:5); "Jesus Christ, the one who pleases God completely" (2:1); "Christ is pure" (3:3); and "There is no sin in him" (3:5). Even Pilate said, "I find nothing wrong with this man!" (Luke 23:4).

Even the best human examples of obedience and purity fail at times. Say thanks to God for the good examples you have in your family members, church leaders, and friends. But keep your main focus on the *perfect* example by filling your mind with the words and deeds of Jesus Christ, the Son of God.

REFLECT: How is Jesus the best example you could ever follow?

PRAY: Tell Jesus you're glad he blazes a trail for you.

11

More than Enough Love to Go Around: Part 1

Bible Reading: 1 Peter 2:21-25
Christ, who suffered for you, is your example. Follow in his steps.
1 Peter 2:21

DOES IT EVER bother you that Jesus lived a perfect life of love—and you don't? Do you sometimes shake your head at yourself and sigh, "What's the use? I'll never measure up to Christ's example"?

Don't be discouraged. Christ *is* perfect in everything, including his love for the Father and for each of us. But even though he encourages us to follow his example (see 1 Peter 2:21), he understands our weaknesses and forgives our imperfection. John wrote about this contrast: "I am writing this to you so that you will not sin. But if you do sin, there is someone to plead for you before the Father. He is Jesus Christ, the one who pleases God completely" (1 John 2:1).

God's standard for us is Jesus' perfection (see Ephesians 4:13), and he is at work making us over into the image of his Son (see Romans 8:29; Philippians 2:13). One day we will be just like Jesus (see 1 John 3:2). Until then, we will always be in the process of learning to love God and others like Jesus loved.

First, *Jesus loved without discrimination*. Jesus spent time with everyone who came to him, even misfits and outcasts. He was at home with both the wealthy and the poor. He ministered to prostitutes, dishonest tax collectors, Roman soldiers, and stuffy Jewish religious leaders. Jesus shows how you can look past physical, cultural, and socioeconomic differences to see every person as someone worth loving.

Second, *Jesus loved without conditions*. He loved people whether or not they accepted him as Messiah and Lord. He showed the same concern for Judas as the other disciples (see John 6:70-71; 17:12). He prayed for those who crucified him (see Luke 23:34). Jesus shows how to love people not because they love you, know you, or care about you at all but because everyone needs God's love—and yours.

Third, *Jesus loved without measure*. Paul prayed we would "have the power to understand . . . how wide, how long, how high, and how deep his love really is" (Ephesians 3:18). Why bother to understand the greatness of Christ's love? Because only then will your love grow wide and long and high and deep enough to meet the love needs of people around you.

REFLECT: How does grasping Christ's great love help you love the way you wish you could?

PRAY: *Jesus, I can't love as perfectly as you do, but I want to grow in my love for God and others. Thanks for being my example.*

12 More than Enough Love to Go Around: Part 2

Bible Reading: Galatians 2:17-21

I live my life in this earthly body by trusting in the Son of God, who loved me and gave himself for me. Galatians 2:20

IF YOU WANTED to be a world-whipping soccer player, who would you rather spend time with: (a) a professional baseball player? (b) a professional couch potato? (c) a professional hockey player? (d) a professional soccer player? Unless you subscribe to some weird theory of cross-training, you would want to be with the one who plays your sport at the highest level so you could pick up skills from his or her example.

Just like that, you need to spend time with Jesus Christ to learn about love. He's "the pro." His example will help you figure out how to love God and others at the highest level. Here is more of what you can learn about Christ's love:

First, *Christ's love is sacrificial.* Paul cheered that Christ "loved me and gave himself for me" (Galatians 2:20). Jesus proclaimed, "I lay down my life for the sheep. . . . No one can take my life from me. I lay down my life voluntarily" (John 10:15, 18). Loving people like Christ loved might cost you time, money, energy, comfort, and convenience. And yet John, known as the apostle of love, issues this challenge: "Christ gave up his life for us. And so we also ought to give up our lives for our Christian brothers and sisters" (1 John 3:16). Christians love even when it costs something because they have experienced Christ's sacrificial love.

Second, *Christ's love kept him connected to people.* He mingled with crowds, lived with his disciples, went to holiday feasts, and spent time in the temple and synagogue. Even though he took time to rest and pray alone, Jesus was a mixer, pouring himself into people. If you want to follow his example, invest your life in others. You might make friends with a new group of kids at school, join a team or club, or volunteer for a committee at school or church. Get involved with people with the goal of being a friend, encouraging them, and sharing the Good News with them. Then you're loving like Christ loved.

Third, *Christ's love was tough.* He wasn't unloving when he blasted the Pharisees for their hypocrisy (see Matthew 23:13, 16, 33). Nor was he unloving when he warned people of the fires of hell (see Matthew 5:22; 18:8). Love doesn't need to be wimpy to be kind. You are following Christ's example of hard-nosed love when God leads you to speak out against a school assignment that violates scriptural principles—or when you question a policy that is dishonest or unfair. You might not like to warn people they're running away from God. But to do anything else is unloving.

REFLECT: What surprises you about Christ's love? Of all the ways Christ loves you, which is the hardest for you to imitate?

PRAY: Ask the "love pro" to teach you his ways for loving those around you.

13 Tapping Into the Power of Love

Bible Reading: 1 Corinthians 13:1-13

When the Holy Spirit controls our lives, he will produce this kind of fruit in us: love, joy, peace, patience, kindness, goodness, faithfulness, gentleness, and self-control. Galatians 5:22-23

THE MEDIA says that true love is what you get when the cutest Hollywood couples stroll up at the Oscars or the Emmys. It's a box-office-busting actress in a show-it-all dress hanging on the arm of her equally box-office-busting man.

The love of Christ looks more than a little different from that. And God's plan is that you display love far deeper than Hollywood romance.

You likely have heard 1 Corinthians 13—the love chapter of the Bible—read at weddings. But studying that passage is a fantastic way to look at Christ's selfless love. Consider what the character of Christ looks like when you insert his name for the word *love* in verses one through eight:

If I speak in the tongues of men and of angels, but have not Christ, I am only a resounding gong or a clanging cymbal. If I have the gift of prophecy and can fathom all mysteries and all knowledge, and if I have a faith that can move mountains, but have not Christ, I am nothing. If I give all I possess to the poor and surrender my body to the flames, but have not Christ, I gain nothing.

Christ is patient, Christ is kind. He does not envy, he does not boast, he is not proud. He is not rude, he is not self-seeking, he is not easily angered, he keeps no record of wrongs. Christ does not delight in evil but rejoices with the truth. He always protects, always trusts, always hopes, always perseveres. Christ never fails.

There's no comparison in the world to the perfection of Christ's love. The astounding thing is that one of God's goals is to build the love of Christ in you. In fact, if you are willing to stop thinking of yourself and allow God's love to flow through you to others, you will receive the power to love as Christ loved.

Christ is God's perfect love in person, and Christ lives in you. If you want to grasp the significance of God's love operating in and through your life—and see what it would look like—copy 1 Corinthians 13 to a sheet of paper. And this time, put *your* name where Christ's name is. Then read these lines to yourself several times as a prayer.

Christ's love is more than a pattern for your life. It gives you the power that enables you to live a life of perfect love. If you know God and are filled with his power, the life of love he requires of you is an absolutely achievable possibility.

REFLECT: Say in your own words what Christ's love looks like.

PRAY: *God, fill me with the love of Christ so I can love others.*

14 Blindsided by Death

Bible Reading: 2 Corinthians 1:3-7
*When others are troubled, we will be able to give them the same
comfort God has given us. 2 Corinthians 1:4*

SEVENTEEN-YEAR-OLD Paige just lost her father to bone cancer after he suffered for eight months. She misses her dad horribly.

Curt, a high school sophomore, was in his friend Ed's car when a truck rammed into the driver's side. Ed died in Curt's arms.

When Cindy went to check on her six-month-old brother during his naptime, Ty was blue and not breathing. When the EMTs arrived, Ty was pronounced dead.

It's indescribably painful and difficult to cope with the death of a loved one or close friend. You might have made that discovery firsthand. Whether it is a parent or a grandparent succumbing to terminal cancer, a friend or classmate killed in a car accident, or any loss of someone dear to you, it hurts. Even if you haven't experienced such a loss, you probably have friends who have—or will. How do you get through that kind of tragedy?

First, when someone close to you dies, you likely will experience a wide range of emotions. You might feel terribly sad, depressed, hopeless, abandoned, frightened, and even angry because of what happened. And you might get intensely angry at the situation, at the person who died and left you alone, at the person(s) you consider responsible for the death, or even at God for allowing it to happen. All these feelings are normal and natural. Emotions are a built-in release valve to help you handle deep inner pain.

Second, your greatest need in the first hours after the death of a friend or loved one is for others to comfort you. That sounds obvious, but what exactly is comfort? It's *not* a "pep talk" urging you to hang in there, tough it out, or hold it together. Comfort isn't an attempt to explain why bad things happen to people. It's not a bunch of positive words about God being in control and everything being okay. All those things can be good and useful in time, but they don't fill our pressing need for comfort.

Real comfort is having people feel your hurt and sorrow with you. You receive comfort when you know you aren't suffering alone. Paul says, "When others are happy, be happy with them. If they are sad, share their sorrow" (Romans 12:15). You sense God's care and concern for you as someone hurts with you, feels sad with you, and cries with you. So when you hurt, find somebody who will hurt with you. It's one of God's huge helps to getting through your sorrow.

 REFLECT: Are you hurting because of the death of someone close to you—recently or in the past? What help do you need from others?

PRAY: Ask God to help you talk to friends and family members about how they can comfort you.

15 Working Your Way through the Pain

Bible Reading: Romans 8:26-30
We know that God causes everything to work together for the good of those who love God and are called according to his purpose for them.
Romans 8:28

A MONTH after Amy's dad died, the friends who were so sympathetic at first didn't seem to care so much anymore. She was still a jumble of emotions when they started saying things like, "It's time to move on" and even, "Snap out of it!" Amy wondered what was wrong with her that she just couldn't shake the pain.

What no one told Amy was that when death takes away someone dear, you go through the same emotional process most people go through after tragedy hits. Your grieving can last weeks or months, and people often whirl through five clearly identifiable stages.

One of the first responses to grief is *denial*. At times you might find yourself unwilling to believe such a terrible thing has really happened to you.

A second stage in responding to grief is *anger*. You grapple with the inevitable question, "Why did this happen?" And when you discover there is no reasonable answer to that question, you might find yourself lashing out. You might aim your anger at people you think are at least partially responsible, at the person who died, and even at yourself, thinking you are partly to blame.

A third stage of grief is *bargaining* with God for relief from the awful event and its consequences. You might try to cut a deal with God, vowing to do anything if he would just bring back your loved one or make the pain go away.

Another stage of grief is *depression*. You realize your loved one is actually gone. You feel overwhelming sadness or hopelessness over the loss. Depression can be accompanied by fear, anxiety, or insecurity about living on without your loved one. Intense loneliness is another side of depression.

The final stage of grief is *acceptance*. As time goes by and the other stages of grief fade, you start to accept the reality of your loss and deal with it constructively.

Most Christian counselors agree that after the death of a loved one it's healthy to experience the five stages of grief. Some of your thoughts or emotions might be new to you—or stronger than ever before in your life. There's nothing wrong with you. You are going through a common response to the very sad event in your life.

Time is one of your best helps in dealing with the death of a loved one. As weeks pass, your sorrow does lessen and your life does feel a little more normal. But time only heals if you don't expect the pain to go away too soon.

REFLECT: What are those stages of grief all about? Could you use that knowledge to help yourself or a hurting friend?

PRAY: Ask God for help in understanding the swirl of emotions you or your hurting friends face.

Bible Reading: Galatians 6:1-5

Share each other's troubles and problems, and in this way obey the law of Christ. Galatians 6:2

"WHEN MY GRANDMA died, it's like I froze," Ryan admitted. "My homework wasn't getting done—especially a huge research paper for history class. But Taylor talked through the project with me little by little. We brainstormed a topic, talked about research sources, and came up with a list of questions to ask the teacher when I got stuck. I couldn't have survived that semester without Taylor's help."

When you lose a loved one through death—or face any other life-altering tragedy—you need more than just comfort to get through the pain. And it's the same kind of help you can offer friends who suffer.

First, you need *support*. What's the difference between comfort and support? People supply comfort when they share your emotional pain. People supply support when they help in practical ways. Life doesn't stop after a tragedy, but the emotional burden you are carrying often saps your energy. You and others in your family probably need help for a while just getting normal tasks done. You need help from people committed to obeying Galatians 6:2, "Carry each other's burdens, and in this way you will fulfill the law of Christ" (NIV).

You might be shocked at the idea of admitting you need help. You might not want to bother others for things you normally do for yourself. Resist the temptation to ignore or push away the support others offer. God put Galatians 6:2 in the Bible because he knows there are times you need the support of others. This is such a time. Let other people do things for you, and be grateful for their help.

So what if you need something and nobody steps up to offer help? Ask for it. There's nothing wrong with telling a trusted friend, a youth leader, or your minister about your need and asking for help.

Second, you need *encouragement*. You receive encouragement when someone does something thoughtful to lift your spirits. Be thankful when people ask how you are doing—or when you receive flowers, cards, letters, or e-mail. Again—if you don't get the encouragement you need, ask for it.

After a loss it takes time to move through the stages of grief, so you will need a heap of comfort, support, and encouragement for a while. Don't expect that you will be ready to dive back into life as usual right away. Let your friends and family care for you as long as you need it.

REFLECT: If you aren't suffering the pain of losing a loved one, keep alert to friends who are. How can you share comfort, support, and encouragement with them?

PRAY: Ask God today to prepare you to share with people around you who suffer from the pain of personal tragedy.

17 Down but Not Out

Bible Reading: Genesis 37:18-28
God turned into good what you meant for evil. Genesis 50:20

JAMAL STOOD UP for what he believed . . . and then he got slammed for it.

Friday night he went cruising with his friends, Tony and Gil, in Tony's car. When Tony spotted his brother's college roommate in the liquor store parking lot, he swerved into the lot. "Hey, Wayne," Tony called. "Do me a favor."

Jamal knew immediately what was going on. Tony was going to persuade Wayne to buy to beer for them—they were underage, but Wayne wasn't. So he spoke up. "Guys, I can't go along with this. Let's do something else."

"Oh, that's right," Tony said sarcastically. "You don't do this kind of thing."

Jamal didn't want to start anything with his friends. But he didn't feel right about what they were doing. He tried to talk them out of it, but Tony gave Wayne the money anyway.

"Tell you what," Jamal said when he saw Wayne go into the store. "I'll get home by myself, okay?" He opened the car door. "I'll see you guys later."

As Jamal walked away from the car, he cringed at the angry words Tony hurled at his back. He had no idea if Tony and Gil would stay mad at him. He knew he should be proud of himself for standing up for what was right. But right now all he felt was stomped on.

It can be lonely to stand up for your beliefs and face rejection and ridicule. If you stick to your convictions—especially about moral and spiritual issues—you might find family members and friends laughing at you or turning their backs and walking away. That's painful.

Joseph, whose high points—and low ones, too—are recorded in Genesis 37–50, knew what it was like to have relationships crumble when he didn't go along with the crowd. His father's favorite, Joseph was hated by his jealous older brothers. They sold him into slavery to get rid of him and then told their father he had been killed by wild animals. Joseph spent many years in bondage before God vindicated him.

Joseph's story shows how God unfailingly sticks with those who stand true to him. A statement is woven through Joseph's story that tells the key to his success: "The Lord was with Joseph." It also reveals the fact that God has a master plan he is working out—a plan that uses both the positive and negative experiences in your life. Even when you feel ditched by family or friends, God hasn't ditched you. And he will use the rejection you feel to help you grow even stronger.

 REFLECT: When have you suffered for doing the right thing? How did you react?

PRAY: *Lord, help me be glad to do the right thing even when people pressure me to do wrong.*

18 Rolling with the Punches

Bible Reading: James 4:7-10

When you bow down before the Lord and admit your dependence on him, he will lift you up and give you honor. James 4:10

JEFF WAS a shy sixteen-year-old who decided to work at a summer camp. He worked hard to connect with campers and staff. Even though starting conversations was hard for him, he did his best to be friendly. But his shyness made him the brunt of jokes from other staff members. The situation was painful, but he kept a good attitude even when he was left out of staff activities.

Halfway through the summer, the director called Jeff into his office. "Jeff, I've been watching you," he said. "I'm happy with how you go out of your way to befriend campers. I'd like to count on you for next year." The director's words really helped Jeff put the events of that summer in perspective and to handle the ugly situation with his fellow staffers positively.

All rejection isn't alike. There are four reasons rejection happens:

One, you might experience *positive rejection*. That's what happens when you hold positive Christian values—the ones clearly indicated in the Bible—and someone mocks you because of them. For example, the Bible tells you to have nothing to do with sexual immorality. So if your friends laugh at you for deciding to stay a virgin until marriage, you're the target of positive rejection.

Two, you may face *negative rejection*. That happens when people exclude you because you do something that bugs them—something not clearly commanded in the Bible. Tyrone thinks it's important to pray before every meal, even when he eats in a restaurant. So when his meal is served, he kneels on the floor and prays aloud, thanking God for the food. Can you see why many of Tyrone's friends won't go to a restaurant with him? That's negative rejection.

Three, you might sometimes experience *self-imposed rejection*. That's when you choose to remove yourself from some objectionable activity. You decide you don't want to associate with someone with a foul mouth or a dirty mind. So you look for new friends who share your values. In the meantime, you might have to cope with loneliness, but your isolation is something you chose.

Four, there are times you face *other-imposed rejection*. Someone decides he or she doesn't want to hang around you because of your Christian lifestyle. He or she might find countless reasons to reject you. That's when you have to ask yourself a tough question: Is that person's "friendship" worth the price of dumping your own values, morals, or beliefs?

REFLECT: When was the last time you felt rejected? Why did people reject you? Is there anything you wish you could have done differently?

PRAY: *Lord, help me stay obedient to you and positive toward others even when they reject me for my convictions or behavior.*

19 Turn to the One Who Understands

Bible Reading: Philippians 4:10-14
*I can do everything with the help of Christ who gives me the strength
I need. Philippians 4:13*

WHEN HANNAH graduated into the high-school group at church, she never clicked—or rather, she never fit into the tight cliques of the group. She started going to another church with a friend, but she always felt like an outsider. Now Hannah has drifted away from church completely—and nobody from either church has even noticed.

You aren't abnormal if you want to have friends and be liked. Like every other human being, you have a built-in need to be significant to others. And unless you are highly unusual, at times you have faced situations that are painful because you are left out. Ridiculed. Or ignored. How you handle those predicaments either makes you stronger or sets you up for further hurt.

Jesus Christ is a friend who knows what rejection feels like. Isaiah described him this way: "He was despised and rejected—a man of sorrows, acquainted with bitterest grief. We turned our backs on him and looked the other way when he went by. He was despised, and we did not care" (53:3). Can you feel something of what Jesus must have felt? He was hated by many. He was slandered by religious leaders—some even claimed that he was the devil! When he was nailed to the cross, he endured ridicule and mockery from heartless crowds. And even those he loved the most turned their backs on him.

So when you are rejected, ridiculed, or ignored by others, your dear friend Jesus knows better than anyone else what you are going through. He's there with you, sharing your hurt and reaching out to comfort, encourage, and strengthen you in brutal times. Jesus not only knows about the loneliness of rejection, but he's also the answer to it. He's the one true friend who will never dump you. He will never reject you. By growing a friendship with him, you gain the greatest source of strength you can ever find. No matter how others trash you, you can always survive because you have a deeply trusting friendship with Jesus. Not only will you survive, but you will thrive and gain new strength through Christ.

Keep this truth in mind: "This High Priest of ours [Jesus] understands our weaknesses, for he faced all of the same temptations we do, yet he did not sin" (Hebrews 4:15). When you're fighting a losing battle, ask Jesus to give you strength. And make this statement from Paul your motto: "I can do everything with the help of Christ who gives me the strength I need" (Philippians 4:13).

REFLECT: Have you felt rejected and alone today? Are you being ignored or ridiculed by a family member or friend?

PRAY: Pour your feelings out to Jesus. He's the one who understands, cares, and acts compassionately on your behalf.

20 The Wisdom of "Foolish" Words

Bible Reading: 1 Corinthians 1:18-20

I know very well how foolish the message of the cross sounds to those who are on the road to destruction. 1 Corinthians 1:18

CHECK OUT these statements from insurance forms—forms where drivers had to describe the details of their car accident in the fewest words possible.

- Coming home I drove into the wrong house and collided with a tree I don't have.
- A truck backed through my windshield and into my wife's face.
- The guy was all over the road. I had to swerve a number of times before I hit him.
- I had been driving for forty years when I fell asleep at the wheel and had an accident.
- To avoid hitting the bumper of the car in front, I struck a pedestrian.
- An invisible car came out of nowhere, struck my car and vanished.
- I was sure the old fellow would never make it to the other side of the road when I struck him.
- I was thrown from my car as it left the road. I was later found in a ditch by some stray cows.
- The pedestrian had no idea which direction to run, so I ran over him.
- The indirect cause of the accident was a little guy in a small car with a big mouth.

Think about this: Sometimes your explanations of Christ and what he has done in your life will sound just as weird to non-Christians as those statements sound to an insurance company—and to us. You claim that Jesus Christ was the Son of God, and people blow you off. You invite people to trust Christ and experience his life-changing power in their lives, and they laugh at you. You explain what God has done in your life, and they insist that you're over-emotionalizing your religion.

You want your non-Christian friends to welcome your life-giving witness, but don't be totally disheartened if they don't. You never know how the Holy Spirit will use your words. And no matter how people react to what you say, you are sharing God's utter wisdom. Give God time to take your words to the heart, where they will make a real difference.

 REFLECT: How can you explain to your non-Christian friends what Christ has done in your life?

PRAY: Ask God for courage to share how you got to know him—even when you fear your friends might mock you.

21 Take It Away, Jesus

Bible Reading: 1 Corinthians 1:21-25
Christ is the mighty power of God and the wonderful wisdom of God.
1 Corinthians 1:24

AN OLD scientist supplemented his retirement income by traveling from university to university with his chauffeur, Bob, and delivering a lecture on his field of expertise. Over the long weeks of travel, the scientist and Bob became friends.

One day as they drove to the next lecture, the scientist said, "I'm getting tired of giving the same lecture every day. You give the lecture this time, Bob."

"Are you kidding?" Bob protested. "I'm no scientist."

"These people don't know that," the scientist explained. "They have never seen either of us before. Besides, you've heard the lecture so many times you practically know it by heart. So you be the scientist, and I'll be the chauffeur."

"But the audience always asks questions after the lecture," Bob argued.

"They ask the same old questions every time, and you have heard me answer them all. Just answer the way I do."

After thinking about it for a moment, Bob smiled. "Okay, I'll do it."

The lecture went off perfectly, and nobody suspected that the "scientist" addressing the audience was really a chauffeur. And during the question-and-answer period, Bob sounded like an expert. He had heard the scientist answer the same questions many times before.

Then someone asked a new question—the most difficult and complex question the chauffeur had ever heard. "That's a great question," Bob said. "It's so simple, in fact, that even my chauffeur can answer it." Nodding toward the front row, he added, "Take it away, Bob."

Bob was a wise man not because of *what* he knew but *who* he knew. As long as the scientist was close by, Bob had nothing to worry about. But if he ever tried to do a lecture without the scientist, Bob would be in trouble.

As a Christian, you may not look wise or powerful to non-Christians around you. In fact, you might choke on some of the tough questions about God and sin and salvation that they throw at you. But you are intimately involved with someone who doesn't just *know* the answers—he *is* the answer. Paul calls Christ "the mighty power of God and the wonderful wisdom of God" (1 Corinthians 1:24). And as long as you live in a close, daily relationship with him, you can count on his power and wisdom to be yours. When the tough questions fly at you, you can always look his way and say, "Take it away, Jesus."

REFLECT: God calls you to tell others about him. How does it boost your confidence to know that Jesus has the total answer to any question?

PRAY: *Jesus, help me prepare well to answer the questions my friends might ask. But help me trust that you always know the answers.*

22 The Futility of Hoop-Jumping

Bible Reading: 1 Corinthians 1:26-31

Remember, dear brothers and sisters, that few of you were wise in the world's eyes, or powerful, or wealthy when God called you.
1 Corinthians 1:26

IF YOU HAD to meet at least one of the following qualifications to earn salvation and enter heaven, which one(s) would get you in today?

☐ Translate the entire Hebrew Old Testament into Swahili.
☐ Write a check to charity from your own bank account in the amount of $50 million.
☐ Run a marathon backwards every day for month.
☐ Figure *pi* to the thousandth place with paper and pencil and no calculator.
☐ Explain existentialism to a group of kindergartners.
☐ Spend a year in a Third World country living on bugs while you build a hydroelectric power plant for the local people.
☐ Donate your body for scientific experiments—while you are still alive.

Aren't you glad God isn't asking you to jump through some of those hoops to qualify for heaven?

The point is, of course, that all of us would be in seriously deep trouble if we had to earn our way into heaven by our own power, intellect, or money. Sure, there might be some people in the world who could pull off one or more of the above. But there probably aren't many who could do five of them, even if they had a lifetime to try. And if there were, they would probably be some of the most egotistical people in the world: "Check out the hydroelectric plant I built for Botswana." "Yeah, well look at my Swahili translation of the Old Testament."

If you had to come to God this way, you wouldn't make it. God designed it that way so he would get the credit, not you. You can enjoy salvation because of what he has done, not because of anything you can do. So there's no room to boast. You might be good, but you're not good enough. You may be wise, but you're not wise enough. So when you talk about who you are in Christ, don't lead people to believe that you had much to do with it. Make sure others understand that you are who you are as a Christian because of what *God* has done.

REFLECT: What difference does it make in your life that you don't have to jump through hoops to get into heaven?

PRAY: Thank God for sending his Son so you could spend eternity in heaven.

23 Being the Right Kind of Friend

Bible Reading: James 1:17-18

Whatever is good and perfect comes to us from God above. . . .
He never changes or casts shifting shadows. James 1:17

A LOT OF people don't know what makes true friendship. Does a true friend have to do the following things to be the right kind of friend? Check (✔) what you think of each statement.

☐ Agree   ☐ Disagree   "If you are my true friend, you will let me copy your homework assignment because I've been too busy."

☐ Agree   ☐ Disagree   "If you are my true girlfriend or boyfriend, you will have sex with me."

☐ Agree   ☐ Disagree   "If you are my true friend, you will quit being friends with the people I don't like."

Should being a friend to others be based on what's right rather than what a friend might want? Absolutely! Some say the only way you know if an action is *right* is if it *works* or *makes someone happy*. But there's more to right and wrong than that. And being a true friend doesn't always mean doing what your friend wants you to do, because what he or she may want you to do might not be best. If it isn't right, it won't be best for you or your friend in the long run.

So how do you know the right way to treat your friends?

Well, you start with what's right—and then you wind up with what works. You start with several indispensable standards of true friendship—like being available to your friends, accepting friends for who they are, and giving friends the support and encouragement they need. These standards for friendship are absolutely right for every situation. There is something about these standards that guarantees they will work to deepen true friendship every time.

You can be sure these standards for true friendship are right for two reasons. First, they are based on the Bible. Second, the standards of friendship in the Bible are right because they come from the heart of God. God himself—his character and nature—shows the standard for what is right and perfect and good. That's how you know that applying these standards—availability, acceptance, support, encouragement—to your friendships really works. They flow from the core of God's character, so you know they're good.

 REFLECT: Why would you want to run your friendships according to God's standards of right and wrong?

PRAY: *God, help me not to crumble when my friends want things that aren't what you want.*

24 A Standard for Friendship

Bible Reading: Isaiah 40:25-31

Those who wait on the Lord will find new strength. They will fly high on wings like eagles. They will run and not grow weary. They will walk and not faint. Isaiah 40:31

MARIA HAD the kind of day at school where she might as well have been the loser in a low-budget action film. She felt like she'd been pummeled in the nose, slugged in the stomach, karate-chopped on the back of her neck, kicked in the kidneys, and stomped in the head. And that was how her friends were treating her.

When your friends let you down, you need a reminder of who God is. When friendship seems like a game you're losing big-time—one you're not even sure how to play—look at God.

God is the *objective* standard of true friendship. Psalm 18:30 reads, "As for God, his way is perfect. All the Lord's promises prove true." God wants to help you be a caring, available friend because he created you—and by nature he's a totally caring, available friend.

God is the *universal* standard for true friendship. Psalm 103:19-20 declares, "The Lord has made the heavens his throne; from there he rules over everything. Praise the Lord, you angels of his, you mighty creatures who carry out his plans, listening for each of his commands." The standard of true friendship is universally right everywhere, under every circumstance, because that standard comes from someone who rules over everything. Accepting others for who they are is right because it's rooted in the character of the God who is accepting, the God who called us into his family when we were unacceptable (see Romans 5:6-8).

And God is the *constant* standard of true friendship. The prophet Isaiah wrote, "How can you say the Lord does not see your troubles? How can you say God refuses to hear your case? Have you never heard or understood? Don't you know that the Lord is the everlasting God, the Creator of all the earth? He never grows faint or weary. . . . He gives power to those who are tired and worn out; he offers strength to the weak" (Isaiah 40:27-29). The standard of true friendship is constant and right for any group of people in any time period because that standard comes from someone who is everlasting and unchanging. You know that caring for others in their joy and sorrow is right because God himself feels our joys and comfort us in our pain (see 2 Corinthians 1:3-4). And God wants to give you strength to be supporting and encouraging of others because God himself is a compassionate God (see 1 Timothy 2:3-6).

REFLECT: If you wanted to show your friends the kind of friendship God shows you, what would you change about the way you treat people?

PRAY: Thank God for showing you what a caring, accepting, supportive, and encouraging friendship looks like.

25 Divorce Is a Dirty Word

Bible Reading: Mark 10:1–9

Since they are no longer two but one, let no one separate them, for God has joined them together. Mark 10:9

MIKE AND JESSICA were both high school students when they met in the supermarket where they worked as clerks. They began dating and fell madly in love. From then on, Mike and Jessica were inseparable. They married before graduation, and Jessica gave birth to a baby within the first year of marriage. But during the second year, Mike and Jessica apparently fell out of love almost as quickly as they fell in. They ended their Cinderella romance with a divorce.

You probably know at least one couple—neighbors, friends, maybe even parents—who became victims of the divorce epidemic that rages in our culture. Divorce happens among Christians, and it's a controversial topic in the church today.

The subject of divorce was a hot issue in Jesus' day too. According to the Old Testament, a man could divorce his wife if "he discovers something about her that is shameful" (Deuteronomy 24:1). But by the time Jesus came, there were two conflicting views about divorce among the Jews, stemming from two interpretations of the word "shameful" in that verse. The Pharisees—the hard-nosed sticklers for detail—said shamefulness referred only to unfaithfulness. The second view interpreted "shameful" as *anything* that displeased the husband. A man could divorce his wife for a simple misdeed like torching his toast or losing a sock in the clothes dryer!

The Pharisees asked Jesus about his interpretation of divorce to find some reason to condemn him and get rid of him. The Pharisees probably hoped that Jesus held the more lenient view of divorce; that way they could discredit him among the religious community for his loose interpretation of Scripture.

But once again Jesus turned the tables on his enemies when they tried to trap him. Instead of siding with one of the two views, Jesus said that in God's view of marriage, divorce is a dirty word. Jesus referenced God's first words on marriage: "A man leaves his father and mother and is joined to his wife, and the two are united into one" (Genesis 2:24). In God's original blueprint for marriage, husband and wife were to be glued together into one inseparable unit. Period. Divorce wasn't even in God's vocabulary.

Divorce is a last resort after all other attempts to resolve conflicts and heal offenses have been tried and retried without success. But your best option is prayerfully to get yourself ready for a marriage that will last a lifetime.

 REFLECT: How are you practicing the kinds of attitudes and actions that will make you a good marriage partner?

PRAY: *God, help me learn the skills I will need someday to stay married.*

26 God's Version of Superglue

Bible Reading: Genesis 2:18-25
A man leaves his father and mother and is joined to his wife, and the two are united into one. Genesis 2:24

IF YOU WANT to have a long-lasting, love-filled marriage someday, you will need one special ingredient: superglue.

Genesis 2:24 commands a man to be glued to his wife. That's what the word "joined" literally means. When husband and wife are glued together with God's superglue, they become one in a marriage that will last.

Falling in love—the emotional side of love—isn't strong enough to glue a couple together. Even in the best marriages, feelings come and go. They don't make an inseparable marriage. The only kind of glue that holds a marriage together is the glue of *commitment.* "Oh," you say, "you mean having a marriage ceremony." No! Saying "I do" to a minister and signing a marriage license are part of it, but commitment is way deeper than that.

Commitment means that you choose to give yourself to your partner in marriage as a permanent gift—and the two of you give yourselves to God as one. That kind of glue puts people together so that they can endure all the pressing, pulling, stretching, and twisting that life inflicts on them. Unless a man and woman are glued together by a commitment made to each other in the sight of God, all the romantic feelings in the world can't keep their marriage secure.

Someday your prince or princess will probably come. You'll see pink hearts explode in the sky. And you'll swear that you're in heaven whenever you're with that special person. That's the falling in love thing, and it's a beautiful experience. But putting a marriage together on that feeling alone is like trying to hold two bricks together with cellophane tape. It can't take the stresses of life.

Because the indestructible glue of commitment is needed to stick two people together in marriage, every person in love needs to wait until the hearts fade long enough to ask himself or herself a huge question before he or she says "I do." Every potential bride or groom needs to pop *this* question: "Am I ready to glue myself to this person for keeps?"

I hope you fall in love someday. But I pray that you stick yourself to your marriage partner with the glue of your wholehearted commitment. To paraphrase Jesus' words, "Don't separate by divorce what God has glued together through your commitment."

REFLECT: What are you counting on to keep your marriage together someday?

PRAY: Ask God to teach you what true, loving commitment looks like.

27 Save Yourself for More than Sex

Bible Reading: 1 Corinthians 6:9-13

Our bodies were not made for sexual immorality. They were made for the Lord. 1 Corinthians 6:13

BY NOW you have noticed there's a difference between boys and girls. And you have also discovered that you are interested in the other sex.

You have probably pondered just how different you are from that other sex—physically, for sure, but in other ways as well. That's okay. It's the way God made you to feel. It's how God made your body to work. It's the physical house he made for your spirit to live in. So your thoughts and feelings about the opposite sex are no surprise to the one who designed you the way you are.

The big problem humans have, though, is as old as Adam and Eve. Remember? The first effect of Adam and Eve's sin in the Garden of Eden was that they became embarrassed of their naked bodies. Ever since, modesty—especially physical modesty—has been an instinct, even among the most primitive peoples. When two people have sex, it's more than just clothes that come off. They also get naked emotionally. But God never intended this kind of "nakedness" to be shared with just anyone. Why? Because when you uncover yourself emotionally, you are in danger of being emotionally wounded.

That's why sex isn't like shaking a stranger's hand. There's nothing casual about sex. Breaking up with someone you have been sexually involved with is so painful because it hurts more than just your body. It's not only your physical body being discarded. *You* have been rejected—all that you are.

Because sex is so personal—going to the core of who you are—it makes sense that God made sex to be enjoyed only within the bounds of marriage. Marriage gives a man and woman who want to share themselves physically, mentally, emotionally, and spiritually the safety of a lifelong commitment.

Everyone wants to get more than physical. You want a deep, intimate relationship. You want to give yourself totally to someone who can accept and love you just the way you are. So when you save sex for marriage, you save more than your body. You save all of yourself for that special someone who will find in you the intimacy and love God created him or her to enjoy in marriage.

It's a package deal. By saving this package until marriage—both body and heart—you will become a priceless gift to someone, just like he or she will be to you.

REFLECT: Why is sex more significant than shaking hands?

PRAY: *God, you made sex a gift that a husband and wife can share. Help me to wait until marriage to enjoy the gift of sex.*

28 The Spirit of Sex

Bible Reading: 1 Corinthians 6:15-20
The Scriptures say, "The two are united into one." 1 Corinthians 6:16

WANT TO KNOW the secret of the world's best sex?

The Bible points out that a husband and wife become "one flesh" (Genesis 2:24, NIV). And here's the secret: The best sex comes in marriage—and after a deep, spiritual relationship has been established.

Sex can affect you in almost the same way knowing God does. God knows you all the way to your innermost being—and he loves you in spite of your faults. Having sex with someone means you reveal yourself at a truly deep level—and not just physically. Sex makes you both more humble and more secure, because you realize your husband or wife loves you in spite of any faults he or she finds in you. And the closer a husband and wife grow spiritually, the more they enjoy their sex life. God blesses sex in a spiritual way and uses it to build up a married couple emotionally.

See it? You get to expect more from sex than the physical. Humans aren't like animals. Ever noticed a female dog in heat and the male dogs around her? It is obvious that the sexual behavior of dogs is purely animal instinct.

For humans, sex involves your mind—your ability to choose. And because your mind and spirit are constantly involved—as are your emotions—sex is always very personal. The relationship between a man and woman is never the same as it was before they had sex. After having sex and then breaking up, many people confess that they feel like they left a part of their self with another person. And they really did. That's what the Bible means when it says that through sex a man and woman become "one flesh."

Someday, when the time comes to give yourself to your husband or wife, that person will know something about you he or she can never forget. And you will know him or her the same way. In fact, that word "know" is the word some translations of the Bible use to describe the sex act, as in Genesis 4:1: "Adam knew his wife" (KJV). Did you know that?

God made sex to be a way a husband and wife say something incredibly special to each other. Every time a married couple shares sex together, they celebrate the vows they made on their wedding day and the oneness they have on all levels—spiritually, mentally, and emotionally as well as physically. As you walk close with Jesus and he leads you in his time to the person with whom you will share all of yourself, you will be able to have every bit of this and even more.

 REFLECT: What kind of oneness does sex celebrate?

PRAY: Thank God for his awesome plan for sex.

29 Locker Room 101

Bible Reading: Romans 13:10-14

Let the Lord Jesus Christ take control of you, and don't think of ways to indulge your evil desires. Romans 13:14

SO HAVE YOU picked up any sex smarts in a locker room or at a slumber party?

You probably know how quickly guy-talk and girl-talk about sex can slide into the category of rudely crude. Some of the jokes are funny, but saying "I love Jesus" and "Did you hear the one about . . ." in the same breath just doesn't go together very well. Even saying "sex is a beautiful gift" doesn't jive with many of the gestures and jokes about sex.

But the knowledge of sex you pick up from your peers is often way worse than disrespectful humor. The jokes and dirty language leave you messed up about what makes great sex—and may even find you buying some outright lies. If you listen to a lot of people, you might begin to think that God is down on those who enjoy sex. Nothing could be further from the truth. Besides, most talk by guys and girls seems to say that great sex is determined by how many times, how often, and with whom you "score." That too is a lie.

For starters, most people don't realize that God is the one who thought up sex. The Bible says that *God* made man and woman (see Genesis 1:27). That fact alone drops some huge clues about whether he thinks sex is a good idea—and it leaves no doubt about who knows best how to help you get the most out of his gift. God didn't declare his laws to limit what you can do but to provide what you truly need for a fulfilled love, marriage, and sexual relationship—and to protect you from the things that could keep you from having all that God intends.

True, one reason God made sex was to populate the planet. Let's face it, without sex you wouldn't be here! But there's another reason why sex between married people is so great, and this is even more important. Sex is God's wonderful way of allowing a husband and wife to express the depth and intensity of their commitment to each other. And they do this in an emotional and spiritual way that is so fulfilling and so full of excitement that it never gets boring. It just gets better and better.

That's God's plan. In a marriage based on commitment and love, sex produces something beautiful for people to enjoy all their lives. But outside this special union of marriage, the sinfulness of people always turns sex into something ugly.

You probably won't hear this fact in a locker room: A lifetime commitment is what makes for great sex.

REFLECT: What false facts have you learned about sex that you need to unlearn?

PRAY: Ask God to change any misguided ideas you have about sex.

30 Claim It and Enjoy It!

Bible Reading: Hebrews 10:12-14
Our High Priest offered himself to God as one sacrifice for sins, good for all time. Hebrews 10:12

"NOTHING IN LIFE is free," Amanda protested. "I've confessed my sins to God, and I've turned away from the bad stuff I used to do. But I figure that sometime when I mess up in the future he's going to say, 'I knew you would mess up again!' I just can't believe forgiveness is free for the asking."

Some Christians think it's a stretch that God actually forgives them when they confess their sins and repent. If that sounds like you, here's how you can experience the freedom of God's forgiveness. Start by taking a few simple steps:

1. *Remember that God loves you unconditionally.* You are God's special child. He willingly paid a high price—the death of his one and only Son, Jesus Christ—to reclaim you as his own.

   When you disobey God, you grieve him (see Ephesians 4:29-32). But his love for you never changes. He might discipline you to pull you close to him (see Hebrews 12:5-12), but his love stays consistent and perfect.

   The problem isn't God's love for you or his willingness to make things right. The problem is your sin. The logical question, then, is, "How can I experience God's love and forgiveness when I sin?"

2. *Confess your sin.* Even Christians can still be hassled by what the Bible calls your "sinful nature" (Romans 7:20-25). And as you let your sinful nature rather than God run your life, the result is disobedience—and a lot of unhappiness. But God has provided a solution, which begins with confession (see 1 John 1:9). To confess means to agree with God that your disobedience and lack of faith are sin. By agreeing that sin is sin, you humble yourself before God and experience his grace and power (see 1 Peter 5:5-6).

3. *Claim God's forgiveness.* Confession doesn't get you more of God's forgiveness. Christ has already forgiven you once and for all through his death on the cross (see Hebrews 10:12-14; 1 Peter 3:18). You can't get more forgiveness. Confession, rather, is claiming and accepting the forgiveness that is already yours.

   Claiming forgiveness is like discovering a treasure that was always yours because it was buried in your own backyard. God's loving forgiveness is already yours. Claim it and enjoy it!

REFLECT: Do you accept that God forgives your sins when you confess them and turn from them? Meditate on the Bible passages that assure you of that fact.

PRAY: *Father, help me to live in the light of your love and forgiveness.*

31 Are You Sure You're Sure?

Bible Reading: Isaiah 12:1-6

See, God has come to save me. I will trust in him and not be afraid.
The Lord God is my strength and my song; he has become my salvation.
Isaiah 12:2

LITTLE RICKY was scared to crawl into bed. He had spooky thoughts as he struggled to go to sleep. He saw creepy shapes float across the ceiling. He feared that monsters hid in the dark shadows of his closet.

Believe it or not, there are scarier things. Satan is always trying to make you doubt your salvation—the fact that you really belong to God. He is the one behind the nagging questions that seem to come from nowhere:

- Am I really saved?
- Has anything really changed?
- Why don't I feel any different?
- Maybe I'm not really a Christian.
- Maybe it didn't "take" with me like it's supposed to.
- Maybe I didn't do it right.

Those doubts are common. But a Christian doesn't have to *feel* his salvation in order to *have* salvation. A Christian doesn't have to *feel* different in order to *be* different, any more than a millionaire has to feel rich in order to be rich. Take a few minutes to absorb the assurance of your salvation from God's Word.

When Satan attacks you and sets creepy doubts about your salvation loose in your brain, read Isaiah 12:2 aloud several times: "God has come to save me. I will trust in him and not be afraid. The Lord God is my strength and my song; he has become my salvation." Then pray this Scripture-based prayer aloud:

Father, you are the one who saves me. Help me to trust and not be afraid. You give me strength and make me sing; you have saved me. Help me to draw near to you with a sincere heart and a sure faith. Let your salvation grab hold of my heart, not only with words, but also with power, with the Holy Spirit, and with sure knowledge that the gospel is true. Thank you for the assurance that I belong to you—today and forever. In the name of Jesus I pray, Amen. (See Isaiah 12:2; Hebrews 10:22)

REFLECT: Do you ever wonder if you are really saved? Spend some time looking up the additional Bible passages listed above.

PRAY: Write out that prayer above. Put it where you can see it often until God's assurance takes hold in your heart.

Close Your Eyes to Blind Faith

Bible Reading: John 8:31-36

You will know the truth, and the truth will set you free. John 8:32

THE PROFESSOR strokes his beard with an air of superiority. "So you're a Christian, are you?" he says to the student standing in front of him.

Luis—a first-year college student—swallows hard.

"Tell me," the professor continues, "can you prove with 100 percent certainty that Jesus rose from the dead?"

Luis's answer comes out in a mousy squeak. "Umm, no."

"You see?" the professor pronounces. "Blind faith. Ignorant, irrational, unreasonable faith."

That professor has the idea that if you can't prove something with 100 percent certainty, it's useless or untrue. He also figures that the Christian faith is a blind faith since things like the Resurrection and Jesus' deity can't be proven with 100 percent certainty. That's a myth. We live in a contingent universe. That means exceedingly few things can be proven with 100 percent certainty, except maybe in the field of mathematics.

Car manufacturers, for example, can't totally prove that their new models are safe. But *the evidence* from tough, repeated safety tests is pretty conclusive. A jury can't prove conclusively that a suspect committed a crime. Even if they possess a confession, there are contingencies. He may be lying to protect someone. He might have been forced to confess. But the jury will weigh *the evidence* to form a conclusion "beyond a reasonable doubt."

Similarly, neither the resurrection of Christ nor his deity can be proven with 100 percent certainty. But that doesn't mean the Christian faith is a blind faith. The evidence for the Christian faith isn't *exhaustive,* but it is *adequate.* The apostle John wrote, "Jesus' disciples saw him do many other miraculous signs besides the ones recorded in this book" (John 20:30). He is saying that Jesus did many other things that confirmed him as the Son of God that weren't recorded. The evidence John provides isn't exhaustive. "But," he writes in the next verse, "these are written so that you may believe that Jesus is the Messiah, the Son of God, and that by believing in him you will have life" (verse 31).

Blaise Pascal—the French mathematician, philosopher, and scientist—said that there is enough evidence for the Christian faith to convince anyone not set against it. But there isn't enough evidence to bring anyone into God's kingdom who won't come.

REFLECT: Why was the argument of Luis's professor flawed?

PRAY: Ask God for opportunities to share with your friends what you know about Christ. Trust the Holy Spirit to reveal the truth to them.

2 Believing Isn't Rocket Science

Bible Reading: Matthew 28:1-7

He isn't here! He has been raised from the dead, just as he said would happen. Matthew 28:6

A MAN and a woman wearing white lab coats enter a laboratory, she with a clipboard and pencil, he with a small white rectangular object clasped in his hand. The man places the white object in a glass tank filled with ordinary tap water. It bobs to the surface. The woman records something on her data sheet.

After performing the event repeatedly in a controlled environment, observing and recording the result, the scientists conclude that a bar of Ivory Soap floats. It has been proven scientifically.

Some people think that if you can't prove something with that kind of repeatable scientific experiment, it's untrue or unbelievable. But that's a myth. The scientific method isn't the only way to prove something. If it were, you wouldn't be able to prove that Abraham Lincoln was ever president of the United States, because you can't repeat that event. It exists only in the past. But Honest Abe's presidency *can* be proven through what is called the "legal historical method" or the "evidential method."

The evidential method proves an event by examining three kinds of evidence: *oral testimony, written testimony,* and *physical testimony.* This is the kind of "proof" offered every day in courts of law around the world, and it's the only kind of proof that applies to an event in history. How can you prove evidentially that Abraham Lincoln was president? If you could find eyewitnesses, you would interview them—that's oral testimony. You would compile copies of letters he wrote, newspapers that reported on him, and books about him—that's written testimony. Finally, you would offer exhibits of physical testimony—such as his pocket watch, photographs of him, his birthplace, or even his sugar bowl.

Some people refuse to believe in the resurrection of Jesus Christ because the scientific method can't prove it. You can't repeat the event in a controlled environment, where observations can be made and data can be recorded.

However, the resurrection of Christ can be proven by the evidential method. You can't find any oral testimony, because no one is still alive from the first century. But you have the written testimony of the disciples in the Bible and the physical testimony of the empty tomb.

Your faith in Christ isn't blind or unfounded. The life and ministry of Jesus, his miracles, and his resurrection can be proven evidentially, and they have been.

REFLECT: How would you respond to someone who said you can't prove the truth of the Christian faith? What do you need to prove a fact evidentially?

PRAY: Tell God how grateful you are that you don't have a blind, unfounded faith.

3 Stewed Tomatoes and Tennis Shoes

Bible Reading: 1 Corinthians 6:9-11
Now your sins have been washed away, and you have been set apart for God. 1 Corinthians 6:11

IF YOU WANT to prove that the resurrection of Jesus Christ two thousand years ago really happened, here's another piece of evidence: the transformation of millions of people when they become related by faith to the person of Jesus. Even though these people come from every walk of life and from all nations of the world, they experience change in remarkably similar ways.

Some say that the changed life of a Christian is just the result of wishful thinking. Or they excuse it by saying it doesn't prove a thing. The subjective experience of a Christian, however, comes from an objective, real cause. This objective reality is the person of Jesus Christ and his resurrection.

For example, suppose a student comes into the room and says, "Hey—I have a stewed tomato in my right tennis shoe. This tomato has changed my life. It has given me peace and love and joy that I never experienced before." It's hard to argue with a student like that *if* his life backs up what he says. A personal testimony is often the subjective argument for the reality of something. So don't dismiss a subjective experience as being irrelevant.

For one person's subjective experience to apply to other people, however, it has to pass two tests. First, what is the objective cause of the subjective experience? Second, how many people have had the same subjective experience from being related to the objective reality?

If you apply these two tests to the stewed tomato in the tennis shoe, what happens? To the first question, the guy would reply, "A stewed tomato." The second question would be put this way: How many people in this classroom, in this school, in this country, on this continent, and so on, have experienced the same love, peace, and joy as a result of stewed tomatoes in their right tennis shoes? The answer would be no one! So this subjective experience is bogus.

But apply those same two tests to the Christian experience. First, the objective reality behind our subjective experience is the person of Christ and his resurrection. Second, millions of others—from all backgrounds and nationalities—have experienced new levels of peace, joy, and victory by turning their lives over to Christ.

The Christian experience is subjective. But it is based on an objective reality. And it has been dramatically duplicated countless times in all kinds of people.

REFLECT: Your changed life is a testimony to the power of the living Christ. Are you allowing him to continue to transform you into his image?

PRAY: *God, change me so my friends can see your power at work. Make my life a convincing display of the power that raised Christ from the dead.*

4 Poor Doubting Thomas

Bible Reading: John 20:24-29
Don't be faithless any longer. Believe! John 20:27

THOMAS HAS been the victim of a lot of bad press. Okay, so his reputation isn't as bad as that of Judas, the guy who betrayed Jesus. He might not even rank with Peter, who denied the Lord three times on the eve of his crucifixion. But Thomas is usually classed among the "bad boys" of the disciples, the twelve men closest to Jesus during his three years of ministry.

Thomas owes his bad-boy reputation to an incident following Jesus' resurrection. Jesus had appeared to the disciples behind closed doors. But Thomas wasn't with them. When they told Thomas the news of Jesus' resurrection, he responded, "I won't believe it unless I see the nail wounds in his hands, put my fingers into them, and place my hand into the wound in his side" (John 20:25). When Jesus later appeared to Thomas, the Lord took him up on his offer. He said, "Put your finger here and see my hands. Put your hand into the wound in my side. Don't be faithless any longer. Believe!" (verse 27).

Many people come down hard on Thomas because of his doubt. But they forget that none of the other disciples believed until they, too, had seen evidence of the Resurrection. Everyone else had already seen Jesus' hands and side. What's more, Jesus didn't say to Thomas, "You should never have doubted." Instead, he showed his disciple the evidence and then said, "Stop doubting." And finally, when Thomas did see the evidence, he uttered one of the great confessions of faith in history, calling Jesus, "My Lord and my God!" (verse 28).

For some reason, we let ourselves think of doubt as only a bad thing. *"Real Christians don't doubt,"* we say. That's a myth. Doubt isn't the opposite of faith; it's the forefather of faith. Doubt doesn't cancel faith; it should give way to faith. In fact, as in Thomas's case, doubt can be the impetus that leads us to the truth.

"Faith grows through seeking truth, and the seeker must ask questions, and questioning means 'honest doubt,' " write Gordon and William Brown in *Romans: Gospel of Freedom and Grace.* "The original meaning of the Greek word for 'doubt,' *skeptikos,* is 'inquirer.' "

The Thomas myth—that real Christians don't doubt—doesn't come from the Bible. The lessons to be learned from Thomas's experience are that doubt is natural, that you can be honest about your doubts, and that honest doubt should give way to faith when Jesus reveals the truth to you. Jesus doesn't want you to hide your doubts from him. He loves you, and he understands your questions.

REFLECT: What doubts keep you from following Jesus completely?

PRAY: Share your doubts with God and allow him to answer them in his own way.

5 What's on Your Price Tag?

Bible Reading: Psalm 91:1-12

He orders his angels to protect you wherever you go. Psalm 91:11

TREVOR'S FIRST assignment in Tech Ed was to make something useful for home. He could pick from a half-dozen designs for napkin holders, recipe boxes, and dresser organizers. But when Trevor received his project back, the grading sheet screamed *F*. At the top of the sheet was scrawled one question: "What is it?"

Do you ever feel like a messed-up school project? If you wanted to find out what you really are, who would you ask? You would go back to the One who made you. If you want a clear view of your true identity, you need to see yourself as God sees you—no more and no less. So how exactly does God see you?

First, *God sees you as eternally lovable.* He is your Father. He created you in his own image (see Genesis 1:26-27). You are the best expression of his creative genius. In response to your faith in Christ, God welcomed you into his family as his child (see John 1:12-13). God has provided for an ongoing, intimate relationship with you because he loves you—and nothing can shrink his love for you.

Second, *God sees you as infinitely valuable.* What is your value to God? At the cross God declared to heaven, hell, and the whole earth that you are worth the gift of Jesus Christ, his dearly loved Son. If you ever put a price tag on yourself, it would have to read "JESUS!" because that's what God paid to save you (see 1 Corinthians 6:19-20; 1 Peter 1:18-19). That tells you how much you're worth to God. If you had been the only person on earth, God would have sent his Son for you. To top it off, having conquered sin, death, and the grave, Jesus returned to heaven to prepare an eternal home for you (see John 14:1-3).

Third, *God sees you as thoroughly competent.* Jesus announced to his disciples, "When the Holy Spirit has come upon you, you will receive power" (Acts 1:8). Because of Christ's promise, Paul could boast, "I can do everything with the help of Christ who gives me the strength I need" (Philippians 4:13). Paul says again where God's power comes from: "It is not that we think we can do anything of lasting value by ourselves. Our only power and success come from God" (2 Corinthians 3:5). God empowers you through his indwelling Holy Spirit and makes you competent to be his ambassador. Think about it: God trusts you so much that he left you on earth to complete the ministry Jesus began. He's given you the job of leading people back to him (see 2 Corinthians 5:20).

 REFLECT: Do you agree that you are lovable, valuable, and competent? What part of your self-image doesn't match what God says?

PRAY: Ask God to bring your self-image in line with his true view of you.

6 Switch On the Light

Bible Reading: Ephesians 5:8-14

For though your hearts were once full of darkness, now you are full of light from the Lord. Ephesians 5:8

IMAGINE BEING in an art gallery where the room lights are on, but the spotlights that shine on the various portraits are off. You can see the portrait frames, and you might be able to make out some of the features of the portraits. But only when the spotlights are turned on can you see all the details—the facial expression, the skin tone, the eye color, the curve of the lips. When the spotlights are on, you can see the painting as the artist intended you to see it.

That's what God's light is like for you. It shines brightly on you and shows you who he created you to be. But you might not see God's portrait of you too clearly. His light has been blocked or dimmed, so your vision of who you are is dim. You need to know how God provided for his light to shine into your life so you can see yourself clearly for who you are.

First, *Jesus Christ is your first source of light.* John announced about Jesus, "Life itself was in him, and this life gives light to everyone" (John 1:4). Jesus called himself the light of the world (see John 8:12). The way you come into the light is to come into personal relationship with Christ. You grow in the knowledge that you are loved, valued, and made competent as your relationship grows deeper through close fellowship with Christ.

Second, *God's Word, the Bible, is another source of the light.* King David wrote, "Your word is a lamp to my feet and a light for my path" (Psalm 119:105, NIV). The more you open your mind and heart to the Word of God, the more light you enjoy. In the light of God's Word you see that God loves you, values you, and makes you competent.

Third, *other believers are a source of God's light.* The One who proclaimed, "I am the light of the world" also told his followers, "You are the light of the world" (Matthew 5:14). Being in relationship with Christ, the Light, fills you with light. As you and your Christian friends share the light of Christ and his Word with each other, you grow in your understanding that God loves you, values you, and makes you competent. That's a big reason why the Bible tells us, "Let us not neglect our meeting together, as some people do, but encourage and warn each other, especially now that the day of his coming back again is drawing near" (Hebrews 10:25). You need interaction with other believers to flood your life with God's light. It's how you spot your true identity.

REFLECT: Do you want to see more clearly who you are in God's eyes? How can you get into the light and see yourself as God sees you?

PRAY: Ask God to flood your life with his light as you read his Word and grow in your relationship with him and other believers.

7 Who's Blocking the Light?

Bible Reading: 1 Thessalonians 5:1-6
You are all children of the light and of the day. 1 Thessalonians 5:5

YESTERDAY ON the way home from school, a passing truck splashed a sheet of mud across Brent's windshield. No big deal—except Brent had let his car run out of wiper fluid. He could see so little through the smears that he almost swerved across the center line into oncoming traffic. Close call.

Your culture is like that mud-splashed windshield. It doesn't always let a lot of God's light into your life. An environment chock-full of apathy or antagonism toward God, the Bible, and Christianity makes it hard for you to see God's truth. And your true identity is one of the first things covered up by the cultural slop.

How? Well, your culture blinds you to truth through the media. The TV shows and movies you watch and the Internet sites you visit splatter you with misinformation about God and his people. They blind you with a view of you that is far from God's view.

Your friends might even toss another blinding bucketful of mud your way.

Ask yourself these questions: What kind of people do you hang out with on a daily basis? What do your friends, classmates, and other members of your peer group think about Jesus Christ and the Bible, the two primary sources of God's light in your life? If you are having difficulty seeing yourself as lovable, valuable, and competent the way God sees you, it might be because God's truth is being blocked from your view by peers who don't see you as God does. They might be covering up the truth of your true identity.

The view you have of yourself is powerfully influenced by your peers because you and every other human being alive wants and needs close, personal friendships. To the extent that your all-important peers keep you from seeing God's view of you, however, they put you at risk of becoming an emotional wreck.

God's portrait of you shows that he sees you as lovable, valued, and competent. But what if your friends and peers don't see you that way? What if many of those close to you treat you as if they didn't give a rip about you? What if your peers subtly or openly avoid you, ignore you, or ridicule you? The more they blind you with lies that you *aren't* lovable, valuable, nor competent, the harder it is to see that you *are*.

REFLECT: Do your close friends see you as God sees you? Is it time to get some new friends?

PRAY: Ask God today to help you allow plenty of his light to flood into your life through your environment and your friends.

8 For Such a Worm As I

Bible Reading: Psalm 86:11-17
You, O Lord, are a merciful and gracious God, slow to get angry, full of unfailing love and truth. Psalm 86:15

JOANNA SUMMED herself up this way: "A worm doesn't adequately describe how I feel about myself. A worm can crawl underground and hide. I'm more like one of the ugly slugs on my patio. Everywhere they go, they leave this horrible trail behind them. That's what I'm like; I mess up everything wherever I go."

What a sad personal description from the mouth of a Christian!

Joanna is clueless concerning her true identity. She makes mistakes like we all do, but she certainly doesn't "mess up everything" wherever she goes.

If you are a believer who isn't convinced of your true identity as God's beloved, valued, competent child, the results in your life can be dismal. You might have a fearful, pessimistic view of the world and your ability to cope with its challenges. You can see new or unexpected situations as threats to your happiness and security. And you might think all your difficulties are purely the result of your own failures.

When you are confused about who you are in Christ, it feels easier to endure what life deals you instead of challenging it or attempting to change it. You might picture yourself as a victim of a hostile environment.

But if you walk in the light of being loved, valued, and equipped by God, you look at the world as a challenge to face and an opportunity to exercise trust in Christ. You can accept the fact that the grace of God in your life empowers you to change your environment for the better. You know that your destiny lies in what God can do through you, and that you will accomplish significant things for eternity even in difficult circumstances.

A faulty sense of identity also affects relationships. A skewed view of yourself puts you on the defensive, so that you compare other people's messages and motives to the inaccurate self-portrait you carry. For example, Joanna has difficulty accepting praise or compliments from others. In her opinion, a slug can't possibly be pretty or helpful or generous. She further reasons, "How can I trust someone with such a messed-up view of me?" Until her inner self-portrait is radically transformed, Joanna will be skeptical of even the most sincere attempts to build her up.

Do you ever find yourself thinking like Joanna? You can be sure that God understands exactly where you are and how you feel—and he loves you completely! He is a compassionate God. He cares.

REFLECT: What does it mean to you that God is compassionate? How could understanding God's compassion remake your life?

PRAY: Respond to God's compassion today with your loving thanks.

9 Turn On the Love Light

Bible Reading: 1 John 4:16-21

God is love, and all who live in love live in God, and God lives in them.
1 John 4:16

KENDALL ATTENDS a large Bible study group nearly every week, but most people around him don't even know he is there. He always sits by himself and heads for the door as soon as everyone says "Amen" to the closing prayer.

One of the group leaders, Dale, noticed Kendall and decided to befriend him. For several weeks, Dale sought out Kendall after Bible study just to say hello. Eventually Dale convinced Kendall to meet him for lunch. After a couple of get-togethers, Kendall began to open up. "No way can God love me," Kendall said one day. "He just puts up with me because I've accepted Christ as my Savior. But God will never love me as his child. I'm just lucky to be saved."

Dale wisely didn't counter Kendall's confession by ramming Scripture verses about God's love down his throat. Instead he gently asked about Kendall's background. He learned that Kendall had grown up in a non-Christian home with a stern father who was quick to discipline him. He couldn't recall that his father ever hugged him or held him or said, "I love you."

So why do people like Kendall fail to see themselves as people unconditionally loved by God? Their sense of belonging is diminished when they don't sense love from God or others. Since they aren't loved by the people from whom they most need love, they often conclude they are unlovable. It's difficult to believe that God can love us if our need for human love has gone unmet.

As long as Kendall kept his distance from others, he wasn't reminded of his unlovableness. Was Kendall unlovable? No way! His inner self-portrait was wrong. He needed more of the light of Christ, God's Word, and God's people to begin revealing who he was.

Dale met with Kendall for a few months. Eventually he convinced Kendall to join a small group. In the group Kendall experienced the love and care of eight other students. As his new friends met his long-ignored need for love, Kendall's idea of his identity was transformed. As he began to experience love through the care of his friends, he began to see his lovableness to God more clearly.

If you shy away from God and people because you can't believe they could ever love you, you need more light on who you really are. Stop pulling away. Instead, draw close to people who love you and let the light of their love illuminate the true picture of who you are.

REFLECT: Have you made it a habit to hide from people because you can't trust their love? How can you let people into your life?

PRAY: Tell God about the hurts that cause you to block people out at times.

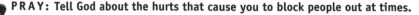

10 Is Anybody Interested in Me?

Bible Reading: John 1:10–14

The Word became human and lived here on earth among us. He was full of unfailing love and faithfulness. John 1:14

KATRINA WAS DESTINED to be a model and an actress before she was born. When Katrina was six months old, Joyce, her unmarried mother, moved them to Los Angeles and enrolled her daughter with a modeling agency to do commercials for baby products. The little girl's childhood was tightly scheduled with modeling classes and competitions, dancing and acting classes, and auditions for commercials and bit parts in television shows. Joyce was determined to keep her daughter on the fast track to Hollywood stardom.

The night Katrina graduated from a posh Los Angeles prep school, she disappeared. She said good-bye to her mother after the ceremony, supposedly on her way to a country club for the senior class all-night celebration. Katrina never came home the next morning. Months later she was found in a shelter for homeless teens in Baltimore, dirty and scarred from street life.

Joyce paid for Katrina to be flown home. "Look at your hair, your skin," Joyce cried at their reunion. "You have ruined your life."

"No, Mother," Katrina shot back angrily. "I have ruined *your* life. I never had a life, not until I left home. You robbed me of my childhood. I was your daughter only when I was posing or performing."

Katrina stayed in Los Angeles and got a job waiting tables. At the invitation of a former classmate, she began attending a small church. She had difficulty at first accepting their hospitality. She had the same misgivings about God, thinking he wouldn't want someone who had done what she had done. Her value as a person had been attached to her appearance and performance for too long.

People like Katrina often feel unworthy when their normal human need for attention goes unmet. We receive attention when people enter *our* world and show interest in the things that interest *us*. By forcing Katrina into her own world of modeling and performing, Joyce failed to meet Katrina's need for attention.

Maybe your inner self-portrait is distorted because you didn't receive the attention you needed growing up. Nobody took a serious interest in what you were about. The good news is that God loved you enough to enter your world. He came from heaven to earth to identify with your human struggles and die for your sins. He is interested in you, and he always will be.

REFLECT: How have the people around you shown interest in your world? How has God proven his interest in you?

PRAY: *God, sometimes I feel like I have to fit into someone else's mold. Thank you for being interested in me just the way I am.*

You Can Do It

Bible Reading: Hosea 2:20

I will be faithful to you and make you mine, and you will finally know me as Lord. Hosea 2:20

REMEMBER JOANNA? When you understand her background, it's no surprise she feels like a slug who messes up everything wherever she goes. Joanna hardly remembered her birth father, who died when she was two. Joanna's stepfather, Buck, was a hardworking provider, but he was also a demanding perfectionist who pushed Joanna to be the best at everything she tried. His prime method of motivation was humiliation. If she didn't make an all-out effort, Buck mocked her.

Joanna grew up with an I-can't-do-anything-right attitude burned into her brain. Flustered under pressure to succeed, she failed to keep her first two jobs. She has managed to keep a low-stress, low-pay job for ten years, but her performance is below average. She can't see herself for who she really is—a competent person loved by God regardless of accomplishments.

You might feel incompetent for some of the same reasons as Joanna. First, *people can feel incompetent when they don't get the encouragement they need from others.* Always being criticized, blamed, or humiliated for what you do shakes your confidence and crushes your motivation. Why try if you can't do anything but fail?

Second, *people might feel incompetent when their need for support from others goes unmet.* Everyone needs a burden-bearer, someone who will come alongside and share the weight of a difficult task or trial.

Third, *people can feel incompetent when they feel unappreciated.* No one is 100-percent competent. Some people struggle to complete tasks with only a small degree of success. But everyone can be appreciated for something—for things like effort, helpfulness, a positive attitude, persistence in adversity, or a willingness to try. Unappreciated people like Joanna find that even their successes are insufficient to erase the labels they have plastered on themselves—like "slug who messes things up."

Maybe you have felt incompetent because you lacked encouragement, support, or appreciation. God doesn't see you as incompetent. He has invited you to join him in the most important task on earth: sharing the gospel with others. You can do what God calls you to do because God has made you competent by filling you with his Holy Spirit. And he is with you to encourage you, support you, and appreciate you every step of the way.

REFLECT: Have others made you feel incompetent? How? Is that the message God wants to send you?

PRAY: Ask God to fill you with confidence that he knows you are competent.

12 Howdy, Neighbor

Bible Reading: Luke 10:25-37

"You must love the Lord your God with all your heart, all your soul, all your strength, and all your mind." And, "Love your neighbor as yourself." Luke 10:27

TRAVIS AND KYLE walked home from school together almost every day, stopping at the MinuteMart to buy a soda. And after Travis finished his soda, he tossed the empty paper cup on someone's lawn—unless he was in front of the Cooks' house, which was next door to his. Kyle couldn't figure this out. He finally asked, "How come you throw your cups on anybody's lawn but the Cooks'?"

"Because," Travis answered, "we're supposed to love our neighbors, and the Cooks are my next-door neighbors. The other people aren't my neighbors, so I don't care if I leave stuff in their yards."

Travis is a few ounces short of a supersized soda. Jesus made it clear that the command to love your neighbor (see Matthew 22:39) isn't limited to the person who actually lives next door. When Jesus was asked, "Who is my neighbor?" he told the parable of the Good Samaritan, who showed love toward a man mugged by bandits (see Luke 10:29-37). The story clearly illustrates that neighbors aren't just people in certain classes, geographical locations, or socio-economic levels. Neighbors are *people in need*—whoever and wherever they may be.

Jesus' command for believers to love everyone wasn't new. Old Testament Jews knew about God's love for all people and his desire that they love as he loved. Moses, not Jesus, was the first to write God's words, "Love your neighbor as yourself" (Leviticus 19:18). God commanded Israel to show loving concern not only for those of their own kind but also for the poor and strangers (see Leviticus 19:9-10) and to seek peace with their enemies whenever possible (see Deuteronomy 20:10-12). God's invitation permeates the Old Testament: "Love people—all people—as I do."

In the New Testament, God's love is offered to all people. Christ died for the whole world (see John 3:16), and God intends for believers to share the good news of salvation with "all the nations" (Matthew 28:19).

So don't limit your love to people like you or people you like. Jesus instructed, "Love your enemies. Do good to those who hate you. Pray for the happiness of those who curse you. Pray for those who hurt you" (Luke 6:27-28). He left no loopholes in the love command. You get to love all people for Christ's sake, because everyone is your neighbor.

REFLECT: Have you ever limited your love to people right around you? How can you stretch your love wider?

PRAY: *Lord, teach me to love all people—not just the ones I like.*

13 All in the Family

Bible Reading: 1 Timothy 5:3-8

Those who won't care for their own relatives . . . have denied what we believe. Such people are worse than unbelievers. 1 Timothy 5:8

"HEY, TRAVIS," Kyle said as the two walked home from school, "has it ever occurred to you that Jesus' command to love your neighbor really means to love everybody—not just the people who live next door?"

"Wow!" Travis exclaimed. "I guess that means I can't go to the movie with you tonight."

"Why not?"

"I have to get to bed early and get my sleep," Travis explained, "because I have six billion neighbors to love!"

Travis is still a few ounces short of that supersized soda.

Yes, Jesus wants you to love everybody, but you can't literally love *everybody*. You don't have enough time, energy, or resources to care for everyone everywhere. If you tried, your love would be spread so thin over so many that it wouldn't mean much to anyone. That's why the Bible gives what might be called "the principle of centralized loving." We are to fulfill the command to love people by starting with those closest to us and working out to the whole world "whenever we have the opportunity" (Galatians 6:10).

The inner circle of your love responsibility is yourself. If you don't take care to provide for your basic needs and protect yourself from damaging influences, you won't be able to love others effectively.

Next to loving yourself, your most immediate love responsibility is to love your own family. Paul wrote on this point, "Those who won't care for their own relatives, especially those living in the same household, have denied what we believe. Such people are worse than unbelievers" (1 Timothy 5:8). Everyone needs assistance, encouragement, prayer, comfort, and counsel from others. You are obligated under God to fill these needs for family members. Loving your parents and siblings is your first priority in the category of loving your neighbor. Caring for extended family members, such as grandparents, aunts, uncles, cousins, etc., is a close second (see 1 Timothy 5:16).

If spending time helping your parents with chores or being with your brothers or sisters is the last item you put on your calendar—or the first to erase when you get too busy—you might need to rethink God's priorities for loving others. God intends your first love commitment to be to those closest to you, and that's your family. If you aren't practicing love there, you aren't living like a Christian.

REFLECT: Are you overwhelmed by God's command to love everyone? Then focus on how you are doing at loving the people closest to you.

PRAY: *Lord, teach me to love the people nearest me.*

14 Let the Love Flow Out

Bible Reading: 1 John 3:14-17

If anyone has enough money to live well and sees a brother or sister in need and refuses to help—how can God's love be in that person?
1 John 3:17

SO YOU'RE supposed to love everybody just like God does. That's the second part of the great commandment to love God and love people (see Matthew 22:37-40). But it's impossible to love everybody in the world, so the Bible gives you priorities for loving your neighbors—those nearest you. Your inner circle is your family—parents, siblings, other extended family members. But our world holds so many more people. After family, where do you start?

The next circle of love is your fellow believers in need. Paul urged, "Whenever we have the opportunity, we should do good to everyone, *especially to our Christian brothers and sisters*" (Galatians 6:10, emphasis added). Outside the circle of your family, your first concern should be the group of believers you learn, serve, fellowship, and worship with—people like your campus Bible study group, your Sunday school class, your youth group, and your ministers and church congregation. Another level might include believers you don't know as well—such as missionaries, denomination leaders, and outreach organizations. At the outer edge of this category are Christians you don't know and will likely never meet—believers in other churches, cities, and countries.

Loving each other like Christ commanded is the heartbeat of your relationship with other Christians. But sometimes Christians put too much emphasis on love within the body of Christ. It's pretty easy to love each other. The real test comes in loving those who aren't much like you—worldly people, unlovely people, hateful people. You might spend so much time with other Christians that you don't leave much time for interacting with your unbelieving classmates and neighbors.

Beyond the circles of family and faith lie "all people" you are to love as you love yourself. This huge category ranges from your literal neighbors—the people next door—to your entire student body to remote tribes you can't even name. Whoever and wherever they are, you get to love them.

Like a pebble tossed into a pond, the big splash of your love will be at the center, to those nearest you—family and fellow believers. But a wave ripples outward to needy unbelievers all around you. Does your love for others spread through all levels of your relationships? Or are you so involved at one level that you don't have time for the rest?

 REFLECT: How could you let God's Spirit show you where your love for others needs to flow more freely?

 PRAY: Talk to God about how you can spread his love to every person you have contact with.

15 Both Soup and Salvation

Bible Reading: James 2:14-18
> *Faith that doesn't show itself by good deeds is no faith at all—it is dead and useless. James 2:17*

"SERVICE PROJECTS?" Ethan scoffed as he looked at brochures for summer missions trips. "I mean, it looks like you talk to people too, but why would I want to waste my time putting up a house for the poor? What good will a house do them when they're going to hell? If I'm not knocking on doors and passing out tracts from dawn till dusk, it's not a missions trip."

Many Christians think the only part of people you should care about is their souls—the part that will live forever. But the Bible demands more.

God wants you to love the people in your world as total persons, not just as souls that need to be saved. Jesus not only talked to people about the bread of life to fill their spiritual hunger (see John 6:35), but he also gave them physical bread for their physical hunger (see John 6:5-11). Every individual is a whole person—soul and body—and those parts are equally valuable to God.

Suppose a local skid row mission invites your youth group to take part in their ministry of "soup and salvation." They want your group to come downtown to present a church service and then serve a hot meal to the homeless. *These are equally loving activities because each is a ministry of love to genuine needs.*

Food, clothing, and shelter alone don't bring people into the kingdom of God. People also need to hear about Christ and trust him as Savior and Lord. But it's difficult for people to listen to your Bible lesson if their stomachs are growling with hunger.

You know what? Caring for physical needs flings wide the door for meeting spiritual needs. And, moreover, the world is watching you. They aren't impressed by your passion to save souls if you neglect painfully obvious physical needs.

Ministries that seek to provide basic physical needs and feed spiritual hunger offer a double helping of the love of Christ. Operation Carelift, a facet of the Josh McDowell Ministry and Campus Crusade for Christ International, is one example. Since 1992 Operation Carelift has collected and delivered food, clothing, medical supplies, and school supplies to the destitute citizens of Russia. With the supplies come Bibles and the gospel message. As one Russian teacher said with tears in her eyes, "That's real love."

 REFLECT: Are you loving the "whole person" in those around you? What can you do to improve the quality of your love?

PRAY: Ask God to give you eyes to see people as whole creatures—and strength to meet both physical and spiritual needs.

16 When Sin Gets in the Way

Bible Reading: John 8:1-11

"Neither do I condemn you," Jesus declared. "Go now and leave your life of sin." John 8:11, NIV

"I KNOW WE'RE supposed to love people where they are," Gabriella said. "But what about Christians who live a sinful lifestyle? I have a friend who's gone off the deep end. She doesn't come to church anymore, and I don't even want to know what she does with her new friends. How can I love her?"

Good question. Love provides what people need and protects them from harm. Disobedient Christians need to be lovingly confronted with their disobedience—with the goal of protecting them from the consequences of their wrong behavior. Suppose you have a Christian friend at school who is sleeping with her boyfriend. She needs someone to lovingly say, "God is pure, and the Bible clearly says that sex outside of marriage is wrong. So I challenge you to stop sleeping with him." She might not want to hear it, but you are acting in your friend's best interest. Love attempts to protect her from possible pregnancy, sexually transmitted diseases, and the burden of regret in a future marriage.

Some people call this "tough love"—risking a relationship in order to turn a fellow Christian away from sin. You do people no favors by blowing off their behavior in order to spare their feelings or maintain your relationship. They are in much greater danger if they continue in the wrong direction. Exercising love comes with no guarantees that your efforts will be well-received. You can only do your best to provide for their good and protect them from harm. How they respond is up to them and God.

"I have a lot of non-Christian friends whose values and behaviors conflict with mine," Doug shared. "How can I love them when we don't agree morally?"

Another good question. You have to separate the person from his or her sinful behavior. Unbelievers have genuine physical, emotional, and spiritual needs. As you have opportunities, provide for their needs without compromising your faith. Then share Christ with them, seeking to protect them from the ultimate harm they face: an eternity without God.

Let's say, for example, you have a non-Christian friend at school who is openly racist. As much as his lifestyle might turn you off, he is a person for whom Christ died. He isn't headed for hell because he is racist; his behavior is a symptom of his need for Christ. Look for ways to be a positive influence and encouragement to him. Pray that God will give you opportunities that will help him ditch sin and turn his heart to Christ.

REFLECT: Do you know any Christians who aren't walking close to God? What can you do to love them?

PRAY: Ask God for wisdom to help you love the tough cases in your life.

17 Thinking about the End

Bible Reading: Colossians 4:2-6

Let your conversation be gracious and effective so that you will have the right answer for everyone. Colossians 4:6

THE WAITRESS arrived with their drinks. Krystal stirred her Diet Coke gently with a straw as she figured out what to say. "I'm worried about my friend Dannie," she said at last. Across the table from her were Doug and Elena, youth leaders at Krystal's church. "Her parents aren't Christians, but she says she's trusted Christ as her Savior. But she's acting strange."

"Is Dannie in some kind of trouble?" Doug asked.

Krystal sighed. "I don't know for sure. She's been really distant for the last few weeks. And I have noticed a few other things about her that worry me."

Doug leaned closer. "Like what?"

"Well, things that make me wonder if Dannie is thinking about suicide."

Elena reached across the table to hold Krystal's hand. "I'm sorry you have to deal with this issue again after what you have been through, Krystal. This must be difficult for you. How can we help?"

Krystal felt tears fill her eyes. She remembered all too clearly her own bout with depression two years ago when she gulped down a fistful of sleeping pills. But Doug and Elena had been there at just the right moment. Krystal would be forever grateful for the love and concern this couple had shown in her darkest hour.

Maybe you, like Krystal, have noticed behavior in a friend that disturbs you. You can't quite put your finger on the problem, but you are wondering if your friend has had thoughts of suicide. Because suicide is the second leading cause of death among students today, you can't shrug off your concern. A staggering sixty-five hundred teenagers die each year at their own hands—that's one every hour and twenty minutes!

Your friend may be entertaining thoughts of suicide if he or she is down or depressed most of the time, often talks and asks questions about death, gives away possessions as if preparing for death, is often fatigued and wants to sleep all the time, or complains about not being able to sleep. You should also be concerned about a friend who takes dangerous risks, such as driving recklessly or playing with knives or guns.

If your friend is exhibiting potentially suicidal behavior, now is the time to do something to make sure he or she doesn't follow through with that impulse! Talk to a trusted adult, like your youth pastor or a counselor at school, and ask for help.

REFLECT: Do you know anyone who is at risk of suicide? How could you work with the adults around you to help?

PRAY: Ask God today to help you minister to your hurting friends.

18 Turning the Dark Clouds Away

Bible Reading: 1 Thessalonians 3:1-8
> *We sent him to strengthen you, to encourage you in your faith, and to keep you from becoming disturbed by the troubles you were going through. 1 Thessalonians 3:2-3*

EVERYONE FEELS gloomy sometimes. But when you think a friend might be depressed—with thoughts of suicide—it's crucial that you act lovingly and prayerfully. People who entertain passing thoughts of suicide usually feel incredibly isolated inside. They often hurt for lack of someone who cares deeply about them, invests time in them, and regards them as significant. When someone you care about battles the despair of aloneness, the most important thing you can share is *you*. Here are several ways to develop a caring relationship that will help your friend feel less alone:

Be concerned for your friend. The best way to deal with a hurting friend is to develop your relationship with him or her and demonstrate your interest and concern.

Be available to your friend. For most hurting people, love is spelled T-I-M-E. Look for opportunities to spend time with your friend.

Keep in touch with your friend. An occasional phone call just to say hello and ask how your friend is doing shows that you care.

Pray for your friend. Ask God to show you ways to build your relationship and meet some of your friend's needs for love and acceptance.

Affirm your friend's identity as a child of God. Depressed people have forgotten their basic value and worth to God. If your friend is a Christian, remind him that he is loved, valued, and useful to God. If your friend isn't a Christian, she is still created in God's image, someone for whom Christ died. Look for ways to affirm your friend's value and worth to God.

Try to instill hope in your friend. The best way to instill hope in hurting people is by focusing on feelings instead of arguing over how they think. Communicate hope by feeling your friend's sorrow and by comforting him or her.

Talk with your friend. Many discouraged, depressed students report that they can't talk to their parents about problems, hurts, and decisions. When you are with your friend, allow her to talk about her life and difficulties. Be sure to respect your friend's opinions without judgment or condemnation, even if they are questionable. It's vital that your friend is free to verbalize his feelings to someone who cares.

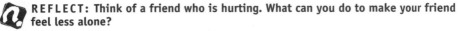 **REFLECT:** Think of a friend who is hurting. What can you do to make your friend feel less alone?

 PRAY: *Lord, help me be a loving and sensitive friend today to those around me who are hurting.*

19 Everybody Is a Priceless Treasure

Bible Reading: Romans 8:15-17

For his Holy Spirit speaks to us deep in our hearts and tells us that we are God's children. Romans 8:16

IF YOU HAVE friends or classmates who are depressed to the point of thinking about suicide, there's no doubt they have an extremely low view of their value and worth. They don't consider their lives worth salvaging. They lack a sense of belonging, worthiness, and competence.

As you work to develop a relationship with your friends, you might want to help them through a Bible study that highlights how God sees us as lovable, valuable, and useful.

If you don't feel confident leading your friends in a Bible study, your youth leader or pastor might be willing to help you. The goal of your Bible study and ongoing input into your friends' lives should highlight three biblical truths:

God sees us as lovable, giving us a sense of belonging. Like everyone else, your friends need to sense they belong to someone. We gain our ultimate sense of belonging when we understand that God loves us unconditionally, just as we are. John 1:12 declares that when we received Christ, we became children of God. He accepted us as his sons and daughters and invites us to call him "Father, dear Father" (Romans 8:15).

God sees us as valuable, giving us a sense of worthiness. Our true worth as persons is proven by the fact that our loving God allowed Jesus Christ, his sinless Son, to die for our sins. Paul said, "But God showed his great love for us by sending Christ to die for us while we were still sinners" (Romans 5:8). Your friend is worth the death of God's Son.

God sees us as useful, giving us a sense of competence. Paul wasn't bragging when he said, "I can do everything with the help of Christ who gives me the strength I need" (Philippians 4:13). Paul simply saw himself as God sees him: gifted and empowered by the Holy Spirit to serve God and others. God wants all believers to realize that he has given each of us specific physical, mental, and spiritual abilities and equipped us to use those abilities successfully. God is so confident in our competence that he has called us to fulfill his great commission (see Matthew 28:18-20).

Do you understand the importance of helping your friends see themselves through God's eyes? A biblical understanding of our identity in Christ might be your friends' lifesaver. The more your friends realize they are lovable, valuable, and useful to God, the less likely they will be to think life isn't worth living.

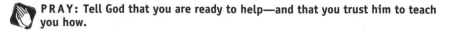

REFLECT: Ask God for ways to share these truths with hurting friends.

PRAY: Tell God that you are ready to help—and that you trust him to teach you how.

20 Upward Mobility

Bible Reading: Mark 10:32-45

Whoever wants to be a leader among you must be your servant.
Mark 10:43

AS JESUS WAS walking with his disciples toward Jerusalem, two of them—James and John, the sons of Zebedee—let their imaginations run wild. Jesus clearly laid out the destiny awaiting him in Jerusalem: rebuke, torture, and death (see Mark 10:33-34). But James and John imagined a totally different conclusion to the journey—a revolution where Jesus would supernaturally oust the Roman military establishment in Jerusalem. In their minds, Jesus and his followers would soon rule Palestine.

The Zebedee brothers were so convinced of their fantasy that they decided to apply early for the top two cabinet positions in Jesus' regime. " 'We want to sit in places of honor next to you,' they said, 'one at your right and the other at your left' " (verse 37). They were totally blind to Jesus' prediction of his coming suffering.

Jesus more or less asked them, "Are you two ready to go through everything I will go through?" (see verse 38). He was thinking about the pain and humiliation of his upcoming trial, beatings, and crucifixion. "Oh, yes," they replied confidently. Jesus was apparently seeing years into the future when he said that they would experience what he would experience (see verse 39). The Master was referring to the fact that James would be rejected and killed for his stand as Christ's disciple (see Acts 12:2), and that John would be rejected and exiled (see Revelation 1:9). Each would indeed taste the suffering that Jesus would soon experience in Jerusalem.

Like James and John, some Christians today have a distorted picture of what it means to follow Jesus. "What am I going to gain from being a Christian?" they ask eagerly. They have a hard time getting the message that the Christian life isn't a smooth-sailing, hassle-free, magic-carpet ride to heaven. We don't get to live the life of a king—at least not here on earth.

If anybody should have lived like a king on earth, it was Jesus. But we live the life of servants, just like Jesus did. So we don't ask what we can *get* from being a Christian—even though the Bible assures us that the rewards and blessings of following Christ are endless. Instead we are to ask, "What can I *give* as a servant of God and of people?"

James and John became great not by rocketing to the position of prime minister in the government of a political revolutionary but by serving Christ and his church selflessly. In Mark 10 they were far from understanding the path to greatness, but they eventually realized that *giving*—not *getting*—is the heart of the Christian life.

REFLECT: What kind of greatness are you expecting in God's kingdom?

PRAY: Tell God you look forward to serving him selflessly today.

21 Mercy, Mercy

Bible Reading: Mark 10:46-52

"What do you want me to do for you?" Jesus asked. Mark 10:51

THE PRESIDENT of the Jericho Chamber of Commerce was concluding his speech at the city gate. City dignitaries, Jesus of Nazareth, and a big crowd of people jostled one another as they listened. "And so we want to express our thanks to you, Jesus, for your brief visit—"

A commotion at the back of the crowd interrupted the speaker. "Jesus, Son of David, have mercy on me!"

"Shut up, you blind fool," one of the dignitaries growled over his shoulder.

The Chamber president continued nervously, "We want to thank—"

"Jesus, Son of David, have mercy on me!" This time the voice from outside the circle was loud and demanding.

"Hush! Be quiet! Be still, old beggar!" several people joined in harshly. But Jesus was visibly moved by the plea. He called the blind beggar forward (a man named Bartimaeus) and healed him.

What caused Jesus to turn his attention away from the crowd to a persistent, blind beggar? Perhaps it was the beggar's cry for mercy. "Mercy" is compassion or pity that leads a person to provide relief for someone in misery, and a "merciful" person is someone who feels the hurts of others deeply and acts to relieve those hurts. Agencies like the Red Cross exercise mercy in an organized fashion. But you also show mercy in simple acts like consoling a littler brother or sister who has skinned a knee.

Mercy is a chief ingredient in God's nature. The Lord said of himself, "I am the Lord, the merciful and gracious God" (Exodus 34:6). Since Jesus was God in a human body, no wonder he was moved by the beggar's cry. Mercy was one of the characteristics of his earthly ministry. His heart was moved by the suffering of people, and his power, as God, allowed him to provide healing and deliverance.

There's no pain, disappointment, confusion, fear, or loneliness that Jesus can't understand. And when you come to him crying, "Master, I need help," Christ responds with compassion. Sometimes you spot his kind deeds when he supernaturally restores someone's health, like he did for Bartimaeus. Other times you spot him through the caring of a concerned Christian friend who prays for you and comforts you in times of trouble. If God is eager to show the kind of mercy Jesus showed poor Bartimaeus, think what he has waiting for you when you call on him for help.

REFLECT: In what area of your life do you need God's mercy? Have you cried out to him for help?

PRAY: Tell God today about your deepest needs—and trust him to meet them.

22 Give Till It Helps

Bible Reading: Mark 12:41–44

They gave a tiny part of their surplus, but she, poor as she is, has given everything she has. Mark 12:44

ESTHER WAS in her late fifties, single, and living alone in a tiny house. In public she was so painfully shy that she was often overlooked in a crowd. Yet she was a faithful Christian who rarely missed a service at her small church. Whenever the pastor or his wife or children had a birthday, Esther quietly presented them with a birthday card and a gift of money. And when the pastor's family took a vacation, Esther always gave them another card with money enclosed.

Years later the pastor learned that Esther had been living on a total of $150 per month—less than if she had been on welfare! One of the most generous people in the church had barely enough to buy the necessities of life. But she generously gave to others as if she were wealthy, just like the poor widow in Mark 12.

The New Testament shows us just one overriding principle about giving. It's not the tithe, although that's a good place to start. (A "tithe" means ten percent.) Instead, everywhere you look in the New Testament you see the open-hand policy. Luke says it this way: "If you give, you will receive. Your gift will return to you in full measure, pressed down, shaken together to make room for more" (Luke 6:38).

Put simply, the open-hand policy means first that the believer's hands are open to give whatever he or she has to whoever needs it. For example, a member of your youth group is too broke to go to camp, so you open your wallet and give him the seven bucks you were saving for spending money. Or a family in the community loses all its possessions in a fire, so you give half your wardrobe to a girl in the family who's your size.

The open-hand policy also means getting ready to receive what God will give you as a result of your generous giving. "Oh, good," you say, "I want to give more so I can get more." That's not exactly how Luke 6 explains the open-hand policy. Give without *thought* of return, and especially without *planning* on the return. *Then* it will be God's good pleasure to surprise you by pouring his gift into your open hands.

It doesn't take a lot—of either money or stuff—to be an open-handed giver. It just takes a little practice. Why not start this week by pulling a dollar or two out of your pocket and asking God to show you where that dollar can do more good than in your possession? Then stand back and let God amaze you at how rewarding it can be to be an open-handed giver.

REFLECT: How have you seen God's generosity in your life? What are you doing to be an open-handed giver?

PRAY: Ask God to help you be as generous with others as he has been with you.

Bible Reading: Mark 14:1-11
Why berate her for doing such a good thing to me? Mark 14:6

BROTHER SUN, *Sister Moon* is a classic movie about the life of St. Francis of Assisi. As the son of a wealthy textile merchant, Francis is destined to live a life of ease as a successful businessman. But after he trusts in Christ, the young man grows uncomfortable with his wealth in light of the poverty that abounds in his community. He feels that since Christ gave up the treasures of heaven to serve others, he must follow suit. He walks away from his father's wealth and lives his life in poverty as he ministers to the needs of the poor.

In Mark 14, you get a glimpse of two individuals. One, like St. Francis, felt money was no object in making a tribute to Christ the King. The other had such a craving for money that it led him to perform the most horrifying deed in history.

Two days before the Last Supper, a woman visited Jesus and poured a bottle of high-priced perfume over his head. It was a loving, respectful recognition of Jesus' lordship. "What a waste!" some of the disciples thought. "We could have sold that bottle and helped a lot of poor people with the money." Not a bad idea, really. But there's a time for using money to help the needy, and there's a time for using money to make a tribute to our Lord and King.

Then there's Judas, whose greed paved the way for his downfall. John tells the truth about Judas: "Not that he cared for the poor—he was a thief who was in charge of the disciples' funds, and he often took some for his own use" (John 12:6). The chief priests recognized Judas's craving for money and paid him to betray Jesus (see Mark 14:11).

So how can you pay tribute to Christ the King like that generous woman did when Jesus isn't here in the flesh? One great way: In Christ's name honor someone who *is* here in the flesh. Here are a few suggestions for paying tribute to Christ through someone else:

- Buy your pastor or youth leader a gift—a book, CD, gift certificate, etc.
- Donate to charity in thanks for Christ's lordship over you.
- Make a sacrificial contribution to your church's building fund.

"Tribute gifts" take on even more meaning to you if you give them anonymously. It's a way to help you keep your focus on the real purpose of the gift—bringing honor to Christ. He will be the only one who knows what you have done. It's a practical, loving way you can declare Christ's lordship with your possessions.

REFLECT: How can you honor Christ by giving to someone right in front of you?

PRAY: *God, build in me a heart that's grateful for everything you have given me—and a heart that recognizes your greatness.*

24 Liar, Lunatic, or Lord?

Bible Reading: Matthew 16:13-19
You are the Messiah, the Son of the living God. Matthew 16:16

"YOU'RE SO STUPID," Sean sneered at Heather. "How can you believe that a dead guy rose? Jesus might have been a good person, but he wasn't God."

Oh? Well, Jesus claimed to be God—period. He didn't leave any other option open. Truth is, his claim must either be true or false. Jesus' question to his disciples, "Who do you say I am?" (Matthew 16:15), has several alternatives.

Was he a liar? If Jesus made his claims knowing he wasn't God, then he was lying to his followers. If he was a liar, he was also a hypocrite—a guy who told others to be honest even while he taught and lived a colossal lie.

That view of Jesus, however, doesn't jive with what we know of Jesus or the results of his life and teachings. Whenever Jesus has been proclaimed, lives have been changed. Nations have repented. Thieves have gone straight. Alcoholics have tossed their bottles. Hateful individuals have become channels of love. Someone whose life had results like that couldn't have been a phony.

Was he a lunatic? If someone told you he was God, you would believe him about as much as if he said he was Santa Claus. You would call him one deluded and self-deceived dude. Yet Jesus didn't display the abnormalities and imbalance that usually go hand in hand with being crazy. Jesus was a guy who spoke some of the most profound words ever recorded—words that have set free many individuals, even some in mental bondage. Jesus Christ was no lunatic.

Was he Lord? If Christ isn't a liar or a lunatic, you only have one option: He is who he claimed to be—the Son of God.

The issue with these three alternatives isn't *which is possible.* Any of the three could be possible. The question is instead, *which is more likely?* Nailing down the identity of Jesus Christ can't be an intellectual exercise. You can't put him on the shelf while calling him a great moral teacher. That isn't a valid option. If he was so great and so moral, then what do you do with his claim to be God? If he was a liar or a lunatic, then he can't qualify as a great moral teacher. And if he was a great moral teacher, then he is much more as well. He is either a liar, a lunatic, or the Lord God. You have to make the choice.

You have two resources to help you make that choice rightly. One is the historically credible record of Christ's rising from the dead. The other is the Bible. Giving you solid reasons to believe is a huge reason God gave you his book. As John wrote, "These are written so that you may believe that Jesus is the Messiah, the Son of God, and that by believing in him you will have life" (John 20:31).

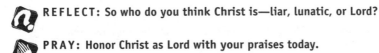

REFLECT: So who do you think Christ is—liar, lunatic, or Lord?

PRAY: Honor Christ as Lord with your praises today.

Bible Reading: 1 John 1:1-4
We saw him with our own eyes and touched him with our own hands. He is Jesus Christ, the Word of life. 1 John 1:1

FOR CENTURIES, loads of the world's philosophers have assaulted Christianity as absurd. Many have simply ignored the central issue of the Resurrection. Others have tried to explain it away through a variety of theories. But the facts of the empty tomb are as convincing today as they were two thousand years ago.

Here are some of the relevant facts:

- Jesus of Nazareth—Jewish prophet who claimed to be the Christ prophesied in the Jewish Scriptures—was arrested, judged a political criminal, and executed by Roman crucifixion.
- Three days after Christ's death and burial, some women who went to his tomb discovered his body was gone.
- In subsequent weeks his disciples claimed that God had raised him from the dead and that he had appeared to them at various times before ascending into heaven.
- From that core of early disciples, the message of Christ spread throughout the Roman Empire and has continued to spread through the centuries.

So did the Resurrection really happen? Was the tomb of Jesus really empty? There are only two possible ways to answer these questions. The resurrection of Jesus Christ was either one of the world's most wicked, vicious, heartless hoaxes, or it is the most remarkable fact in human history.

Think about the witnesses for a moment. The New Testament accounts of the Resurrection circulated during the lifetime of men and women who were alive when the event happened. Those people could have easily confirmed or denied the accuracy of the accounts. The writers of the four Gospels either had witnessed these events themselves or were relating the accounts of eyewitnesses.

Had the writers of the Bible books of Matthew, Mark, Luke, and John made up the story of the Resurrection, their report never would have lasted past the first century. But even people who hated Jesus and wanted to disprove the Resurrection couldn't refute what everybody else knew to be fact: the tomb was empty and Christ was alive.

You didn't see the empty tomb or the risen Christ, but you have the reliable, time-honored testimony of the New Testament writers. Christ is risen!

REFLECT: How would you answer a non-Christian friend who said the Resurrection never happened?

PRAY: Pray for a friend who doesn't believe the truth of the Resurrection.

26 You Can't Get Around the Empty Tomb

Bible Reading: Acts 1:1-5

During the forty days after his crucifixion, he appeared to the apostles from time to time and proved to them in many ways that he was actually alive. Acts 1:3

FOR FORTY DAYS after his crucifixion, Jesus showed himself to his disciples to prove that he had really risen from the dead. Yet some folks argue that a fate far less miraculous befell the body of Jesus.

Some say the disciples went to the wrong tomb on Easter morning—an empty one. But if that were true, officials needed only to open up the right tomb and point to the dead body to disprove the Resurrection. That didn't happen. Others insist that the disciples stole Christ's body. But a handful of disciples would never have gotten by the elite Roman troops guarding the tomb. Still others believe that Jesus didn't really die on the cross—that he was just unconscious from exhaustion and lack of blood, then revived in the cool tomb. But had the whipped, wounded, and weakened Christ somehow been able to break out of his own tomb—a laughable theory given the size of the stone that sealed him inside—he would hardly have looked like the conqueror of death his disciples claimed he was.

So what exactly happened after the lifeless body of Jesus was taken down from the cross? About one hundred pounds of aromatic spices mixed into a gummy or cement-like substance were applied to the linen cloths wrapped around the body to form a kind of "body cast" weighing about 120 pounds.

After the body was placed in a solid-rock tomb, the historical account points out that a huge stone closed the entrance of the tomb—not just any huge stone, but one that weighed approximately one and a half to two tons. Then a Roman guard unit of sixteen highly disciplined fighting men was stationed to guard the tomb.

But three days later the tomb was empty, and the followers of Jesus claimed he had risen from the dead. They reported that he appeared to them over forty days. Paul the apostle recounted that Jesus appeared to more than five hundred of his followers at one time, most of whom were still alive and could confirm—or contest—what Paul wrote. No one can accurately say that Jesus appeared to just an insignificant few.

Christians believe Jesus was bodily resurrected by the supernatural power of God. Because of the historical evidence, it's harder *not* to believe in Christ's resurrection than it is to believe.

 REFLECT: That is the evidence. The verdict? Jesus Christ actually rose from the dead and he lives today. How does that affect how you live your life?

PRAY: Tell God you want to live in a way that shows you believe Jesus' resurrection is true.

Bible Reading: Philippians 3:7-11
*I have discarded everything else, counting it all as garbage, so that
I may have Christ and become one with him. Philippians 3:8-9*

HERE'S HOW you get to know the facts of any event in history: You dig into the testimony of eyewitnesses. And the most enlightening testimony regarding the resurrection of Jesus Christ is the life of the early Christians. You have to wonder what
made them go everywhere telling the message of the risen Christ.

Ponder this: Were there any benefits to be gained from their efforts—things like
prestige, wealth, increased social status, or material benefits—that might account for
their wholehearted and total allegiance to this "risen Christ"? Not unless you consider getting beaten, stoned to death, thrown to lions, tortured, and crucified to be
opportunities for career advancement.

These early Christians didn't react like you would expect. They didn't fight back.
They forced their beliefs on no one. Instead, they laid down their lives as the ultimate
proof of their total confidence in the truth of their message.

It's important to remember that at first even the disciples didn't believe in
Christ's resurrection. But once they were convinced—in spite of their doubts—they
never again doubted that Christ was raised from the dead.

Can you imagine the odds of the twelve disciples and dozens more of Christ's
followers, all knowing the Resurrection was a lie, not crumbling under the torture
and pressure to admit their deception? That's crazy! They wouldn't suffer like that
for a hoax, not all of them. Somebody would have cracked, spilled the truth, and
blown their cover-up plot.

It's unbelievable that a deliberate cover-up—a plot to perpetuate a lie about the
Resurrection—could have survived the violent persecution of the apostles and the
atrocious purge of the first-century believers who were thrown by the thousands to
the lions for refusing to renounce the lordship of Christ. If the Resurrection was a
hoax, don't you think at least one of the apostles would have renounced Christ before being beheaded or stoned to death or crucified? Wouldn't someone have sold
out to the authorities to spare his life and possibly gain a generous reward?

Nothing less than the real deal—the undeniable appearance of the resurrected
Christ—could have caused these people to maintain to their dying day that Jesus is
alive and that he is Lord. The ultimate proof of Christ's life and lordship is in a personal relationship with him.

REFLECT: Do you think the disciples would have died for a lie? Why or why not?

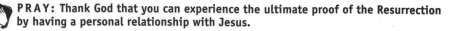

**PRAY: Thank God that you can experience the ultimate proof of the Resurrection
by having a personal relationship with Jesus.**

28 Is It Good for You?

Bible Reading: Deuteronomy 10:12–16

*What does the Lord your God require of you? He requires you . . .
to obey the Lord's commands and laws that I am giving you today
for your own good. Deuteronomy 10:12-13*

DO YOU EVER wonder why God takes such a tough stance against premarital sex? You feel those urges. And the opportunities to answer those urges are certainly available. But the Bible says no. Is God just some spoiler of all things fun?

Any time God warns you not to do something, he's trying to take care of you. He wants to protect you from the negative consequences of your actions. He also wants to make sure you can enjoy the huge benefits that come from obedience.

Physically, God wants to protect you from a dangerous run-in with more than fifty different kinds of sexually transmitted diseases. More than a million teenage girls get pregnant every year. He doesn't want you to be one of them. Babies are beautiful things, but he doesn't want you to have to live with the heartache and problems that pregnancy creates outside of marriage.

Emotionally, God wants to guard you from the negative emotions that plague a person involved in sex before marriage, fears like: "What if my parents find out?" "What if we break up?" "What if we get caught?" He wants to spare you the guilt that comes the morning after, the shame from being known as "easy" or "cheap," and the doubt about your self-image, your relationship with God, and whether you're being loved for yourself or used for your body.

Relationally, God wants to protect you from breakdowns in communication. If you're sleeping with your boyfriend or girlfriend, often your relationship focuses on your sexual involvement instead of on each other as persons. Although most people don't realize it, you carry all your past experiences and relationships into your future marriage. That can create problems. Your spouse may feel super-insecure, always wondering if you are comparing him or her to your past partners.

Spiritually, God wants to protect you from feeling far from him. Not only can premarital sex blow your testimony for Christ among your non-Christian friends, but you can also feel like God is a million miles away from you. You have damaged your fellowship with him and with other Christians because you feel like a hypocrite. God loves you, and he doesn't want you to experience that pain.

God wants to make sure you get the best. By waiting you guarantee your physical health, emotional maturity, relational happiness, and spiritual growth. And you can't lose when you follow God's ways, which he gives you "for your own good."

REFLECT: What good reasons does God give you to wait until marriage for sex?

PRAY: Talk to God about how you are dealing with your sexual desires.

29 Out with Bad Thoughts, in with Good Thoughts

Bible Reading: Ephesians 4:17-24

Throw off your old evil nature and your former way of life, which is rotten through and through, full of lust and deception. Instead, there must be a spiritual renewal of your thoughts and attitudes.
Ephesians 4:22-23

HERE'S A QUIZ from chemistry class: What's the best way to force gas out of a test tube? If you answered, "Pour liquid into the test tube," you're right. You get gas out by pouring liquid in. It's called displacement. One element pushes out the other because they can't both occupy the same space.

Here's a similar principle for dealing with lustful thoughts: Get rid of them with pure thoughts.

You can inject in pure thoughts in many ways. Turn on a Christian CD and focus on the music and lyrics. Open a Christian magazine or book, turn on a Christian video, or call up a Christian friend for a clean conversation. But the most effective way to displace bad thoughts is by memorizing and meditating on Scripture. Here's a pattern you can follow:

1. *Decide to memorize at least one verse each week.* Here are some good ones to start with: Psalm 51:10; Psalm 119:9, 11; Romans 12:1-2; 1 Corinthians 10:13; Philippians 4:8; Colossians 3:1-3.
2. *Memorize the verse word for word.* Find a Bible translation that helps you understand the verse clearly, then memorize that version. Don't make up your own translation. Write the verse on a small card you can keep in your pocket and look at it often until you have it memorized.
3. *Meditate on this verse.* Meditating means thinking deeply and continuously about the verse. Ask yourself what the verse means and what God is saying to you through it. Think about each word separately and what it means to the verse as a whole.
4. *Apply the verse to your life.* Complete the statement: "As a result of this verse, I will . . ."
5. *Review.* Go over the new verse every day for two months. Then once a week after that.
6. *Use what you have stored away.* Whenever impure thoughts hassle you, pull up one of your memory verses, review it, and meditate on it until the good thoughts force out the bad thoughts.

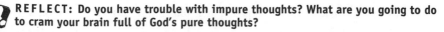 **REFLECT: Do you have trouble with impure thoughts? What are you going to do to cram your brain full of God's pure thoughts?**

 PRAY: Ask God to purify your mind through the Scriptures you memorize and meditate on.

30 A Way Out

Bible Reading: 1 Corinthians 10:12-13

When you are tempted, he will show you a way out so that you will not give in to it. 1 Corinthians 10:13

DARYL'S YOUTH PASTOR told him that when he was tempted by sexual sin, he should pray about it. "But then I just think about it more," he moaned. "Endlessly praying about it doesn't seem to help."

The pressure to conform to culture's view of sex is strong. You feel pressed by the media, your friends, and your own desires. And prayer is just one piece of your strategy for dealing with sexual temptation. Here are a number of helps that can serve as God's "escape route" from sin:

Set standards beforehand. Determine right and wrong based on God's Word. Then make sure your date knows about them before you go out.

Be accountable. Keep another person informed about your actions, thoughts, and attitudes—someone of the same sex, someone more mature spiritually, someone you respect. If you start to slide in your standards, let him or her help you get back on track.

Let your lifestyle show. Say no to sexual pressure by your words, your body language, and your actions. Let your whole life declare, "I'm going God's way."

Keep your mind pure. What you feed your mind determines what you think about, so be careful about what you let into your mind through your eyes and ears.

Avoid sex-oriented media. Make it a habit to shut out TV programs, videos, movies, books, magazines, music, or software that violates your standards.

Dress to reflect your convictions. Both girls and guys need to dress modestly. Pick clothes that look good but that aren't cut for their turn-on effect.

Choose your companions carefully. Hang out with people who have the same convictions you have. Get involved in groups that support your right choices.

Seek the wisdom of others. Choose good role models. Talking with older, more mature people—parents, pastors, or youth leaders—can help you sort out confusing emotions.

Break off relationships. If you are getting pressured or giving in to pressure from someone, backing off from or ending that relationship relieves the pressure.

Make a fast, strategic exit. Be honest about your weakness. If you think you can't handle a situation, head for the door.

Ask God to help. None of these other strategies will work unless you realize that you really do need help. God doesn't want you to be a lone ranger. Use prayer as your first step—and all along the way.

REFLECT: What strategies do you want to put into action in your battle against sexual pressures?

 PRAY: Spend time today talking to God about the sexual pressure in your life.

How to Get There from Here

Bible Reading: Psalm 119:57–64

I pondered the direction of my life, and I turned to follow your statutes.
Psalm 119:59

IT'S HARD to have any sympathy for these oddballs:

Girl genius Lotta Graymatter graduated from the university and entered law school at age twelve. But in seven years of law school, Ms. Graymatter has failed every class she has taken. "Law books are so heavy, and they don't have pictures," Lotta explained to her disappointed family. "I'll just have to become a lawyer my own way."

With his dying breaths, a scientist dictated to his assistant, Sinus Naselmeister, a secret formula that would cure the common cold and surely win Naselmeister a Nobel prize. After typing the formula into his computer, Naselmeister shut down the machine and began experimenting. His best medicine so far is a cough syrup that tastes so bad even lab rats won't take it.

You can't become a lawyer if you don't read the textbooks and pass the bar exam. And you can't develop a cure for the common cold if the formula is rotting on your hard drive.

No one is that dense—but some folks come close. It seems like a lot of Christians make the same mistake as our two weird friends above. We want to find God's direction for our lives, but we overlook the most obvious directional device God has provided: the Bible. It's our textbook for wisdom and understanding. It's our formula for dealing with problems. If we don't turn to the Bible for direction, we're worse off than both those dunces rolled together.

God's direction for your life—or his "will"—can be divided into two categories: his *universal will* and his *specific will.* God's *universal* will is clear and indisputable because it is spelled out in his Word. It's God's will, for example, that you trust Christ for salvation, obey your parents, share your faith, remain sexually pure, pray, and so on. God's *specific* will includes details like whom God wants you to date and marry, what college you should attend, and what career God wants you to choose.

You won't find a verse in the Bible that says something like, "Thou shalt attend State University and prepare for a career as a fruit-fly breeder," or "Thou shalt date and marry that cute girl from chemistry class." But as you commit yourself to following the *universal* directions God put in the Bible, he can start showing you his *specific* directions for you.

 REFLECT: How do you feel about the fact that God loves you enough to give you all the direction you need for your life?

PRAY: Spend some time sharing your appreciation with him.

2 Finding Your Way One Step at a Time

Bible Reading: Psalm 119:105-112
Your word is a lamp for my feet and a light for my path.
Psalm 119:105

ON THE TV drama *Early Edition,* character Gary Hobson prevents life-threatening tragedies each week because he knows about them hours before they happen—thanks to the mysterious "early edition" newspaper left on his doorstep.

Think of the advantages to knowing the future. You could study for all those surprise quizzes in school, and you wouldn't waste money on dates you know will be duds.

Wouldn't you like to know in advance the details of God's specific will for the major matters of your life? Wouldn't life be less stressful and complicated if you knew for sure where you will attend college, what you will do for your career, and whom you will marry?

In his wisdom and love, God chooses to keep the future hidden. He chooses instead to reveal his specific will for your life one day at a time, one step at a time.

The critical first step to discerning God's step-by-step direction for your life is *God's Word.* King David wrote, "Your word is a lamp for my feet and a light for my path" (Psalm 119:105). The Bible is like the little flashlight you take on a late-night hike. It helps you see a few steps ahead of you—and that's about it. But if you fail to keep the light trained on the trail at your feet, you'll likely fall on your face and never get where you hope to go.

A second step to finding God's specific direction is *prayer.* You can start by praying like Christ taught us: "May your will be done here on earth, just as it is in heaven" (Matthew 6:10).

A third step is the *counsel* of mature believers. Getting wisdom from others helps prevent rushed, emotional decisions and makes up for your lack of experience.

A fourth step is *circumstances.* As Paul discovered, God often opens and closes doors through circumstances (see Romans 1:13). But you have to balance the direction you draw from circumstances with a knowledge of Scripture, sincere prayer, and wise counsel.

As you follow what God has shown in Scripture as his universal will and seek his specific direction through prayer, counsel, and circumstances, you can take the next step: *Do what you want to do.* Psalm 37:4 promises, "Take delight in the Lord, and he will give you your heart's desires." What your heart desires is likely what God desires for you too. And if it isn't, he will make it clear to you.

 REFLECT: What would your life be like if God had left you to find your way in the world alone?

PRAY: Talk to him now about areas in your life where you need his direction.

3 Don't Ever Buy a Compass That Points South

Bible Reading: Psalm 119:33-40
Turn my eyes from worthless things, and give me life through your word. Psalm 119:37

THE AUDIENCE goes crazy with applause as the emcee glides to center stage. "Welcome to the annual Compass Awards show for the Home Guidance Network," he says. "As you know, the Home Guidance Network provides programming to help members of the viewing public find direction for their lives. Tonight we will honor the most deserving of these programs with the coveted Compass Award." The host displays the gleaming, oversized, gold compass statue, stirring the audience to enthusiastic applause.

"This year's first nominee is the spirited program *Direction from the Dark Side.* This weekly show highlights occult practices—from horoscopes to tarot cards to psychics—by which people make important decisions.

"Our second nominee is the ever-popular program *Do What I Do*, where rich, famous, and successful people tell how they live so our viewers can copy them.

"Next is the warm and wonderful program *If You Can't Trust Your Friends, Who Can You Trust?* where viewers are encouraged to direct their lives solely on the advice of their friends.

"Our fourth nominee is the runaway hit *Keeping Up with the Culture.* The hosts of this great show remind us that if you guide your life by what you see on TV, in the movies, and in other media, you will find success.

"And our final nominee is the heart-wrenching drama *As My Feelings Turn,* the show that says, 'If it feels right for you, it probably is right for you.' "

The host produces a large, sealed envelope and begins to tear it open. "And the winner of this year's Compass Award is—"

Wait a minute! There's no such thing as a Home Guidance Network—and even if there was, who really cares which of these "programs" wins? *They're all worthless!* The practices they preach—seeking occult insights, copying the lifestyles of famous people, depending on your friends to tell you what to do, doing what the culture does, or following your feelings—aren't God's way to provide direction for your life.

The Bible is your directional map. God's Word reveals his universal will, and reading it is the indispensable first step in determining his specific will for your life. Everywhere you turn there are useless and dangerous methods of seeking direction. Like King David, continually ask God to turn your eyes from those worthless things and give you life through his Word.

REFLECT: Have you ever relied on one of these worthless ways to guide your life? What happened?

 PRAY: Tell God you want *him* to guide your life.

4 Getting the Word on Tough Choices

Bible Reading: Psalm 119:97-104
Your commands make me wiser than my enemies, for your commands are my constant guide. Psalm 119:98

YOU'VE BARELY gotten comfortable in lit class when your teacher drops a bomb: "Class, I need to record who completed last week's reading assignment. I'm sending around a sheet of paper. Sign it, then put yes or no."

Way to go, dog brain! you think. *I should have finished reading the book on Friday instead of sitting semi-comatose in front of the computer for four hours.* Panic sets in. The sheet of paper is getting closer. No way do you want to write no next to your name, but . . .

Hey, I read more than half of those pages, so I could write yes, you reason. *Besides, I read more of it than most of the kids who are going to sign yes.*

The paper suddenly lands on your desk. You sign your name confidently, then hesitate over the space where you must write either yes or no. What will it be? How will you decide?

You face choices like that every day. How do you decide what's true and what's false, what's right and what's wrong? Some decisions are no-brainers, but how do you make the call when the line between right and wrong looks fuzzy?

King David says that God's "commands"—another term for God's Word, the Bible—are vital to gaining the wisdom and guidance you need for puzzling decisions. One way to put God's Word to work in your tough choices is a process you can remember as the Four Cs. Here's how it works:

C-1: *Consider the choice.* Every decision you face is an opportunity to pick God's will or your own way. Your choice isn't between what *you* think is right or wrong—it's between what God says is right or wrong.

C-2: *Compare it to God.* Compare your choice to God's *precepts.* Are there Bible passages that tell you what to do in this situation? Compare your choice to God's *principles.* Does this choice violate biblical principles like honesty or purity? Compare your choice to God's *person.* How would he respond to this choice?

C-3: *Commit to God's way.* Consciously decide to turn from your selfish way and do what God and his Word show you to do.

C-4: *Count on God's protection and provision.* God's care doesn't mean everything is going to be rosy. But living God's way brings things like freedom from guilt, a clear conscience, the joy of sharing Christ, and, most important, God's blessing on your life.

REFLECT: What decisions about right and wrong have you faced lately? Do your choices stand up to the four-C test?

PRAY: Thank God that we can trust the Bible for guidance.

5 Rare Book

Bible Reading: Psalm 119:137-144
> *Your promises have been thoroughly tested; that is why I love them so much. Psalm 119:140*

DURING THE LAST few days you've figured out some huge facts: (1) the Bible is your primary source for direction in life; (2) the Bible reveals God's *universal* will and plays a vital role in helping you discover God's *specific* will for your life; and (3) the Bible is your guide for making right choices in life.

But suppose you're talking with a friend. He says, "But how can you trust the Bible? It's just like any other religious book." How would you answer that?

Some significant facts about the Bible contribute to its reliability. Together, these facts are true *only* of the Bible. These facts don't prove that the Bible is true, but they prove that the Bible is *unique,* which is the first step in considering the reliability of what the Bible teaches.

The Bible is unique in its unity. The Bible was written over a 1,600-year span by over forty authors from every walk of life—kings, fishermen, poets, and statesmen. It was written on three different continents (Asia, Africa, and Europe) in three different languages (Hebrew, Aramaic, and Greek). Yet the Bible speaks with amazing unity and conformity on hundreds of controversial subjects. No other book can make that claim.

The Bible is unique in its circulation. The Bible is the world's all-time best-seller by far, with more than *2.5 billion copies!*

The Bible is unique in its translation. The Bible has been translated in part or in whole into more than 1,600 languages. It is available in the languages and dialects of 95 percent of the earth's people. No other book can make that claim.

The Bible is unique in its survival. Six hundred and forty-three manuscript copies of Homer's *Iliad* have survived to today. That might seem like a lot, but the *Iliad* is only a distant second among ancient books to the New Testament's 24,633 surviving manuscripts—despite many attempts by skeptics over the centuries to destroy God's Word! Voltaire, a famous French skeptic in the eighteenth century, predicted that Christianity would die out within one hundred years. But fifty years after his death, the Geneva Bible Society moved into his house and used his printing press to produce thousands of Bibles that were distributed worldwide. Voltaire faded into history, but not the Bible! No other book can make that claim.

Why has this unique book survived? Because its Author loves you and wants you to have the guidance you need to get going on a successful and rewarding life.

REFLECT: How would you explain the reliability of the Bible to a non-Christian friend?

PRAY: Thank God today for giving you his utterly reliable Word.

6 Are You Bowing under the Pressure?

Bible Reading: Romans 15:5-7
Accept each other just as Christ has accepted you. Romans 15:7

SCHOOL STARTS in ten minutes, so you figure it's about time to roll out of bed and get ready. You look in your closet and pull out a black shirt, black pants and belt, black socks, and black shoes. You take one glance in the mirror. *Perfect.* As you race through the kitchen, you bump into Mom. She takes one look at you and screams. Near hysteria, she rants about the way you look.

Undisturbed—you've been through this many times before—you tell her, "Mom, this is how all my friends dress." As you jump into the car you ask yourself, *Why am I dressed this way? It's the dumbest look I've ever worn!*

Why do you wear what you wear? Probably because of your peers—the same people who try to dictate the words you use, the people you associate with, the places you go, and the attitudes you hold. Peers press you to conform to their standards even if you don't want to. Depending on where your friends are coming from, peer pressure can either help you or hurt you.

In the 1960s, the most powerful influence in a teen's life was his parents, followed by teachers and then peers. But ever since the 1980s, peer pressure ranks first, followed by parents, and then the media. It's not like peer pressure didn't exist when your parents were kids, but the intensity wasn't the same. Your dad being pressured to smoke a cigarette out in the school parking lot is nothing compared to the pressure on you to smoke crack. Nor can your mom's one experience with her boyfriend wanting to take her "parking" compare to the pressure you get to go all the way because it's supposedly what everybody does today. Because the intensity levels are light-years apart, some parents find the peer pressure you face hard to understand.

Peer pressure is so powerful because every single person on earth has a God-given need to be loved and accepted. God wants to fulfill this drive first in your love-relationship with him. He wants you to be secure in how much he loves and accepts you as his chosen child. He knows that if you aren't secure in him, you will look to friends for acceptance. The greater your insecurity, the greater your need for acceptance, and the more the opinions of your friends matter. For some, a friend's opinion becomes the driving force of life.

Christ accepts you totally. Romans 15:7 confirms it. The more you experience his acceptance, the less you will need your friends' opinions to help you feel accepted.

REFLECT: How has pressure from your peers shaped your life this week? Are you okay with that? Is God?

PRAY: Thank God today for his unconditional acceptance and ask him to increase your awareness of his deep love for you.

7 Coming On Strong

Bible Reading: 1 Thessalonians 4:3-8
God wants you to be holy, so you should keep clear of all sexual sin.
1 Thessalonians 4:3

WHAT WOULD you guess is the number one pressure on a girl to become sexually active? If you guessed guys, *you're wrong.*

The greatest pressure on a girl often comes from her own girlfriends. If you find yourself in a situation like that, remember there are some things you can give away only once. Your virginity is one of them.

Don't sacrifice the things that are eternal on the altar of the immediate. Translation: Don't give away something you can never give away again to some guy—who buys you a lousy hamburger—just because your girlfriends are pressuring you. The next time they hassle you, shoot back at them what one young woman said to her friends: "In five minutes, I can become like you. But try as hard as you can, you can never again become like me."

And guys, you might feel pressured to get sexually involved with your girlfriend by friends who say things like, "It's natural when you're in love." It's also natural to burp in public. But do you do that? No. Not everything natural is proper in every setting. Some things offend others. And to get sexually involved with your girlfriend, even if she wants to, offends other people and breaks God's laws.

Think about how your actions would affect her parents if they ever found out. Or her future husband. Or what about her future children? Your actions would hurt them deeply. What are you going to tell her dad when he comes banging on your front door? "But, sir, it was the natural thing to do"?

When the Bible talks about love, the first characteristic it mentions is patience. First Corinthians 13:4 says, "Love is patient." Real love can always wait to give. Lust, however, is different—it can never wait to get. If your boyfriend or girlfriend is pressuring you to have sex, he or she might have confused lust for love.

You don't have to put up with the pressure. Your boyfriend or girlfriend may insist that love is his or her motivation. Tell your boyfriend or girlfriend that true love waits. That puts the pressure back on him or her, where it belongs.

You may feel embarrassed or uncomfortable sharing with God your thoughts and feelings about sex. But if you recall, he invented it. Nothing you can think, feel, or do about sex will embarrass him, and he stands ready to help you deal with the pressure you feel in this area.

REFLECT: How would you answer someone who said that sex before marriage is the "natural" thing to do?

PRAY: Tell God your concerns about sex.

8 Under Control or Out of Control?

Bible Reading: Proverbs 23:29-35

Don't be drunk with wine, because that will ruin your life. Instead,
let the Holy Spirit fill and control you. Ephesians 5:18

DO YOU HAVE friends who constantly try to make you a poster child for a "Got Beer?" ad campaign? Do they say things like, "So why don't you go drinking with us?" or "Come on, there's no harm in a little brew. You might like it"?

When people ride you hard because you don't drink, what can you say to make them back off?

Tell them it's not fear that keeps you from drinking. It's brains. Proverbs 22:3 says, "A prudent person foresees the danger ahead and takes precautions; the simpleton goes blindly on and suffers the consequences."

Here are some of the consequences that people who drink stumble into: After heart disease and cancer, alcoholism is America's largest health problem. It affects 10 million people, costs 60 billion dollars, and is implicated in 200,000 deaths annually. Alcohol is involved in 50 percent of deaths by motor vehicle and fire, 67 percent of murders, and 33 percent of suicides. It contributes to death in some cancers and to scores of diseases of the endocrine, cardiovascular, gastrointestinal, and nervous systems. Research says the suicide rate of alcoholics is between six and twenty times higher than that of the general population.

That's some scary evidence—so scary that if alcohol were presented for legalization as a drug today, it wouldn't be approved. And there are more ill effects. Physically, alcohol can damage your liver, put undue stress on your heart, and impair your memory. Emotionally, it can create anxiety, cause you embarrassment from stupid behavior, and cause family hassles, guilt, and poor self-image. Alcohol destroys your freedom by limiting your ability to make right decisions and act on them.

If you want a personality makeover, drinking does a bang-up job. Some shy people become the life of the party once they get drunk. Others try to kill themselves. So if you really want a personality makeover, try Ephesians 5:18 instead. Coming under the influence of either alcohol or the Holy Spirit will cause you to act differently. You might not know what alcohol will make you do, but you can be sure how the Holy Spirit will make you act—just like Jesus.

Don't give in to your friends' pressure. Hold firm. Instead of caving in to their pressure to drink, surrender to the Spirit's promptings in your life. Let him control you, lead you, and empower you. Your friends will be shocked to see the new you.

REFLECT: How are you going to react when people tease you about not drinking?

PRAY: Pray that you and your friends will seek the control of the Holy Spirit in your lives.

9 How to Turn to the Right

Bible Reading: Deuteronomy 6:20-25

The Lord our God commanded us to obey all these laws and to fear him for our own prosperity and well-being. Deuteronomy 6:24

"LADIES AND GENTLEMEN, feast your eyes on this magnificent bottle of pills. Just one capsule a day and you will automatically know the difference between right and wrong. That's right—you'll never make a bad choice again. Who will be the first to pay one hundred dollars and take home this bottle of miracle pills?"

How hard would it be to part with a mere hundred dollars to make sure you made the right choice in every decision of life? Not very. Whenever friends pressure you to do something and you don't know if it's right or wrong, wouldn't it be great to pop a pill and instantly know the answer?

Well, there's no such wonder drug. But asking yourself these questions will help you make the right choice:

1. *The Personal Test:* Will doing what my friends ask make me a better or worse Christian?
2. *The Practical Test:* Will doing it likely bring desirable or undesirable results?
3. *The Social Test:* Will doing it influence others to be better or worse Christians?
4. *The Universal Test:* Suppose everyone did it. Would it be good for everyone?
5. *The Scriptural Test:* Is it expressly forbidden in the Bible?
6. *The Stewardship Test:* Will doing it waste the talents God has invested in me?
7. *The Missionary Test:* Will doing it help or hinder the progress of the kingdom of God on earth?
8. *The Character Test:* Will doing it make me stronger or weaker morally?
9. *The Publicity Test:* Would I want my friends to know about it?
10. *The Common Sense Test:* Does it reflect good, everyday common sense?
11. *The Family Test:* Will doing it bring credit or dishonor to my family?

God has put you here on planet Earth and released you to have a great time. He wants you to experience life to the fullest. But that's why he made certain things off-limits. He knows everything isn't good for you. So let him guide you in your choices by helping you choose what is right.

REFLECT: Do you believe that God is looking out for what's good for you? What evidence do you see?

PRAY: Talk to God about his desire to protect you and provide for you.

10 Trapped in the Middle

Bible Reading: Romans 7:18-25
*Who will free me from this life that is dominated by sin? Thank God!
The answer is in Jesus Christ our Lord. Romans 7:24-25*

WHEN YOU HEAR convicts and drug addicts tell how they came to believe in Jesus, you might figure your testimony is too tame to interest anyone. Actually, *not* having a gory personal story is a good, God-glorifying thing. And you might not know this: *Every Christian has an exciting story to tell.*

First, before you received Christ, you were a slave to sin and Satan. You were blind to the truth about Jesus Christ. The world, the flesh, and the devil jerked you around as surely as if you were chained to them. To see a vivid description of your old self, check out Ephesians 2:1-3.

Second, before you committed your life to Christ, you were the hopeless, helpless victim of what the Bible calls your sinful or fleshly nature. "When we were controlled by our old nature," wrote Paul, "sinful desires were at work within us, and the law aroused these evil desires that produced sinful deeds, resulting in death" (Romans 7:5). Satan and sin engineered the dissatisfaction, pain, guilt, and frustration that characterized your life without Christ.

Third, the moment you trusted Christ and committed your life to him, you were set free from your captivity to Satan and sin (see Romans 8:1-2). Christ broke the power of your old nature to control you. You are free from the control of your former masters—Satan and your sinful nature.

"But," you might be saying, "my life hasn't always run smoothly since I trusted Christ. I don't always live like I know a Christian should. I blow it!"

True. You are free from sin's control, but Satan, the world around you, and the habits of your old nature work together to keep you from enjoying the freedom, peace, and satisfaction of knowing Christ. Even Paul experienced the frustration of struggling with sin. "When I want to do what is right, I inevitably do what is wrong. . . . Oh, what a miserable person I am!" (Romans 7:21, 24).

Maybe you have felt the frustration Paul wrote about—becoming so bogged down by guilt from old habits that you wonder what good it does to be a Christian. Well, God didn't create you to go through life feeling frustrated and guilty. He wants you to feel satisfied. How do you get that way? Paul asked that same question: "Who will free me from this life that is dominated by sin?" (Romans 7:24). He also knew the answer: "Thank God! The answer is in Jesus Christ our Lord" (Romans 7:25). And that's the great part of your story God is still writing.

REFLECT: What would you tell someone who asked you about the pros and cons of being a Christian?

PRAY: Ask God to take you to new depths in knowing him—and new heights in experiencing freedom from sin.

11

Getting Back on Track

Bible Reading: 1 Peter 5:5-7

Humble yourselves under the mighty power of God, and in his good time he will honor you. 1 Peter 5:6

"I BELIEVE in Christ, but he doesn't have a lot to do with my daily life," Trent admits. "It's not like I don't want to read the Bible to figure out what God wants, but I don't have time. God never seems as close as other people say he is. I still know that he cares for me, though, so when I hit a big problem, I pray hard."

Life can be a struggle when you call the shots. You lack joy, at times your anxiety level is high, and peace is in short supply. You don't have much power over temptation, and you probably get discouraged more than you care to admit.

So where are you in your relationship with God? Do you decide each day to give Christ the leadership of your life? Are you letting God's Word break through to grow your faith? Your relationship with God still might not always be all you would like, but that's the path to finding spiritual satisfaction.

If you feel like a half-hearted, bogged-down Christian, here are some practical steps to help you get going:

Remember that God loves you unconditionally. You are his special child. When you disobey God, you grieve him (see Ephesians 4:29-32). You might feel his discipline (see Hebrews 12:5-12), but his love for you never changes.

Confess your sin. Letting your sinful nature dominate your life results in disobedience—and a lot of disappointment. Admit your sin to God and ask him for help to move on. After all, a mature Christian isn't someone who never falls down. A mature Christian is someone who gets back up and keeps going (see Philippians 3:12-14).

Count on God's forgiveness. It's hard for most people—Christians included—to fathom how God could welcome us back like the father in Jesus' story about the prodigal, wandering son (see Luke 15:11-32). But Christ's death on the cross has already purchased your once-for-all forgiveness (see Hebrews 10:12-14; 1 Peter 3:18). Accept God's forgiveness. It's already yours!

Turn to God in trust. Trusting God means changing your attitudes and actions and making a decision to turn to God instead of continuing to think or do things that cause you to drift in your relationship with Christ. On your own, it's impossible to change. But by trusting in God, you depend on his power and strength to live the Christian life (see 2 Timothy 2:22). And as you yield to him each day, you experience the radically remade life he planned for you all along.

REFLECT: How are you doing in your relationship with God? What's the next step you can take to grow closer?

PRAY: Tell God you want to get closer to him—and tell him you want to do your part.

12 Tapping Into Your Power Source

Bible Reading: Ephesians 3:14-19

I pray that from his glorious, unlimited resources he will give you mighty inner strength through his Holy Spirit. Ephesians 3:16

DO YOU THINK of yourself as a disciple? "Not me," you might answer. "It's too cold where I live to wear sandals. And wearing bathrobes all day long is really out of style this year. Besides, I can't drop out of school to follow Christ full-time."

Know it or not, if you have chosen to follow Christ, you *are* a modern-day disciple. And the way God wants to work in and through you is just like how he has worked in and through his disciples for the past two thousand years.

Still, there's a lot to learn about being a disciple. Lesson number one? Discovering exactly how God works in you by his Spirit.

The Bible teaches that the Holy Spirit is God's Spirit. The Holy Spirit isn't a thing or an it or a ghost but a living being and one of the members of the Trinity—God the Father, God the Son (Jesus Christ), and God the Holy Spirit.

When you became a Christian, God's Spirit entered your life (see Romans 8:9; 1 Corinthians 3:16). How? Because the Holy Spirit is God, he is omnipresent. That means he can be everywhere at once. He can live in you and in other Christians around the world at the same time.

And it's through the Holy Spirit living in you that God remakes your life. The Holy Spirit, for example, enables you to understand the Bible (see John 14:26). He gives you courage and the words you need to share Christ with others (see Acts 1:8). And he develops in you the qualities that make you a winner in your relationship with God and others. Those qualities—love, joy, peace, patience, kindness, goodness, faithfulness, gentleness, and self-control—are what the Bible calls "the fruit of the Spirit" (Galatians 5:22-23, NASB).

There's another great thing the Holy Spirit does. When you trusted Christ, the Holy Spirit claimed and sealed you for God (see Ephesians 4:30; 2 Corinthians 1:21-22). You belong to God now, and Satan has lost you forever. But while Satan no longer owns you, he doesn't stop trying to neutralize you as a Christian. He wants to demolish your faith to the point that you are ineffective in serving God (see Ephesians 6:10-12).

How do you deal with Satan's clever tactics to take you out? You can spot the answer in Paul's prayer for young Christians. He asked God to *strengthen each of them with power through his Spirit in their inner being* (see Ephesians 3:16). The point is simple but radically deep: You get the strength to live your Christian faith from God's Spirit.

REFLECT: What does the Holy Spirit have to do with your daily life and faith?

PRAY: Pray today to receive the Spirit's strength.

13 Fill 'Er Up at the Soda Fountain

Bible Reading: Ephesians 5:15-20

The believers were filled with joy and with the Holy Spirit. Acts 13:52

THE BASICS of tapping into the Holy Spirit's power for your daily life aren't all that different from filling a soda at your favorite fast-food place: The cup has to be in the right spot, the lid has to be off, and once the flow starts you can expect some considerable fizz.

God designed you to be filled and led by the Holy Spirit. You need these three simple steps to have that happen.

1. *Confess your sin* (1 John 1:9). The Holy Spirit can't lead you when you live far from God. Whenever you realize that you've been disobedient and seized control of your life, you need to agree that your independence is wrong. Give thanks for the forgiveness you have through Christ.

2. *Trust God to fill you and lead you by his Spirit.* What do you do to be filled with the Holy Spirit? First, present every area of your life to God (see Romans 12:1-2), and tell him you want him to be your boss in each area. Second, ask the Holy Spirit to fill you. God commands you to be filled with the Holy Spirit (see Ephesians 5:18), so *asking* to be filled is something he *wants* you to do. Third, once you have asked, believe that he has filled you. The Holy Spirit is a gift free for the asking. As you tell God you want to be filled, God promises to answer (see 1 John 5:14-15).

   So will you feel different when you're filled with God's Spirit? Not necessarily. Being filled with the Spirit isn't so much about feelings as it is about facts. God fills you because he promised in his Word that he would. That's fact! Feelings come and go. The biggest signs of God's control in your life are the peace, power, and fruit of the Spirit you will experience.

3. *Keep walking in the Spirit.* Just because you trust God to fill you with his Spirit doesn't mean you'll never blow it through disobedience or lack of faith. No one is perfect. When you blow it, confess your sin on the spot and turn back to God. Ask him again to fill you, and trust him to do it. Keep building your faith through prayer and studying God's Word (see Romans 10:17). Yes, you have to be ready for spiritual conflict with the world, the flesh, and Satan. But if you respond to the conflict by relying on God's Spirit working in you and through you, you will conquer.

Get yourself in the right spot to get filled with the Spirit—and get set for God to fill you to overflowing!

REFLECT: What step does God want you to take to let his Spirit fill your life?

PRAY: Tell God today your desire to be a Spirit-filled disciple.

14 Filling Up the Train to Heaven

Bible Reading: 2 Peter 3:9-16
[The Lord] does not want anyone to perish, so he is giving more time for everyone to repent. 2 Peter 3:9

"I'M REALLY not interested in hearing how special God thinks I am," Megan protested. "People who focus on themselves end up totally selfish. I can't see how thinking about me helps me glorify God and show the world how great he is."

God wants you to see yourself like he sees you: lovable, valuable, and useful to him and to others. But why? Is it just to make you feel warm and fuzzy? Could he possibly want to feed your selfish side? No and no. God wants you totally convinced that you are loved and valuable because he has a far deeper purpose for fixing your faulty self-image—but it's because he has work for you to do.

You might not realize this incredible fact about yourself: You are God's gift to the world. If that wasn't true, you'd just be taking up space. God could have zoomed you straight to heaven the moment you trusted Christ. The fact that he chooses to have you hang around on earth even after you belong to him proves that you have a distinct purpose for being here.

So what's your purpose in life? I like how one young guy answered that question. "My purpose in life," he said confidently, "is to go to heaven and take as many people with me as I can." That guy knew that Christ had made *him* alive and set *him* free so he would be equipped set *others* free.

I hope you have the same burning desire to be part of God's plan of redemption. When you get the picture that God created everyone in his image and sent Christ to die for everyone, you want to share his love with them. And when you realize that you too are lovable, valuable, and competent, suddenly you give from a heart jammed with the love of Jesus.

You may say, "If the whole reason I'm here is to lead people to Jesus, then I'm a rotten failure. Hardly anyone—no one—has come to Christ from my telling them about him." That might be true. But it's also likely to be true that a bunch of people are on their way to trusting Christ because of who you are in Christ and how you love them.

If as a Christian you see yourself as God's valued child, you are communicating something of the gospel to others. As you live out your faith—and learn to speak up for Christ when the opportunities arise—you will likely see even more people come to Christ.

 REFLECT: Say it in your own words: How does knowing you are lovable, capable, and competent *not* make you a selfish person?

PRAY: *Lord, I want my purpose in life to reflect your purpose of reaching out and telling the world of your love.*

15 Excuses, Excuses, Excuses!

Bible Reading: Matthew 5:13-16

Let your good deeds shine out for all to see, so that everyone will praise your heavenly Father. Matthew 5:16

"WHOA—telling people about Jesus?" you might think. "I have to get my act together first before I can talk about Christ."

You might be one of a huge number of Christians convinced that their lives aren't good enough for them to say anything about Christ. That's a huge problem. How come? You will never completely get your act together. You will always fall short—and always feel guilty, frustrated, and hopeless.

"I'm not good enough" isn't the only misguided attitude that keeps people from speaking up about Jesus. Some people fear ugly reactions if they tell others about Christ. They don't want to anger or offend people, so they clam up. Others fear their tongues will knot up if they try to share the gospel. They don't want to confuse people with anything less than a perfect, complete, persuasive answer.

Each of those attitudes will keep you from being part of God's massive, exciting work in your world. Here are some ways to rethink those attitudes and see yourself as useful to God—which is exactly how he sees you:

If you think you aren't "good enough" to witness for Christ, you have a limited sense of God's love for you. The more you see yourself like God sees you—unconditionally accepted, forgiven, created in his image—the less you will let your imperfections be a barrier to sharing. God wants to use you even while you are "in process," growing as a Christian.

If you fear the negative reactions you might face as you witness, you have a limited sense of your worth to God. Depending too much on others for approval suggests you have a low view of your worth to God. God thinks so highly of you that he allowed his Son to die for you. You are valued by the King of the universe. Even if everyone refuses to listen to you, you are still of high value to God.

If you are reluctant to witness because you fear you will say the wrong thing, you have a limited sense of your competence in Christ. If you fear stumbling over your words, you're saying to God, "I know you want me to witness, but you'll need to use somebody more skilled and confident, because I'm not any good at this."

Witnessing doesn't start with what you say or how well you say it. Your starting point is knowing who you are in Christ. You are God's beloved child—unique and useful to him just the way you are.

REFLECT: What keeps you from speaking up about Christ? Is there anything about how you see yourself that God wants to fix?

PRAY: *God, I just want to be who you created me to be. Help me to share my faith the best I know how and leave the results to you.*

16 For Goodness' Sake

Bible Reading: Galatians 6:7-10
Don't get tired of doing what is good. Galatians 6:9

SEVENTEEN-YEAR-OLD Antonio and his family live next door to a disabled elderly man. When Antonio mows the lawn at his house, he also mows the neighbor's yard and keeps it looking nice. He does this to be kind, not because the neighbor pays him—because he can't afford to. The elderly man has been more responsive to Antonio's invitations to church since he began his good deeds.

Mindy volunteered during her junior year to tutor freshmen struggling in math. She spends four to six hours a week helping Jordan get up to speed in algebra. Jordan and his parents can't believe the progress he is making, and they are enormously grateful to Mindy for her sacrifice of time. Mindy keeps praying for the right opportunity to share her faith in Christ with Jordan and his family.

A major part of sharing Christ with the world is simply doing good to others. All through the Bible you can read instructions to do for others what is right and good. "If we do what helps [others]," Paul wrote, "we will build them up in the Lord" (Romans 15:2). Elsewhere he wrote, "Whenever we have the opportunity, we should do good to everyone, especially to our Christian brothers and sisters" (Galatians 6:10). He encouraged us, saying, "Don't get tired of doing what is good" (Galatians 6:9). When you do good things for other people, they get the chance to see the Savior in you.

Besides revealing himself through your doing good things for others, God can also show himself to other people when you jump on every situation as an opportunity to do your best. Paul challenged the Galatian Christians, for example, with these words: "Be sure to do what you should, for then you will enjoy the personal satisfaction of having done your work well, and you won't need to compare yourself to anyone else" (Galatians 6:4).

Wanting to do *your best* isn't the same as wanting to be *the best* at something. Trying to be the best means you are comparing yourself to others—something the Bible discourages. Doing your best for others peels people's eyes off of you and lets people see God in your actions.

And here's a truth to rely on: When you use your gifts, talents, and abilities in the power of the Holy Spirit, it doesn't matter how people respond in the short run. God will make the most of your efforts to draw people to himself.

 REFLECT: Are you committed not only to sharing your faith but also to living it through your good deeds toward others?

PRAY: Tell God about your commitment right now.

17 What's Love Got to Do with It?

Bible Reading: 1 Corinthians 13:1-13
Love is patient and kind. 1 Corinthians 13:4

"HERE SHE IS, ready to answer all your questions about love—Dr. Leva Salone." The audience erupts in applause as the counselor enters the studio.

"Let's get right to your questions," Dr. Salone says, pointing to a young man.

"Dr. Salone, is there such a thing as love at first sight?"

"Good question. Love as it is described in the Bible is not based on looks or even romance. Real love is based on commitment and deep understanding of the other person. There is such a thing as *attraction* at first sight, which can grow into real love. But true love cannot be determined at first glance."

Dr. Salone nods to a high-school junior in the front row. "Dr. Salone, I have such strong feelings for my boyfriend. Does that mean I'm in love?"

"Real biblical love produces strong feelings," Dr. Salone begins, "but strong feelings don't necessarily mean you are in love. Feelings come and go quickly, depending on the mood you're in. To know if your love is real, avoid focusing on your feelings. Look instead at the depth of commitment you have for each other."

Another guy stands. "Isn't sex the ultimate expression of love, Dr. Salone?"

"There are few things more beautiful than sex in the context of a loving marriage relationship," Dr. Salone says. "But sex as an expression of love is more the result of a committed marriage relationship than the cause of it. Sex was made for two people to enjoy and deepen their love within marriage. That's why the Bible instructs us to save sex for marriage."

"Dr. Salone," calls out a girl in the back, "how can I know if my love is mature enough to make a relationship last?"

The doctor steps closer to the audience. "Let me share with you seven characteristics of mature love to help you measure your own love. One, mature love is spelled G-I-V-E. It is always giving. Two, mature love shows respect for one another. Three, mature love has no conditions for acceptance. Four, mature love is realistic. It doesn't live in a dream world. Five, mature love takes responsibility for its loved one. Six, mature love is demonstrated in a sustained commitment. And seven, mature love never stops growing."

How would your love life stack up against the fictional Dr. Leva Salone's list? If your love needs a reality check, spend some time meditating on 1 Corinthians 13. God invented love. The more you understand what his Word has to say about it, the more loving you will be in your relationships.

REFLECT: How do your attitudes and expectations of love measure up to this biblical definition of love?

PRAY: *God, teach me to love—to really love as you defined it.*

18 Don't Settle for Anything Less

Bible Reading: 1 John 4:7-12
Anyone who does not love does not know God—for God is love.
1 John 4:8

EVER HEARD that old song about infatuation and marriage? The words go something like, "Infatuation and marriage, infatuation and marriage—go together like a horse and carriage."

If you're hip to the sounds of golden oldies, right now you're saying, "It's not *infatuation* and marriage, it's *love* and marriage." And you're correct. But in everyday life, loads of people get the two words mixed up. What's the difference?

Infatuation has been defined as the emotional impulse of love, untested by time or circumstance. Since infatuation can lead to real love, sometimes it's tough to tell the difference. The characteristics below, though, highlight the huge difference between infatuation and true love. How does your love measure up?

Infatuation	True Love
Develops suddenly	Grows with time
Up and down emotionally	Consistent
Fickle	Faithful
Breaks up when irritated	Does not panic when problems arise
Emphasizes looks	Emphasizes character
Gets	Gives
Based on my feelings	Based on the other's needs
Self-centered	Self-controlled
Physical first	Spiritual first
Expects to find happiness	Expects to work at happiness
Asks, "How am I doing?"	Asks, "How are you doing?"
Focuses on the other's performance	Unconditionally accepts the other
Possessive	Allows the other to relate to others
Idealizes the other person	Realistic about strengths and weaknesses
Avoids problems	Works through problems

Do those characteristics of true love remind you of someone? They should, because they reflect the characteristics of God's love for you. You are the object of that selfless, unconditional love every day. And when you start to live out those traits in your relationships, you mirror God's love.

REFLECT: Are your attitudes toward the opposite sex more like infatuation—or like real love?

PRAY: Ask God to help you express his love to others every day.

19 The Temple of Love

Bible Reading: 1 Corinthians 6:18-20
You must honor God with your body. 1 Corinthians 6:20

YOU BE the judge: Are the people who make these statements massively confused about the meaning of love? "I love to eat." "I love my new outfit." "I love that new band, Braindead Tse-tse Flies." "I love doing homework."

Looking at that list, you might get the impression that love could mean any sort of affection for just about anything. So what in the world do people mean when they say they *love* something or someone? What is true love anyway?

Trying to define true love can get pretty confusing. The first step is to understand what true love *isn't*.

First, *true love isn't the same as lust.* Our culture often mixes up love and lust. How can you tell the difference? Love gives—lust takes. Love values—lust uses. Love endures—lust flames out. If your interaction with someone of the opposite sex is based on intense sexual feelings and physical gratification, lust might be masquerading as love in the relationship.

Second, *true love isn't the same as romance.* Romantic feelings are amazing in close guy-girl relationships. God wired you to experience those feelings in special relationships with the opposite sex. But you can't equate the excitement and warmth of romance to love. Romance is a feeling. True love is far more.

Third, *true love is not the same as sex.* Many students—many adults, too—confuse intense sexual desire with true love. Sex as God intended it isn't wrong. It was designed by God for procreation and fulfillment within the bounds of marriage. But sex and love are distinct:

- You can have sex without love and love without sex.
- Love requires constant attention. Sex takes no effort.
- Love takes time to develop and mature. Sex needs no time to develop.
- Love requires emotional and spiritual interaction. Sex requires only physical interaction.
- Love deepens a relationship. Sex without love dulls a relationship.

God wants you to enjoy sex in its proper time and context for your life—*marriage.* You might be in love long before then, but even if that is the case, you should welcome the opportunity to honor God with your body by waiting.

REFLECT: Have you ever told God your feelings and struggles over lust, romance, sex, and love? Why or why not?

PRAY: Start on that talk right now.

20 No Strings Attached

Bible Reading: John 3:16-21

God so loved the world that he gave his only Son, so that everyone who believes in him will not perish but have eternal life. John 3:16

IF LOVE is more than lust, romance, or sex, you might be thinking, *how do I know if I'm in love?*

Big question—especially when you find yourself magnetized by a member of the opposite sex. There are three relationship behaviors people often label as love:

"I love you if . . ." If love is *conditional* love. It is given or received only when certain conditions are met. The only way to get this kind of love is to earn it by performing the right way. People who are dating or married might withhold love *if* their partner fails to do or be what they want. *If* love is basically selfish. It's a bargaining chip offered in exchange for something desired.

If love isn't true love. If you sense pressure to perform a certain way to gain the love you desire, the relationship isn't based on true love.

"I love you because . . ." The second kind of love—*because* love—is a close cousin to *if* love. One person loves another because of something he or she is, has, or does. Someone might say, "I love you because you are so beautiful" or "I love you because you make me laugh." *Because* love sounds pretty good. Almost everyone likes to be loved for who they are or what they do. It's certainly preferable to *if* love, which you constantly have to work hard to earn.

Because love still isn't true love. You might find yourself attracted to someone because of his or her personality, position, intelligence, skill, or ability. But sooner or later those things change—or your tastes change. If your love isn't founded on more than what that person has or does, it won't last.

"I love you, period." The third kind of love is love without conditions. This kind of love says, "I love you no matter what you might be like deep inside. I love you no matter what might change about you. You can't do anything to turn off my love. I love you, period!" That's the kind of love God has for you—the kind that prompted him to give his Son, Jesus, to die for your sins.

Love, period isn't blind. It can—and should—know all it can about the other person. God knows all about your sin, but he loves you anyway. *Love, period* might spot someone's failures, shortcomings, and faults. Yet it totally accepts him or her without demanding anything in return. There's no way you can earn this type of love, nor can you lose it. It arrives with no strings attached.

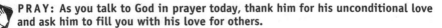

REFLECT: Do you love the people around you with "love, period" kind of love? What would it take to base your guy-girl relationships on that love without strings?

PRAY: As you talk to God in prayer today, thank him for his unconditional love and ask him to fill you with his love for others.

21 The Right Stuff

Bible Reading: Hebrews 13:1-4
> *Give honor to marriage, and remain faithful to one another in marriage.*
> *Hebrews 13:4*

JEREMY CRIED as he watched Julie's dad steer the heavy rental truck down the street. The one perfect woman for Jeremy had just moved out of his life. Life as he knew it was over. He would never love again.

Tough break for a second-grader.

Does God have just one person picked out for you to marry—or does he have a gallery of possibilities for you to choose from?

You don't have to be a rocket scientist to figure out what general type of person you would like to spend the rest of your life with. So go ahead and eliminate from your list of possibilities everyone who doesn't fit in that group. Then ask yourself, "Does God want me to marry *the* right person or *a* right person?" Some folks say God wants you to marry *the* right person, meaning he has one—and only one—person picked out for you to marry. Others think the world contains many people God would consider a suitable mate for you. God, they say, wants you to marry *a* right person.

Let's cut through the controversy and confusion with a practical solution: Of all the possible people to marry, pick the best one for you! Then you have the best of both options. If God only has one picked out, you can be sure you have landed with him or her. On the other hand, if there are several right ones out there, then you just got the best one possible. And as you wonder if you have found the right person for you, keep these vital pointers in mind:

Evaluate how well and for how long you've known each other. Real love is based on a thorough knowledge and understanding of the other person.

Determine if that person loves you with "love, period" love. Read 1 Corinthians 13:4-8 and see if it describes how your prospective marriage partner loves you. Stay objective by asking a friend if he or she agrees.

Take the steps to discern God's will you would take for any other big decision, making the most of the guidance God gives through Scripture, prayer, wise advice—including advice from your parents, who want the best for you—and the open and closed doors of circumstances.

One final thought: Be more concerned with *being* the right person than *finding* the right person. Becoming the kind of person someone else will consider the best possible choice is the only way to be prepared for finding *your* best choice.

REFLECT: How are you getting ready to find the right mate?

PRAY: Even if you don't want to think about marriage yet, it's not too early to pray about it. Talk to God today about being and finding the right person.

22 Wise Investing

Bible Reading: Matthew 6:19-21
Don't store up treasures here on earth. . . . Store your treasures in heaven. Matthew 6:19-20

AS HIGH SCHOOL juniors, Steve and Nolan took jobs bagging groceries in the same store. Steve wanted to make wads of money so he could buy a car and enjoy a great social life. Nolan's goal was to have enough money for school expenses and a few social activities, but staying faithful at church and getting ready for college were more important to him than his job.

By the end of his senior year, Steve drove one of the nicest cars at school, and he could afford to go out with friends two or three nights a week. But in the process of grabbing hold of his goal, Steve's church life and school life slid to the bottom of his priorities. By fall, Steve lacked both the grades and the savings to start college, and his busy social schedule had pushed all church activities out of his life.

Nolan also reached his goal by graduation. He hadn't earned nearly as much money as Steve, but he finished high school with a 3.5 GPA and won a scholarship for college. He had been a leader in his youth group and seen several of his friends trust Christ through the group. Because of his staunch dedication to the youth group, his church awarded him with an oldish but dependable used car. They also promised prayer and financial support for college.

Jesus' warning about storing up wealth on this earth hits Steve's and Nolan's situations—and yours—head on. It's simple economics. Where can you get the best return on your investment of time and energy? You can sell out for a job that fills your pockets with the bucks to buy all the things you want—CDs, clothes, cars, video games, computer equipment, and more.

But ponder this: Where will all that stuff be a mere year from now? The clothes will be out of style, the electronics obsolete, and the car needing a fix. And in just a few more years, it will all be dust. If stuff is all you can show for your efforts, you won't have much to show.

You have the chance to make a wiser choice—to invest your time and effort in things that will last beyond the next couple of years. And *people* are the things that ensure the highest return. The treasures Jesus said you could store up in heaven have a vital connection with loving people in a way that results in them trusting Christ and growing as his disciples. Those are treasures that will never lose their value or become obsolete. And that's an investment opportunity too good to pass up.

REFLECT: Where are you investing your life right now? What are you doing that will last forever?

PRAY: *Lord, help me to invest my life wisely in things that matter.*

23 What's So Funny about Money?

Bible Reading: Matthew 6:22-24
You cannot serve both God and money. Matthew 6:24

DID YOU HEAR about Fred and Frank, the two bungling counterfeiters? These dim-wits printed a pile of money, but this phony currency was *really* phony. Instead of printing $20, $50, or $100 bills, they printed thousands of $18 bills.

"How are we going to spend our money?" Fred said to Frank. "Everybody around here knows that our $18 bills are fakes."

"I have an idea," said Frank. "Let's haul the money way out in the backwoods. Maybe they'll change some of our bills for real money."

So Fred and Frank took a sack of phony money and started driving into the hills. Eventually they drove up to an old, broken-down general store. "These people won't think twice about changing an $18 bill," Fred and Frank agreed.

They walked into the store and approached the old clerk behind the counter. "Would you be able to make change for us?" said Fred.

"I reckon I will," said the store clerk. "What do you need?"

Frank answered, "Well, can you change this $18 bill?"

"Sure enough," the store clerk said, reaching for the till.

Fred turned to Frank and winked. Their plan seemed to be working.

"By the way," said the store clerk, "which kind of bills would you like in return—two nines or three sixes?"

If money is always at the center of your life, you will have more problems than Fred and Frank.

Money can be a demanding master. The more you accumulate, the more you want. The more stuff you acquire with money, the more stuff you itch to have. And the more you stockpile money and stuff, the less you want to share with others.

Jesus put it all on the line: You can't serve God and money. When money is your master, you want to grab and hoard and spend on yourself. When God is your master, you learn to share with people in need and to give to others. For Christians, money is simply a tool to serve others. That doesn't mean you have to give away all your money and possessions. It just means you don't let money or your desire to stuff yourself with stuff tell you what to do with your life.

If the only things dancing in your head right now are all the things you want to *get* this Christmas, you might be serving the wrong master. Let God change your heart as you contemplate all you can *give* to others at this giving time of the year.

REFLECT: What is dominating your thoughts right now—giving or getting?

PRAY: *Father, build in me the kind of giving heart that you have—the one that was so selfless that you sent your Son to earth.*

24 Nativity Trivia

Bible Reading: Luke 2:1-7
She gave birth to her first child, a son. Luke 2:7

DO YOU REALLY know the Christmas story? Test your knowledge by circling the correct response to each of the following items of Nativity trivia. Check your answers at the bottom of the page.

1. Joseph was from . . .
   a. Bethlehem   c. New Jersey
   b. Nazareth   d. None of the above

2. A manger is a . . .
   a. stable for domestic animals   c. feeding trough
   b. wooden hay storage bin   d. barn

3. Who told Mary and Joseph to go to Bethlehem in the first place?
   a. Caesar Augustus   c. An angel
   b. An angel in a dream   d. A travel agent

4. The wise men found Jesus in a . . .
   a. stable   c. Holiday Inn
   b. manger   d. house

The most important thing about the Christmas story isn't your mastery of those facts. At the center of Christmas is the birth of your Master. Think about it: The God who created heaven and earth—the God who created you—came to earth in the form of a human baby born to a peasant couple and named Jesus. God, who is Spirit, took on flesh just like yours. God, who isn't confined to time and space, slipped into human history and forever changed our relationship with himself and our relationships with one another.

And God did all of that because he loves you and wants a relationship with you. The greatest gift God ever gave you was himself—in the form of his Son. The greatest gift you can ever give him is yourself—so you can enjoy the relationship God created you for.

REFLECT: How are you going to give yourself to God in thanks for all that he has given you?

PRAY: Talk to him today about your desire to be a gift to him.

ANSWERS:
1. a (Luke 2:3-4); 2. c; 3. a (Luke 2:1); 4. d (Matthew 2:11)

25 Peace on Earth!

Bible Reading: Luke 2:8-14

Glory to God in the highest heaven, and peace on earth to all whom God favors. Luke 2:14

EVER SINCE the angels appeared on the hillside with their great news of joy and peace, Christmas has been a time for singing. You've probably sung each of the following Christmas songs below—except that the titles have been changed just to mess with your mind. See if you can figure out the real titles—the first one, for example, is "Deck the Halls."

1. Embellish the interior passageways.
2. Listen, the celestial messengers produce harmonious sounds.
3. The Christmas preceding all others.
4. Move this way, entire assembly of those who are loyal in their belief.
5. Expectation of arrival by mythical, masculine perennial gift giver.
6. The first person nominative plural of a trio of far eastern heads of state.
7. Small masculine master of percussionistic cylinders.
8. Natal celebration devoid of color, rather albino.
9. Jovial yuletide desired for the second person singular or plural by us.
10. Nocturnal time span of unbroken quietness.

The angels sang, "Peace on earth," and Jesus Christ is the Prince of Peace (see Isaiah 9:6). He came to bring peace to a world in turmoil. He came to bring peace into your life when things seem to be falling apart. God's brand of peace starts with trusting Christ personally and allowing his peace to rule your life. It spreads to others as his peace transforms your life.

Jesus came to be the great peacemaker, and as you grow in his peace you become a peacemaker too. The peace that Jesus provided—the peace that you can experience today—is the peace of forgiveness and reconciliation. That's what Christmas is all about: God reconciling with his human creation so that you can be friends again with him and others.

Spread God's peace. That's a birthday present Jesus will really appreciate.

REFLECT: How will you share the peace of Jesus today?

PRAY: *Jesus, you brought real peace to my world. Make me a peacemaker too.*

ANSWERS:
1. Deck the Halls; 2. Hark, the Herald Angels Sing; 3. The First Noel; 4. O Come, All Ye Faithful; 5. Santa Claus Is Coming to Town; 6. We Three Kings; 7. Little Drummer Boy; 8. White Christmas; 9. We Wish You a Merry Christmas; 10. Silent Night

26 The Gifts That Really Count

Bible Reading: Matthew 6:25-33

Your heavenly Father . . . will give you all you need from day to day if you live for him and make the Kingdom of God your primary concern. Matthew 6:32-33

THIS YEAR you played it smart. You wanted to make sure everything you received was the right size and color, so your Christmas list was short and sweet. It looked something like this:

- a gift certificate to my favorite clothing store
- a gift certificate to my favorite music store
- a gift certificate to my favorite computer and software store
- a gift certificate to my favorite video store
- a five-pound box of money

But as you sit surveying your opened gifts, you are seriously depressed. All your hopes and dreams for Christmas have turned into a nightmare.

- Your dad gave you a complete bowling outfit—ball, bag, shoes, and two brightly colored bowling shirts. You don't even bowl.
- Mom bought you a cello and a series of instructional videos. But you're tone-deaf.
- Your grandmother gave you another pair of polka-dotted flannel pajamas—your sixth pair in six years—which are two sizes too small.
- Dear Uncle Smedley gave you a year's subscription to *Exceptional Student* magazine and promised you fifty cents for every A you get this year.

Okay, maybe it wasn't that bad. But you probably didn't get everything you wanted for Christmas, did you? Unrealized expectations are something all of us have to deal with.

But God has a gift for you that you won't want to return. In Matthew 6:25-33, God promised to provide everything you *need* for the coming year. It might be difficult to admit you can survive without that five-pound box of money, but somehow you'll make it. In the meantime, God knows your real needs—spiritual, relational, emotional, and material—even those you aren't aware of. And he loves you so much that he will make sure you never lack those things. Your task is to continue living for him and watching him fill your life with his absolute best.

REFLECT: What kind of gifts are you looking for God to give you? Are you looking for his best?

PRAY: Talk to God about your disappointments about stuff—and set your heart on things that count.

27 Why Pray When You Can Worry?

Bible Reading: Matthew 6:34

Don't worry about tomorrow, for tomorrow will bring its own worries.
Matthew 6:34

AS YOU THINK about the upcoming new year, are you worried about what might happen? Are you afraid of a worldwide economic collapse, sending humankind back to bartering chickens? Are you tense that you might be asphyxiated by pollution or vaporized by another terrorist attack?

You can worry all you want about those things, but it won't do you any good. Just look at what a few wise people say about the futility of worry:

- Worry never robs tomorrow of its sorrow, it only saps today of its joy. *Leo Buscaglia*
- Worrying is wasting today's time cluttering up tomorrow's opportunities with yesterday's troubles. *Anonymous*
- Don't worry about the world coming to an end today. It's already tomorrow in Australia. *Charles Schultz*

The most significant word about worry, of course, comes from Jesus. His instruction? Don't. Paul echoed that thought in Philippians 4:6: "Don't worry about anything; instead, pray about everything. Tell God what you need, and thank him for all he has done." The apostle Peter adds, "Give all your worries and cares to God, for he cares about what happens to you" (1 Peter 5:7).

Sure, there will be plenty of things about next year you won't like—natural disasters, world tension, community strife, and conflicts with parents or friends. God never promised you a life without problems. And when scary things loom, you feel a sudden knot of worry in the pit of your stomach that paralyzes you.

That knot is your internal reminder that it's time to pray. When you feel yourself wound tight with anxiety, don't let it paralyze you. Instead, let it *prayer*-alyze you. Tell God straight up how you feel. Fill him in on all the issues or people or circumstances that worry you. Invite him to take control of them and you. Keep praying until the anxiety settles down. And when your nervousness comes back, pray again . . . and again . . . and again.

When you interpret worry as a natural nudge to pray instead of an impossible burden to carry, troubling circumstances won't be so scary. You won't see them as incidents that terrify. You will take them as opportunities for God to work as you hand them over to him in prayer.

REFLECT: What worries you most about the next few days? The next month? The next year?

PRAY: Cast all your concerns on God, because he cares for you.

28 Time to Settle In

Bible Reading: John 15:1-4
Remain in me, and I will remain in you. John 15:4

HERE WE GO again, Jared thought with disgust. He had become way too skilled at packing up his room for a move. His family had never stayed in one place for more than three years, and this time they hadn't even come close to that record. Jared had hoped this time they would stay put. But then he heard the words he dreaded: "I've been transferred again."

"You'll love Madera!" his mom had said. *Madera!* This suburb of Fresno in the steamy central valley of California didn't sound exciting in the least. Jared had heard summers were so hot you could actually fry an egg on the sidewalk! But realizing he had no choice, he continued to pack his room.

Moving once or twice in a lifetime is hard enough. It's even harder when your moves uproot you every two or three years. Even though Jared struggled year after year with painful relocations, he learned a crucial lesson. Here's an excerpt from his journal, written shortly after arriving in Madera.

Here I am again, Lord—a new place, surrounded by strange things and unknown people. I miss my friends and my life back home. I wonder if this new place will ever be my home. I wonder if I will ever be able to really settle in here.

At least I have you, Lord. At least I know that wherever I go, you are still with me. You have made your home in me. You have settled in, and you're not going to be transferred and leave me alone. And I have made my home in you. Wherever I go, we will be together. Thank you, Jesus, for that promise.

Jared had discovered an amazing truth you need to know too. When Christ was raised from the dead, he returned to his home in heaven to be with his Father. But the Spirit of the living Christ now makes his home in you, and he wants you to make your home in him. In Revelation 3:20, Jesus invites us: "Look! Here I stand at the door and knock. If you hear me calling and open the door, I will come in, and we will share a meal as friends."

You might move from place to place. Your friendships might change from year to year. All sorts of upheavals might make your life tomorrow look radically different from your life today. But one fact is sure: Jesus will never leave you. He is totally at home in you, and he invites you to be at home in him.

 REFLECT: What difference does it make to you that Jesus will never leave you, no matter what changes today brings?

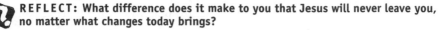 **PRAY:** Take some time today to thank the living Christ for being your dearest and most abiding friend.

29 "I Want to Be like Mike"

Bible Reading: John 15:5-8

Those who remain in me, and I in them, will produce much fruit.
For apart from me you can do nothing. John 15:5

A MAJOR SPORTS-drink company once ran an ad campaign encouraging people to "be like Mike," as in NBA basketball legend Michael Jordan. The phrase, "I want to be like Mike" was everywhere. Kids said it. Adults sang it.

Why do ad campaigns work? Every button-push of the TV remote or flip of a magazine page bombards you with pressure to be like Mike or Garth or Cindy or Gwyneth or another big star. Splash on this cologne, dial that long-distance number, slip into these boxers, and—*shazzam!*—you will be a celebrity. And since everybody dreams of being gorgeous or rich or famous or talented, you might take the bait and buy the product. And if you do, you probably don't stop to wonder if the celebrity actually uses the product he or she endorses.

Unless you know someone personally, you will never know what he or she is really like—and, as a result, you will never really be like that person. If you want to be like Mike, you have to get to know the real Mike, not the Mike you spy in TV ads. You have to spend time with him and get thrashed in a game of one-on-one against him. You have to know Mike to be like Mike.

Just like that, you have to know Jesus Christ personally to have any hope of becoming like him. If you want to be like Christ in character, you have to get to know the real Jesus Christ to the point that his character impacts your life. He said it best: "Apart from me you can do nothing" (John 15:5). Philippians 2:5 tells us, "Your attitude should be the same that Christ Jesus had." Unless you are growing in an intimate relationship with the living Christ, you can't identify his attitude. You can't adopt his attitude. And you can't bear the fruit of Christlike character.

So how can you get to know Jesus Christ up close and personal? You can always listen to what other people say about him, but is that enough? Not really, because you are only hearing about how *they* know him. Just listening to your pastor or youth leaders tell you about Christ is not enough. You have to go farther. You have to go one-on-one with Jesus.

Other people can't get close to God for you. They can't read, study, memorize, and meditate on the Word of God for you. They can't invest time for you in daily, personal, private interaction with Christ. They can't pray and pour out your heart for you or listen as Jesus pours out his heart to you.

It's your choice—and challenge—to get to know him. And when you do, you will become like him.

REFLECT: What are you going to do in the upcoming year to keep getting to know God personally?

PRAY: Thank Jesus for his invitation to know him and bear fruit.

30 "If It Weren't for Emily . . ."

Bible Reading: John 15:9-13

I command you to love each other in the same way that I love you.
John 15:12

"NICE OUTFIT, Karen. What did your mother do with the other half of your grand-mother's old curtains? Did your brother get an outfit too?"

That verbal slam echoed so loudly through the hallway that Emily couldn't help but overhear. Emily knew it was hard for people to be friendly to Karen, who was quiet, reserved—and brilliant. She lived in the library and wouldn't know a gym if she wandered into one and fell on the floor. And her style of dress was, well, slightly behind the times. Guys wouldn't be caught dead with Karen. Girls who talked to her risked becoming a social outcast like her, so no one did. Karen even sat alone when she attended her church youth group.

But Karen's situation was getting to Emily. Just last Sunday her youth pastor had taught on 1 John 4:20: "If someone says, 'I love God,' but hates a Christian brother or sister, that person is a liar; for if we don't love people we can see, how can we love God, whom we have not seen?" Emily couldn't ask for a more obvious op-portunity to do what Jesus wanted her to do. And so—as her fellow students watched and snickered—Emily approached Karen in the cafeteria and asked her to join her for lunch. For the first time since fifth grade, Karen had a friend.

Emily remained Karen's friend through high school, even though it cost her many other friends. When they graduated, Karen was named valedictorian of their senior class. As she began her speech, she did her best to thank her parents and her teachers for their support. Then she choked and began to cry. Recognizing that her friend was losing it, Emily stepped onto the stage to stand by her side.

Holding her friend's hand, Karen continued through her tears. "Most of all, I want to thank Emily. When I was at my lowest point—alone, rejected, and ready to give up on life—she showed me what it means to be a friend and what it means to love unconditionally. If it weren't for Emily, I wouldn't be alive today."

Loving others as Christ loves you is costly. Think about the price Jesus paid to love us. He left the glory and splendor of heaven. He came to earth and was ridiculed, rejected, beaten, spit upon, and crucified. Loving us wasn't comfortable or conve-nient for him. It cost him everything.

Jesus calls us to love others in the same way. So what are you willing to "spend" to love others? Will you give up your convenience, popularity, time, energy, or money? Will you step outside your comfortable world to get into the lives of people like Karen?

 REFLECT: Will you love the people that the world doesn't love? What will it cost you? Are you willing to pay that price?

PRAY: Ask God today whom he would like to begin loving through you.

31 What Do You Want to Be When You Grow Up?

Bible Reading: John 15:14-16

I appointed you to go and produce fruit that will last. John 15:16

MEET DREW, the swimmer. Drew joined her first swim team in third grade and never looked back. She won nearly every event she entered—freestyle, butterfly, breast-stroke, and relays. In high school she won titles at state and junior national competitions. Two years into a brilliant college career, she qualified for the Olympic team. Next summer Drew will compete in her first Olympics.

Meet Pete, the Christian. Pete is a talented individual, especially in theater. He loves to sing, act, and perform. In high school he won the lead in several plays and musicals. He was also a featured performer in his church's drama ministry. Everyone who knows Pete expects to see him on Broadway or in the movies some day. He was offered a full scholarship to a prestigious acting school in New York, but he turned it down to attend missionary training school. In six months he will be traveling to the Philippines on an evangelistic drama team.

Two students, two totally different goals. For Drew, personal achievement is the focus of life. Everything centers on excelling and winning. Pete is different. He also has special skills, high goals, and notable achievements. But unlike Drew, Pete's accomplishments don't define Pete. He isn't Pete the actor or Pete the musician; he is Pete the Christian who acts and sings. To Pete, serving Christ is more important than his personal goals. He sees his gifts and talents as instruments for serving Christ, and his choices confirm his beliefs.

No matter what skills and talents you possess, God's first call on your life is to use those skills and talents to "produce fruit that will last." In the Bible, fruit refers both to your inner character qualities and to the impact of those qualities on the watching world. Pete's first goal is to be the person Christ wants him to be so his life will bring others to Christ. He knows that fame and fortune won't last forever, but people who trust Christ through the witness of his character and message will.

So does that mean that a Christian can't be an Olympic athlete or a Broadway actor? Absolutely not. Just don't let your identity be defined by these pursuits. If you have trusted Christ, you are a Christian first, last, and always. Anything else you do and anything else you achieve is temporary at best. Be filled with the living Christ. Be focused on his purposes for your life. Then go do your best at anything and everything he has gifted you to be.

REFLECT: Have you let your talents—rather than your faith in Christ—define your life? How might God want to reshape your priorities and goals?

 PRAY: *God, I put you first. Help me focus first on your purposes for my life.*

Journal Notes

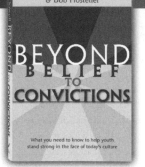

BE CONVINCED OF WHY YOU BELIEVE

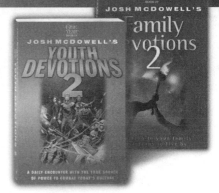

Josh McDowell's Youth Devotions 2
Josh McDowell's Family Devotions 2
to Youth/Families

"We are not fighting against people made of flesh and blood, but against the evil rulers and authorities of the unseen world . . ." (Ephesians 6:12, NLT). More than ever our young people need a spiritual defense. This second installment of Josh's best-selling youth and family devotions offer 365 daily devotional encounters with the true Power Source to strengthen your family spiritually and provide your young people with a resource that will help them combat today's culture. ***Josh McDowell's Youth Devotions 2*** 0-8423-4096-3
Josh McDowell's Family Devotions 2 0-8423-5625-8

The Deceivers **Book to Youth**

Written in the popular NovelPlus format, this book combines the adventures of Sarah Milford and Ryan Ortiz and their search for meaning, along with Josh's insights found in sections called "The Inside Story."

In dramatic fashion *The Deceivers* explains that unless Christ is who he claims to be—the true Son of God—then his offer to redeem us and provide meaning to life can't be real. This book presents not only the compelling evidence for the deity of Christ but also how God's plan is to transform us into a new creature with an intimate relationship with him. ***The Deceivers*** 0-8423-7969-X

Children Demand a Verdict **Book to Children**

Children need clear and direct answers to their questions about God, the Bible, sin, death, etc. Directed to children ages 7–11, this question-and-answer book tackles 77 tough issues with clarity and relevance, questions such as: Why did God make people? How do we know Jesus was God? How could God write a book? Is the Bible always right? Are parts of the Bible make-believe? Why did Jesus die? Did Jesus really come back to life? Does God always forgive me? Why do people die? Will I come back to life like Jesus? ***Children Demand a Verdict*** 0-8423-7971-1

BE COMMITTED TO WHAT YOU BELIEVE

Video Series for Adult Groups

This 5-part interactive video series features Josh McDowell sharing how your young people have adopted distorted beliefs about God, truth, and reality and what you as adults can do about it. Step by step he explains how to lead your kids to know "why we believe what we believe" and how that is truly relevant to their everyday lives. This series provides the perfect launch for your group to build the true foundation of Christianity in the lives of the family, beginning with adults.

The series includes 5 video sessions of approximately 25 minutes each, a comprehensive Leader's Guide with reproducible handouts, the *Beyond Belief to Convictions* book, and a complimentary copy of *The Deceivers* NovelPlus book. (Also available on DVD.)
Belief Matters Video Series 0-8423-8018-3

Video Series for Youth Groups

Combining a powerful message, compelling video illustrations, and captivating group activities, this series will enable you to lead your students to this convincing conclusion: the ways of the world do not produce true meaning in life—only Christ as the true Son of God can transform our "dead lives" into a dynamic and meaningful life in relationship with him. Josh and Ron have created this interactive series to incite a revolution—a revolution to transform your young people into a generation of sacrificial and passionate followers of Christ. As a foundational building block of Christianity this series offers overwhelming evidence that Christ is the Messiah and challenges each student to commit totally to him.

The series includes 5 dramatic video illustrations, Leader's Guide of teaching lessons with reproducible handouts for group activities, and *The Deceivers* NovelPlus book. (Also available on DVD.) ***The Revolt Video Series*** 0-8423-8016-7

Begin Your **CROSSCULTURE**™ Revolution at www.BeyondBelief.com